Studia Fennica
Litteraria 8

The Finnish Literature Society (SKS) was founded in 1831 and has, from the very beginning, engaged in publishing operations. It nowadays publishes literature in the fields of ethnology and folkloristics, linguistics, literary research and cultural history.

The first volume of the Studia Fennica series appeared in 1933. Since 1992, the series has been divided into three thematic subseries: Ethnologica, Folkloristica and Linguistica. Two additional subseries were formed in 2002, Historica and Litteraria. The subseries Anthropologica was formed in 2007.

In addition to its publishing activities, the Finnish Literature Society maintains research activities and infrastructures, an archive containing folklore and literary collections, a research library and promotes Finnish literature abroad.

Studia Fennica Editorial Board

Pasi Ihalainen, Professor, University of Jyväskylä, Finland
Timo Kaartinen, Title of Docent, Lecturer, University of Helsinki, Finland
Taru Nordlund, Title of Docent, Lecturer, University of Helsinki, Finland
Riikka Rossi, Title of Docent, Researcher, University of Helsinki, Finland
Katriina Siivonen, Substitute Professor, University of Helsinki, Finland
Lotte Tarkka, Professor, University of Helsinki, Finland
Tuomas M. S. Lehtonen, Secretary General, Dr. Phil., Finnish Literature Society, Finland
Tero Norkola, Publishing Director, Finnish Literature Society
Maija Hakala, Secretary of the Board, Finnish Literature Society, Finland

oa.finlit.fi

Editorial Office
SKS
P.O. Box 259
FI-00171 Helsinki
www.finlit.fi

LIEVEN AMEEL

Helsinki in Early Twentieth-Century Literature

Urban Experiences
in Finnish Prose Fiction 1890–1940

Finnish Literature Society · SKS · Helsinki

Studia Fennica Litteraria 8

The publication has undergone a peer review.

VERTAISARVIOITU
KOLLEGIALT GRANSKAD
PEER-REVIEWED
www.tsv.fi/tunnus

The open access publication of this volume has received part funding via a Jane and Aatos Erkko Foundation grant.

© 2014 Lieven Ameel and SKS
License CC-BY-NC-ND 4.0 International

A digital edition of a printed book first published in 2014 by the Finnish Literature Society.
Cover Design: Timo Numminen
EPUB Conversion: eLibris Media Oy

ISBN 978-952-222-548-1 (Print)
ISBN 978-952-222-743-0 (PDF)
ISBN 978-952-222-567-2 (EPUB)

ISSN 0085-6835 (Studia Fennica)
ISSN 1458-5278 (Studia Fennica Litteraria)

DOI: http://dx.doi.org/10.21435/sflit.8

This work is licensed under a Creative Commons CC-BY-NC-ND 4.0 International License.
To view a copy of the license, please visit http://creativecommons.org/licenses/by-nc-nd/4.0/

A free open access version of the book is available at http://dx.doi.org/10.21435/sflit.8 or by scanning this QR code with your mobile device.

Contents

Prologue   9

1. Introduction   10
    An Eternal Cinderella?   10
    Selected Material   12
    Earlier Writings on Helsinki in Finnish Literature   13
    Real and Imagined Cities   14
    Outline   15

2. Ways of Writing and Reading the City   17
    Perspectives on the City in Literature   17
        Dichotomies   18
        Ambiguity   19
    Metaphorizations of the City   20
    Towards a Poetics of Movement   23
        Trajectories through Space and Narrative   25
        Focalization and the *Flâneur*   26
        Walking as Enunciation   27

3. The Shock of Arrival. Expectations and First Impressions of the City   30
    Arrival in the City in Juhani Aho's *Helsinkiin* (1889)   31
    Mobility and the Degenerating City   34
    The Young Man/Woman from the Province   38
    Expectations and First Experiences of Helsinki   40
        Competing Visions   40
        Restlessness and Rootlessness   42
        Arrival and the Paralyzing City   46
        An Experience of Shock: Conclusion   49
    Helsinki 1890–1918: A Short History   53

4. The Fateful Esplanade. The Stratification of Public Space   56
    A Shorthand Expression for the City   57
    A Male Bourgeois Ritual   60
    The Gaze and the Right to the City in Eino Leino's *Jaana Rönty* (1907)   65
        Jaana Rönty   66

Public Space – Public Women? 67
The Experience of Helsinki's Public Space under the Aegis of the "Frost Years" 70
    The Esplanade as Agent Road 73
Uneasy Encounters 74
Traces of *Flânerie* Beyond the Esplanade 76

5. Experiences of a Metropolis in Motion. Changing and Disappearing Helsinki 81
    A Panoramic View of the City 82
    Helsinki in Arvid Järnefelt's *Veneh'ojalaiset* (1909) 86
        A Novel about the Land Question 87
        City of Sin: the Brothel Scene 88
        Tentacular City 91
    Helsinki in Transformation 92
    Intimations of Apocalypse 96
        Nocturnal Outing to the Fortress 97
        "All culture is swaying, all forms are inverted" 100
        The Whore of Babylon 106
    Towards a Sense of Belonging 107
        A Fully-fledged Helsinki Novel 111
    Helsinki 1917–1940: A Short History 115

6. Aestheticizing the City. The Internalization of a New Helsinki 117
    The Internalized Urban Experience in Mika Waltari's *Suuri illusioni* (1928) 118
    City Archaeologies 124
        Thoughts Breaking off in Mid-Sentence 129
    The Nocturnal Car Drive 131
    Aestheticizing "New Helsinki" and Helvi Hämäläinen's *Säädyllinen murhenäytelmä* (1941) 136
        Helsinki as Urban Pastoral 142
        Conclusion 145

7. Towards the Margins. Cumbersome Movement through the Urban Fringes 147
    Krokelby in Joel Lehtonen's *Rakastunut rampa* (1922) 148
    Henkien taistelu (1933): the Margins of the City as Testing Ground 150
        A Deformed Landscape 152
        From Carnivalesque to Grotesque Landscape 153
        "Like meat on a grill" 155
        The Slaughterhouse 159
    Mapping a Socially Divided City: Place Names 160
    The Loss of the Centre 166
        The Shop Window and the City as a "Bordello of Consumption" 167
        The Centrifugal City 168
    Hampered Mobility 171

A Divided City: Class and Gender   173
 A Home in the Margins?   176

Conclusion   179

Notes   183
References   216
 Primary Sources   216
 Secondary Sources   219
Abstract   238
Index   239

*To the inhabitants of Helsinki,
past, present and future*

Prologue

To date, Helsinki and its literature have received surprisingly little attention. In the traditional view of Finnish literary history as a slow descent from the forest to the city, the late arrival of urban landscapes in literature seemed to be not more than logical. Literary Helsinki has been described, in the words of V. A. Koskenniemi, Maila Talvio and others, as a Cinderella, a young girl without respectable history, an eternal parvenu.

This study proves such negative views of literary Helsinki wrong, and demonstrates that complex and fascinating experiences of Helsinki have been present in prose literature written in Finnish from the very beginning. In the literature of the late nineteenth and early twentieth centuries, a varied literature of the city appears that has set the tone for the future. The rich variety of themes and generic perspectives in Helsinki literature developed in dialogue with international contemporary traditions and age-old images of the city, and was also defined by events typical of Helsinki's own history.

The literature of Helsinki is examined here in the first place through the experiences of literary characters, rather than as a set of immobile images. Particular attention is paid to descriptions of movement through public space. The analyzed corpus consists of more than sixty novels, collections of short stories and novellas, several of whom have received little attention until now. This study offers also new insights into more canonized literary works thematizing the Finnish capital. The close reading of these Helsinki novels and short stories provides a naturally evolving story of the development of city experiences, from the arrival in the disconcerting metropolis to feelings of deep attachments to the urban environment. This study, the first monograph that examines Helsinki in literature written in Finnish, is based on my doctoral dissertation *Moved by the City: Experiences of Helsinki in Finnish Prose Fiction 1889–1941* (Ameel 2013a). Readers interested in the more detailed theoretical and methodological frameworks of my analysis of literary Helsinki are referred to this doctoral dissertation.

Helsinki, February 2014

1. Introduction

> and the city takes a breath, stony and pitiless,
> on her barren peninsula,
> embraced by the open sea and the pale sky
> (Waltari 1936: 234)[1]

An Eternal Cinderella?

Helsinki has long been defined by what it seems to be lacking. It has been claimed that it has little or no history, that it is an artificial construction that is not representative of the Finnish nation and its culture.[2] In the narrative of Finnish literary history, the Finnish capital has long been relegated to a marginal role. As late as the 1990s, it has been claimed that "there are hardly any significant Finnish novels that are set in Helsinki".[3] The idea of Finnish literature as largely lacking a rich imagination on the city would recur time and again throughout the twentieth century, most explicitly in Kai Laitinen's essay "Metsästä kaupunkiin" ("From the Forest to the City"), which reduced the "grand tradition" of Finnish prose literature to a journey from the forest to the city (Laitinen 1973). This evolution logically emphasized the "unnatural" character of the city in the Finnish cultural context, and the late arrival of a complex urban imagination in literary representations. This study demonstrates that complex and fascinating experiences of Helsinki have, on the contrary, been present in prose literature written in Finnish from the very beginning: they appear only a few decades after the first prose works written in Finnish began to be published.

Typical for the negative tone which was long predominant in describing Helsinki's literature is V. A. Koskenniemi's 1914 essay on Helsinki's literary representations in the book *Runon kaupunkeja* ("Literary Cities"). His text presents Helsinki side by side with the likes of Bruges, Weimar and Verona, but comparing unfavourably to such well-established literary cities:

> Stockholm has Strindberg, St. Petersburg has Dostoevsky, Berlin has Kretzer, Hamburg has Frenssen, Oulu has Pakkala and Rauma has Nortamo – but who is Helsinki's poet? Who has claimed for Helsinki the admission ticket into the society of literary cities?[4]

Who is the poet of Helsinki? The answer, in Koskenniemi's opinion, was disheartening: Finnish literature had not yet produced a "synthetic literary work about Helsinki, a novel or an epic, in which this Northern capital would live in its totality with all those characteristics which nature, race and culture have bestowed upon her" (Koskenniemi 1914: 89).[5] In his view, Helsinki lacked as yet a writer who could capture its particular nature and characteristics, and a poetical work that would present this vision. It is a vision of Helsinki and its literature that is as old as it is persistent: the image of an eternal Cinderella, forever under age, waiting to be allowed to go to the ball.[6]

Perhaps the literary representation of turn-of-the-century Helsinki did not live up to the expectations of contemporaries, but a close look at the rich material available reveals a surprisingly manifold variety. In the two centuries since 1812, when Helsinki became the capital of Finland, and in particular from the late 1880s onwards, when Finnish prose literature came into bloom, the city has spawned a complex literary imagination, which as yet remains largely unstudied. An extensive analysis of how Helsinki is experienced in Finnish literature is not available, and addressing this hiatus is the main aim of this book.

How does Helsinki appear in Finnish literature? What kinds of experiences has it evoked and provoked? Through what processes was this literary city constructed, in terms of both its relationship to international urban discourses, genre and period conventions, and its particular social, political and also military history? What kinds of relationships are formed between Helsinki and the fictional characters in these novels and short stories? Or, to phrase one overall question that informs all of the above: how is the experience of urban public space rendered in Finnish prose literature from the late 1880s until the beginning of the Second World War?

The experience of public space and representations of mobility hold the key to the experience of the city in Helsinki literature. Questions of mobility, both social and physical, define the experience of the city in this period, and they lie at the core of the research questions tackled in this study. The turn of the century and the decades that followed have not without reason been called the "vertigo years" (Blom 2008), years defined by an ever-increasing, dizzy-making speed, acceleration, and expansion. Finland was no exception: situated at the fringes of Europe, and as a country that had a long way to catch up on technological, industrial and urban innovations, the all-embracing changes of the age were arguably even more tangibly felt here than elsewhere, since they were so much more condensed in time and space. In addition to the burgeoning technological and urban developments visible in the Finnish capital, Helsinki's cityscape witnessed a number of far-reaching social and political disruptions that infused the literary descriptions of (public) urban space with an added sense of tension and urgency: the 1905 General Strike, the 1906 rebellion of the Russian soldiers at the fortress of Viapori/Suomenlinna, the 1918 Civil War, the Prohibition during the 1920s, and the depression and political radicalism of the 1930s.

This book makes a contribution, first of all, to the field of Finnish literary studies, in which the city as cultural artefact and generator of literary images has received relatively little attention. Contrary to the deprecating view presented by Koskenniemi and others, Helsinki emerges around the turn of the twentieth century as a complex literary space in Finnish literature, combining the strong echoes of a wide range of international discourses of the city. In a more international context, this study makes a contribution to research on literary cities in general, especially as a reminder of how powerful the images and experiences evoked by smaller cities and capitals on the margins of the Western literary field can be. By analysing a relatively small capital on the fringes of Europe, it becomes possible to add fresh insights to the research of urban space in literature, which has been mostly concerned with a small group of metropolises. Whereas much of the ever-more expanding literature on the classical literary cities (Paris, London, New York, L. A.) seems to merely add to an idiosyncratic debate, the study of smaller cities and peripheral urban centres can make, in my opinion, real and tangible contributions to an understanding of the potential inherent to city discourses and images. These may be used as sources to energize and revitalize everyday living spaces, to establish a sense of community and belonging, and to foster liveable neighbourhoods and urban environments. Literary scholars are particularly well placed to analyse and gauge the potential for images and discourses of the city, and to contribute to how these can be brought to bear on the actual city in everyday contexts, both through recent trends in city (and neighbourhood) branding, and at the grass-roots level of individual streets and building blocks. Studies on such issues, which have been largely monopolized by cultural geography and urban studies, can be greatly invigorated by added insights from literary studies. A more concerted cross-insemination from all relevant academic disciplines has been called for by such social geographers as David Harvey, who has stressed that "[t]he geographical imagination is far too pervasive and important a facet of intellectual life to be left alone to geographers" (Harvey 1995: 161).

Selected Material

The prose literature which constitutes the corpus for this study consists of a selection of books and short stories published in Finnish between the late 1880s and the beginning of the Second World War. This period constitutes what is in effect the first half century of literary representations of Helsinki in literature written in Finnish, starting with the very first texts thematizing the Finnish capital (Juhani Aho's "Helsinkiin" ["To Helsinki"; 1889], and some of Aho's other short prose) and ending with the disruption caused by the Second World War. This is the period in which the foundations of literary Helsinki were laid, constructing a varied literature that has set the tone for later descriptions.

A number of potentially interesting prose texts were excluded. Popular literature (crime novels, for example) and children's literature will not be referred to, or only in passing.[7] Historical novels published during these years but set in an earlier period have also been excluded, unless as background material.[8] Theatre plays and works of poetry are largely excluded. For a number of reasons, Finnish literature written in Swedish was not included.[9]

I chose to include prose texts from a relatively long time frame, spanning the period of the turn of the twentieth century as well as the inter-war period. Many of the earlier studies on Finnish texts foregrounding the city in this period have focused on placing them in their immediate frame of genre and period, which has tended to obscure the continuous development of the literary images of Helsinki. Analysing literary texts from a more extensive corpus makes it possible to re-appraise the thematics and importance of individual novels in the light of a continuity that would otherwise remain less clearly visible. In total, some sixty novels, collections of short stories and individual short stories were selected. Some authors, such as Mika Waltari and Maila Talvio, are present with as many as half a dozen texts or more, while other authors, such as Hilda Tihlä, are included with just one.

Earlier Writings on Helsinki in Finnish Literature

In 2000, Helsinki celebrated its 450th anniversary, and an overview of recent publications featuring the Finnish capital appeared under the slightly laconic title "450 vuotta – entä sitten? Korkea pino kirjoja" ("450 years – and then what? A big pile of books"; Laurila 2001). The article listed a wide range of texts celebrating, evoking and studying Helsinki: collections of poetry, photo books, anthologies, novels, city guides, historical works and academic contributions. No comprehensive study of how Helsinki appeared in literature, however, featured on the list. This had not changed by 2012, when celebrations related to the bicentenary anniversary of Helsinki as the capital of Finland caused a new outpour of Helsinki-related publications.[10] Finnish literary history has generally shown little interest in city thematics (see also Laine 2011: 155). Compared to other capitals within Europe in general, or Helsinki's most immediate large neighbours, Stockholm and St. Petersburg, there are remarkably few articles and monographs on literary Helsinki.

To date, the most important study on Helsinki in Finnish literature is arguably still Raoul Palmgren's *Kaupunki ja tekniikka Suomen kirjallisuudessa* ("The City and Technology in Finnish Literature"; 1989), a book which aims to provide an overview of all relevant references to cities and technology from the very beginnings of Finnish literature to the date of its appearance. The only recent monographs dealing with literary Helsinki, Arne Toftegaard Pedersen's evocative *Urbana odysseer* ("Urban Odysseys"; 2007) and Alessandro Bassini's 2012 doctoral dissertation *Notes from the Suburb: the Image of Helsinki in the works by Kjell Westö* (Bassini 2012), focus on Helsinki in Finland-Swedish prose in the 1910s and in the work of one author – Kjell Westö – respectively. They mention texts written in Finnish only tangentially.

In the course of the last century, a small number of articles have appeared on Helsinki representations in literature. A small set of articles was published in connection with, or closely following, the centenary anniversary of Helsinki as the capital of Finland in 1912 (Schildt 1912; Koskenniemi 1914; Saarenheimo 1916). Compared to Koskenniemi's and Schildt's engaged and insightful contributions, many of the later articles devoted to the literary representations of Helsinki were content with enumerating plots and extensive quotations of descriptive passages. This is the case, in particular, for the fairly general studies that appeared in the 1940s, 1950s and 1960s (Castrén 1947; Anttila 1956; Liuttu 1963; Havu 1965).

The 1990s witnessed the appearance of a handful of articles on Helsinki (and Finnish cities in general) in literature, pointing at new vistas of research and a renewed interest in the study of literary space, in part inspired by innovative approaches from other academic disciplines (Karkama 1998; Karjalainen & Paasi 1994).[11] In addition to these contributions, a number of articles have traced Helsinki representations in the work of one specific author, text or context (see, for, example Nieminen 1974; Laurila 1982a; Envall 1992; Riikonen 1994; Karjalainen 1995; Korsberg 2008). Scattered references to city representations in Finnish fiction can also be found in a number of monographs on specific themes or authors (see Envall 1994: 11–44; Hapuli 1995; Nummi 2002: 253–293). The recent dissertation by Silja Laine on the question of skyscrapers and urban architecture in Helsinki in the 1920s features an extensive overview of some of the central developments concerning the image of Helsinki in literature, but with a special focus on representations of architecture and high buildings (Laine 2011: 137–183).

Real and Imagined Cities

The strong link between historical cities and their literature is so obvious and forceful that it has sometimes obscured how complex the relation is between imagined and "real" cities. We can go on a literary walk in Dostoevsky's St. Petersburg; Paris is evoked by the writings of Zola, Balzac and Proust; Prague markets itself as the city of Kafka, and Lisbon is packed with Pessoa paraphernalia. The practice of inflating an author's image of a city with the geographical city of the same name has been criticized from various perspectives, and any study on city representations would be well informed to position clearly what is, in fact, the prime object of the study involved. Is this the actual, historical city as reflected in the "mirror" of literary representation, or the imagined city as a semi-autonomous cultural artefact, or any of the various ways in which the actual city and its literary representation interact with each other and with other literary city representations? This question was taken up by Virginia Woolf in her first review for the *Times Literary Supplement*, entitled "Literary Geography" (1905). In Woolf's words: "to insist that it [a writer's city] has any counterpart in the cities of the earth is to rob it of half its charm" (Woolf 1905/1986: 35; see also Johnson 2000: 199). There is indeed something profoundly reductionist in equating the literary city with its geographically locatable counterpart, and I would agree with Burton Pike's claim that "Dickens' London and London, England, are located in two different countries" (Pike 1981: 13). But, like most scholars, I would also agree with Marco Polo's assertion in Calvino's *The Invisible Cities* that, while "the city must never be confused with the words that describe it", nevertheless "between the one and the other there is a connection" (1972/1997: 61).

Scholars studying the literary city can be roughly divided into two groups, with the extreme sides of the axis insisting on either a direct relation between the "actual" and "fictional" city, or treating the literary city as a completely independent world. William Sharpe calls these opposing poles respectively "formalists" and "historicists" (Sharpe 1990: xii), and insists that, despite heated debates, "the study of the city and its art is not a matter of 'either/or', of embracing one approach to the exclusion of others" (ibid.). More to the point, the difference between these perspectives reflects different kinds of research interests in the literary city. After all, there are a great many things a literary text can "do", and all of these can be legitimate objects of study.

In order to analyse the urban experiences in a given novel, it will be necessary to look at the processes involved in the creation, or "making" of a particular literary city. Building on Nelson Goodman's theory of worldmaking (see Goodman 1978; Nünning 2010: 216–217), one can say that in order to "make" an imagined city world, a literary text will draw on a whole variety of pre-existing cities, and recycle prefiguring material as the plot evolves. In the case of the literary city of Helsinki in a particular prose text, the narration will combine at least some of the following elements in its "citymaking": architectural and historical fragments from the "actual" city of Helsinki; a wide range of images belonging to other literary cities (such as Paris, London, or St. Petersburg); conventions of genre and period; and archetypal images of the city. The imagined city of Helsinki in literature appears, then, as a variety of different possible cities, with their own particular value systems. It is these cities that are at the focus of this study.

The complex relation between the literary city and the "actual", geographically locatable city is one of the reasons why no existing maps of the historical city of Helsinki during this period are included in this study. To facilitate the readability for readers unacquainted with Helsinki, two tailormade maps of the Helsinki peninsula were added. These provide information on places and districts that are thematized in literature in this period, and are not intended as scientific maps of historical Helsinki. The first map, depicting Helsinki around 1900, can be found on page 29, immediately preceding Chapter 3. The second map, depicting Helsinki around 1930, can be found on page 114, preceding Chapter 6.[12]

Outline

The most important research subject in the present study is not so much the *city* itself, or even images of the city, but the *experience* of the city in literary texts. In the chapter "Ways of Writing and Reading the City", I will introduce the theoretical perspectives on the city in literature most relevant for this study. The analysis of city experiences in literature will require a methodology or what one might call a poetics of movement. Such a tentative poetics of movement, drawing on the thinking of Charles Baudelaire and Walter Benjamin, but also on more recent thinkers such as Michel de Certeau, will serve as a theoretical framework with which to investigate urban trajectories through space and narrative.

The analysis of the selected corpus is divided into five chapters, loosely following a chronological order, and structured thematically. The first three chapters focus on literature from the turn of the century, extending into the

1910s, while the fourth and fifth analysis chapters analyse experiences of the city in novels published in the 1920s and the 1930s. In every chapter, one key text will be used as a window from which to approach particular thematics. Using a key text to approach the material provides the opportunity to contextualize one author and text in more detail, and to present a more thorough reading of at least one particular text than otherwise would have been possible. In the course of the respective chapters, additional relevant primary texts will be linked to the themes taken up in discussing the key text.

The third chapter, entitled "The Shock of Arrival", traces the first experiences of literary Helsinki in Finnish prose texts, focusing on arrival in the city. The key text in this chapter is Juhani Aho's novella, *Helsinkiin* ("To Helsinki"; 1889).

The fourth chapter, entitled "The Fateful Esplanade", studies literary experiences and images connected to the Esplanade, concentrating on representations of walking and moving through urban public space. It reveals the profound stratification of urban public space, in particular from the perspective of gendered space, taking into account the notions of socially, politically and linguistically divided space. The key novel in this chapter is Eino Leino's *Jaana Rönty* ("Jaana Rönty"; 1907).

While the third chapter examines the first experiences of people moving to the capital, and the fourth chapter follows the footsteps of literary characters roaming the streets of Helsinki, Chapter 5, "Experiences of a Metropolis in Motion", analyses how developments in the built environment have their effects on literary characters' experiences. This chapter, in which Arvid Järnefelt's *Veneh'ojalaiset* ("The Family Veneh'oja"; 1909) will be treated as a key novel, examines how literary Helsinki appears as a rapidly transforming city, in which the accelerating processes of modernity become responsible not only for (re)generating, but also for erasing parts of the cityscape.

The sixth chapter, entitled "Aestheticizing the City", discusses the internalization and aestheticization of the city experience in Finnish literature from the late 1920s and 1930s. I will use Mika Waltari's cult novel *Suuri illusioni* ("The Great Illusion"; 1928) to approach these thematics, and to analyse how, during these years, the city experience was also described through new stylistic features and techniques. In addition to *Suuri illusioni*, one other novel obtains a more privileged position in this chapter: Helvi Hämäläinen's *Säädyllinen murhenäytelmä* ("A Respectable Tragedy"; 1941).

The seventh and final chapter, "Towards the Margins", examines how, in particular during the 1930s, but starting in the late 1910s, a parallel writing on the city develops at the fringes of the city. The key novel in this chapter is Joel Lehtonen's *Henkien taistelu* ("Battle of the Spirits"; 1933). Particular attention will be given to how characters' movement through the city is described as inhibited by the characters' social (and/or gendered) background. Even though the novels discussed in this chapter repeatedly describe (sub)urban spatial environments and particular characters' movement through the city in terms of deformity, the socially marginalized protagonists in these prose texts are often profoundly at home in the city, and express feelings of strong attachment, in particular in relation to their local neighbourhoods.

2. Ways of Writing and Reading the City

> the city as a phenomenon –
> an outrage, a spectacle,
> an emblem of human ingenuity
> that seems frankly superhuman
> (Joyce Carol Oates 1981: 18)

Perspectives on the City in Literature

All literary texts on Helsinki are in some way or another linked to the vast thread of international city literature which extends all the way down to the very beginnings of Western literature. From the very first preserved texts in Western history, one can find city images in all their ambiguous complexity: as nodes of creative and destructive energy, as beacons of utopian possibility and of moral warning. As Burton Pike points out, "[w]e unthinkingly consider this phenomenon modern, but it goes back to early epic and mythic thought. We cannot imagine *Gilgamesh*, the Bible, the *Iliad*, or the *Aeneid*, without their cities, which contain so much of their energy and radiate so much of their meaning" (Pike 1981: 3). In the forms of the metropolis and the capital, in particular, the city has become a powerful artefact of the human cultural imagination, endowed with complex powers of representation, and evoking a plethora of images. In the history of the novel, cities have played a particularly crucial role (Bradbury 1976/1986: 99), and the development of literary movements such as realism, naturalism, symbolism and modernism is intimately intertwined with the history of the cities that helped shape them.[1]

In the course of the last half century, a vast body of international research on literary cities has come into being. Several of the most influential studies present a linear model to trace the evolution of city representations in Western literature.[2] Typical in this respect is Richard Lehan's *The City in Literature* (1998), which sketches the well-established and highly canonized evolution of city literature in European and American literature as marked by a shift from romanticism to realism and naturalism, advancing through symbolism to reach its zenith in the high modernist texts of writers such as James Joyce and Virginia Woolf, and further advancing into postmodern prose.

The periodical typology of highly canonized and hegemonic literary traditions cannot, however, be applied to a peripheral literary tradition such as the Finnish one without some caveats: not all thematic preoccupations, repertoires of stylistic features, or literary motifs from the canonized tradition will have their immediate equivalents in Finnish literature, and some aspects specific to culture, to the country's socio-political situation in this period, and also to language, will have to be taken into account. This study, then, illustrates the rewards as well as the limitations of a comparative literary studies approach towards city images in a peripheral context.

In addition to diachronic studies, a profusion of studies on city representations in the work of particular authors, and historical or literary periods, or structured around a thematically, periodically or geographically defined selected corpus have appeared.[3] Such studies add a number of important insights, in particular in relation to peripheral and medium-sized cities that have often been neglected by more teleological and diachronic studies.[4]

In most, if not all, of the existing studies, a strong emphasis on historical periods and literary movements is immediately apparent. The representation of cities in literature has always been closely related to the genre and period conventions in which any given literary text is conceived: particular historical periods give rise to specific ways of seeing and experiencing the city, and these in turn result in particular literary paradigms. As Cedric Whitman points out, it does not really matter whether Homer ever saw Troy, since he would have had to describe it as he would have any other Bronze Age city, on the basis of the generic conventions available to him (Whitman 1958: 27; see also Pike 1981: 11). Conventions of genre and period will be of considerable importance for the present study: in the period 1890–1940, the realist, naturalist and symbolist movements, in particular, exhibited particular visions of the urban experience that were highly influential on the Finnish literature of Helsinki.

Dichotomies

While the development of city images has often been described in terms of linear developments, most of the comparative and diachronic studies are to a greater or lesser extent structured on the basis of polarizations. Generally speaking, there is a strong tendency to describe evolutions of literary representations of the city as a swinging back and forth, like a pendulum, between dichotomies: alienation and belonging, community and individual, enchantment and disenchantment, euphoria and dysphoria, etc.[5]

In many respects, one of the founding polarizations from which to approach the city has been the dichotomy country-city. It is a binary opposition that is at least as old as Horace, and that has provided the title and subject matter of an early ground-breaking study of the literary city, Raymond Williams's *The Country and the City* (1973). While a number of insights from Williams's work have undiminished relevance, in particular in the context of English literary studies, the dichotomy on which this work is based has, as Burton Pike claims, drawn attention away from the "enormous power the image of the city has exercised on the human imagination by itself, independently from that tradition" (Pike 1981: xiii–xiv). It is a dichotomy which has a major place in thinking on the city in Finnish literature (see Laitinen 1973), but with which the present study is not concerned, and which, I believe, again following Pike, belongs more to the tradition of the pastoral than to the study of the literary city proper (Pike 1981: xiv).

More pervasive, and much more relevant for the present study, are the founding opposites of Babylon and Jerusalem.[6] In Western literature, the moral implications of this dichotomy grounded in Biblical references to the city have had a particularly strong resonance (see Sharpe 1990: 1; Pike 1981: 5–8). In this tradition, which can be traced all the way back to

Saint Augustine, the image of the city oscillates between views of the city as utopia, and of it as the ultimate spatial embodiment of all evil. It is an image that pervades to some degree all writing on the Western city since Augustine, including the Finnish literary texts in the period discussed here (1890–1940).

Even in profoundly pessimistic narratives, both world views of this polarizing dichotomy can often be found – one as possibility, the other as fictional reality. Most importantly, the pervasiveness of Biblical images of the city should not obscure the fact that the polarization between Babel and (New) Jerusalem is but one of the potential dichotomies structuring the experience of the city. The temple was only one of the three institutions that have been traditionally described as essential to the city, the other two being the market and the fortress (see Lehan 1998: 13), and the city always had a number of other important functions.[7] The positive image of the city as a centre of learning, for example, gained strength during the Middle Ages, in part thanks to the founding of universities in important cities (Pleij 2009: 128–131). From 1828 until Finnish independence (1917), Helsinki was the location of the only university in the country, and the double image of seat of learning and cesspit of vice appears, in particular, in the literary genre of the student novel.

Ambiguity

Ultimately, it is not necessary to resolve the tension between city dichotomies or to try to impose on one particular city in literary (or other) representations one of the poles of a spectrum it will necessarily represent as a whole. The way in which literary experiences of the city evolve is constructed not so much as a straight line from one side of the spectrum to the other, but rather in the continuous and dialectic movement back and forth, from alienation to belonging, from paralysis to frantic movement, from worldly to godly, with neither of the extremes ever being separated from the equation. In this respect, it is good to bear in mind Saint Augustine's words – in quite a different context – on the non-separable nature of the two opposing imaginary city communities: that of the city of God and the city of the world, Jerusalem and Babylon:

> How can these two cities be distinguished? We cannot separate them from one another, can we? No, they are intermingled, and they continue like that from the very beginning of the human race until the end of the world. (Augustine 2001: 265)

Much of the enduring fascination of the city is directly linked to its very ambiguity and to the often confusing diversity it tends to harbour.[8] This ambiguity, rather than the dichotomies which emanate from it, is arguably the key to understanding how city experiences are rendered in literature. In Burton Pike's words, it is "the most powerful constant associated with the idea of the 'city' [...], the inability of strong negative and positive impulses towards a totemic object to resolve themselves" (Pike 1981: xii). In urban history, urban studies and urban sociology, in particular, ambiguity and diversity have been seen as the key terms with which to understand the urban experience. Lewis Mumford, in his classical study *The City in History*, saw ambivalence as a central part of the city's nature. David Harvey, speaking from a distinctly different perspective than either Pike's or Mumford's, has evoked the fleeting and seemingly contradictory characteristics of the city as follows:

> It is a place of mystery, the site of the unexpected, full of agitations and ferments, of multiple liberties, opportunities, and alienations; of passions and repressions; of cosmopolitanism and extreme parochialisms; of violence, innovation, and reaction. (Harvey 1989b: 229)

But how, to continue with Harvey, are we to "penetrate the mystery, unravel the confusions, and grasp the contradictions?" (Harvey 1989b: 229–230) A critical geographer, Harvey turned repeatedly to metaphors and images, amongst others drawn from literary representations, to "penetrate the mystery" of the city. Similarly, looking for ways to grapple with the complexity of the American city in their article "Symbolic Representation and the Urban Milieu", the sociologists Richard Wohl and Anselm Strauss turned to representations of the city, insisting that "[t]he complexity of the city calls for symbolic management" (Wohl & Strauss 1958: 523). In literature, as well as in literary studies, sociology, and urban studies, the "symbolic management" carried out to come to terms with the ambiguity and contradictory complexity of the city repeatedly takes the shape of a range of metaphors with which to approach the city.

Metaphorizations of the City [9]

As James Donald has pointed out, the city is "always already symbolized and metaphorized" (1999: 17).[10] In what follows, a number of city metaphorizations will be discussed: ways of describing that structure urban experiences of the city in literary representations of the city, but that can also be found in thinking on the city in the fields of urban history, critical sociology and literary studies.[11] If there is one persistent metaphor used to describe the city, it is that of a living, natural creature or an organic being, with its own life cycle, its birth, growth and death.[12] Cities tend to be thought of as being born, as growing up, and as gradually dying or decaying; of having an organic life cycle, which can end in death. It is often death, and the dying processes of cities, that have exerted the greatest fascination.[13] Apocalyptic perspectives have potently informed the city writings of Dickens, Dostoevsky, and Joyce (see Alter 2005: 66, 81, 122), and particular cities have particular myths concerning their future destruction. Amongst these, the apocalyptic discourse on St. Petersburg is of particular interest for literary images of Helsinki in literature. The end-of-days undercurrents at work in literary representations of the city will be one of the themes discussed in the fifth chapter, which focuses on experiences of the city during the first decades of the twentieth century, a period in which accelerating modernization and the volatile socio-political situation result in an image of a city under threat.

In the case of Helsinki, the idea of the city as growing and maturing is most clearly visible in the persistent perception of the Finnish capital as a young, immature city. Rome was already eternal two millennia ago; Helsinki was still under age a century back. In writings on the Finnish capital, its age is repeatedly conceived to be that of an immature youngster. The Finland-Swedish author Runar Schildt (1912), for example, likens the city to a clumsy youngster and to a parvenu, and both V. A. Koskenniemi (1914) and Maila Talvio (1936) describe Helsinki as a Cinderella. A well-known illustration published on the occasion of Finland's participation in the Paris *Exposition Universelle* of 1889 shows Helsinki, in the allegorical figure of a young girl crowned by the St. Nicholas' Church, arriving in Paris, which is depicted as a matron-like woman of middle age (Smeds 1996: 245). The image of Helsinki as a young girl was consecrated as the official image of Helsinki in the form of the statue *Havis Amanda*, the daughter of the Baltic, erected in 1908 between the central Market Square and the Esplanade.[14] Helsinki's image as sprung forth from the Baltic is reminiscent of the genesis of Venus, and like Venus, Helsinki in literature is repeatedly associated with a sea shell: Eino Leino described Helsinki, in his poem "Meren kaupunki" ("City of the Sea"; 1908), as a sea shell, as did Topelius, in the collection of stories *Vinterqvällar* ("Winter Evenings"; 1881/1882: 17).[15]

This identification of the city with a young girl is closely linked to two other central metaphors related to the city: the city as body, and the feminine nature of the city. The body is one of the most potent metaphors with which the city can be conceptualized.[16] Especially from the eighteenth century on, when growing scientific knowledge of the body was combined with urban planning, planners began to speak of the city in corporal terms (Sennett 1994: 263). Terms such as "arteries" and "veins", for example, came to be used when discussing and planning the canalization of urban traffic (ibid.: 264 ff.). In some texts, both literary and historical, the metaphor of the city-body is taken to extremes, attributing to the city a mouth, digesting systems, and intestines. It is a metaphorization which more often than not has economic implications, positing the city as a body feeding on the produce of the surrounding country or colonies. But the metaphor of the body is also used in a sense that equates the city with the body politic, attributing perceived diseases in society to the ailing organic structure of the city.[17] This metaphorization allows for the concept of the city as a diseased body, or as an "excrescence" of the body politic.[18] In Finnish realist and naturalist literature, the image of the city as a diseased and degenerative body feeding on its surroundings has severe consequences for how the urban environment is experienced by newcomers to the capital. It is a metaphorization which functions as the vehicle for social critique in turn-of-the-century Finnish novels, and can be used to render a profoundly misanthropic vision of society as a whole, most prominently in Joel Lehtonen's grim satirical *Rakastunut rampa* ("A Cripple in Love"; 1922) and *Henkien taistelu* ("Battle of the Spirits"; 1933), novels that will be analysed in the final analysis chapter.

While the equation of the city with the body politic reveals some of the profoundly pessimistic world views that were attributed to the urban environment, it is a metaphorization that could also have more positive repercussions. The fascination with the city is tied to its potential to symbolize abstract concepts that lie beyond the city boundaries: the intangible concepts of community, citizenship, or the nation state. In literature in particular, the city "has become metaphor rather than place" (Bradbury 1976/1986: 97; see also Lynch 1960: 5). Bradbury echoes earlier thinking which vests the city with the potential to reflect not only itself but much larger and even more complex entities: the community of believers in Augustine's *City of God* (2007), the Empire and its citizens in the case of Rome, the order of rational reasoning in the baroque city plan or the centralizing nation state emerging during the nineteenth century. The image of the city is also an *imago mundi*, constructing the citizens' "representation of space as a whole, of the earth, of the world" (see Lefebvre 1974/1991: 243–244). By looking at the metropolis, one might claim to metonymically see the world (or at least *a* world) in its totality.

The image of the city as a human body is closely related to the image of the city as a fundamentally feminine figure, as mentioned above.[19] This metaphor of the female body allows for an enormous variety of specific adaptations in discourses about the city: the city may be described as a motherly figure, but it can as easily be portrayed as a harlot (see for example Prendergast 1992: 136), as a "most delicious of monsters" – the female figure with which Paris is described in Zola's *Ferragus* (as quoted in Brooks 2005: 133) – or as the Whore of Babylon of the Apocalypse (for Berlin, see Bergius 1986). Equating the city with the feminine body sustains the idea that the city can also be conquered, seduced, or raped; a metaphorization that can be found in fields as diverse as (literary) history and the spatial practice of graffiti.[20] The city is from its very beginnings a profoundly gendered symbol, something which will be discussed in relation to the figure of the *flâneur* and *flâneuse*, in Chapter 4.

The city can be seduced and conquered, and it can also, conversely, appear in terms of a seductive figure: the image of a mysterious, alluring female figure, appealing yet disconcerting. Even saints such as Augustine and Jerome confessed to having been "allured and teased by sensuous images of Rome" (Mumford 1961: 246), and for a wide range of authors writing on the city, the city represented "both lure and trap"; the London of Dickens is a case in point (Lehan 1998: 38). The disconcerting, seductive female city is akin to the image of the sphinx, half-animal, half-woman, guarding the secret of the city (see Wilson 1991). By welcoming and challenging the newcomer, the city acts in this metaphorization as an accelerator of the unconscious, and is thought to awaken atavistic instincts and dormant desires. It is an image of the city which will be of particular relevance to Helsinki literature of the turn of the twentieth century, which focuses on arrival in, and early experiences of, the city.

In addition to the sphinx, one other mythical figure is associated with the city: the Minotaur. Half-man, half-bull, a horror-invoking figure lurking in the labyrinth, this is the shape in which the city appears when the city's accumulative, feeding functions take over: the city as a Moloch, demanding regular sacrifice. From the late nineteenth century onwards, when industrialization begins to radically transform Western cities, the metaphorization of the city as Minotaur and the related image of the city as machine gain ground, especially in writings that examine the city's social and economic conditions. Little wonder that a Marxist thinker such as Henri Lefebvre claims the city is "in effect a constantly burning blazing furnace" (Lefebvre 1974/1991: 93), evoking a Moloch-like image that is already persistent in turn-of-the-century literature on the industrial city.[21] The Minotaur's habitat is the maze or labyrinth, which is yet again a metaphor frequently used for grasping the city.[22] Both the figures of the sphinx and the Minotaur presuppose that the city is a labyrinthine space containing a mystery to be solved – in other words, that it is a text that can be read and decoded.

Seductive and waiting to be conquered, artificial yet organic; a symbol of death and of life itself[23] – no city in literary representations is totally free from earlier city myths and archetypal city images. The city as a moral touchstone grounded on Biblical precursors; the city as labyrinthine text, inhabited by the brooding figures of the Minotaur and the sphinx; the city as a living being, growing, developing and decaying; the city as a seductive figure, awakening desires and yet putting them to sleep; the city as disorientating, alienating yet stimulating – all these metaphorizations will have to be taken into account when looking at a particular city in literature.

The dichotomies, ambiguity and metaphorizations outlined above will all be instrumental in guiding the analysis of experiences of Helsinki in the course of my analysis chapters. As a theoretical guideline, however, this approach would be incomplete without taking into account the profound paradigm shifts that have taken place during the last three decades in a wide variety of academic disciplines. These changes and the consequences they have for the study of city representations in literature will be the subject of the next section and will allow for a better understanding not so much of the image of the city, but of the experience of the city.

Towards a Poetics of Movement

> We live in spacious times
> (Ford Madox Ford 1905: 59)

A considerable number of literary studies of the city have taken as their overt aim the study of *images* of the city, metaphorizations such as those discussed in the previous chapter. In recent decades, however, there has also been a growing interest in studying *experiences* of the city – the sensations that arise from a personally and subjectively lived urban place. This study falls into the latter category: it analyses the kinds of relationships which literary characters construct with regards to Helsinki, and the terms in which their experience of the city is rendered. The growing interest in experiences (personally lived as well as shared experiences) of space is in part inspired by developments within geography, and humanistic geography in particular.

In the decades following the end of the Second World War, and in the 1970s in particular, thinkers within the field of geography had been advancing a return of human relations and experiences to the centre of a field of study that had become increasingly preoccupied with positivism, facts, figures, maps and statistics (see Brosseau 1994: 334). The result was the development of humanistic geography, as a field of enquiry marked by interest in personally lived "place", rather than absolute "space". Pioneering works in this field were Yi-Fi Tuan's *Topophilia* (1974) and *Space and Place* (1977).

The advent of a humanistic geography, with its focus on lived "place", meant that geographers became more interested in new material such as diaries, travel stories, memoires, and literature. From the 1970s onwards, literary texts became gradually accepted as objects of study for humanistic geographers (see Tuan 1978; Brosseau 1994; Hubbard et al. 2002: 129), and a number of essay collections appeared to give voice to this humanistic-geographical interest in literary material (see Pocock 1981). Interestingly, literature was often used to study regional geographies, in particular in relation to landscapes (Mallory & Simpson-Housley 1987; Porteous 1990).

More or less contemporary with humanistic geographers, Henri Lefebvre and other scholars within Marxist thought and critical social studies worked to reassert the importance of space as a fundamental category to be studied in its own right. Their innovative contribution rested in part on a reappraisal of the nature of space as something relative rather than absolute – a view that runs parallel to the increased focus on "place" over "space" in humanistic geography. In Lefebvre's view, space is not something that simply "is", either absolute or a priori. Space, on the contrary, is always experienced and perceived, always dependent on a subject and thus, on a body (Lefebvre 1974/1991: 162).

Henri Lefebvre and (Marxist) scholars inspired by him were interested in the way in which imagined spaces were intertwined with the production of everyday space. This is expressed in Lefebvre's famous threefold taxonomy of space, which distinguishes between spatial practices, representations of space, and representational spaces (Lefebvre 1974/1991: 33, 38–39). Most interesting for the study of space in literature is Lefebvre's category of representational spaces, which includes elements in the built environment with symbolic functions (such as the belfry in the medieval village; ibid.: 42, 45), but that also encompasses images of space in literary and other representations (ibid.: 38–39).[24] In a review of studies in urbanism and literature, John M. Ganim has called Lefebvre's spatial triad "famously difficult", but he concedes that it enables one to speak of factual cities "in a dialectical relation to ideas and literary representations" (Ganim 2002: 372–373). From a literary studies perspective, one of Lefebvre's major contributions is that he has drawn symbolic representations of space into the larger framework of the processes involved in the production of space, giving city representations and their study a potentially crucial position within the overall study of space.

Many of the innovative insights of humanistic geography and critical geography have spilled over into other disciplines, resulting in "a veritable flood of spatial discourses proliferating across the disciplines" from the 1990s onwards (Friedman 2005: 192).[25] In literary studies, questions of space have until fairly recently been marginalized.[26] In part, this is due to the subsuming, in classical narratology, of space under the category of description (see Buchholz & Jahn 2005: 555) – a category which in itself occupied a marginal position (see Bal 2006).[27] Space in narrative, however, is much more complex than the description of spatial environments (Zoran 1984: 313). What kinds of theoretical concepts should be brought to bear on the study of space in narrative fiction to account for the experience of urban space as a study object that is in flux, and that is characterized by its production and constant becoming? The German comparative literary scholar Otmar Ette has strongly argued that there is no immediate need for more spatial concepts *per se*, but rather for a vocabulary with which to analyse movement and mobility. Echoing Lefebvre's call for a study of rhythms in space (Lefebvre 2003: 190–198, see also Lefebvre 1974/1991: 87), Ette calls for "a poetics of movement" (Ette 2005: 18–19). Other literary scholars, too, have stressed the fact that any study of space in literature will necessarily amount to the study of space *and* movement in literature.[28]

Trajectories through Space and Narrative
One way to carry out a study of mobility in literature is to start out from the trajectories of literary characters. In the *Atlas of the European Novel* (1998) and *Graphs, Maps, Trees* (2005), Franco Moretti has convincingly shown the range of innovative research conclusions that can be drawn from such an analysis. Spatiality, as Moretti points out, is not a matter of narrative embellishment, but functions as "an active force that pervades the literary field and shapes it" (Moretti 1998: 3 ff.). The spatial movements of literary protagonists have a singular importance in shaping the history of the novel, as well as the experiences of literary characters in particular novels (ibid.) Trajectories through space can be tied, for instance, to the advent of a particular genre (the *Bildungsroman*) as well as to phenomena related to specific historical periods (for example the nineteenth-century era of nation building) (Moretti 1998: 11–74). Both of these implications of spatial trajectories in literature will be of relevance in my analysis of characters' movements to and through the Finnish capital. The importance of trajectories through space as guiding narrative devices that propel the action and the protagonist forward in the narration is particularly relevant for the third chapter of this study, entitled "The Shock of Arrival", in which protagonists' moves to the capital are traced.

The importance of such lines of flight in literature, not only as descriptions of journeys of the protagonists on a spatial plane, but also as means to tear through layers of time, as indicators of ambition, and as reflecting much broader categories (the construction of the nation state, social and moral trajectories), has been demonstrated not only by Franco Moretti, but also in the work of Hans Ulrich Gumbrecht (2006), Hilary Dannenberg (2007, 2008), and Teresa Bridgeman (2007), amongst others.

In specific genres and periods, particular modes of mobility gain prominence: the journey by train to the capital, for example, has a noted impact on the spatial experience in the genre of the student novel and in narratives of the "Young Man/Women of the Provinces" (see Chanda 1981). In the literature of modernity, the description of movement and mobility has been related to the appearance of formal and stylistic innovations (see Borg 2011: 30). Certain kinds of trajectories within the city invite a distinctive set of stylistic features relevant to the novel's overall aesthetics, and may have a considerable importance for the resulting literary techniques with which the urban environment is rendered. A prototypical example from Finnish literature of how a mode of movement has its effect on the style of narration is the Parisian tram journey in Juhani Aho's *Yksin* ("Alone"; 1890/2003; see Nummi 2002: 185 ff.), but examples of the resulting "impressionist" style can be found in the work of later authors, too, in particular in relation to the motif of the car speeding through the city at night, which becomes prominent in the late 1920s, as will be analysed in detail in Chapter 6.

FOCALIZATION AND THE *FLÂNEUR*

A heightened interest in spatial trajectories in literary texts should not obscure the importance of who is experiencing and who is focalizing the experience of mobility. In order to examine mobility and/in literary space, it will be necessary to pay special attention to the individualized perspective of the spatial experience – in other words, the focalization of the narration (cf. Nünning 2009: 39–44). This is, incidentally, also an aspect of narration which is frequently marginalized by scholars outside of literary studies who make use of literary texts. Paying attention to shifts in focalization and to the way in which the focalized perspective is framed can shed light on aspects of the spatial experience that would otherwise remain out of sight, such as the engendered dimension of space and questions of power, surveillance, and the right to public space.

A crucial view of the city is that of the city walker. It constitutes one of the founding visions of the emerging cities of (early) modernity. The theoretical apparatus that has come into being during the last century and a half or so around the figure of the *flâneur* constitutes one of the most well-established "poetics of movement" in relation to the literary city. In the texts of Charles Baudelaire (1857/1998; 1863/1964; 1869/1989), and of Edgar Allan Poe (1840/1912), the city walker as a *flâneur*, the detached observer who goes looking for fleeting impressions on the spur of the moment, and who listens to the incessant pulse of the city and the city crowd, has become synonymous with modernity and with the new modes of literature it inspired. The *flâneur* has become a crucial concept for understanding the cities of modernity and their literature.[29]

In this study, nevertheless, the concept of the *flâneur* will be relegated to a secondary role, although it will serve as a valuable theoretical boundary marker and point of reference for discussing modes of urban movement. The first reason not to use the *flâneur* as a key concept is methodological: since the *flâneur* is traditionally a male (and arguably middle class)figure, it is a concept which has been argued to marginalize or even ignore the experiences of the working class, of women and of minority groups.[30] The last decades have seen a heated debate concerning feminist and gendered interpretations of the *flâneur*, initiated by Janet Wolff (1985) and Griselda Pollock (1988), and further developed by Leonore Davidoff (2003), D'Souza

& McDonough (2008), and others. I will return to the discussion concerning the *flâneuse* in Chapter 4, which deals with the gaze and the stratification of public space in early twentieth-century Finnish prose.

Most crucially, the *flâneur*, in the limited definition of Baudelaire and Benjamin, is largely absent from literature written in Finnish in the period examined here. The defining characteristic of the *flâneur*, that he goes "looking for that quality which you must allow me to call 'modernity'; for I know of no better word to express the idea I have in mind", as Baudelaire put it (Baudelaire 1863/1964: 12), is profoundly at odds with the way patterns of walking and mobility are played out in Finnish literature of this period. A more detailed discussion of the relevance, for literary experiences of Helsinki, of Benjamin's aesthetics of shock, and of images of *flânerie*, respectively, will be given in the conclusion to Chapter 3, and in the final part of Chapter 4.

Walking as Enunciation

A more inclusive and less contested (though hardly less opaque) theory of city walking is provided by Michel de Certeau in his essay "Walking in the City", which provides a useful alternative (or corrective addition) to the older conceptual framework built up around the *flâneur* (de Certeau 1984: 91–110; see also Prendergast 1992: 209–210). De Certeau begins his essay with a panoramic view of New York as seen from the top of the World Trade Center, and contrasts this comprehensive and totalizing bird-view perspective with the very different urban texture that comes into view when one descends to ground level. Here, one is confronted with an infinite "chorus of idle footsteps" performed by everyday activities (de Certeau 1984: 97); an invisible urban "text" which is constantly written by city walkers, but which eludes direct legibility.

An innovative aspect of de Certeau's approach is his way of understanding movement through space as a form of communication, and as *enunciation*. Drawing on John R. Searle's (1969) thoughts on the speech act, de Certeau argues that walking can be analysed by means of speech act theory as an act of enunciation similar to that of producing an utterance: the "act of walking is to the urban system what the speech act is to language or to the statements uttered" (de Certeau 1984: 97). Walking acts out a place, turns it into a lived space (ibid.: 97–98).[31] Movement through urban space, in de Certeau's understanding, is a dialogic enunciation, a view which resonates with Barthes's idea that "the city is a discourse and this discourse is truly a language: the city speaks to its inhabitants, we speak our city, the city where we are, simply by living in it, by wandering through it, by looking at it" (Barthes 1986/1997: 167).[32]

One of the characteristics of walking in de Certeau's understanding is that it has epistemological underpinnings (see also Borg 2011: 117–124). Walking is much more than a mere way of transporting oneself on foot – it can be a fundamentally sense-making operation, a way of getting to know one's environment. In this sense, walking is a way of ordering a complex totality, something which was also argued by Kevin Lynch (1960: 96; see also Sielaff 2004: 69 ff.). In literature, descriptions of a particular character's high mobility can be indicative of a profound knowledge of the urban space through which he/she is moving; the frantic movement, for example, of some of the characters in Finnish literature of the 1920s and 1930s, can be understood as directly linked to their readiness to go looking for knowledge of the urban geography, and the success with which such endeavours are carried out. Conversely, a sense of impeded mobility can stem from a character's limited understanding of the city. The uncertain first strolls taken by a newcomer to the metropolis, and the difficulties a literary character experiences when moving through his or her new environment can be understood as resulting from the ungainly epistemological process that is being carried out.

Heightened mobility does not, however, necessarily equal a heightened awareness of place, or vice versa. The relatively extensive mobility provided by movement by horse-drawn carriage, for example, typical of Finnish literature around the turn of the century, is far from being concomitant with an intimate knowledge of the space through which the character is moving. Walking (and, more generally, moving) through space does not only have an epistemological dimension, but also an ontological one. Applying the thinking of de Certeau on walking as enunciation, urban movement is also a means of expression of the self. Impeded mobility, for example in the case of characters in several prose texts of the 1920s and 1930s, goes hand in hand with an intimate and accurate (if often highly local) knowledge of the city. The cumbersome ways in which the characters move about, then, is not indicative of an epistemological shortcoming, but rather of the socially marginalized status of these characters in the story worlds in question (see Chapter 7).

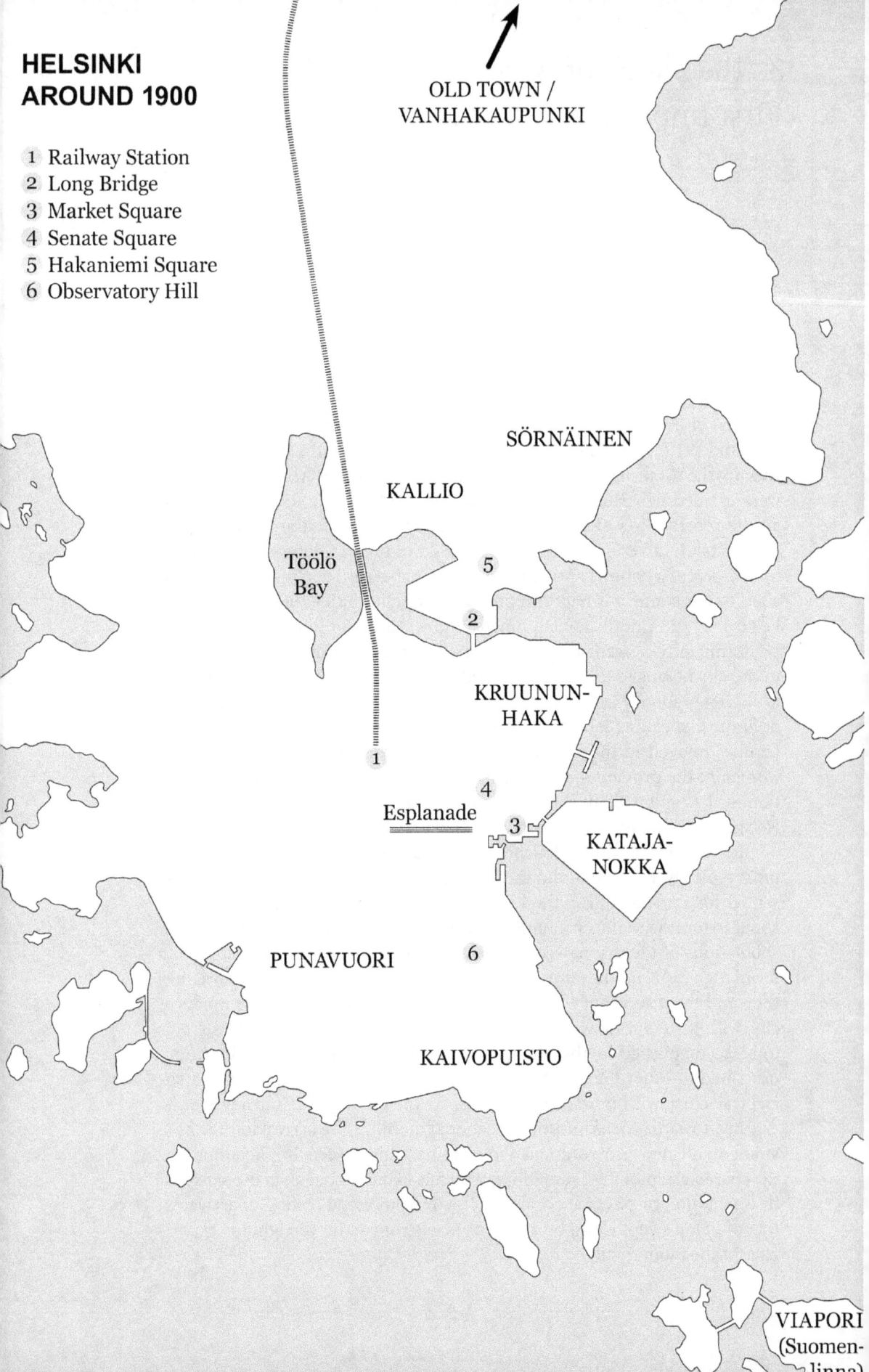

3. The Shock of Arrival: Expectations and First Impressions of the City

The first and most defining experience of Helsinki in Finnish literature at the turn of the twentieth century is that of arrival. In the period between 1889 and 1919, several novels and short stories describe the travel to, and arrival in, the Finnish capital. By the year 1911, five stories had appeared that were entitled "To Helsinki" ("Helsinkiin") (Liuttu 1950: 35, 47).[1] Almost all the protagonists of Finnish prose texts in this period are strangers to the capital. In a very concrete way, Helsinki in the period was, as the nineteenth-century national-romantic author Zacharias Topelius had claimed, "alien to the country it had to represent" (Topelius 1885/1986: 21; see also Veivo 1997: 28): until the late nineteenth century, the Finnish capital was predominantly a Swedish-speaking city, and most of the Finnish-speakers in the city belonged to the uneducated lower classes.[2] This situation began to change gradually towards the end of the century, when growing numbers of Finnish-speaking labourers, as well as students, civil servants and their families, moved to the capital. The experiences of these young men and women of the provinces, who constitute the first Finnish-speaking generation in the capital, form the raw material of a considerable number of the Helsinki novels and short stories that appeared in this period.

The description of the journey to the capital – on foot or by boat, or, most typically, by train – and the first hours and days in the capital are essential for understanding the kind of relationship literary characters are about to form with the city. In the experiences of arrival, many of the future tribulations of literary newcomers to the city can be found in embryonic form: high expectations, intoxicating excitement, alienation and disorientation, and the discrepancy between the dizzying experience of the modern city, with its tempting worldly pleasures, and the demanding tasks set out to be accomplished by the protagonist. The journey to the capital is often described in other than merely geographical terms: it is depicted as a social trajectory with moral implications. As the climax of a journey that is directed towards social and/or educational mobility, the arrival in the city's strange and new environment typically has unforeseen implications for the characters' mobility, something which is expressed in an acute sense of disorientation or physical paralysis. The overpowering feeling of arrival is that of being swept along by a violent maelstrom – the vertiginous experience of the modern city.

This chapter examines experiences of arrival in the city in Finnish literature in the late nineteenth and early twentieth centuries and explores how such experiences are informed by, and often juxtaposed with, earlier expectations. In the descriptions of the journey to, and the arrival in the city, the newcomers' confrontation with the urban world becomes visible in a condensed form. I will concentrate first on a reading of Juhani Aho's novella, *Helsinkiin* ("To Helsinki"; 1889), which will be complemented by a comparison with other turn-of-the-century Finnish prose texts featuring the arrival of a provincial protagonist in the capital. The most important other literary works discussed in this chapter are Arvid Järnefelt's novels *Veljekset* ("Brothers"; 1900), *Veneh'ojalaiset* ("The Family Veneh'oja"; 1909) and *Nuoruuteni muistelmia* ("Memories from my Youth"; 1919); Eino Leino's *Jaana Rönty* ("Jaana Rönty"; 1907) and *Olli Suurpää* ("Olli Suurpää"; 1908); Kyösti Wilkuna's *Vaikea tie* ("The Difficult Road"; 1915). Other novels will be mentioned in passing, amongst others Maila Talvio's *Tähtien alla* ("Under the Stars"; 1910) and *Kultainen lyyra* ("The Golden Lyre"; 1916).

Arrival in the City in Juhani Aho's Helsinkiin *(1889)*

The arrival of an outside individual in the city is one of the most potent *topoi* used in literature in the late nineteenth and early twentieth centuries (see Keunen 1999: 359, 2001: 427). It is a movement that Peter Brooks sees as one of the main instigators of what he calls the realist impulse, "the need, to describe, to account for, to perform a kind of immediate phenomenology of one's new surroundings" (Brooks 2005: 131). Throughout the nineteenth and into the twentieth century, an impressive cavalcade of European literary characters can be seen travelling from the countryside and from provincial towns to the capital, to be immersed in a strange and often estranging urban environment – from Dickens's Victorian London to Zola's Paris of the Second Empire, to the St. Petersburg of the Russian novel. It is an evolution which is also present in many Finnish novels at the turn of the twentieth century and beyond, which (sometimes literarily) trace the road to Helsinki.[3]

The first and in many respects still the most compelling literary description of the journey to and the arrival in the capital in Finnish literature is Juhani Aho's *Helsinkiin*.[4] *Helsinkiin* belongs to a literary genre which, in Finland at least, bears special relevance to the confrontation between the individual and the city in the late nineteenth and early twentieth centuries: the student novel. This genre in Finnish literary history is characterized by the arrival of a provincial character in the metropolis to pursue his/her studies, and the subsequent rise (and often fall) of the hero.[5] Originally, the Northern European student novel, a subgenre of the *Bildungsroman*, had presented student life in a positive, euphoric light. In the mid-1870s, however, a shift can be seen away from romantic ideals, towards more critical and pessimistic descriptions; a shift which was marked in Sweden by the appearance of Strindberg's short-story collection entitled *Från Fjärdingen och Svartbäcken* ("From Fjärdingen and Svartbäcken"; 1877) and in Norway by Arne Garborg's novel *Bondestudenter* ("Peasant students"; 1883). In Finland-Swedish literature, a similar shift can be noticed with the publication of K. A. Tavaststjerna's novel *Barndomsvänner* ("Childhood Friends"; 1886) (Söderhjelm 1916/1920: 118–120).[6] The change in the descriptions of student life in the city coincides with the growing influence of French naturalism, with its emphasis on degeneration and its interest in sexuality and prostitution (see Lyytikäinen 1997: x–xi). *Helsinkiin* can be seen as one of the literary examples of Finnish naturalism (Saarenheimo 1924: 166; Alhoniemi 1972: 89; Rossi 2007: 49). When the student novel appears in the prose literature written in Finnish near the last quarter of the nineteenth century, this paradigm shift was well underway, and many of the descriptions of student life in the city are consequently infused with a pessimistic vision of the city and what was seen as its dangerous, degenerating influence.

Helsinkiin recounts the story of young Antti Ljungberg, a Finn of Swedish-speaking background from the provincial town Kuopio, who travels to Helsinki by steam boat and train in order to pursue his studies at the Helsinki University – the only university of the autonomous Grand-Duchy of Finland. Upon arrival at the railway station in Helsinki, he is driven to the restaurant Kappeli, from where, at the end of the story, he is taken along, completely intoxicated, to an ill-reputed part of the city. What makes Aho's student novella particularly interesting is the fact that it was originally conceived by the author as a full-scale novel, but was eventually published as a condensed novella (Kopponen 1980; Lyytikäinen 1997: ix; Rossi 2007: 48–49). The text at hand presents the reader with a student novel in miniature form, with premonitions of the future developments of the protagonist, which lie outside of the horizon of the novella itself.

Aho's novella offers not just one possible vision of a young student's development vis-à-vis the city: the protagonist Antti is surrounded by a whole range of students, presenting the reader with a number of differing social and moral trajectories for a provincial student in the city. Amongst Antti's fellow students, Pekka is Antti's positive double: a diligent and serious student, whose example Antti is unlikely to follow. Kalle and eternal student Nieminen are Antti's negative doubles, foreshadowing Antti's possible future course, and his probable turn towards becoming a pleasure-loving, debt-amassing student (Kalle), and showing the consequent threat of becoming a physically, mentally and financially ruined elder student (Nieminen). The representation of a variety of possible student fates in the city is typical of the student novel, recurring in most if not all student novels at the turn of the century. Student doubles are symbolic of the guidance the protagonist needs when initiated into the modern world, and of the importance of sharing the disorientating experiences of modern urbanity. Student doubles and their differing trajectories also constitute the core of Tavaststjerna's novel *Barndomsvänner*, whose title, "childhood friends", hints at the dichotomy between the fates of main character Ben and his unreliable childhood friend, Syberg.[7]

As mentioned above, *Helsinkiin* was written after the Nordic student novel had made a turn towards more critical descriptions of student life, in a literary climate influenced by the negative connotations linked to the city in the realist and naturalist literature of the late nineteenth century. Pessimistic undertones are strongly visible in the description of the journey, which takes up the largest part of the novella's pages. Such negative premonitions are, however, juxtaposed with positive expectations towards Helsinki in Antti's daydreams of future success, and in the vision of Helsinki as a merry city of light and (sensuous) delight: Antti thinks of the capital as "that dizzying, dazzling Helsinki, which had been said to grow year by year grander and merrier" (Aho 1889/1997: 56).[8] But the optimistic visions are almost immediately offset by hints at the city's degenerative influence. The journey to Helsinki in Aho's novella is for the most part described as a slow descent into a dangerous hotbed of vice and sin. It should be noted that the description of this downward trajectory, tragic in itself, is for the most part infused with irony from the part of the narrator, and contains several highly comic elements.[9]

As Antti approaches Helsinki, he gradually falls prey to the three main dangers that infest the late nineteenth-century literary city, and that threaten the male outsider: wine, debt, and women. The latter danger carries special meanings in the genre of the student novel, since it is linked both to the thematics of coming-of-age, and to one of the most central themes in the Finnish student novel: that of the problematic relation between lower class women and the student (see Molarius 1996b; Rojola 2009: 19–21; Melkas 2009: 123–129). In literary texts drawing on naturalism and decadence, the city embodies, more than anything else, an atmosphere of immorality and seductive sexuality. This aestheticization of the moral and physical depths of the city can be traced to Baudelaire, and is typically related to the female body. In *Helsinkiin*, female figures feature prominently in the way Antti imagines his journey to Helsinki as a heroic quest rooted in medieval romance. Such figures include the idealized Alma, who does not reciprocate his love, as well as the more obliging waitresses on the boat – in *Helsinkiin* as well as in a whole range of prose texts in this period waitresses are repeatedly described as receptive to the advances of enthusiastic students. There is also the figure of Helsinki herself, which is described in relation to Antti's earlier visit to the city, in terms of a female figure with arms wide spread for an embrace (Aho 1889/1997: 17).[10] The thought of the capital, then, carries strong sexual undercurrents, and the journey to Helsinki is filled with anticipation. In Antti's conversations with fellow student and man-of-the-world Kalle, there is exciting talk of the famous café Kappeli and indirect mention of Helsinki's brothels and prostitutes (ibid.: 62–63).

The sensual undertones attached to the city in Aho's *Helsinkiin* reach a climax in the passage quoted below, in which young Antti imagines the capital he is hastening to. Spurred on by the alcohol-drenched talk of his more experienced companions, an exciting mirage of Helsinki starts to appear in his imagination:

> Helsinki began to loom in front of him like a dark red room decorated with velvet sofas, diffusing an enchanting perfume and with loosely clad creatures roaming about in the secretive semidarkness, moving ever closer to him, sitting

down on his knee, wrapping one arm around his neck while with the other, they played piano and sang that light, fiery tune – the same tune that Kalle was humming: "frallallalla, natten ä' bra!" [...]

His [Antti's] face had gone white, and when he took his glass, his hand was shaking noticeably. (Aho 1889/1997: 63)[11]

Helsinki is conjured up before Antti like a sensuous brothel, suggestively set in clair-obscure ("dark red room" [...] "semidarkness"), containing soft fabrics ("velvet sofas") and intoxicating all the senses. It is an enchanting environment pregnant with expectation, and the vision, in conjunction with the alcohol Antti has been consuming, has an immediate numbing effect on the protagonist, who has grown pale and whose hand is shaking. Both elements can be considered to be indications of the turn for the worse Antti's fate is gradually taking. Similar ill-bearing premonitions can be found throughout the novella, multiplying as Antti draws closer to the city. When stirring his "rum toddy", Antti is satisfied to notice he does it so skilfully that it almost seems he has a *"predisposition"* for it; the italicization is the narrator's, and one of the many ironic asides present in this story (ibid.: 54). After a night of heavy drinking on the ship to Helsinki, the sight of Lake Saimaa and the healthy beauty of nature contrast unfavourably with Antti's hangover and his dirty clothes, and he fears degeneration has already set in (ibid.: 72–73). When his hangover is washed away by the first schnapps, Antti's cheeks start to glow like someone suffering from consumption (ibid.: 74). All these references can be seen as portentous omens. The journey to the city has a gradual corrupting and immobilizing effect on the young student protagonist.

Mobility and the Degenerating City

During most of the events described in *Helsinkiin*, the protagonist is on the move, and much of his sensations of mobility can be linked to his expectations of life in the city, to his hopes for a future social and academic rise, and to his implicit, subsequent fall. In Aho's novella, symbols of mobility and speed take on important roles. Aho has been considered as the "painter of modernization *par excellence*" in Finnish literature (Lappalainen 1998b: 80), and in much of his work, he uses vehicles of mobility, such as trains and trams, as multi-layered literary motifs (for example in *Rautatie* [*The Railroad*; 1884]; *Yksin* ["Alone"; 1890/2003]) to express the altered sense of time and space that resulted from the accelerating processes of urbanization and modernization.[12] In *Helsinkiin*, the pace of the journey has a direct effect on the way the narration is constructed: the rhythm of the journey to Helsinki, which starts off at a rather leisurely pace on the boat from Kuopio, seems to gradually move towards an almost sexual climax when Antti and his fellow students board the train at Lappeenranta. Sensuous adventures seem to be promised by every whistle of the locomotive:

> And this promise [of future adventures] could already be felt in every passionate whistle of the locomotive, and in the raging motion of the train and in all those

stations rapidly moving away behind them – all those things which meant that the journey becomes shorter every moment and their destination Helsinki is coming closer and closer. Helsinki! towards which they are racing with the speed of an ever accelerating stream, and which awaits like a quiet pool, boiling with bubbles, ever more greedily swallowing up the stream. (Aho 1889/1997: 76–77)[13]

The acceleration felt by Antti as he approaches Helsinki is reflected in the narration by ever denser sentences, which seem to be running almost out of breath ("in every passionate [...] and in the raging motion [...] and in all those stations [...] all those things"), and which come to a climax with the triumphal mention of Helsinki. The effect of the narration is further enhanced by a change to the present tense ("Helsinki *is* coming closer"; "towards which they *are racing*" [my emphasis]). The capital is described here as the nexus of Antti's mobility, the goal, "boiling with bubbles", of the mighty stream which transports the masses of the people. The metaphor of the city as a vibrant centre, while the countryside consists of still and forgotten waters, is developed further when the narrator describes the provincial town of Savonlinna and some of its inhabitants, students of old, who are described as having stepped outside of the "flow of people streaming down to the big world" and who are left aside in a small and silent bay beside the stream (ibid.: 55).

Antti's emotions change from the one extreme to the other as he approaches the city. When he hears somebody mention Helsinki, the name has a menacing sound, and he is frightened (ibid.: 78); but the first view of Helsinki is that of dancing people at the Alppila restaurant (ibid.: 80), and when the train arrives at Töölö Bay, the lights of Helsinki become visible, illuminating the sky ahead so that it is "blazing red like a fire" (ibid.: 80).[14] At this point another restaurant becomes visible, Kaisaniemi restaurant, and Antti is again seized by a chilling anxiety. The appearance of restaurants in quick succession, while entirely plausible when taking into account the actual train trajectory referred to, can be seen as symptomatic of the protagonist's view of the city as well as of his possible future.

The views of Alppila and Töölö Bay offer the first glimpses of the actual city, which had loomed large in the background of Antti's thoughts during the whole journey south. Particularly telling is the sudden opening of the cityscape when the train enters the area of Töölö Bay, presenting a near-panoramic view of the capital. This view presented the first sight of the metropolis to generations of people moving to the capital, and in the first decades of writing on Helsinki, it was much more prominent than the view now considered to be the quintessential one of arrival in Helsinki, namely, the skyline viewed from the sea. The view of the city, with its menacing, near-apocalyptic sky with lights as of fire, combined with the sensation of the speeding train and glimpses of dancing couples observed from the coach window, give the whole scene a grim ambiguity, reminiscent of the skeleton dances of late medieval imagery. It conveys an impression of a city of both leisure and light, but also of fiery fire, consuming newcomers, the idea of the city as a "blazing furnace" (Lefebvre 1974/1991: 93), which will return, in particular, in the writings of L. Onerva (see Chapter 5).

When Antti arrives in the capital, the predominant sensation related to his arrival is not that of independent movement, but of being taken along. In bouts and fits, Antti has grown increasingly paralyzed during the journey, and upon arrival at the Helsinki railway station, his sense of frightened expectation culminates in complete immobility when the train comes to a standstill:

> When the train came to a stop under the glass roof and he had to emerge from the carriage, he felt he couldn't move. His knee-joints were like jelly, and they didn't want to carry him. (Aho 1889/1997: 80)[15]

The confusing sense of arrival in a large city's railway station is a central convention of the city novel, "a founding scene of urbanization" as Arne Toftegaard Pedersen calls it in his discussion of an arrival scene at the Helsinki railway station in a poem by Tavaststjerna (Toftegaard Pedersen 2007: 84–85). Hana Wirth-Nesher points out that in such scenes, the train station "conventionally signifies change, movement, promise, or escape, and it offers an intensified form of the city street"; it constitutes "the city's seam, a place of crossing over, mingling, romance, adventure and intrigue" (Wirth-Nesher 1996: 39–40). For Antti Ljungberg in *Helsinkiin*, the experience of arrival is both climactic and paralyzing, and an important step towards the unmasking of his idealist illusions of future success. He becomes completely dependent on others for movement, is swept along by the stream of passengers, after which he is dragged along and forcefully taken to the Kappeli restaurant, which is announced from afar by the loud music of its orchestra, playing on the bandstand in front of the restaurant (Aho 1889/1997: 81–83).

In a long paragraph, the dazzling spectacle of Helsinki's most famous restaurant is described. It is as if Antti has arrived, at last, in the brothel of his earlier imagination, or in the "quiet pool" of the earlier simile, although the effect is very different and much more disconcerting:

> In a daze, as if swept down a foaming waterfall, Antti found himself seated after a moment on a soft sofa in a green room with a many-splendoured cut-glass chandelier, paintings on the walls and a huge mirror. It was as if he'd fallen into a quietly hissing pool, but not a restful one, a frothing maelstrom that a moment later would hurl him down another waterfall, still lower, with no end in sight. He felt he was being whirled round and round, his head spinning, with the blood going to his brain and flushing all sense of direction from his eyes. For a moment Antti had no idea where he had come from and where he was going. (ibid.: 84)[16]

The move to the city is described as a river gathering force, flowing downward; a symbol of the debasing turn Antti's life has taken when moving to the city. Helsinki appears as a series of violent rapids and waterfalls, hurling Antti lower and lower, "with no end in sight". Like the brothel of his earlier imagination, Kappeli is a space that combines gentle textures ("a soft sofa") with disorientating light effects (the "many-splendoured cut-glass chandelier", the "huge mirror"). Most strikingly, it is a space in movement, as if the accelerating journey to the capital has never really stopped, but continues at an even faster pace, even though physically speaking, Antti has come to a standstill. The resulting disorientation is taken to a point where the protagonist is not only incapable of reading his environment, but utterly unable to remember "where he had come from and where he was going". The protagonist's characterization as passive driftwood in the maelstrom of the modern world, rather than as an energetic actor, is one of the traits that link *Helsinkiin* to the poetics of naturalist fiction.

The figurative language used by Juhani Aho to describe the experience of Helsinki is remarkably similar to how Marshall Berman and others have described the experience of the city in modernity. The image of the maelstrom, in particular, is used on numerous occasions in Berman's *All That Is Solid Melts Into Air*, and Berman claims that to "be modern […] is to experience personal and social life as a maelstrom" (Berman 1982/1989: 345–346). Berman wants to describe the actual experience of modernity, but repeatedly turns to literary texts for his dissection of modern experiences. His analysis of Rousseau's *Julie, ou la nouvelle Héloïse* (*Julie, or the New Heloise*; 1761), recounts a sense of shock similar to the one felt by Antti in Aho's *Helsinkiin* and described above:

> This atmosphere – of agitation and turbulence, physic dizziness and drunkenness, expansion of experiential possibilities and destruction of moral boundaries and personal bonds, self-enlargement and self-derangement, phantoms in the street and in the soul – is the atmosphere in which modern sensibility is born. (Berman 1982/1989: 18)

Like Rousseau's *Julie, ou la nouvelle Héloïse*, and like so many novels featuring young protagonists from the province moving to the capital, Aho's *Helsinkiin* is bound up with a distinctly new kind of experience – the experience of modernity, grounded in the ever-more accelerating life in expanding cities. This is one way in which Antti's experience of shock can be understood: a sense of profound disorientation that stems from the violent confrontation with the agitating rush of modernity, embodied here in the city; what Pertti Karkama, in his study of modernity in Finnish literature has called the "modern crisis experience" (Karkama 1994: 192–208).

The scene in Kappeli is not the final stage of Antti's downward trajectory. After recovering for a moment with the help of some drinks and sociable chatter, he becomes tired and sleepy, blinded by the dazzling light of the chandelier (Aho 1889/1997: 88–89). By now almost completely numbed, Antti lends some money (which he had received from his mother as precious extra pocket money) to one of his new friends, and is taken along outside. Horse-drawn carriages are ordered, and when trying to board one of the carriages, Antti at first falls. He succeeds a second time; and the last thing the reader sees of Antti is his white student cap, which disappears in the Helsinki night (ibid.: 90).[17] The address which is given to the driver – *Tarkk'ampujankatu 15* – does not seem to carry any implicit meanings for Antti, but for the surrounding students, and certainly for the contemporary reader, there was no doubt where Antti was heading at the very end of the story: to a brothel in Helsinki's seedy district Punavuori.[18]

The Young Man/Woman from the Province

In the decades following the appearance of *Helsinkiin*, dozens of subsequent novels and short stories describing the arrival of provincial newcomers to the Finnish capital appeared, drawing on the prototypical features of arrival present in Juhani Aho's novella, and adding new elements. Most of the protagonists travelling to the capital in literary works of the late nineteenth and early twentieth centuries share some characteristic traits with Antti Ljungberg, but many of their experiences of the city are put in further perspective by a profound sense of uprootedness, and by descriptions of the specific climatic conditions accompanying arrival. Similarly to *Helsinkiin*, the first experiences and expectations of the city in subsequent short stories and novels can be directly related to images of mobility, both in the sense of geographical mobility and in the sense of social and moral trajectories.

Several of the novels discussed below are, like *Helsinkiin*, student novels, but the generic framework of the student novel alone does not provide a sufficient analytical tool with which to attempt a comprehensive view of the confrontation with the city in Finnish turn-of-the-century literature.[19] This is due first of all to the fact that it fails to offer a typology that could connect the experience of Helsinki in Finnish literature with the relevant urban imagery in other literary traditions in this period. Moreover, by concentrating on the experiences of only one particular group in society, it excludes a considerable number of urban experiences in Finnish prose. Juhani Aho's Antti Ljungberg and the other students featuring so prominently in Finnish prose of the late nineteenth century are by far not the only group in society whose move from the provinces to the capital is depicted in literature. At the end of the nineteenth century, Helsinki was one of Europe's fastest-growing capitals, attracting people from all social classes. For all these people, the city constituted the nexus of their expectations, the hub of the wheel upon which their fortunes were made or broken.

One larger and more inclusive typology is provided by that of the "Young Man from the Provinces", which was first introduced by Lionel Trilling in his foreword to the novel *The Princess Casamassima* (1948) by Henry James, and explored in detail by A. K. Chanda (1981).[20] In his article, "The Young Man from the Provinces", Chanda attempts to define an ideal type of the literary character of the Young Man, drawing from a range of British, American and French novels, mostly from the nineteenth century, but with references to earlier literature (such as picaresque novels) and to twentieth-century examples. Summarizing the most important features, Chanda's Young Man is a provincial person moving to the city, a "romantic social climber" who rejects his pastoral past and who "possesses innate aristocratic refinement" (Chanda 1981: 339). The Young Man's meteoric rise in society, which is reversely connected to his moral development, is followed by his "irreversible tragic fall" (ibid.). Although Chanda consistently speaks about the Young *Man* from the provinces, female heroes are also included in his typology.

In order to apply Chanda's typology to the Finnish context, a number of reservations will have to be made. In Finland before independence, social rise for speakers of Finnish was defined and obstructed by three central factors: Russian oppression, the unceasing, although gradually diminishing, concentration of political and cultural power in the hands of the Finland-Swedish elite, and the historical absence of a large Finnish-speaking urban middle class. These factors have far-reaching consequences for the social, political and geographical mobility of young Finnish men and women trying to make their mark on history, and on the representations in literature of their endeavours. Due to these restraining factors, a number of Chanda's features that are characteristic for the Young Man from the Provinces are absent or appear in a modified form in Finnish prose. In particular, this is the case for the hero's spectacular rise in society, to the heights of the high nobility. In the Finnish context, the magical stroke of luck, brought about by some powerful benefactor, and the subsequent meteoric rise, are out of the question.[21] Another feature which Chanda deems essential for the Young Man is his "innate refinement, the charm and personal beauty which enable him to adapt himself to, and be adapted to, high society" (Chanda 1981: 328), features which are hard to find in descriptions of the Finnish Young Man from the Provinces.

Although the Finnish Young Man from the Provinces lacks innate aristocratic features and generally does not experience a meteoric rise in society, he is not merely a parvenu. According to Chanda, what sets the Young Man apart from the parvenu is a "certain fineness of spirit, a yearning for the rich possibilities of life, which raises him above mediocrity" (ibid.: 329). This is certainly true for a number of Finnish young provincials moving to the capital: sensitive heroes eager to embrace the opportunities offered by the city can be seen in several novels by Santeri Ivalo, Arvid Järnefelt, Kyösti Wilkuna and Maila Talvio.[22] For several protagonists in Finnish Young Man novels, sensitivity lies close to sensibility: they are romantic dreamers, to the point almost of becoming sentimental heroes. In Juhani Aho's *Helsinkiin*, moreover, the journey of young Antti attains almost Quixotic dimensions. Antti ironically resembles a knightly hero, in whose quest all conventions of late medieval romance are turned upside down. *Helsinkiin* can in fact be read as a reversed "novel of ordeal", a genre which in Bakhtin's words is "constructed as a series of tests of the main heroes, tests of their fidelity, valour, bravery, virtue, nobility, sanctity, and so on" (Bakhtin 1986/2004: 12). Antti's virtue, fidelity and valour are continuously tested, and in every test he fails.[23]

In their confrontation with the city, the immature sensitivity of the Finnish Young Men is juxtaposed with the merciless modern world of the city, with which it is utterly out of tune – typical in this respect is the story of Juuso, the eponymous "Stepchild of his Time" of Ivalo's *Aikansa lapsipuoli* ("Stepchild of his Time"). Juuso arrives to the city with high hopes, both personally and politically, but all his idealistic endeavours end in failure. Divorced by his wife and completely disappointed with life, he ends up in a mental institute after an unsuccessful attempt to kill his cynical nemesis Heikki.

Apart from the satirized residue of medieval romance mentioned above, three important features of the Young Man (as defined by Chanda) can be singled out for their relevance to how the confrontation with the city is given form in Finnish prose texts around the turn of the twentieth century. These are the rejection of the Young Man's provincial and often impoverished roots, the fact that the Young Man is a social achiever who rises and who, in most cases, also falls, and finally, that in his rise, he is accompanied by a *Doppelgänger*. We have seen how in *Helsinkiin*, Antti is surrounded by a whole range of student doubles, and in Finnish late nineteenth- and early twentieth-century novels featuring provincials in the city, doubles abound. Examples of such doubles can be found in a number of contemporary novels featuring arrival in the city, such as Järnefelt's *Veneh'ojalaiset* (Hannes and Hinkki) and *Nuoruuteni muistelmia* ("Memories from my Youth"; 1919; the female doubles Hilja and Sanna), Ivalo's *Aikansa lapsipuoli* (Juuso and Heikki), Talvio's *Kultainen lyyra* ("The Golden Lyre"; 1916; the female doubles Helmi and Martta).[24]

Expectations and First Experiences of Helsinki

Competing Visions

What kinds of expectations and first experiences related to arrival in Helsinki can be found in the prose texts featuring Young Men and Women from the Provinces in the late nineteenth and early twentieth centuries? One striking feature is the fact that the experience of the capital is often initiated by juxtaposing positive and negative expectations of the city. In the case of Aho's *Helsinkiin*, such polarizing expectations had been mostly filtered through the thoughts of the main character. In a number of later texts, conflicting opinions on the city are typically voiced by characters surrounding the protagonist. In Hilda Tihlä's story *Leeni* (1907), for example, the female protagonist Leeni is given a distinctly pessimistic image of the city as a cesspool of vice by her grandmother, while her grandfather gives a more positive appreciation of the city as a place with tens of churches and hundreds of priests.[25] A similar dichotomy between two conflicting visions of Helsinki, those of a city of worldly pleasures and a city of godliness, respectively, is present in Maila Talvio's short story "Helsinkiin" ("To Helsinki"; 1896), in which the young maid Anna-Kaisa is given the opportunity to work in the Finnish capital. The woman who offers Anna-Kaisa the job evokes conflicting images of the city; to Anna-Kaisa, she recounts how she "will become a perfect beauty when she dresses up in the right clothes, and that everybody is going to like her; she will take part in the dances and the fun of the capital, as much as she ever wishes to" (Talvio 1896: 174).[26] On the other hand, Anna-Kaisa's worried family and fiancé are assured that "there are beautiful churches in Helsinki, in which every day of the week Mass is said, and there are such good priests" (ibid.).[27]

In both examples, the expectations of the city are structured as alternative versions of the protagonist's future development, in a way that resembles Antti Ljungberg's student doubles in Juhani Aho's *Helsinkiin*. Presenting such alternative futures constitutes what Hilary Dannenberg has called "temporal orchestration": a narrative strategy that creates suspense in the way it invites the reader to speculate about the coming events on the basis of conflicting or alternative futures (see Dannenberg 2008: 42, 45–52). I would add that temporal orchestration also activates the readers' awareness of genre and period conventions, since the competing versions will be perceived as more or less plausible depending on the presence of conventional motifs or themes. In Maila Talvio's "Helsinkiin", for example, the fact that Anna-Kaisa has lent such a receptive ear to the talk of nice clothes and great fun in the city does not bide well for her future social and moral trajectory, and the reader will be inclined to believe that once in the capital, she will be looking more for the nearest party than for the nearest church. However, in the case of this particular story, a third, implicit possible future would seem to be even more probable. The interest of a young working-class woman for worldly pleasures and beautiful clothes is a common generic premonition in Young Woman of the Provinces -novels, which tends to come to degenerating fruition in the form of a descent into prostitution. In the case of Maila Talvio's "Helsinkiin", possible futures are all the information the reader is left with: the short story ends when Anna-Kaisa leaves her home village, and she is told to be already "on the verge of taking the first steps into its [Helsinki's] enchanting circle" (Talvio 1896: 180).[28]

Similar contrasting versions of future urban experiences informed by Biblical images of the city (as well as by genre- and period-related conventions), are also present in Santeri Ivalo's prototypical student novel *Hellaassa* ("In Hellas"; 1890), which opens with a description of the protagonist's sense of frightened expectation as he ponders the impending move to the capital:

> His old mother had already been grieving over him for going so young to that Babylon – as she put it – where so many good boys had come to grief. – Hm… There were always dangers, of course, especially for weak characters, who threw themselves unthinkingly into the stream. It was said that the atmosphere that reigned there was bad, too – an air of decay. (Ivalo 1890: 2)[29]

To young Eljas, the protagonist of *Hellaassa*, the city represents a morally dangerous place, characterized by an air of decay. He also implicitly thinks, however, that the city is particularly dangerous for "feeble characters", thus implying contrasting alternative futures for his own development in relation to the capital. Since he is endowed with a healthy self-esteem, Eljas retains high hopes of success in the city. His ambitions, however, are very different from those of Antti in *Helsinkiin*, whose ideas of self-advancement and sexual adventures are in stark contrast to Eljas's naïve conception of self-sacrifice in the service of a Fennoman programme he will find to be obsolete. The Biblical connotations of the confrontation with the city can also be linked to the name of the protagonist: Eljas as a Finnish rewriting of the prophet Eliah, who fought the false prophets of Babylon.[30]

In the quote above, there is a second juxtaposition, in addition to the implicit dichotomy success-failure: the opposition between quiet countryside-waters and the violent stream of the capital, which is couched in figurative language similar to the one used in Aho's *Helsinkiin*. Significantly, while Eljas ponders the danger of letting himself be swept along by the stream of the capital, he is surrounded by the still waters of an inland swamp (Ivalo 1890: 1–2). This juxtaposition of still countryside waters and the violent downhill stream of the city is further accentuated in the opening scene of the fourth chapter, which is set one third into the novel. This chapter, set immediately after a time lapse during which Eljas has settled down in Helsinki, is introduced by a long metaphor of down-pouring snowy water, streaming unrelentingly down the eaves into the "black, deep, dark sewers", portraying the degenerating and paralyzing effect the city has had on the idealistic protagonist (ibid.: 54).[31] As in the case of *Helsinkiin*, the city is symbolized by raging waters, and its centrifugal power will have a disorientating and degenerating effect.

In *Hellaassa*, Eljas's arrival in the city is not narrated; the narration shifts directly from the quiet countryside environment to a lively bar scene in Helsinki. To a certain extent, however, this environment presents a shock similar to the one found in Aho's *Helsinkiin*; the frantic scene at the bar conveys a testing ground that will give a first indication of which of the earlier alternative futures Eljas will be most likely to take. The bar scene also reveals the meaning of the enigmatic novel title "In Hellas", which a reader might first have thought to relate to Eljas's optimistic ideas of future educational success. "Hellas", however, is not the cradle of learning embodied in Helsinki's University, but the name of a derelict bar at the outskirts of the capital, where Eljas's dreams will turn out to be illusions. It should be added that these dreams are related not so much to projected high social status, love, fame, or financial gains, as in many of the international Young Man/Woman novels discussed by Chanda, but must be seen in the context of the Finnish national-romantic ideals of the provincial student's task in the nation's history. In a number of crucial scenes set in the bar Hellas, it becomes clear that Eljas, too, is one of the "feeble characters" he contemptuously derided at the outset of the novel, and that his high ideals are utterly out of tune with the cynical reality in the city.

Restlessness and Rootlessness

In Ivalo's *Hellaassa*, Talvio's "Helsinkiin", and Tihlä's *Leeni*, the actual experience of arrival is glossed over. A shocking sense of arrival in the city is narrated more explicitly, in terms that bring to mind Juhani Aho's prototypical rendering, in a number of other turn-of-the-century prose texts. The shock of arrival is not always linked to the very first time a character arrives in the city; Antti Ljungberg, too, had been to Helsinki once before the momentous journey described in *Helsinkiin*. Even to literary characters who know the capital, a return to the city could incur a profound shock. At the outset of Kyösti Wilkuna's student novel *Vaikea tie* ("The Difficult Road"; 1915), young Markus Kaarlela arrives in Helsinki to continue his studies. The opening lines of the novel describe his contradictory and anxious sentiments upon arrival:

> The hands of the tower clock approached two in the afternoon, when student Markus Kaarlela, walking down Nikolainkatu, arrived at the House of Estates. When he noticed that one of the benches in the small park was unoccupied and sheltered from the blazing sun, he walked to the bench and sat down puffing and panting. [...] He sensed a vague restlessness and strange excitement in his nerves, similar to what everyone feels who has just arrived from the quiet country life to the noise and the disparate bustle of the capital. The rattle of the carts, the shrill shouts of the newspaper sellers and the foul squealing of the trams turning a corner unpleasantly preyed on his nerves, while the blunt angularity of the stone buildings rising up everywhere around him, and the stylized beauty of the cramped little parks oppressed his mind, which was accustomed to nature's freer forms. (Wilkuna 1915: 5–6)[32]

The stimuli that are experienced as most disturbing to Markus are related to elements that emphasize the difference between the feverish city and the quiet countryside; elements that can be considered as symptomatic of the time-space compression typical of the modernizing city, such as the (daily) newspapers and the tram.[33] Significantly, the very first word of the novel refers to the hands of the clock tower that set the urban day apart from the more cyclical time of the countryside. The architectural formality of the environment, as well as the limited natural space of cramped and stylized parks, has a further unpleasant effect upon the young student. The result is, not, however, entirely negative, but instead, Markus feels a "vague restlessness" and a "strange excitement" – the Finnish original of the latter word ("kiihottuneisuus"), in particular, bears strong sensuous connotations.

The most pressing reason for Markus's sense of restlessness and insecurity is the physical lack of a home in the city. It was a condition in which he was not alone: it was common for students to return to the country for the summer months and to search for new quarters upon return to the city at the beginning of the academic year (see Kervanto-Nevanlinna 2003a: 353). While Markus searches for a student room, guided through the city by announcements in a newspaper, his earlier time in Helsinki is recounted in a flash-back. Markus had originally arrived in the city full of good intentions, but things have not gone as planned: like so many Finnish students, "immersed in the life of the capital, he had been like a tree wrenched from its roots, without any certainty to turn to, and susceptible to every gust of wind" (ibid.: 6).[34] The University, too, has given him an alienating impression, not in the least because the dominant language there is still Swedish. All in all, the contact with the city has had a paralyzing effect on Markus: "with some of his closest friends, he had led an apathetic and vegetative life" and especially during the cold and rainy autumn nights, he had spent as much of his time as possible in bars and restaurants "where alcohol and music muffled his paralyzed mind like fluffy feathers" (ibid.: 7).[35]

The dreary autumn weather mentioned on the first pages of *Vaikea tie* can be found in many other Finnish novels of the time, correlating intensely with the gloomy emotions of the protagonist arriving in the capital. The connection in literature between arrival in the city and gloomy weather is not wholly coincidental: for many urban classes, city life naturally started or resumed at the end of the summer. The first extensive impressions of the city, then, are often infused with the dreary September and October weather unfortunately still typical for Helsinki. The autumn weather does not always lead to despondent sentiments in Helsinki novels. Maila Talvio's *Tähtien alla* ("Under the Stars"; 1910) gives a vivid impression of the rain-drenched Helsinki streets in the beginning of October, again with repeated references to violently downpouring waters. But the description continues more cheerfully: "People got used to life without the sun, the moon or the high stars. They filled the bars, theatres, restaurants and conference rooms [...] and dedicated themselves completely to those activities and distractions, which Helsinki has so amply in store for the autumn." (Talvio 1910: 5)[36]

The description of autumnal nature carries a particular meaning within the decadent and naturalist frame of reference, accentuating notions of decline and degeneration. Gloomy weather conditions accompany the protagonist's return to Helsinki at the end of the summer in Arvid Järnefelt's panoramic novel *Veljekset* ("Brothers"; 1900), in which the main character, Henrik, goes through events remarkably similar to those befalling Markus in *Vaikea tie*. Henrik's return is set at the beginning of the third and final part of the novel, after more than 400 pages of travelling through different parts and cities of Finland. The protagonist's unhappy feelings upon return to the capital are reflected in the gloomy weather conditions: "[...] the weather had become very grim. Cold, fierce autumn winds gusted through the streets, raising dust clouds in the air and causing the yellowish linden leaves on the sidewalks to whirl about" (Järnefelt 1900: 411).[37] One typical urban sound – now long forgotten – adds to the depressing atmosphere: that of the telephone network, whimpering above the city. The people of Helsinki are described in terms that recur frequently in literature of this period, and that are still commonly used today: "hastily going to and fro on business of their own, without paying attention to anybody else" (ibid.).[38] The most depressing and urgent matter, however, is the lack of a physical home in the city, which gives Henrik a feverish sense of forlornness when he returns to his hotel room after a useless search:

> Nothing was left now of the grandeur with which he had arrived in the city. His new mood was forgotten and all of a sudden, amidst this tiring, restless fever, he again became the insecure Henrik of old. He was unable to think of anything else, all he could do was to agonize over this lodging business. (ibid.: 413–414)[39]

In Henrik's case, as in the examples mentioned earlier, the high expectations entertained by the main character are crushed by the realities encountered in the city. The effect is disorientating to first-comers, but even to people who know their way in Helsinki, arrival in the city in turn-of-the-century Finnish prose texts embodies an immediate, disconcerting and paralyzing shock, which impairs the characters' senses and their mental facilities.

An all-pervading sense of homelessness in the city is common to many of the Young Men and Women of the Provinces arriving in the city. It is a homelessness that is typically related to the uprootedness of the paternal home in the countryside, which either precedes the arrival of the Young Man in the capital, or occurs not long after his arrival. In Järnefelt's *Veljekset* and equally in *Veneh'ojalaiset* ("The Family Veneh'oja"; 1909), the violent disappearance of the elderly home or home lands acts as one of the prime movers of the narrated action, and a wish to re-create the lost home constantly and feverishly spurs on the main characters. In Eino Leino's *Olli Suurpää* ("Olli Suurpää"; 1908) the imaginary loss of the fatherly mansion looms large in the subconscious of Olli, while in Leino's *Jaana Rönty* ("*Jaana Rönty*; 1907), rootlessness is what defines the background of the protagonist Jaana and her family (see Molarius 1998c).[40] Maila Talvio's *Tähtien alla* (1910) features an auctioning of the furniture of the elderly home similar to the one described in Arvid Järnefelt's *Veljekset*.[41] In Talvio's earlier novel *Aili* ("Aili"; 1897), the death of the father of the protagonist immediately precedes Aili's move to Helsinki, while in Arvid Järnefelt's *Isänmaa* ("The Fatherland"; 1893), Santeri Ivalo's *Aikansa lapsipuoli* and Kyösti Wilkuna's *Vaikea tie*, the death of the father completes the protagonist's sense of rootlessnes that had accumulated during his years in the capital.[42]

The examples above clearly illustrate that the experiences of Helsinki in Finnish prose literature of this time are exclusively those of an outsider to the city. Until the appearance of Arvid Järnefelt's *Veneh'ojalaiset*, there are no clear examples of literary characters that can be considered as natives to Helsinki in literature written in Finnish. All protagonists are strangers to the capital, as were the authors of the first Helsinki novels and short stories. It is a generation of in-between people: the first generation of Finnish-speakers aiming at a university education, the first generation of countryside labourers moving into the industrializing centres, the first generation to make the move from physical to spiritual work (see Melkas et al. 2009).

The sense of shock inherent to crossing the perceived divide between a backward, slow-moving Finnish-speaking countryside and mesmerizing, cultivated, active and originally Swedish-speaking capital is further informed by the context of turn-of-the-century literary movements such as naturalism and decadence, which have particular relevance to many of the short stories and novels discussed here. Drawing on new insights from the natural sciences and inspired by Darwinist thinking, fin-de-siècle literary and cultural movements had an outspoken interest in entropy, decline and degeneration.[43] In the struggle for life in the modern city, it was thought that one and the same generation could not jump social classes; the move from the working class living in the countryside to the educated class living in the city had to be performed over a period spanning many generations, and if an individual wanted to enjoy the fruits of future generations too early, this carried an almost inevitable danger. For a member of the Finnish "race", with its non-urban background and its specific nature-bound racial features, a move too quickly upward in society was thought to lead to degeneration. Not surprisingly, in this context, we find the protagonist of *Hellaassa*, an idealist-turned-cynic, sometime after his arrival in Helsinki reading Max Nordau, one of the most famous exponents of the Darwinist-inspired theories of decline and degeneration.

In a number of stories of the 1910s, this social Darwinist dimension of the shock of arrival, which was visible in earlier writings, becomes explicitly spelled-out. In Maila Talvio's *Kultainen lyyra* ("The Golden Lyre"; 1916), the two competing positions concerning the protagonist's, Helmi's, imminent move to Helsinki are voiced by stereotypical characters given opposing speeches at the protagonist's graduation party. While the local agronomist attacks the city and its degenerating influence, a young female native of Helsinki defends the importance of the capital for the nation. The speech criticizing the city accuses Helsinki of bleeding the countryside dry, and warns that moving to the city is not without its dangers:

> [...] the displacement from a class which practises physical work, to the class which practises mental work, is certainly not always, for the persons in question, anything easy or pleasant. It can in fact be dangerous both for body and soul. That displacement, that displacement, and that new soil – not all saplings are able to endure that. (Talvio 1916: 38)[44]

In reaction to this speech, the city girl Pirsta (Birgitta) accuses provincials of considering the city as an abscess that has to be operated from a healthy body; in her opinion, the city constitutes the brains to the body, made up of the countryside (Talvio 1916: 39).[45] The terms in which Pirsta defends the city make use of the metaphorization of the city as body, a metaphorization which is frequently used to couch criticism of the city, and appropriated by the young city woman in defence of the capital. In *Kultainen lyyra*, competing views of the city inform the narrative from the beginning to the end. Eventually, Helmi, utterly fatigued by her exertions in the city, returns home to die at the farmstead of her parents, the same house that had been the setting for the graduation party. In a delirium, she imagines how at her funeral, the agronomist reiterates his earlier warnings: "Do you see it now; she could not stand the displacement. Even trees need a schooling time before they can adapt. She couldn't stand it." (Talvio 1916: 181)[46]

The shocking and debilitating experience of arrival in turn-of-the-century Finnish literature is thus closely related to the naturalist and decadent paradigms on which these novels and short stories draw. The idea of the Young Man or Woman from the Provinces as a young sapling displaced violently from its native (and Finnish-speaking) soil, into an alien ground, and of the necessary shock this transplantation must have for the individuals in question, is found repeatedly in Finnish prose stories as well as in poetry in the early twentieth century (see Molarius 1998a: 103–106).[47] The recourse to metaphors or similes from nature to describe this urban experience ("saplings" and "soil") further adds to the sense of displacement from a natural environment, as in the excerpt from *Vaikea tie* quoted earlier, in which the protagonist, Markus, is described as "a tree wrenched from its roots, without any certainty to turn to, and susceptible to every gust of wind" (1915: 6).

Arrival and the Paralyzing City

In Aho's *Helsinkiin*, the disorientation and immobilisation of the main character had been initiated during the railway journey to Helsinki. The description of the first confrontation with the Finnish capital in terms of an immobilising experience recurs in several Finnish prose texts from the turn of the twentieth century. One notable example is provided by Arvid Järnefelt's *Nuoruuteni muistelmia* ("Memories of my Youth"; 1919), a novel written under the pseudonym of Hilja Kahila.[48] *Nuoruuteni muistelmia* is a work of popular fiction, which recycled a number of earlier motifs from the Young Man/Woman from the Provinces repertoire. In this novel, the young protagonist Hilja travels by train to Helsinki in search of work, and in search of the boy she secretly loves. As in a number of other Finnish Young Man/Woman from the Provinces novels, the arrival in the city comes quite late, some 100 pages into the novel. In Hilja's imagination, which is fed by the stories of her more experienced friend Sanna, Helsinki appears as an exciting, fairy-tale like world, constituted by contradictory elements: a "magic mixture of winter and summer, of night and day, of the sun and of white lamps" (Järnefelt 1919: 78).[49] The train journey to the capital constitutes Hilja's initiation into the big unknown, and the disorientating effect is immediate and drastic. The swiftness of the movement, the strange sounds and the unknown future ahead all combine into an overwhelming feeling of alienation, unrest and disorientation:

> It was the first time I travelled by train. The strange rattle and the frightful bustle I could see through the window were about to make my mind go mad, when everything was already completely topsy-turvy in my head: the unknown future, my receding home, the spectre of the city drawing near […] Eventually I couldn't understand anything anymore, couldn't remember where I was taken; I was unable to grasp the terrible rattle below and above and around me, and was incapable of thinking at all. (Järnefelt 1919: 99)[50]

The all-encompassing strangeness of the events, concertedly made up of sounds, movement and visual impressions, renders even thinking and trying to make sense of the received impulses impossible.

One concept with which to describe the loss of agency of the protagonist during the journey visible in the citation from *Nuoruuteni muistelmia* is that of the "agent road", a concept proposed by Hans Ulrich Gumbrecht in connection to Zola's Rougon-Macquart series (Gumbrecht 2006). Following Gumbrecht, the concept of the "agent road" can be defined as a road which takes on the character of a narrative function, defining the protagonists' movements as well as providing them with a sense of purpose or direction (Gumbrecht 2006: 641). A loss of agency from the part of the protagonists is involved in this process of mobility: the road, as it were, takes over the initiative, and the protagonists are assigned a passive role; the agent road itself dominates the direction in which the narration moves. Gumbrecht uses the examples of feverishly onwards marching insurgents, and of the train engine let loose at the end of *La Bête humaine* (*The Beast in Man*; 1890). There are numerous examples of agent roads connected to Helsinki in Finnish turn of the century prose texts, and the railway to the capital features most prominently amongst these. The railway taking Antti Ljungberg to Helsinki, in Juhani Aho's *Helsinkiin*, takes on aspects of agency and leaves the protagonist bereft of initiative or any sense of directions, and the same can be said of the road taken by Hilja in the extract above. Perhaps the clearest example of the railway leading to Helsinki as an agent road is found in Arvid Järnefelt's student novel *Isänmaa* (1893/1997), in which the protagonist, Heikki, returns to Helsinki in the middle of the novel, full of a sense of doubt and foreboding. Until the last moment before boarding the train, he is unsure whether he should, in fact, leave his home behind, but the urgency of the waiting train leaves him no free choice: "The train decided in his stead" (Järnefelt 1893/1997: 14).[51] Heikki boards the train to fulfil his destiny in the capital.

Significantly, in a number of novels, the loss of agency is not only set in motion when the protagonist sets out for the capital, but continues upon and after arrival. Further restrictions on free movement and independent decisions await the protagonist in the city, where his or her future course is set out by pre-determined factors. When Hilja, in Järnefelt's *Nuoruuteni muistelmia*, arrives in Helsinki, her self-confidence is not decisively shaken by the disorientating impressions endured during the train trip. On the contrary, she feels excitement when, together with her friend Sanna, she walks to the large door opening towards the "murmuring city" (Järnefelt 1919: 103).[52] The two young women are not able to freely discover the city, however: Hilja and Sanna are awaited by some men in whom the reader can easily discern police constables come to arrest them for the thefts Sanna has committed during the journey. Hilja does not realize what is going on when they are taken to the police gaol, even when she eventually gets locked up. Her inability to read the environment during the train trip continues and is taken to a next, potentially more dangerous level, and although Hilja is soon released without much further ado, the episode bodes ill for her future developments in the novel. During Hilja's first days in Helsinki, she follows her mistress, Mrs. Johansson, around town, and her feelings of disorientation continue unabated. Her impressions of the city are described as if she were numbed or sleep-walking (ibid.: 110–111), and the effect of these sentiments of disorientation and alienation is a hatred of the urban spectacle, and an acute homesickness (ibid.: 117).

In Eino Leino's novel *Jaana Rönty* (1907), which will be discussed in more detail in the next chapter, the arrival of the protagonist Jaana also culminates in an introduction into disorientating urban space. Like Hilja (and like Anna-Kaisa in Maila Talvio's "Helsinkiin", or Hilda Tihlä's Leeni), Jaana is a poor girl from the countryside. Jaana comes to Helsinki alone, not knowing where she is going to find work or lodging. For a long day, she wanders through the strange city. Amidst an unknown urban environment, Jaana is like a child taking its first steps, and her feeling of being unable to relate to this new environment is increased by the fact that people in Helsinki speak a language she does not understand (Leino 1907/1998: 189–192). Her first experiences in the big city are crushing: in a few days, "her self-confidence had disappeared completely" (ibid.: 192).[53] Through a chance meeting, she is offered a job, and Jaana is excited and delighted at the prospect that her insecurity has come to an end. To the reader, however, it soon becomes clear that she has been sent to a brothel. Her utter unfitness for this new environment is stressed by the transformation she has to undergo: as if she is prepared for the role of sacrifice – a role which she will eventually be forced to take on – she has to change clothes and her name is transformed into a more fitting "Hildur" (ibid.: 197–198, 209). Jaana is saved before anything tragic can happen by an elderly gentleman, Baron Manfelt, who will play a considerable role throughout the novel, during strikingly similar, but much more eventful crises that will be discussed in the next chapter.

An Experience of Shock: Conclusion

In the course of the journey to the capital, various distances are crossed. There is, of course, the geographical distance between countryside (or provincial town) and the capital, the social divide between the family's and the individual's world, and the temporal distance between the past and the future. There is also the distance between two visions of the fatherland: the idea of service to the fatherland through education and work in the capital, and on the other hand the idea of service to the fatherland on what literally is the "father's land", the farmland awaiting the return home of the master's son (see Järnefelt's *Isänmaa*; 1893).[54] In the experience of arrival, such juxtaposing visions of the protagonists' future development are put to the test, and most commonly, ill-bearing premonitions appear. A number of factors conspire to construct a profoundly negative experience of arrival in most of the Finnish prose texts in this period: arrival in Helsinki is often related to gloomy autumn weather conditions, and the sense of alienation and disorientation felt by Finnish-speaking newcomers is further augmented by the added effect of hearing foreign languages spoken in the capital. The insecurity felt by so many of the protagonists in these texts is partly due to a very physical insecurity: the lack of a home in the city, a condition that was enhanced by the loss of the parental home in the countryside. Moreover, the disorientation and alienation felt by the protagonists can be seen on a broader level: their in-betweenness in the capital was that of a whole new emerging class in society.

The prose texts analysed in this chapter vividly illustrate how the first experiences of the city are defined by a sense of shock, resulting in inability to move independently or freely, and even in a sense of paralysis. In *Helsinkiin*, Antti Ljungberg feels he is unable to move and his knee-joints feel like jelly when he arrives in the capital (Aho 1889/1997: 80); in *Vaikea tie*, Markus descends into apathy after returning to Helsinki, and he leads a "vegetative life", muffling "his paralyzed mind like fluffy feathers" with alcohol and music (Wilkuna 1915: 7); Hilja, in *Nuoruuteni muistelmia*, is so overwhelmed by the train journey to Helsinki that she becomes "incapable of thinking at all" (Järnefelt 1919: 99). The disorientating effect of the city is all the more striking given the fact that a sense of mobility is what defines the Young Men and Women arriving in Helsinki around the turn of the century. They are brought to the capital and transported within it by the new mobility offered by the railway network and trams, and it is the dreams of an upward social mobility that spurs them on. In many of the crucial Finnish texts thematizing the experience of the city in this period, modes of transport and images of mobility acquire more than mere symbolic status. They are central to the development of the provincial protagonists in the city. Franco Moretti has aptly stated that what differentiates the city – and in consequence, also urban literature – from other forms of human residence and their literary representations, is "that its spatial structure [...] is functional to the intensification of *mobility*: spatial mobility, naturally enough, but mainly social mobility" (Moretti 1983/2005: 111). Although the journey to the city is often experienced as exciting and encouraging by the protagonist, potentially foreshadowing the social rise he or she hopes for, the images of speed and mobility are also connected to the protagonist's future downfall – to his or her alienation and degeneration.

The idea that the experience of the modern city is essentially an experience of shock can be considered as a classical assumption in writing on urbanity, going back to Walter Benjamin's writing (Benjamin 2006), which in turn were partly inspired by Georg Simmel (1903/1969). In their writings, an experience of shock amounts to the quintessential condition of urban life. Walter Benjamin's development of what has been called a "theory of shock" (Jennings 2006: 14–15) and even an "aesthetics of shock" (Alter 2005: 25; Borg 2011: 46–50) to define the modern urban experience has become widely influential for the way the city in literature is read, to the extent that it has been called by Franco Moretti the "sancta sanctorum of literary criticism" (Moretti 1983/2005: 109).

For Benjamin, Simmel and theorists writing in their wake, the shock of urbanity is something which is part of the *everyday* experience of the city – something city dwellers are used to encounter on an almost daily basis, and which they could even rejoice in. The shock inherent to the urban experience was for Benjamin related to the experience of the *flâneur*, a figure defined by free urban mobility and by aimless trajectories through the city performed while "botanizing on the asphalt" (Benjamin 2006: 68). Such an essentially mundane urban experience can be considered the exact opposite of the shock experienced by Young Men and Women arriving in the capital. The shock felt most profoundly by the literary protagonists in these novels and prose texts is not the shock related to the everyday experience of the modern city, grounded in the mobility of the *flâneur* who is able to rejoice in it. It is a shock felt by characters crossing the threshold into modernity, the dizzying experience of the metropolis' violent maelstrom. As such, it has a tremendous impact on their mobility, and on their ability to orientate themselves: in the middle of the disconcerting modern urban spectacle, earlier directions and guidelines lose their meaning, and new bearings have to be taken.

The descriptions of arrival in the Finnish capital found in Juhani Aho's *Helsinkiin* and in prose of the turn of the century are further developed in the prose of the 1920s and 1930s. Scenes of disorientating arrival in the capital appear, for example, in Arvi Kivimaa's *Hetki ikuisen edessä* ("A Moment before Eternity"; 1932: 25), and several of Mika Waltari's Helsinki novels feature an incapacitating shock of arrival in the Finnish capital. The most extensively described example is the arrival, in *Surun ja ilon kaupunki* ("City of Sorrow and Joy"; 1936), of an unnamed provincial at the Helsinki railway station:

And now he walks along the platform, one person amongst the busy chaos of a few hundred other arrivals. The shadow of the canopy disheartens him, in a flash he feels inconsolably the meaninglessness of all his endeavours, his strength abandons him, he blackens out and he slumps as he follows the crowd of travellers to the broad granite stairs. The square opens up in front of him, he stops at the foot of a giant pillar, the sun shines into his eyes like a blinding fire, he is lost and timid. [...]

There are a quarter of a million people around the unknown man, within a range of a few kilometres, as he leans against the granite pillar of the railway station, exhausted, abandoned by his strength, and without hope. (Waltari 1936: 18–19)[55]

The image of arrival in the utterly disorientating and paralyzing capital has remained influential throughout the twentieth century and into the present one, both in renderings of Helsinki in literature, as well as in movies and popular literature.[56] Many of the later descriptions of paralyzing arrival can be considered at least partly as conscious pastiches of the *topoi* that had come into being at the turn of the twentieth century. One of the more recent examples is the opening scene of Mikko Rimminen's 2007 novel *Pölkky* ("Woodblock"), which is structured as a page-long description of a (supposedly provincial) character's arrival at the Helsinki railway station, and his utter inability to conform to the urban texture he is confronted with.

A Helsinki Panorama

Pauli Tapani Karjalainen and Anssi Paasi, in their article on representations of Helsinki in literature, open with the image of Helsinki approached by the sea, and quote the author Bo Carpelan: "Helsinki must be approached from the sea [...]: this is the classic image of Helsinki, dear both to travellers and to the people of the city" (Karjalainen 1994: 59–60). For generations of Finns moving to the capital, however, the view of the city as seen from a train window was the first and most crucial image. It was much more prominent than the view now considered to be the quintessential one of arrival in Helsinki: the skyline viewed from the sea. The more traditional panoramic view from the Töölö Bay area, as seen from the bridge at Linnunlaulu ("Bird Song") is present, amongst others, in Maila Talvio's *Tähtien alla* ("Under the Stars"; 1910) and much more recently in the culminating scene of Mikko Rimminen's Helsinki novel *Pussikaljaromaani* ("The Six-pack Novel"; 2004), a novel that offers a distinctly Joycean panorama of Helsinki and its working-class district Kallio.

Urban Maelstrom

Turn-of-the-century Finnish prose repeatedly uses the word maelstrom ("pyörre"/"pyörteet") to describe the experience of the city. In Maila Talvio's novel *Tähtien alla* ("Under the Stars"; 1910), Helsinki life is described as a maelstrom experienced by the newly arrived girl Hilja (Talvio 1910: 71). Several reviews of Talvio's novel *Niniven lapset* ("Children of Nineveh"; 1915), describe the protagonists' move to the capital as a descent into the city's maelstrom (Saarenheimo 1915; H.S-M 1915). In a review of Eino Leino's *Jaana Rönty* (1907), the Finnish capital's degenerating nature is described similarly as "Helsinki's maelstrom" (lrv 1908: 282). In his 1899 report of his journey to Russia to meet Tolstoy, Arvid Järnefelt describes the whirl of people in the streets of the Russian capital with the word "a maelstrom of people" ("ihmispyörre") (as quoted in Karkama 2010: 219). In Eino Leino's *Pankkiherroja* ("Bank Lords"; 1914), Helsinki nightlife is described as "a world of decay, an endless abyss and maelstrom of filthy passions" into which the protagonist throws himself (Leino 1914: 106).[57] In Toivo Tarvas's novel *Eri tasoilta* ("On Different Levels"; 1916a), young provincial students are described as people who, without a home, end up in "the drowning maelstrom of the city so rich in pleasures" (Tarvas 1916: 210).[58]

"Nervousness and Urban Life"

Early theories of urban sociology were not unknown in turn-of-the-twentieth-century Finland. An interesting newspaper article from 1903 discusses theories put forward recently by the Berlin nerve doctor Albert Moll, with special reference to the dangers of the urban condition to the nervous system: "the regular move from one apartment to another [...], the rumble of trams and other vehicles, the cautious attitude with which streets have to be crossed, the increased speed while moving across greater distances, even the need to have to wait for a tram", all strain the nerves of the city dweller (Anon. 1903a; see also Anon. 1903b). The author concludes that in the future, cities might have to ordain specific legislation to protect the nerves of their inhabitants (ibid.). In a 1909 article describing the Helsinki Esplanade, Santeri Alkio argues that the urban crowd forces the modern stroller to keep a keen outward gaze, if only because otherwise he would be knocked over by hurrying passers-by. The urban noise "engendered by all-day long terrible banging, pounding, and bellowing greatly directs the attention outwards", and movement in the metropolis becomes, by consequence, "a kind of struggle for life" (Alkio 1909: 265).

Helsinki 1890–1918: A Short History

In 1812, Helsinki had become the capital of Finland, at that time an autonomous Grand-Duchy in the Russian Empire. From 1828 onwards, Helsinki became also the seat of the only university of the country. Helsinki's population grew explosively in the century following 1812, making it one of the fastest-growing European cities. The population spiralled from a mere 4,000 souls at the beginning of the century to almost 30,000 in 1870, 93,000 in 1905, and more than 150,000 in 1920 (see Palmgren 1989: 22, 38). In the second half of the nineteenth century, Helsinki grew not only in numerical terms, it also modernized at a fast pace. Technological innovations included the application of gas lighting in 1860 and rail traffic, first by horse-drawn trams, and from 1901 by electric trams (Bell & Hietala 2002: 96; see also Tommila & Hirn 1980; Pöyhönen 1992). Connections between Helsinki and the Finnish hinterland, as well as with cities abroad, were improved considerably: Helsinki was linked by train to Hämeenlinna in 1862 and to St. Petersburg in 1870, and the movement of people to the capital was enhanced by the freedom of trade and migration, legislated in 1879 (see Bell & Hietala 2002: 71; Kervanto-Nevanlinna 2003a: 342).

Politically, life in Helsinki in the period 1890–1918 was dominated by three struggles. First, there was the struggle of the Finnish-speaking majority of the country to translate numerical dominance into political, cultural and economic capital at the expense of the Swedish-speaking minority. Helsinki had been predominantly Swedish-speaking, but as its population grew, the balance gradually tipped in favour of the Finnish-speaking population. Around 1900, Finnish- and Swedish-speakers had become equal in numbers, although Swedish-speakers continued to dominate cultural, political and economic life. In addition to the language question, there was also the struggle of the Finnish people to uphold the nation's constitutional rights in the face of increasing Russian oppression; and third, there were the increasing clashes of interests between the organizing working classes and the entrenching bourgeoisie.

In Russo-Finnish relations, two periods of increased tension can be singled out, during which the Russian authorities tightened their grip on Finnish society. The first of these, which has become known as the "Frost Years" ("Routavuodet") or even the "cursed years" (Aspelin-Haapkylä 1980), was set in 1899–1905, and was almost immediately followed by the second period, which constitutes the decade leading up to Finnish independence (1908–1917). The starting point of the first period of oppression was the February Manifesto, issued in 1899 by Nicholas II, Czar of the Russian Empire and ruler of Finland (see Laati 1955: 115–128). The aim of the Manifesto was to draw Finland more firmly within the administration of the Russian Empire. Political opponents were exiled, political gatherings and newspapers were banned; institutions such as the Finnish army, the Finnish customs, postal and money services were dismantled, and measures were taken to strengthen the position of Russian as an official language. The February Manifesto and the oppression it embodied caused a shock wave throughout Finnish society. The first literary reaction to the Manifesto, a reaction which can be considered programmatic, was the poem "Helsinki sumussa" ("Helsinki in the Mist") by Eino Leino, an author whose prose literature will be discussed in depth. "Helsinki sumussa" was published in the newspaper *Päivälehti* ("Daily Paper") on 18 February 1899, only a few days after the February Manifesto was issued. It was the first time Leino would choose Helsinki as a literary setting (Larmola 2000: 21). In the poem, the monumental heart of Helsinki, centred upon the Senate Square, is gradually covered by a menacing mist, and a number of potent images are attached to the capital. As the political centre of the country, Helsinki becomes a metaphor for the nation as a whole, and an affliction at the heart of the city functions as a symbol of the nation's social and political sickness. But in Leino's poem, the cityscape is more than just a representation of the powers that brought it into being; it becomes also the expression of the mood of the city's inhabitants, presenting a troubled face when the citizens feel perturbed.

If Nicholas II's February Manifesto was the starting point for a dramatically heightened tension in Finland at large and in Helsinki in particular, the following pivotal moment in Helsinki's history was constituted by the shooting of Finland's Russian Governor-General Bobrikov. The assassination was carried out on the staircase of the Finnish Senate, at the very site of the symbolically charged environment described in Leino's poem. By a stroke of strange coincidence, the day on which these shots were fired happened to be the day James Joyce would choose for the setting of *Ulysses*: 16 June 1904. The events in Helsinki are actually referred to in Joyce's *Ulysses* (1922/1993). The importance of this day as a turning point in Helsinki's history and for the (literary) discourse on the city may well be illustrated by the fact that Kjell Westö puts the opening scene of his acclaimed Helsinki novel *Där vi en gång gått* ("Where we once walked"; 2006), on the day of the first anniversary of Bobrikov's murder.

The tension of the Frost Years, running up to this murder, culminated in events that were to pass during the following years. In 1905, the Russian Empire, Finland included, was struck by revolution and a general strike. The Great Strike and the changes in its wake – universal suffrage, amongst others – would transform Finland's power structures irreversibly (see Ruutu 1980; Palmgren 1989; Kujala 2003). In Finnish literature and the media, it gave rise to a wave of pamphlets, articles, short stories, poems and novels (see Haapala et al. 2009). The Great Strike made the deep socio-political division in Finnish society and within Helsinki painfully visible. Bourgeois forces and the working classes had different interests at stake and different goals in mind and in the absence of normal law enforcement during these tense days, both sides organized their own civil guards (Laati 1955: 129–137).

In Helsinki, a violent aftershock of the Great Strike was felt in 1906, when the Russian garrison at Helsinki's fortress islands of Viapori revolted (see Salomaa 1965; Jussila 1979: 112–147).[59] The revolt created a particularly tense and acute situation for the Helsinki citizens. There was the possibility that the Russian rebels would shell the city to force it to join the rebellion, and there was no consensus within the Finnish capital as to what course should be taken. The Red Guard favoured joining the rebellion, while the

Civil Guard did not believe in the chances of success. Blood was shed during a confrontation at Hakaniemi, which started when tram traffic was obstructed by supporters of the rebellious fortress; several people were killed in the ensuing gun fight between Red Guards and Russian sailors and the bourgeois Civil Guard (Laati 1955: 135).

The Russian authorities strengthened their grip soon after the Great Strike, and it was as a country firmly within the fold of the Russian Empire that Finland entered the First World War. In November 1917, and in part as a consequence of the Russian February and October revolutions and the successive disintegration of the Russian Empire, Finland declared independence. The various parties and movements within Finland were profoundly at odds as to what direction should be taken, and Civil War broke out in January 1918. Helsinki was rapidly occupied by the Red Guard, while bourgeois ("White") forces rallying around General (future Marshall) Mannerheim found a stronghold in the north-western coastal area of Ostrobothnia, and a front line north of the city of Tampere came into being. The heaviest urban fighting took place in and around the Red stronghold of Tampere. In comparison, Helsinki suffered relatively lightly when it was taken on 12–13 April by the advancing German army and navy – the Germans had joined the war at the side of the White Army in March 1918. The following day, a Victory Parade was staged by the German Army in the centre of Helsinki (see Viljanen 1955: 191–206). The Civil War ended on 16 May 1918, but the events had inflicted deep wounds that would affect Finnish society for decades to come. Eino Leino's non-fiction account of these days documents this resentment with particular vivacity (Leino 1918/1929; see also Koskela 1999a: 226). As elsewhere in the country, "Reds" were imprisoned in inhuman conditions awaiting their trial. In Helsinki, the fortress of Viapori, renamed Suomenlinna, was turned into a provisional prison camp (Klinge & Kolbe 1999: 94–95).

4. The Fateful Esplanade
The Stratification of Public Space

> Both of us are falling, like two ripened apples, from the Finnish family tree. And where do we fall? World culture! That is where we belong, not the asphalt of the Esplanade. (Leino 1960: 42)[1]

When Eino Leino[2] wrote these lines in 1908 in a private letter to fellow author (and beloved) L. Onerva, the figure of speech he used in the last sentence was a well-established one. In the letter, the asphalt of the Esplanade is used to refer to the whole of the Helsinki Esplanade, which in turn refers to Helsinki itself. It was a figure of speech that could be used to various effects: in this particular case, the Esplanade refers not only to Helsinki, but more generally to the provincial literary and cultural circles in Finland, as opposed to the international cultural movements to which Leino and Onerva felt attracted. In all of the manifold uses that will be discussed in this chapter, the metonymical relationship remains the same: Helsinki is repeatedly identified with what amounts to its most prominent public space – the centrally located Esplanade.

Physically and geographically speaking, the elegant Northern and Southern Esplanades, and the park running between them, are situated at the heart of the city's centre, parallel to one of the main streets (Aleksanterinkatu). Located immediately at the eastern edge of the Esplanade is the Market Square, one of the commercial landmarks of the city, which around the turn of the century presented a particularly bustling scene in the mornings (in literature, see for example Tihlä's *Leeni* ["Leeni"]; 1907: 110–112; Leino's *Pankkiherroja* ["Bank Lords"]; 1914: 201). Someone standing in this period in the middle of the Market Square would see to his or her immediate north the famous hotel Seurahuone (today the City Hall), which features as the setting for sumptuous dinners in several prose texts (for example Ivalo's *Aikansa lapsipuoli* ["Stepchild of his Time"]; 1895: 248–252; E. Leino's *Olli Suurpää* ["Olli Suurpää"]; 1908/1998: 337, 498). Passing the statue of *Havis Amanda*, the embodiment of Helsinki, which was erected in 1908, the city walker could stroll to the restaurant Kappeli, a few steps away, opposite of which stood a band stand which provided the soundtrack of numerous evening walks described in literature. Lining the Esplanade on both sides were a number of cafés, restaurants and music halls that constitute the setting for Helsinki's colourful social life. Turn-of-the-century literature evokes the Esplanade's nightlife through descriptions of music hall shows at the restaurant Princess (Wilkuna's *Vaikea tie* ["The Difficult Road"]; 1915: 42), dinners and drinks at Kämp (E. Leino's *Olli Suurpää* [1908/1998]: 394–396), and passionate talks of the young avant-garde at the famous café Catani

(E. Leino's "Päivä Helsingissä" ["A Day in Helsinki"]; 1905: 55–70).[3] Along the route, a leisurely stroller would also see the very first statue in the capital, that of the national poet J. L. Runeberg, erected in 1885.[4]

This chapter analyses how Helsinki's public space was experienced through the prism of the Esplanade, in particular in relation to representations of walking – that "network of [...] moving, intersecting writings" (de Certeau 1984: 93), performed by city walkers in literary texts in the late nineteenth and early twentieth centuries. In the literature written during these years, the Esplanade appears as an iconic spatial environment, but also as a highly stratified space to which multiple meanings are attached, with profound social, linguistic, political and gendered implications. After an introductory exploration of the Esplanade and its function as a setting for a bourgeois (and male) ritual, the experiences of the female protagonist in Eino Leino's novel *Jaana Rönty* ("Jaana Rönty"; 1907) will be analysed in detail. Comparing one particularly revealing scene set at the Esplanade in this novel with other experiences of Helsinki's public space in literature will enable a reconstruction of the unwritten rules, conventions and expectations that inform the use of public space in literary Helsinki around the turn of the century.

A Shorthand Expression for the City

In novels and short stories set in Helsinki around the turn of the century, the Esplanade is omnipresent. It appears as a prism through which one approaches the Finnish capital: a metonymical representation of the whole city. Literary cities tend to contain one or more iconic spatial environments that are recognized immediately by the intended audience, and that are understood to represent the city as a whole. In their discussion of symbolic representations of American cities, Richard Wohl and Anselm Strauss call such a metonymically used space a "coded, shorthand expression" for the city, and they give the New York skyline as a prototypical example from the American context (Wohl & Strauss 1958: 526). A novel which opens with such an iconic setting immerses the reader or spectator in a specific geographical location, but potentially also in a social and/or political context, and in a recognizable narrative environment: the case of the New York skyline, for example, might entail expectations of a story of arrival in the city. In a wide range of Finnish prose texts, the Esplanade functions as a similar "shorthand expression", a means of spatially framing the narration in a succinct and comprehensible manner. This holds true in particular when the setting of the Esplanade is placed immediately at the beginning of the novel or short story, or in relation to the first mention of a particular character. An early example of the way in which the Esplanade is metonymically used in literature can be found in Arvid Järnefelt's student novel *Isänmaa* ("The Fatherland"; 1893), in which the protagonist, Heikki, imagines the Finnish capital to which he will return the following day. The images he evokes are those of the autumnal Esplanade:

But now the summer drew to a close. Tomorrow he would have left these quiet regions and a restless city wind would be blowing around him. Autumn clothes, hats, gloves and the Esplanade with its restaurant Kappeli and its electric lights – – ! (Järnefelt 1893/1997: 151)[5]

Together, these seemingly disconnected references (autumn fashion, modern electric lights, the Esplanade and its famous restaurant Kappeli) crystallize into an image of a modern and European metropolis, which is experienced as an unnerving and hectic environment ("restless city wind"). In the passage quoted, the ambiguous nature of the city and the conflicting promises and premonitions attached to it are summed up by an evocation of the Esplanade. It is a setting that also constitutes the central locality in the prototypical first experiences of Helsinki described in Juhani Aho's *Helsinkiin* ("To Helsinki"; 1889), which is discussed at length in the previous chapter.

In the example from Järnefelt's *Isänmaa*, the use of a shorthand spatial setting functions as a device to plunge the reader in the midst of a (supposedly) familiar environment. Typically, the Esplanade and the atmosphere that happens to reign there – either climatic, or with reference to the crowds walking and gathering there – is juxtaposed with the mood of the protagonist, in a description that either correlates or contrasts with his or her feelings. In a number of texts, a juxtaposition between the Esplanade's atmosphere and the characters' mood occurs at the very beginning of the narration, in which case it provides a whole condensed story, past or future, of the protagonist's relationship in relation to the city and the urban community. Such a juxtaposition was sometimes used to describe the mood of the protagonist in unison with that of the urban crowd at the Esplanade, but it could also be used to convey the opposite effect, and to describe the protagonist's sense of loneliness.[6]

The opening lines of a short story written by Kasimir Leino, published in 1889 and thus one of the earliest instances from literature written in Finnish, provide an illustrative example. The title, "Neron tähteet. Kuvaus pääkaupungista" ("The remains of a genius. A description of [or from] the capital"), gives crucial information concerning the background of the protagonist (he is a former genius), but also on how the reader is supposed to view the text: it is a "description of the capital". The opening lines of the story do not give a panoramic view of the city, but focus on a very limited spatial environment:

> There he sat again, hunched up in his habitual place next to the music pavilion in front of the Esplanade's Kappeli. The weather was not exactly favourable… a silent drizzle was constantly pouring down from the sky. And this was also the reason why there were not a lot of people to be seen, listening to the music. Those who were about ushered themselves hurriedly under the roof, ordered a glass of warm "rum toddy", hot punch or something similar, so as to remain warm at all. And they were not content with that, but told the […] wine chef to bring one of those simple blankets, which the people at Kappeli used to wrap around their legs in cold weather.
> But that man, cloaked in his long and shabby, black overcoat, just sat there freezing on his hard and wet bench. (K. Leino 1889)[7]

As the title suggests, the old man sitting in the cold in front of Kappeli is not more than the remains of a musical genius, poor and alone, with nothing left but to listen to the music being played at the music pavilion. The gloomy weather conditions contrast with the cosy spirit of people huddling together under the roof of Kappeli, which in turn contrasts with the lonely, excluded protagonist, cold, and only flimsily protected against the fury of the elements. Bearing in mind that the subtitle of the story is "a description of the capital", Helsinki is put down as an inhospitable place with dreary weather conditions. This vision would return time and again in literary descriptions of Helsinki, which set the first experiences of a protagonist arriving in the city against the background of grim autumn weather.[8]

In terms of imagined community and of geographical reality, Helsinki is conjured up at the beginning of Kasimir Leino's short story as a very limited social and physical space: a small, exclusive group of bourgeois men gathering in the centre of Helsinki's society life. This is one vision of the microcosm of the capital that would remain prominent in literary (and other) representations: Helsinki as a city of bourgeois leisure centred on the Esplanade. In "Neron tähteet", the setting at the Esplanade serves to underscore the divide opening up between the lonely protagonist and the more successful inhabitants of the city. The mood of the protagonist and the scenery at the Esplanade could equally be used to convey the opposite: the confidence of a successful protagonist navigating the cold and unwelcoming Esplanade. This is the case in the opening lines of *Olli Suurpää*, a Helsinki novel written by Kasimir Leino's younger brother, Eino Leino. Eino Leino uses a number of elements reminiscent of Kasimir Leino's "Neron tähteet" to juxtapose a literary protagonist with a cold winter evening at the Esplanade. The description of the protagonist and his surroundings, and its implications for the reading of the city as a symbolic space are strikingly different from "Neron tähteet":

> A strong and freezing wind blew through Helsinki's boulevards. It was winter, but the snow had melted over and over again, and had eventually completely receded to the other side of the clouds. The chilly cars of cabmen rolled over the cold cobble stones.
>
> There were not a lot of people around, even though it was the normal hour for the evening walk, the moment just before the start of theatre plays and concerts. Families preferred to stay inside. Bachelors quickly slipped inside through pub doors.
>
> Attorney-at-law Olli Suurpää sailed safely along the Northern Esplanade in his large Petersburg fur jacket. He had somehow supplied his mortal part perfectly against all the fluctuations of hot and cold. Nevertheless his eyes, too, were fixed particularly intensely on the two burning electric lamps in front of Kämp, lamps that he was able to discern already from afar as standing out from the light bundles projected outwards from the shop windows. He was on his way to a small, secret party meeting. (E. Leino 1908/1998: 333)[9]

Olli Suurpää, like Kasimir Leino's "Neron tähteet", starts out with a description of the Esplanade as a Helsinki microcosm: the Finnish capital is reduced to its boulevards, and those, in turn, culminate in the bright lights of Kämp, to which all eyes are set ("his eyes, too"). It is a city of leisure and bright shop windows: of theatre plays, concerts, and cafés. But Helsinki is also, in this novel, a city with secretive forces jockeying for position in an increasingly volatile political climate. The season is not autumn, the time of decay and melancholy, but winter, a fitting setting for what in effect is a political allegory with the aim to depict Helsinki in the "Frost Years" ("routa-vuodet"), the years of Russian oppression at the beginning of the twentieth century. The seasonal conditions besetting the city can be linked to the afflictions at the heart of the body politic – the repressive policies of the Russian authorities, as well as the appeasing attitude of some of the Finnish political forces. In contrast to the first story, the protagonist has managed to supply "his mortal part perfectly against all the fluctuations of hot and cold", but the ironic description may instil an observant reader with a sense of doubt as to how safely, really, Olli Suurpää is "sailing along the Esplanade". It is particularly tempting to read the reference to the Petersburg fur jacket allegorically. In the chilly political climate which sets Finns against each other and against the Russian oppressors, Olli feels not in the least uneasy about protecting himself against the cold by an import from the Russian capital. This may be read as a premonition of future plot developments: towards the end of the novel, Olli Suurpää betrays the Finnish cause by accepting a position in the Russian-run administration.

In the two extracts above, Helsinki is introduced metonymically by way of the Esplanade, but in very different terms. In Kasimir Leino's "Neron tähteet", it appears as a cold city of leisure, exclusion and personal despair, centred on the Esplanade. In Eino Leino's *Olli Suurpää* similar elements recur (city of leisure and artificial lights; geographically and socially confined environments; freezing cold), but with a political undertow.

A Male Bourgeois Ritual

In texts on Helsinki's history or architecture, the Esplanade, the "nerve centre of the city's mental life" (Suolahti 1949: 310) is described almost invariably through its physical appearances: the majestic buildings lining the thoroughfare, the music stand in front of Kappeli, the exotic touch added by the presence of palm trees around the turn of the twentieth century (see Järvenpää 2006), the restaurants which were often operated by foreign bakers, and the like. In literary texts, what receives most emphasis are the spatial narratives that stress the Esplanade's role in Helsinki citizens' interaction with each other. The Esplanade appears as a public space in which citizens' need for display was channelled into a highly programmed ritual of walking, with distinct social, political and gendered implications. In prose texts of this period, walking the Esplanade appears as a crucial ritual with which to create and exhibit a sense of belonging to the capital – an enunciation with which the walker voices his inscription into a particular imagined society. In an early novel by Juhani Aho, *Papin rouva* ("The Parson's Wife"; 1893/2000), for example, one of the characters is defined almost exclusively by mentioning that he is one of those who walk at the Esplanade at the appropriate time (Aho 1893/2000: 249).

In the fragment from *Papin rouva*, the Esplanade-walker mentioned is identified by a term that is frequently used to describe a man strolling along the Esplanade: "keikari", a word which is a close relative of the dandy. In a newspaper sketch describing the spectacle at the Esplanade, the fashion-savvy men strolling the Esplanade are described as *flâneuring* ("flaneeraavat") and, echoing Baudelaire, the author of the text claims ironically that they, who spend their time idling, are in fact fulfilling their duty in "following their time" (Mikko 1893: 135). The ritual of walking the Esplanade is most often performed by individuals and families from the upper and middle classes, but in the literature of this period, it also carries gendered meanings: the walker on the Esplanade at the turn of the century is almost unvaryingly male.

Building on the thoughts of Michel de Certeau concerning spatial narrations and the everyday, the Esplanade can be considered as a synecdoche not only in the way it represents, physically and geographically, the city of Helsinki, but in the way it is used by Helsinki citizens to enunciate their belonging (or endeavour at belonging) to a larger urban community. De Certeau argues that everyday activities are enunciative, that they are practices that speak in similar ways as words that are uttered.

De Certeau points out that if walking is approached as an enunciation, particular kinds of walking can be interpreted as figures of speech; he notes, in particular, the peripatetic figures of speech of the *asyndeton* and the *synecdoche*. In relation to the Esplanade, the latter concept, which "expands a spatial element in order to make it play the role of a 'more' (a totality)" (de Certeau 1984: 101) is of particular interest. The Esplanade is used as a shorthand reference for Helsinki, and drawing on de Certeau's terminology, a walk along the Esplanade can be seen also as a synecdochic spatial practice with which to carry out a dialogue vis-à-vis Helsinki. By walking the Esplanade, literary characters in a number of prose texts around the turn of the century can be seen to create a relation to urban public space in its totality: seeing and being seen, they inscribe themselves into a particular discourse on what it is to be a Helsinki citizen.

De Certeau's concept of the synecdoche entails a process of knowledge gathering: in the complex and profoundly ambiguous context of the city, taking a part for the whole is an epistemological process of the first order (see Prendergast 1992: 210). The shorthand reference to the Esplanade at the beginning of a novel or short story has epistemological significance, first of all, for the reader, who is introduced to a larger context which is made knowable through reference to a (presumably) representative part. The synecdochic walk is also an epistemological endeavour from the part of the character who, by his enunciative walk, is becoming acquainted with the urban environment, and making his presence known in the process.

A telling example of walks as complex ways of enunciation can be found in a long soliloquy at the centre of Eino Leino's novel *Olli Suurpää* ("Olli Suurpää"; 1908).[10] As seen above, *Olli Suurpää* begins with a description of the eponymous protagonist walking along the Esplanade on his way to

Kämp. As the novel proceeds, it becomes clear that a regular walk along the Esplanade at the appropriate time constitutes a central element in the everyday practices with which Olli tries to instil his life with a sense of stability; a bulwark against the troubling political and emotional upheavals he is faced with. Olli Suurpää is acutely aware of the importance of his everyday rituals, and in a long monologue he explains to himself that his claim to be a "real native of Helsinki" – even though he is not born in the city – is based on a set of everyday practices, amongst which a carefully performed and timed walk features prominently (Leino 1908/1998: 420–425). The internal monologue is rendered by the narrator in a profoundly satirical tone, which conveys to the reader an understanding that Olli's routines are in reality not more than futile and superficial attempts at mental and social stability. The satirical element is taken to comic heights when Olli's poodle, Matti, voices his opinions, and, echoing his master's words, praizes the Esplanade as the ideal environment to network and to "develop one's soul through diverse and interesting conversations with the most noble dogs of the city, in whose company I, too, walk every day from the one end of the Northern Esplanade to the other, as solemn as my master does with his briefcase under his arm" (ibid.: 425).[11]

With their highly programmed walk along the Esplanade, Olli and his dog enunciate a particular kind of belonging to Helsinki bourgeois circles. Typical of similar highly programmed walks along the Esplanade in literature of this period, Olli Suurpää's leisurely promenade is not without its political undercurrents. The walk along the Esplanade, carefully timed to conform to the expected routines of a law-abiding citizen, constitutes a clearly understandable enunciation of support for the government in charge and for the political status quo. This is explicitly stated by Olli's poodle, who in his part of the monologue strongly defends the political authorities in a statement that closely mirrors his master's monologue:

> But my sympathies are in this matter completely at the side of the legal authorities, which I see represented by so many of my equals at the Helsinki Esplanade. As long as the official institutions function, as long as the hand of the law performs its task meticulously and the people are unwaveringly faithful to the Emperor and to the Fatherland, I do not see any sensible reason why a peaceful citizen would turn to rebellious solicitude concerning the fate of the people and society. (Leino 1908/1998: 425–426)[12]

By performing his daily walk, Olli Suurpää and his dog are enunciating not only their desire to belong to Helsinki's imagined urban community, but also their inscription into a particular political party programme: that of appeasing the Russian authorities, rather than choosing the headlong confrontation advocated by the Young Finn party to which Eino Leino himself was affiliated.[13] In several novels by Arvid Järnefelt, the punctual and bourgeois Esplanade walker is similarly described as a representative of the conservative forces in society; this is the case in *Maaemon lapsia* ("Children of Mother Earth"; 1905: 137) as well as in *Veneh'ojalaiset* ("The Family Veneh'oja"; 1909/1996: 258–259, 263).

Taken to the utmost extreme, a small shift in the spatial synecdoche of walking the Esplanade, such as the change from one sidewalk to the other, could entail a drastic change in the city walker's political sympathies. This happens in a short story by Juhani Aho, which describes the opportunistic shifts in allegiance from Swedish-speaking to Finnish-speaking sympathies, acted out on the asphalt of the Esplanade. The struggle between Finnish- and Swedish-speaking parties for predominance is among the most prominent themes in Finnish literature of the late nineteenth century, in particular in student novels. Historically speaking, the language divide ran straight through the middle of the Esplanade: the Finland-Swedes were accustomed to walk the Northern Esplanade – the sunny side of the street – while the Finnish-speaking population would walk along the Southern Esplanade (Järvenpää 2006). One notable example in literature can be found in which explicit reference is made to the language question, and in which the Esplanade appears as a metonymical image of the field of Finnish party politics: Juhani Aho's "Mallikelpoinen" ("An Exemplary Character"; 1890). In this short story, a walk along a particular part of the Esplanade symbolizes subscription to a whole political discourse.

The "exemplary character" who is the subject of Aho's satirical short story is Mauritz Ahlfelt; a young, ambitious and unscrupulous character from a Swedish-speaking background who is ready to make all necessary concessions to further his political career. The very first thing the narrator mentions about Mauritz is that he can be met regularly at the Esplanade, and the Esplanade constitutes a key part in this character's daily routines.[14] It also functions, however, as a metonymical space symbolic of his political ambitions and for the direction he is going to take in the ongoing party-struggle. Towards the end of the story, the narrator concludes that it will not take long until Mauritz will move away from the Northern Esplanade to the "Finnspång" – a Swedish-language term which literally means the "Finnish path", a term given to a stretch of the Southern Esplanade where the leaders of the Finnish-minded party were known to walk (Forsman et. al. 1925–1928: 895–896; Paunonen 2010: 162). Through reference to a minimal change in spatial practices in this highly symbolic space, the transfer from the Northern to the Southern Esplanade, a monumental political move is made tangible: for opportunistic motives, Mauritz joins the Finnish-speaking circles, where he will have better possibilities of advancing his career.

As is clear from the examples above, a walk along the Esplanade was not only far removed from the uninhibited wanderings of the *flâneur*, it was also anything but a challenge to existing hegemonic spatial strategies. Walking, similarly to any other everyday utterance or enunciation, can contest power structures as well as support them. This is something which de Certeau is clearly aware of, when he argues that "[w]alking affirms, suspects, tries out, transgresses, respects, etc., the trajectories it 'speaks'" (de Certeau 1984: 99). Later critical geographers and literary scholars inspired by his (and Lefebvre's) writings, often show an uninhibited optimism in their views of peripatetic practices, and tend to see everyday enunciations as positively marked ways of appropriation and contestation, set against the totalizing space of the city (see for example Borg 2011: 119). The numerous descriptions of walks along the Esplanade as a programmed bourgeois ritual in Finnish turn-of-the-century literature attest, however, to everyday enunciations' potential to uphold power structures. It should be noted in this context that in several of the cases discussed above, the literary characters' uncritical attitude towards totalizing spatial practices is generally not shared by the narrator. Mauritz Ahlfelt and Olli Suurpää are severely ridiculed, described in a satirical manner, and characterized as social and political arrivistes ready to compromise.

The laying out of the Esplanade as a central pedestrian promenade channelling the movements of the citizens has its counterparts in international and much larger urban projects: Stockholm's Esplanade system (see Borg 2011: 72–85), and, of course, the massive remodelling of Paris by Baron Haussmann, and the London of John Nash. The grand-scale redevelopments of London and Paris, in particular, were an illustration of urban planning harnessed for socio-political purposes to channel potentially subversive pedestrian (and other) movement (see Lefebvre 1974/1991: 308; Harvey 1989b: 182; Sennett 1994: 329–332). Compared to these international examples, the scale encountered at the Esplanade was microscopic, but political and social dimensions were clearly present on the asphalt of the Esplanade in turn-of-the-century literature. Several male, middle class city walkers of the Esplanade are explicitly seen as upholding and enunciating a particular socio-political ideal, and the function relegated to the working-class crowds is to be in awe of the spectacle that is daily performed. This is expressed, for example, in a passage in the student novel *Hellaassa* ("In Hellas"; Ivalo 1890), in which a description of the well-to-do at the Esplanade is juxtaposed with the mention of "a considerable percentage of the capital's maids and servants", who "were standing in a densely grouped bunch in front and around the [Kappeli] bandstand" (Ivalo 1890: 109–110).[15] Different classes were given very different roles in the daily spectacle at the Esplanade: in a space where such an importance was attached to the ritual of seeing and being seen, the roles of watchers and people being watched were clearly defined.

A tangible example of the social divisions witnessed on the Esplanade, and the way these depended on particular times of the day, can be seen in Hilda Tihlä's novel *Leeni* ("Leeni"; 1907). In a descriptive passage, several pages of length, the narrator scrutinizes how the Esplanade changes during the course of one day, and how it caters for several functions of the city, but with a distinctive undertow of social stratification. In the early morning, Helsinki is at first silent and clean; gradually, the city wakes up, and becomes busy with life in the bustling Market Square, located at the eastern end of the Esplanade. Around midday, the economic function of this public space, which is described as socially diverse, suddenly comes to an end when "the heart of the city" becomes the scene of the bourgeois walking ritual already described (Tihlä: 1907: 110). Not everyone is welcome any longer; working-class men are only few and far between; and when a "dark beauty from the outskirts of the city" joins the crowd, her presence is felt to be awkward – people would rather have her gone (ibid.: 110–111).[16] When a young working-class boy strays on the Esplanade, his presence is not appreciated, and "he soon runs off to a place away from the centre, where he can breathe safely" (ibid).[17]

The Gaze and the Right to the City in Eino Leino's Jaana Rönty (1907)

The bourgeois ritual performed at the Esplanade is far removed from the spontaneous wanderings of Baudelairean *flâneur*, which were spurred on by a fascination for urban phenomena of modernity. This does not mean, however, that the considerable literature that has evolved around the *flâneur* and the *flâneuse* does not have any relevance for understanding the encounters in public space found in the literature analysed here. One of the *flâneur*'s most important characteristics has undiminished relevance: the gaze. In Baudelaire's quintessential essay "The painter of modern life", the observer of modernity is endowed with a particular way of looking – a child-like "animally ecstatic gaze" grounded in "deep and joyful curiosity" (Baudelaire 1863/1964: 8). The readings of Baudelaire by Walter Benjamin have further enhanced the importance that has been attached to the *flâneur* gaze in the (late) nineteenth-century urban experience. One of the quintessential literary examples of the *flâneur* gaze is provided by Baudelaire's poem "À une passante" ("To a Passer-by"; Baudelaire 1861), which describes the exchange of meaningful glances between two chance passers-by (see Benjamin 2006: 40, 75–77; Brooks 2005: 134–135).

The polyphonic dialogue of gazes, glances and stares in urban public space is also indicative of the social and gendered power relations that permeate this space. During the last decades, the gendered dimension of the gaze has received particular attention, inspired in part by new perspectives offered by feminist film criticism and art history.[18] The *flâneur* and the male gaze have been seen as the quintessential symbol of "men's visual and voyeuristic mastery over women" (Wilson 1992: 98). The poem "À une passante" and its subsequent reading by Benjamin have been central to a number of re-readings of urban modernity in relation to the female city walker, to the extent even that the *passante* has been equated with the *flâneur* himself: the woman being passed on the street is "an enigmatic icon of the cityscape", and her ability to answer the gaze makes her a "mirror image of the male observer" (Parsons 2000: 72 ff.; see also Wolff 1985: 42).

If the *flâneur* is largely invisible on the Esplanade, the male "gendered gaze" referred to in feminist (or more generally gender-inspired) readings of the male city walker is pervasively present, and in some instances in Finnish turn-of-the-century literature, a particular gendered gaze constitutes the first step in a chain of events leading to aggression, violence, and even rape. In the following, a pivotal scene in Eino Leino's *Jaana Rönty* will be examined as a crucial example of gendered and social stratification of urban public space.

Jaana Rönty

Jaana Rönty is one of the three novels that together constitute Eino Leino's Frost Year Trilogy ("routavuosiromaanit"). The triptych is intended to give complementing views of society: first, that of a student from a provincial background (Tuomas Vitikka), second, that of a working-class woman (Jaana Rönty), and third, that of a civil servant (Olli Suurpää). *Jaana Rönty* was the most successful of the three: it received favourable reviews, was awarded with a state literary prize, and, quite exceptionally for a Finnish novel, it was reviewed positively in the British newspaper *The Tribune* in the very year it was published (Anon. 1907; H. S. 1908: 58). Interesting from the perspective of urban writing, *Jaana Rönty* was praised by contemporary critics across the language divide for the way it depicts Helsinki from a Finnish-speaking lower class perspective (Schildt 1912). During recent decades, *Jaana Rönty* has received considerable attention as a novel that depicts the pulse of its time, and which displays the changing attitude of the intelligentsia towards the common people in the early twentieth century.[19]

Jaana Rönty is one of the typical young men and women of the provinces whose first encounters with the city have been the object of analysis in the preceding chapter. She is a young woman from a poor and provincial background who moves to the great city, where she awakens as an individual, but where severe misfortunes befall her, and where eventually she degenerates. Like many Finnish Young Man/Woman novels, a substantial part of the novel is set in the countryside, but the most consequential and detailed scenes take place in the capital, which can be considered as the catalyst of turning points in Jaana's life. In the background of Jaana's downward evolution we find not only the strained political conditions in Finland which gave to Eino Leino's trilogy the name "Frost Year Novels", but also the rapid economic development of Finland's capital and the nation's socio-political upheavals, which periodically gave rise to violent eruptions in urban public space.[20]

The first encounters of Jaana with the Finnish capital are disconcerting: unable to orient herself, Jaana wanders the city aimlessly, alienated by the unfamiliar surroundings. To newcomers, however, the city is not only a disorientating and paralyzing space, but also the arena for social advancement. Years after her arrival, Jaana has become a young city maiden, with her clothes, her work and her little home to prove her new status. The "social text of the city street" (Lefebvre 2003: 91), however, remains largely foreign to her, made up of enunciations she finds it difficult to read and understand. When she tries to appropriate the spatial language of the city, her peripatetic enunciations are misread with dramatic effect. The crucial moment in Jaana's development in the city comes on a beautiful spring evening, when she is walking along the idyllic Esplanade. Typically for Helsinki novels of this period, the description of the setting juxtaposes the climatic circumstances on the Esplanade with the protagonist's inner thoughts and feelings. The air is filled with expectation: Jaana is about to meet her "cavalier" – a young man she has met close by where she lives, and they are supposed to go to the circus together.

> Outside, it was a warm spring evening. Music could be heard at Kappeli. Jaana's steps felt so light that her heels were constantly trying to jump up in the air. Her lips were smiling, and her eyes glittered. (Leino 1907/1998: 219–220)[21]

A fateful chain of events unfolds when Jaana's acquaintance does not appear, and when gradually, the spectacle offered by the Esplanade starts to draw Jaana's attention. Fascinated by the numerous people strolling about, she starts to copy the way other women walk the Esplanade. A police officer eventually notices Jaana, accosts her and asks her with what right she walks there. When she is unable to give him a satisfying answer, she is taken to the police station, where she is raped.

The critic Viljo Tarkiainen argues that Jaana's rape (in addition to many other events in the novel) is not more than a sad coincidence (Tarkiainen 1907: 494). The fatal events that befall Jaana at the Esplanade are, however, anything but random: they are revealing of the tense political atmosphere in contemporary Helsinki, the prevailing socio-political strains, and the social and gender-related stratification of urban public space. In particular, they illustrate two questions that were intimately interconnected with the social and gendered stratification of urban space, and that were thematized in media discussions and the literature of the time: the woman question and the question of morality in society. In both questions, for reasons that are clearly unknown to Jaana, but that must have been common knowledge for most of the novel's readers, the Esplanade featured prominently.

Public Space – Public Women?

The Esplanade was not only a place for male bourgeois showing-off, but also one of the most important Helsinki spaces in which courtship and flirtation, in all its subtle and less subtle forms, were staged. Amongst many other things, this was the place where men from the higher social circles came to watch the young maidservants taking a walk in their free time. In a passage in Santeri Ivalo's novel *Hellaassa*, for example, a young student tells the others how the "maids' parade" at the Esplanade had been unbelievably good the other day (Ivalo 1890: 20–21).[22] The reference to the "maids' parade", the spectacle of young working-class girls strolling along the Esplanade in their spare time, is relatively harmless, although it illustrates the different roles assigned to men from the higher classes and women from the lower classes, which constituted at the Esplanade – and all through the city's public space – a continuous area of tension. In another student novel written by Ivalo, *Aikansa lapsipuoli* ("Stepchild of his time"; 1895), two of the characters descend upon the Esplanade after a heavy lunch at Seurahuone, to watch how "spawning was at its hottest" (Ivalo 1895: 252).[23]

When night began to fall, the playful courting rituals took on a more merciless and uninhibited form: the Esplanade was also the central area for Helsinki's street prostitution.[24] In Finnish literature, there are several direct references to the sinful nature of the Esplanade, such as the following passage from Wilkuna's *Vaikea tie* ("The Difficult road"; 1915), which describes the closing-time scene unfolding before the protagonist's eyes on the Esplanade around the turn of the century:

The men leaving the bars were joined by street nymphs, who, like nightly butterflies, had left their hiding places on the outskirts of the city and had now, protected by the midnight shadows, dared to come to the finest parts of town to prey. The shameless barter was accompanied by loud bursts of laughter and rude jokes. Police officers, muffled up in their overcoats, were silently walking back and forth in the middle of the street like living statues. (Wilkuna 1915: 85)[25]

In this passage, the nightly Esplanade turns into a maze of glances and gazes: prostitutes and men exchange furtive glances, and the police officers in the background, in their turn, keep an eye on the proceedings. It is a passage which reveals the socially divided and gendered geography of the city. The centre of the city is not the everyday habitat of these "nightly butterflies", rather, the dwellings where they are said to hide are situated at the "outskirts of the city" and they come only at night time to this "finest part of the city". Lower class women are in the roles of prostitutes, upper middle class men are categorized as the potential clients; respectable women are not to be seen. The implication is that respectable women have no place in the whole scene, and indeed, the Esplanade, like other public spaces in Helsinki where street prostitution was practised, was generally understood to be an environment where unaccompanied women could be freely approached from a particular time of the day onwards (see Häkkinen 1995: 30).

The play of glances and gazes could lead to painful misunderstandings: recognizing potential clients and possible prostitutes in the middle of a crowded street was no easy matter, especially in the case of the Esplanade, where (at daytime and in early evening) many people went about on their daily chores.[26] References to such misunderstandings are encountered in a number of sources: in Arvid Järnefelt's autobiographic work *Vanhempieni romaani* ("The Book of My Parents"), for example, there is a mention of an encounter at the Esplanade in which a prostitute approaches the son of acquaintances of the Järnefelt family (Järnefelt 1928–1930/1944: 393–394). In Järnefelt's novel *Nuoruuteni muistelmia* ("Memories from my Youth"; 1919) the protagonist, Hilja, a girl who has just moved to Helsinki, is mistaken for a prostitute when she goes for a walk at the Esplanade in the evening.

Awareness of what time and place was considered acceptable for a solitary (female) walker is central to a woman's ability to navigate urban public space, and ways of dressing and moving had to be taken into account as well. A prostitute could not necessarily be recognized by her clothing only, but when a poor woman dressed too luxuriously, this could be perceived as a clear sign.[27] The elements which lead to the fatal chain of events at the Esplanade in *Jaana Rönty* are constituted by Jaana's clothing, the moment and the place of the events (the Esplanade at dusk), but also, and crucially, by Jaana's body language. A particular kind of walking was associated with public women, and there are numerous instances in literature in which the way a woman walks is interpreted as a clear sign of indecent intentions. In Maila Talvio's novel *Tähtien alla* ("Under the Stars"; 1910), a man approaches the main character Hilja at the Railway Square in Helsinki and grabs her by the arm; when Hilja is taken aback by this sudden event, the gentleman blames the way she walks: "'Why did you walk so slowly, then?!' He retorted with an air of rightful anger, and pulled back" (Talvio 1910: 283).[28] It was a situation which was not only typical of Helsinki; similar events were witnessed in other cities as well, both in Finland and, of course, internationally. In Finnish novels situated in the urban environments of Oulu and Kuopio, women, even young girls, drew male attention to their own corporality by the unusual way in which they walked (see Lappalainen 1998a: 110). Inability to conform to the steady pace of the metropolis has also been noticed in the context of women's respectability in nineteenth-century London. In Victorian London, country girls received unwanted attention by the unusual speed with which they walked (Nead 2000: 65), and respectable women who wanted to move through urban public space without being accosted had to demonstrate their dignity by the gracious and purposeful pace of their movement (Walkowitz 1992: 51).

Interestingly, Leino's novel offers a detailed description of the way Jaana walks immediately preceding the challenge by the police officer, and of how she tries to adapt to a particular kind of walking she sees performed at the Esplanade. In de Certeau's terms, Jaana tries to appropriate the spatial language of the Esplanade, but she is unaware of the strong undercurrents of meaning which her imitation carries. The narrator describes at length how Jaana becomes gradually fascinated by the "ladies" she sees walking at the Esplanade. Although Jaana realizes that they are not real upper class ladies, she seems to be unaware that they are, in fact, prostitutes. She notices how they walk in a particular way, and how they "tripped about so nice and neatly, taking smaller steps than the others and carrying their skirts differently than other women" (Leino 1907/1998: 221). Jaana tries to imitate them, and when she realizes what she is doing, "she started to copy them ever so eagerly, this time on purpose and self-consciously" (ibid.).[29]

From the moment Jaana forgets the reason why she is walking along the Esplanade, she starts to notice the spectacle performed there, and to actively take part in it. But she underestimates to what extent she herself has become part of that very spectacle. Jaana, as an outsider to the city, is not able to read correctly this "subtlest but least well-defined system of signs" – the city street (Lefebvre 2003: 91). Her appearance and the way she walks are understood, however, by others on the Esplanade as part and parcel of the social text, and her behaviour is interpreted accordingly. When Jaana copies the movements of other women, her own steps, in turn, are followed attentively:

> A police officer, standing on the corner of the street, had for some time been following Jaana's steps with his eyes. Now he decidedly went after her, and at a dark gateway, he grabbed the girl by the arm.
> "Why are you walking here?" he asked. (Leino 1907/1998: 221)[30]

Significantly, the challenge of Jaana's right to walk is accompanied by a shift in focalization. The narration is no longer recounted through Jaana herself, but through another focalizer: the police officer. In this case, it is indeed the panoptic and controlling gaze of the upholder of public order who scrutinizes Jaana and who classifies her on the basis of the gendered and social signs made up by her clothing, outlook, and way of walking. Here, as in other instances from contemporary literature, it is not merely outward appearances that give away a woman as not belonging to the surrounding environment, but rather the way she walks and the very steps she takes: the man "had for some time been following Jaana's steps".[31] On the basis of Jaana's body language, the police officer comes to the conclusion that she is a prostitute.

The Experience of Helsinki's Public Space under the Aegis of the "Frost Years"

Seen in the light of the political context in which Eino Leino wrote the Frost Year Novels, the police officer on the Esplanade takes on a more complex character than that of the mere gatekeeper and controller of a particular gendered geography of fear.[32] The extremely volatile conditions reigning in Helsinki in the early years of the twentieth century put an unmistakable stamp on the way urban public space is rendered and experienced in Finnish literature. In Runar Schildt's words, the Finland-Swedish generation responsible for the breakthrough of urban images in literature is a generation "marked first and foremost by the Frost Years and the Great Strike" (Schildt 1912), and this is also true of the Helsinki novels written in Finnish that appeared in this period. Compared to the development of city images in other literary traditions around the same period (such as the developments in the urban literature of Stockholm, see Borg 2011), the experience of Helsinki is permeated and defined by a sense of urgency related to the grave political conditions.

These were the "cursed years" (Aspelin-Haapkylä 1980), during which the acutely felt threat to the nation and the suffocating political repression were lying almost universally on the Finnish minds and hearts, and in particular on the capital, where the political, cultural and social forces were concentrated. In the Finnish novels, short stories, poetry and newspaper articles that were published during these years, spatial surroundings were repeatedly imbued with allegorical qualities. Due to the enforced Russian censorship in this period, Finnish authors often had no other choice than to make use of allegorical images and historical reminiscences to voice their criticism of the Russian repression (see Leino-Kaukiainen 1984: 238–239; Lyytikäinen 1999: 211).[33] Eino Leino was a master in couching political preoccupations, worries and programmes in allegorical language: in his very first literary text on Helsinki, the poem "Helsinki sumussa" ("Helsinki in the Mist"; 1899), all of the Helsinki centre appears as an allegory of the political situation, and in the two other Frost Year Novels he wrote in addition to *Jaana Rönty*, the strained political climate is repeatedly described as being felt so tangibly on the Esplanade that it profoundly disturbs the daily routines of otherwise malleable male bourgeois characters: in the novel *Tuomas Vitikka* ("Tuomas Vitikka"; 1906), those of the eponymous protagonist's father, in *Olli Suurpää*, those of the protagonist Olli.

In *Jaana Rönty*, both Helsinki public space and the protagonist's fate take on allegorical dimensions related to the ongoing political struggle. Jaana is portrayed as a representative of the Finnish nation, and the police attack can be read as an allegory for the rape of Finland during the Frost Years. This is clearly also the way in which many contemporary readers understood this passage (see Anon. 1907; Järnström 1908: 153). The police officer who stops Jaana uses Russian words ("Nietu" ["no"]; "Da da ["yes"]) alongside Finnish in his conversation with Jaana, and he speaks Russian to officers arriving on the scene (Leino 1907/1998: 222–223). Furthermore, the "cavalier" whom Jaana is supposed to meet at the Esplanade is, in fact – as readers realize by then – in the service of the Russian secret police, and it is the friend of this cavalier, also a secret police officer, who rapes Jaana at the police station. Identification of the police with the Russian oppressors is also made in other novels, for example in Wilkuna's *Vaikea tie* (1915), in which the main character Markus is stopped by a police officer when he staggers home drunk after a nightly bar crawl. He calls the officer a "Ruskie devil"[34] and ends up in the police gaol, where most of the police officers speak either Russian or Finnish with an Estonian accent (Wilkuna 1915: 137).

A comparison between these instances in Wilkuna's *Vaikea tie* and Leino's *Jaana Rönty* is revealing in another sense: Jaana's confrontation with the police officer is the critical moment which propels her on a downward course, while in *Vaikea tie*, the protagonist Markus continues cheerfully onwards on the chosen path, largely undisturbed by the encounter. The difference between the two passages lies, of course, in the gender and social standing of the protagonists in question: a male representative of the upper and middle classes could rise above such incursions on his freedom to roam the city. In the case of Jaana Rönty's movement through the city, other rules apply, and the events on the Esplanade lead to a social and moral descent which is also reflected in Jaana's personal social-geographical map of the city, as seen through her respective dwelling places and work places. At the beginning of the novel, she is as yet a stranger to the working-class district and to the city's brothels, into which she strays unwillingly. In the course of the novel, however, Jaana's downward trajectory takes on the form of a journey through the social layers of the city, from the asphalt of the Esplanade to her later dwellings in the working-class district of the city, and her work as a sauna washer on the outskirts of the city.

The fact that the unwritten rules governing Helsinki's urban public space apply differently to people from different classes and gender is explicitly visible in *Jaana Rönty*. In the novel, there are four instances in which a character's right to walk the city is challenged. All the important characters in the novel take part in these events: Jaana Rönty, the elderly Baron Manfelt, whose trajectories through Helsinki repeatedly intersect with those of Jaana, and (through the secret and regular police) also the Russian authorities. The very first instance in which a city walker's right to walk is questioned in *Jaana Rönty* is of considerable importance, since it initiates Jaana's acquaintance with her future "cavalier". Jaana has noticed that a young man walks up and down the street close to where she lives, and when this young man approaches her, Jaana asks him, in wordings remarkably similar to the police officer's later question: "Why are you always walking here?" (Leino 1907/1998: 215)[35] The man first answers playfully that he has been instructed by the doctor to walk, but he finally answers more seriously that he has "official business to attend to" (ibid.). Jaana does not believe this explanation, but the man is in fact, telling the truth, since he is occupied by the Russian government to spy on the students who live in the same house as Jaana.

Immediately following the scene in which Jaana is arrested by the police officer on the Esplanade, there is another, third passage in which a city walker's right to walk freely is challenged. When Jaana is dragged violently to a waiting police carriage, an angry mob forms, and an old man shouts at the officers, one of whom threatens the man with his scabbard, telling him to move on. The old man, however, is not to be threatened so easily: "'I will go when I want to,' he barked." (ibid.: 224)[36] After an exchange of words, the old man tells his name and rank:

> I am baron Manfelt, major-general, resigned from duty, with the right to carry a uniform. Living in this city. (Leino 1907/1998: 225)[37]

The stunned police officer apologizes and the Baron walks on, with unabated freedom to move through urban space: as a male member of the nobility and as a former army officer his authority is sanctioned – ironically – like that of the secret police, by the Czar himself. Significant for the role of Baron Manfelt in the novel is the fact that in this passage, the focalization shifts again, this time to the Baron himself, who gets to say the last word on the situation. As he is walking away from the scene, he considers for a moment whether he should interfere or not, but decides that it is no use: "every day similar things happened, and a lot worse, too" (ibid.: 225).[38] To the Baron, this is not more than an "insignificant street incident" (ibid.).[39] Intriguingly, the incident triggers the Baron's memory: he realizes that he has met a similar-looking girl (in fact, the very same girl) in a brothel at the outskirts of the city, who told him the story of her life and family. The next chapter in the novel presents the story of Jaana's rural background, and the framing of the story suggests that it is told as Baron Manfelt remembers and reconstructs it – the Baron does not only keep the authorial gaze over the scene at the Esplanade, but also over the very life of Jaana on the level of the narration (see Rojola 2008: 232–234).

Jaana Rönty is an allegorical story of the Finnish nation under Russian attack, but also a Frost Year version of the story of a young working-class woman succumbing to the vices of the city (see Railo 1907: 170–171; rv 1907), a standard *topos* in realist-naturalist literature (Lappalainen 1998a; Aalto 2000: 142). The fact that Baron Manfelt is repeatedly used as a focalizer reveals that this is also a story concerning the upper classes' perspective of the working classes, and a reflection of the former's responsibilities towards alleviating the plight of the latter. The very first encounter between Jaana Rönty and Baron Manfelt is instructive in this respect: they meet at the brothel into which Jaana is unwittingly introduced, on which occasion the Baron "saves" her. In the scene at the Helsinki Esplanade, Baron Manfelt has the opportunity, again, to save Jaana, but he eventually prefers to walk on: he and the other representatives of the intelligentsia in the novel are described as either impotent or unwilling to really interfere with the plight of the poor and the repressed.

The Esplanade as Agent Road

As a story of descent into moral corruption and prostitution, *Jaana Rönty* resembles the prototypical naturalist narrative of a working-class woman's evolution in relation to the modern city. Parallels in other novels and short stories in the same period abound, and Eino Leino's elder brother Kasimir had written a remarkably similar short story, "Emmalan Elli" (1884), in which the degenerating environment is not constituted by Helsinki but Oulu. Both in *Jaana Rönty* and "Emmalan Elli" (and several other contemporary texts), the protagonist's background and roots bode ill for her future development, but the move to the city plays a decisive role. In *Jaana Rönty*, Helsinki has a crucial role in awakening the dormant instincts that lie in waiting for Jaana, and the Esplanade, as the most important synecdoche of the Finnish capital, is the spatial environment that functions as an accelerator of this process. The programmatic walking rituals performed at the Esplanade "activate", as it were, the predispositions and the gendered roles that are held in store for Jaana. In this sense, the Esplanade can be considered an "agent road", a spatial narrative function that defines and inspires the protagonist's movements (see Gumbrecht 2006). Similar to the experience of the journey by railway to the capital, described in the previous chapter, the experience of the Esplanade is defined by a loss of independent movement, and agency is transferred from the protagonist to the road itself, and to the moral and social trajectory it implies.

For working-class women, a walk on the Esplanade is repeatedly described in this period as inevitably involving the fatal first steps on the trajectory towards prostitution and degeneration. Exemplary of such a vision of the Esplanade as an "agent road" is a 1902 sketch from urban life published under the pseudonym Maija in the woman's magazine *Kodin ystävä* ("Friend of the Hearth"). In the text, entitled "Elämän todellisuudesta" ("The Realities of Life"), the I-narrator recounts the fate of a young girl, Hanna, who moves from Oulu to Helsinki, and who, following the lead of another young woman, "a poor frivolous girl, corrupted by Helsinki", starts walking the Esplanade in the evening.[40] At this point, nothing has as yet occurred, but to the narrator, the consequences of these first steps are obvious enough: "Poor Hanna, she did not understand to what kinds of dangers such a life could lead…" (Maija 1902)[41] On a warm August evening, Hanna is approached by a gentleman, invited to his home, and (the story is not conclusive on this account) raped, after which she descends into prostitution. Hanna is the clear victim, but the narrator does not point the finger to anyone in particular as the one to blame: all characters are described as enacting their pre-determined roles, which are activated on the asphalt of the Esplanade. Rather than involving a moral outcry, the sketch extends a general warning on the dangers of the modern city for innocent newcomers.

In short stories and novels of the 1920s and 1930s, the importance of the Esplanade diminishes, but the idea of the urban road as a degenerative "agent road" in relation to young working-class women remains prominent. For a young girl, walking the city roads continues to entail fateful consequences. In Toivo Tarvas's aptly named short story "Asfalttikukkanen" ("Asphalt Flower"; 1920), from the collection *Kadun lapsia* ("Children of the Street"), the protagonist Saara receives words of warning similar to the one expressed above when she is on her way to meet a student acquaintance. The old lady with whom she lives notices how Saara is about to leave the house particularly well-dressed, and warns her: "Oh, poor child. Beware, pitiable girl, of evening walks, it can become a habit, from which you cannot let go even though you would want to. There are more than enough streets in this city; so many that you cannot walk them to the end in one lifetime." (Tarvas 1920: 121)[42] Saara is seduced by the student; she subsequently becomes the mistress of an elderly engineer, and eventually she degenerates into an abject state of prostitution. The short story ends with Saara's suicide.

Similarly, in Unto Karri's 1929 novel *Sodoma* ("Sodom"), the street is seen as exacting a direct influence on young women, and it is again an old lady who expresses worries about the "dirt of the street" which attracts young girls "like a giant magnet" (Karri 1929: 51–52). Regardless of earlier warnings, young Alli, one of the novel's main characters, feels in her soul the "call of the street" (ibid.: 91).[43] The reader is hardly surprised when she finds work in a bar of slightly dubious nature, begins a close relation with a frivolous student, and eventually becomes pregnant. In *Sodoma*, the Esplanade has not lost its position as the centre of Helsinki's street prostitution: a close friend of Alli recounts how she is being kept as a mistress by a rich man she met at the Esplanade. In the exchange of words between Alli's friend and the gentleman in question, the woman had told him quite frankly that at present, she organizes her "reception" at the Esplanade, but that she is looking for more quiet quarters – in other words, she wants to make the move from being a street prostitute to being a kept woman (ibid.: 99–100).

Uneasy Encounters

As the examples above illustrate, the turn of the century saw in Finland – as elsewhere – a vivid discussion concerning the woman question, morality in society, and prostitution, in close relation to questions such as the rise of the working class, and the urbanization and industrialization witnessed in the metropolis.[44] The way such worries were couched in prose narratives repeatedly takes the form of descriptions of uneasy encounters in urban public space, in which a male protagonist is confronted with a disconcerting figure rising from the city crowd. Such figures are typically familiar-looking, yet hard to recognize. Unlike Baudelaire's *passante* or Poe's man in the crowd, they are no complete strangers but turn out to be ghosts from the past. The passages in question force the usually male protagonist into agonizing soul searching and a contemplation of his earlier choices and ethical values. The setting for these encounters is typically a safe and familiar urban surrounding, not uncommonly the Esplanade.

A typical example can be found in Arvid Järnefelt's *Veneh'ojalaiset*, in which the protagonist Hannes meets a repellent drunken woman in the street. Too late he realizes that the despicable woman is in fact the same person as the girl he once promised, in his teens, to save from prostitution. The encounter can be considered as a reminder of his inactivity and incompetence in the face of social and gendered inequality. An even more disturbing event in the same novel is a strange encounter on the Esplanade which resembles, on a number of accounts, the events described in "À une Passante". In Baudelaire's sonnet, the lyrical I meets a woman in the street who is dressed in mourning; he is overcome by the shock of the meeting and by regret, because he will most likely never meet this woman again: "O you whom I could have loved, O you who knew it too!" (quoted in Benjamin 2006: 76). The poem reverberates with a sexual desire directed to, and emanating from the crowd. As Benjamin points out, this desire is "imperious", and the detail that the woman is in mourning adds an extra titillating and decadent touch to it (ibid.). The shock felt by the lyrical I in this poem is, in Benjamin's reading, one of the fundamental experiences of modern urban life, a reading which resonates far and wide in the study of city experiences in literature (see for example Berman 1982/1989: 146–147).

The event in Järnefelt's *Veneh'ojalaiset* differs on a number of crucial aspects from the encounter in "À une Passante". Hannes sees a woman walking, dressed in mourning, but he is unable to look her in the eyes and even actively tries to avoid doing so, since he has devoted his life to the stern teachings of Tolstoy and Epictetus (which is one of many comic elements in the novel). Hannes prefers to cross the street, rather than run the risk of being overcome by the shocking desire that so upsets Baudelaire's *flâneur*. But when he meets the mysterious woman again (she, too, has crossed the street) and looks her in the face, he recognizes not a desire that beckons to an unrealizable future – he sees the results of his earlier and already consummated desire.[45] The woman is not a stranger to him, but his beloved Kerttu, who is in mourning for their lost child, born out of wedlock, and abandoned by Hannes. This encounter, then, is not a call for impossible and anonymous love in the big city, but a call to marry. Soon after the encounter, Hannes goes to see Kerttu, they marry and establish a family. Like other encounters in Helsinki's public space, this encounter with a mysterious woman is not a personally perceived shock emanating from the modern urban crowd, but a social and/or moral wake-up call to help another character, with whom the protagonist turns out to be familiar.

In a number of prose works referred to earlier in this chapter, the gendered and social inequality reigning in public space is thematized, rather than merely mentioned in passing. In the quoted works written by Järnefelt, this theme is explicitly visible, for example in *Nuoruuteni muistelmia* ("Memories of My Youth"; 1919), but also throughout the novel *Veljekset*. In a revealing scene, the protagonist in *Veljekset*, Henrik, walks the streets of Helsinki, pondering what task he should devote himself to in the city. Looking around, he sees a prostitute, and considers giving his energy to these "children of the city that most need it" (Veljekset 1900: 441).[46] He soon realizes, however, that this will be a daunting task: "If I should be obliged to treat everyone of those women like my own sister, I would not have the time to do anything else, – I would not even be able to walk along the streets" (ibid.).[47] To his dismay, the woman approaches him, and half-heartedly, he tries to bring her to change her life. It transpires that they have met earlier, and later on, Henrik finds out that she is, in fact, the sister of his own brother's wife. The girl is eventually saved when she marries a friend of Henrik's.

Like Henrik in Järnefelt's *Veljekset*, young Markus in Kyösti Wilkuna's novel *Vaikea tie* tries to save a prostitute he met accidentally and who equally turns out to be an earlier acquaintance. Markus does not succeed; although the girl – Sandra – goes back to her home village on Markus's behest, she returns to Helsinki towards the end of the novel. Markus meets her again in front of the statue of Runeberg at the Esplanade – a clear indication that she has taken up her old profession.[48] Markus's concern for the harassment of working-class women in Helsinki's public space runs like a red thread through *Vaikea tie* from the moment Markus approaches two working-class girls in the Old Church Park. The angry reaction of one of the girls acts as an awakening to Markus – about whom we learn a few pages later that he was drunk at the moment – and, realizing the dire conditions of working-class girls moving through urban public space, he joins the socialist ranks and writes an article in the socialist paper *Työmies* ("The Labourer") criticizing the behaviour of students towards women.[49] Although he returns to the bourgeois ranks during the Great Strike, he is eventually engaged with the same working-class girl he met at the Old Church Park.

The passage from Talvio's *Tähtien alla* quoted earlier, in which the main character Hilja is mistaken for a prostitute when walking slowly across the Railway Square, is equally linked to the broader thematic field of the novel, in which questions of morality are of a first order. In the novel, Hilja enters into a close, but harmless friendship with a young student – the son of a farmer – living in with the family, a relation which fatally tarnishes the reputation of both Hilja and her family. A similar misunderstanding affects the platonic love affair between student Eljas and bar girl Anna in Ivalo's debut novel *Hellaassa* (1890). Their untimely public appearance results in Eljas's removal from the city's circles of prominence and his noble plan – to save Anna from the dangers of prostitution – fails miserably.

Traces of Flânerie Beyond the Esplanade

Generally speaking, characters in turn-of-the-century literary Helsinki do not display an eagerness for the creative, Baudelairean surrender to the city crowd. Most of the time, bourgeois literary characters in fact prefer not to walk at all and choose instead to take a horse-drawn carriage to travel even the smallest distances. The distance between the railway station and Kappeli, covered by Antti by horse-drawn carriage in Aho's *Helsinkiin*, for example, is less than a kilometre. Whenever walking the streets of Helsinki acquires a certain air of self-confidence, it is a practice that is rigidly regulated and stratified, as in the case of the programmed stroll along the Esplanade. One of the possible reasons for the conspicuous lack of *flâneurs* in Helsinki in this period is, of course, the Finnish capital's size. At the turn of the century, Helsinki was so small, both in geographical terms and in terms of its population, that many of the upper (middle) class people walking its central streets would necessarily know each other at least remotely, a condition which translates into the repeated instances in literature of coincidental encounters at the Esplanade.[50] When Hannes, the protagonist of Järnefelt's *Veneh'ojalaiset*, returns to Helsinki after years in St. Petersburg, he is delighted to notice that in his home city, he recognizes every second or third person on the street (Järnefelt 1909: 125). In such circumstances, surrendering to the crowd or indulging in urban anonymity could hardly be considered a reasonable option for aspiring Helsinki *flâneurs*. Even in Joel Lehtonen's *Henkien taistelu*, which is set in the capital around the turn of the 1930s, one character states that "in the small town Helsinki" people run into each other almost unavoidably (Lehtonen 1933: 448), and the protagonist is indeed repeatedly described running into acquaintances on the Esplanade or the street Aleksanterinkatu.

The peripatetic exploits in Helsinki at the turn of the twentieth century, then, seem to lack most of the features of the walk in the city of modernity as exemplified by Baudelaire and Poe. Finnish writers at this time did not, however, lack interest in the *topos* of the *flâneur*, nor were they unable to render him in prose. Descriptions of urban wanderings, bearing clear marks of *flânerie*, can be found in works such as Juhani Aho's *Yksin* ("Alone"; 1890/2003), Maila Talvio's *Tähtien alla* ("Under the Stars"; 1910) and V. A. Koskenniemi's *Kevätilta Quartier Latinissä* ("A Spring Evening in the Quartier Latin"; 1912, see Pääjärvi 2006). In all three cases, the Baudelairean surrender to the crowd and to the frenetic pace of urban movement is set in Paris. Not only was the environment found lacking, but so were the potential city walkers: most of the Finnish-speaking characters in Helsinki novels of this period belong to the lower and lower-middle classes and have a provincial background, and would thus fit awkwardly with the image of a self-confident city dweller with plenty of time to spare.

When taking into account Finland-Swedish novels from around the same period, the modes of walking the city, however, have a dramatically different outlook, and it becomes clear that the lack of the *flâneur* in literature in Finnish is not determined by the characteristics of the historical city of Helsinki, but by prevailing aesthetic preferences. In Finland-Swedish literature, the idle city walker would take firmer root; influenced by Hjalmar Söderberg's and other Swedish authors' literature of Stockholm, the so-called *dagdrivare* generation would build a rich imagery of literary Helsinki, in which the lonely, male city walker would take a central place (see Toftegaard Pedersen 2007). This generation was actively involved in discussing new developments in *flâneur* writing that appeared in Sweden (Borg 2011: 182). The Finland-Swedish *dagdrivare* or idler cannot, however, be equated outright with its close relative the Baudelairean *flâneur* (as happens in Laitinen 1991: 301–302; Molarius 1998b; see Ameel 2010). The *dagdrivare* saw the idleness of his life as an unfortunate condition, rather than as an accomplishment worth striving for (see Pettersson 1986; Ciaravolo 2000: 172–173).

For the *flâneur*, there is something profoundly euphoric about a "voluntary up-rooting, of anonymous arrival at a new place" (Wolff 1985: 40). As seen in the previous chapter, the condition of being uprooted, and of anonymous arrival in the capital, constitutes, on the contrary, a debilitating shock to the Young Men and Women from the provinces converging in Helsinki in the literature written in Finnish of the late nineteenth and early twentieth centuries. The effects of this shock continue to have their effect once literary protagonists settle down in the city: even for a short trip, characters usually prefer a horse-drawn carriage rather than walk, a decision that also reflects a desire to uphold a particular status.

In descriptions of leisurely walks in turn-of-the-century Helsinki novels written in Finnish, nature tends to play a more important role than the urban spectacle. Inhabitants setting out for a stroll (or for a trip by car or horse-drawn carriage) quickly find themselves either on the seashore or in the forest. As the character Albert Hagen, in Toivo Tarvas's *Eri tasoilta* ("On Different Levels"; 1916a), exclaims: "Really, this beloved Helsinki is small, after all. [...] Just when we start to get going, we already bump into the sea or the forest" (Tarvas 1916a: 82).[51] The close presence of both the countryside and the sea gives the leisurely movement of Helsinki citizens distinct characteristics. The sea, in particular, is closely bound up with Helsinki's perceived identity, in historical, journalistic as well as literary writings.[52] A fascinating example of a solitary walk performed in connection to Helsinki's seascape is found in the novel *Aikansa lapsipuoli* (Ivalo 1895), in which the protagonist, after a session of heavy drinking, suddenly feels oppressed by the stifling atmosphere in a centrally located Helsinki café. In need for fresh air, the protagonist leaves the place – and sets out for an odyssey on the frozen sea:

> Otto started to talk with some new friends, and in the meantime Juuso slipped out of the bar. He walked to the sea, went down on the ice and took a long walk far on the frozen sea, where the sun shone bright on the snowy surface and where the fresh sea wind blew freely. There he tried to gather and organize his thoughts. (Ivalo 1895: 159)[53]

In the same novel, the scene of a beautiful winter holiday is described, when the whole city empties, and the citizens set out for winter outings on skis, horseback and sledges:

> The inhabitants of the capital, young as well as old, were today on the move in the snow-covered nature, some walking, some on horseback, many, the younger ones in particular, on skis. From all sides, and through all the customs barriers, they could be seen skiing out of the city in small groups, some in the direction of the open sea to the islands, others in the direction of the forests and the hills. (Ivalo 1895: 73)[54]

The protagonist, too, is on the move with a small group of friends, on their way to the "Old Town" (Vanhakaupunki), a district of scenic beauty which also in later decades features as a destination for Helsinki citizens (see

Lehtonen 1922: 58). Towards the end of the novel, the protagonist, utterly disillusioned with life, becomes "a fervent walker, [and] moving in the open air seemed to calm his mind and entertained his thoughts" (Ivalo 1895: 275).[55] Typically of the Helsinki walker in this period, however, becoming a fervent walker does not amount to becoming a *flâneur*: usually, he "made long walks out of the city", and even when he stays inside the city boundaries, the lonely expanses of the sea seen from the park Kaivopuisto constitute his favourite environment (ibid.).[56]

City walking in the Finnish capital was thus closely bound up with the nature of the city – the sea shore, the parks, the forest and bays close to the city. Environments of natural beauty that frequently function as the background setting for a leisurely stroll in Finnish prose texts are, amongst others, the Observatory Hill, which offered a view of both the city and the sea (in Järnefelt's *Veneh'ojalaiset*, Wilkuna's *Vaikea tie*); the Kaivopuisto park, and the surroundings near the Töölö Bay (in Ivalo's *Aikansa lapsipuoli*; Talvio's *Tähtien alla*; Tarvas's *Kohtalon tuulissa*).

Flâneurs are scarce in Finnish literature in the period 1890–1940, but they do exist. The earliest explicit references appear in the work of Toivo Tarvas, which also in other respects pioneers aestheticizing descriptions of Helsinki. Albert Hagen in Toivo Tarvas's *Eri tasoilta* (1916a) is a *flâneur par excellence*. A native of Helsinki, he feels a close bond with the city, but also a sense of loneliness and alienation which he actively cultivates. Solitary walks in the city are his favourite pastime, and in his love for the urban crowd, he resembles Baudelaire's painter of modern life, who enjoys "to set up house in the heart of the multitude" (Baudelaire 1863/1964: 9). When Albert, after a period of convalescence towards the end of the novel, is able to walk through the city again, he is overwhelmed with joy that he "can walk in the bustle of the crowd, and feel he belongs to the crowd"; "[i]t is sweet to be in the crowd and to imagine, that they feel the same as you do" (Tarvas 1916a: 250).[57] Several *flâneurs* can be found in the work of Toivo Tarvas; in *Eri tasoilta*, the second male character, Urho, surrenders at times to drifting through the Helsinki crowd, and in the collection of short stories *Häviävää Helsinkiä* ("Disappearing Helsinki"; 1917) the protagonist of the framing story "Suomenlahden helmi" ("Pearl of the Baltic") is an aestheticizing city walker, as well as an ardent observer of the urban spectacle.

During the 1920s and 1930s, the texts of one Finnish author, in particular, can be singled out as evocations of Helsinki *flânerie*: the novels, short stories and poems of Iris Uurto. The *flâneur* attitude is described most explicitly in her debut collection of short stories and poetry *Tulta ja tuhkaa* ("Fire and Ashes"; 1930), in which the protagonist of the first short story, "Gretan päiväkirjasta" ("From Greta's diary"; Uurto 1930: 5–18) writes down a eulogy to her home city and to walking through its streets:

> I have a special love for this city. I love its streets, its windows, houses, movement. The best pastime, the purest pleasure, is for me to walk along the streets, especially in the evening. [...] If only I may move one foot in front of the other, slowly and carefree. And at the same time I direct my gaze at faces, people, everything. (Uurto 1930: 7)[58]

If a *flâneuse* does indeed exist, she certainly resembles Greta in *Tulta ja tuhkaa*, with her "special love" for the city and her desire to walk Helsinki's streets and to gaze at the spectacle it provides, in conscious or unconscious imitation of Baudelaire's "perfect idler" and "passionate observer" (Baudelaire 1863/1964: 9). But walking the city is for her more than a mere pastime. Benjamin notes that the *flâneur* "seeks refuge in the crowd" (Benjamin 2006: 40), and Greta's promenades are inspired by a longing that makes her want to forget herself in the crowd:

> I am homeless and I try to forget myself in the bustle of the street. This wandering is a true image of myself. A stranger to everything, an observer without a leading star. With a restless longing in my heart. (Uurto 1930: 9-10)[59]

Several of the characters – both male and female – in Iris Uurto's later prose are given to an aestheticizing wandering through the Helsinki streets: Paula in *Ruumiin ikävä* ("The Longing of the Body"; 1931) and Lauri in *Kypsyminen* ("Maturing"; 1935) have the strongest penchant for *flânerie*, and their experiences of the city will be analysed in more detail in Chapter 6, which explores the aestheticization of the city in 1920s and 1930s prose literature.

Walking the Finnspång

The "Finnspång" was the stretch of the Southern Esplanade where the leaders of the Finnish-minded party were known to walk (Forsman et. al. 1925-1928: 895-896; Paunonen 2010: 162). Several Finnish literary texts from the turn of the twentieth century make reference to the Finnspång. Eino Leino's short story "Päivä Helsingissä" ("A Day in Helsinki"; 1905), for example, features an elderly teacher whose political affiliation with the conservative party is mentioned in parallel with the mention of the man's daily walk at the "Finnspång": "Now he was one of the conservative party's leaders and walked his half an hour at the 'Finnspång' just like the other men." (Leino 1905: 34)[60] The Finnspång also plays a crucial role in the life of Mauritz Ahlfelt, the prototypical arriviste in Juhani Aho's sketches "Mallikelpoinen" ("An Exemplary Character"; 1890) and "Hätääkärsivien hyväksi" ("For the Benefit of the Needy; 1891). As a symbol of the conservative Finnish party, the Finnspång also features in another short story by Juhani Aho, "Nuori sielu" ("A Young Soul"; 1896), in which an idealistic provincial at last returns to Helsinki after years in the countryside, and is described in a profoundly ironical light by the narrator as he tours the sights of the capital (see Molarius 1991: 83-84). One of these sights is the Finnspång, which the narrator shows him. The provincial's reaction is filled with admiration:

> "- No really, so here is that splendid... well well, so here it is... so here they walk and meet each other and decide the matters of the country and the people.
> He felt like walking on the Finnspång, he wanted to see what 'they' looked like." (Aho 1896: 117)[61]

5. Experiences of a Metropolis in Motion
Changing and Disappearing Helsinki

This chapter examines the appearance of literary Helsinki as a space in motion, and the ongoing interaction between the changing built environment and the development of literary characters. The first decades of the twentieth century are years in which the economic and demographic growth of the city is punctuated by major upheavals such as the Great Strike of 1905 and the Viapori Rebellion of 1906, events with a far-reaching influence on the literary image of the city as a space of extreme possibilities as well as extreme danger. In the literary representations of this period, Utopia and Apocalypse lie closely together. Perhaps surprisingly, this is also a period in which literary protagonists express a growing sense of belonging to the city and to the particular parts of the city they begin to call their home.

I will start out with a brief discussion of Arvid Järnefelt's novel *Veljekset* ("Brothers"; 1900) to illustrate how this period presents a more panoramic vision of the city.[1] Järnefelt's kaleidoscopic *Venehojalaiset* ("The Family Venehoja"; 1909) will be approached as a key novel and will be discussed in more depth. In this novel, new, emerging aspects of the literary city can be seen to function on a variety of narrative levels. Thematically, the city appears as a profoundly apocalyptic environment and as the stage for speculation and development driven by opaque financial and economic forces. In terms of the plot development, Helsinki functions not so much as a passive background, but as an active force enabling tremendous possibilities of self-fulfilment: drawing on a distinction used by Burton Pike, one can say that the city in this novel has irreversibly become a "presence" rather than a mere "setting" (Pike 1981: 8). Finally, in terms of the attributes that are attached to the city by the literary characters, *Venehojalaiset* presents a break with most of the earlier literature of Helsinki: regardless of the novel's apocalyptic overtones, the protagonists express a profound sense of belonging to the Finnish capital.

In Järnefelt's *Veljekset* and in *Venehojalaiset*, as well as in a number of short stories and city novels from the 1910s, two important approaches within which the urban space operates serve as indications that a new relationship is being forged between the city and the urban protagonist. The first approach is that of the panorama, a narrative strategy used to impose a totalizing order and a measure of comprehensibility on the complex and ambiguous cityscape.[2] Complementary with this panoramic view is a relation with the city that is acted out in transitory experiences on ground level, through an invisible "chorus of idle footsteps" (de Certeau 1984: 97). It is arguably in the syncopated interaction between both perspectives that a complex experience of the city is grounded. The ground-level experiences of literary characters in this period, moreover, increasingly express a heightened sense of mobility when compared to earlier instances from Finnish literature. Literary characters such as Henrik in *Veljekset*, Hannes and Hinkki in *Veneh'ojalaiset*, and a number of characters in the 1910s prose texts written by Maila Talvio, Eino Leino and Toivo Tarvas, are shedding the limited mobility typical of the earlier Young Men and Women of the Provinces. Increasingly, they experience the city environment through everyday walking.

A Panoramic View of the City

Arvid Järnefelt's novel *Veljekset*, a multi-perspective depiction of Finnish society in the late nineteenth century, opens with an extensive panoramic description of Helsinki.[3] The sweeping view of the city in the following quote reaches beyond the superficial modern city of leisure and light, and displays an acute concern with life at the urban fringes and the margins, as well as a heightened awareness of the city's ongoing transformations:

> Henrik lived on the outermost fringes of the capital, where because of the rocks there were no more regular streets, or where a street grid had but only recently been planned and laid out amidst the remains of stones broken by explosions; – behind those and a few barren, wave-battered rocks, the sea, continuously rumbling, widened into an open expanse, with no land in sight at the horizon. From his window, Henrik could see at his right an institution for fallen women and an incredibly tall brick tower, constantly pouring out a thick black cloud of smoke, which indicated which way the wind blew. It was the electric lighting power centre, thanks to which in the boutiques of the city, in the public institutions, the festival halls, and in the streets, bright lights flared up when a small lever was switched. On the left, one could see first a maternity hospital, then, in the direction of the sea, the ramparts of Kaivopuisto, and in the direction of the land, the green pinnacle of the Catholic Church, and behind that, the first orderly features of the city. (Järnefelt 1900: 5)[4]

In contrast to other (both contemporary and earlier) descriptions with which Helsinki novels and short stories opened, the city is portrayed here from a perspective that is at once all-encompassing and still very selective. In the novels and short stories discussed earlier, the experience of the city presents a narrow physical and social urban reality made up of the asphalt of the Esplanade and the interiors of bars, clubs and restaurants, with very few references to factories, working-class districts, or even shops. The panorama seen from Henrik's window in *Veljekset*, on the contrary, does not present the reader with the centre of the city, but with the urban fringes. It is a first indication that the narrator in this novel is particularly concerned with dissecting the social and moral problematics of the people living on the margins of society.

In the panoramic view of the city with which *Veljekset* opens, the physical features of Helsinki are endowed with important symbolic functions, and the way in which they are described reveals a keen understanding of the city's complexity. Helsinki is described as an expanding city, laid out in an ongoing process of planned destruction. The first building Henrik sees, and hence the feature of the city that gains the greatest weight in this selective ordering, is the institute for fallen women, a reflection of Järnefelt's interest in what Elizabeth Wilson has called "the great fear of the age" (Wilson 1992: 92), prostitution, and in the moral dangers of city life. Next to this, the power station is situated, the hidden force centre providing the energy for the brightly lit city. The plume of smoke emanating from its chimney literally and symbolically indicates which way the modernizing winds of change are blowing. Almost all contemporary descriptions of Helsinki feature mentions of dazzling electric lights; the panoramic view in *Veljekset* aims beyond such superficial appearances of the modern city, to suggest the hand that switches the lever. In relation to the two buildings first mentioned, the maternity hospital seems an almost logical extension of a particular series of urban institutions: by virtue of its being mentioned immediately in relation to the earlier buildings, it is almost as if the children are produced at the hospital in a similar way as the electricity in the power centre – for the sake of the city's energy. Further off in the panorama, two other images and archetypal functions of the city appear: that of the temple (the Catholic Church) and the fortress (the Kaivopuisto ramparts). Helsinki is constructed in this passage as a space defined by planological and technological dynamics, but also as part and parcel of social and moral problems.

The strategy of describing the city from a bird's eye perspective is a technique typical of nineteenth-century and early twentieth-century novels which, as Bart Keunen points out, "tend to emphasize the deterministic relationship between protagonist" and environment (Keunen 2001: 426–427). This deterministic relationship can be found in a number of realist-naturalist (city) novels of the nineteenth century such as the Paris novels by Balzac and Zola, and drawing on Bakhtin's study of the *Bildungsroman* (Bakhtin 1986/2004), Keunen argues that novels functioning within such a deterministic and documentary, realist-naturalist paradigm read "buildings, streets, works of art, technology and other social organizations as signs that refer to historical developments" (Keunen 2001: 425); signs of the massive changes witnessed in the cities of the nineteenth and early twentieth centuries.

The panorama is the literary image which translates these complex processes into a single comprehensible vision. As pointed out by Michel de Certeau and, following de Certeau, by Christopher Prendergast in the latter's study of Paris in the nineteenth century, the panorama constitutes an almost Olympian perspective of the city which constitutes "the very image of a certain urban rationality" (Prendergast 1992: 209). The panorama presents urban conditions as a comprehensible totality with its own centre and inner logic. But it is also a way in which the urban text is totalized – a way of producing a "fiction of knowledge" (de Certeau 1984: 92). The panoramic vision is related to what Nicholas Freeman has called, in his study of literary London, an empiricist reaction to the city, grounded in the "positivist belief that the city could be mapped and eventually understood by processes of painstaking investigation and analysis" (Freeman 2007: 26).

In Finnish literature of the first decades of the twentieth century, the panorama becomes a prominent means of approaching the city in a totalizing way, often with strong moralizing undercurrents. In the opening pages of Maila Talvio's *Niniven lapset* ("Children of Nineveh"; 1915), for example, Helsinki is seen from the third-floor window of the apartment of the family Ståhle, which presents a view that suggests both promises and threats:

> There truly was something radiant and electric in that white city. In between the city's clusters of houses, one could see the friendly rippling blue inlets of the sea. Seen from the third storey, where the apartment of the counsellor was situated, the city was resting calm and smiling at their feet, as if it was handing pleasures left and right to all those hundreds and thousands that asked them from their city. The buildings were grouped around the white church in proud and regular groups. The air, full of dust, the smell of asphalt, and street noise, was saturated with irritating life. The green colour of the trees, which formed groups here and there in the city and along its fringes, had that strange and dark glow, which accumulates in plants before they wither. (Talvio 1915: 6–7)[5]

Following an enumeration of positive attributes ("radiant and electric"; "friendly"; "calm and smiling") in this passage, the reader is confronted with a number of portentous omens. The street noise is "saturated with irritating life", and the colour of the trees displays an ominous "strange and dark glow, which accumulates in plants before they wither". The decay visible in the trees foreshadows the descent of the family Ståhle, only recently arrived in the capital, into moral and financial bankruptcy, but also the coming fate of Helsinki as a "New Niniveh" on the verge of the Great War (See Viinikka-Kallinen 1997: 25).[6]

The panoramic opening view in *Veljekset*, and in other Helsinki novels in its wake, is symptomatic of an endeavour to present a totalizing understanding of the city, aimed at identifying and questioning its social, economic and moral complexities. The acute awareness of processes underlying urban space is central to the thematics addressed in the novel as a whole, in which moral questions are of the first order. Towards the end of *Veljekset*, when the protagonist, Henrik, considers that he feels, finally, at ease and content in the city, he realizes that one of the main reasons for this is the fact that he is free "from those real city activities that made his life so agreeable, such as the many and indispensable physical urban activities: sweeping the streets, watering, building, coach driving, and so on" (Järnefelt 1900: 438).[7] Few of the Esplanade walkers discussed in the earlier chapters would have cared if they were not able to take part in all aspects of the city's activities, but to Henrik, who has experienced a moral awakening, the city appears as a larger chain of causes and effects that all have to be taken into account.

In the panorama at the beginning of *Veljekset*, there is a reference to an urban environment in the process of being violently destroyed, levelled and built: Henrik lives on the fringes of the city, "where a street grid had but only recently been planned and laid out amidst the remains of stones broken by explosions". It is a descriptive detail that bears relevance for the understanding of the novel and its protagonist. Henrik's life, too, is being disrupted and is informed by a sense of insecurity, and he is looking for ways to create a home and to find a purpose in life (see also Niemi 2005: 143–146). Eventually, he becomes attached to his lodgings in the capital and to the room from which the panoramic view above is seen. But this home, like Henrik's paternal home in the countryside which has been lost after the untimely death of his father, is not to last. The wooden house in Helsinki in which he lives has to make way for the forces of urban development that were seen encroaching upon the panorama in the novel's opening pages. He has to move out and when, on a fine day in the spring, Henrik walks through Helsinki towards his old quarters, the view he sees is one of "great destruction": half of the house is already ruined, and shrivels of wallpaper, with the decorative patterns he knows by heart, are swaying in the wind.[8] Henrik immediately connects the destruction of this home in the city with the destruction of the paternal house, the old vicarage, which had been violently "torn from his heart" (Järnefelt 1900: 436–437).[9] Like that of so many other characters in turn-of-the-century Finnish literature, Henrik's rootlessness is linked to the destruction of the paternal home in the countryside. When the political situation becomes more critical (the February Manifesto is obliquely referred to), Henrik's sense of homelessness is juxtaposed against the plight of the whole nation, but, perhaps surprisingly, not without positive repercussions. Destruction offers the possibility of starting again with a clean sheet, without earlier dependencies on past dreams or affiliations:

> The home vicarage and his earlier image of life was not more than something like a broken eggshell, from which he had emerged. And having to leave that confined abode, which first had grieved him, turned into a feeling of triumph, when the ceiling of his new home opened into the arching sky, and the walls receded into a blue haze. (Järnefelt 1900: 532)[10]

Henrik's sudden feeling of epiphany and relief comes while he is in the train on his return journey to Helsinki. It is a feeling in which the reader finds hints of the optimistic pantheism which permeates many of Järnefelt's works, and of Tolstoyan ideas concerning the rejection of the material world. But other ideas are at work in conjunction with these: despite earlier feelings of rootlessness, alienation and discomfort in the city, Henrik has become attached to the capital, which he begins to call his home. In large parts of the novel, he is still described as ill at ease when moving independently in city space. Gradually, however, everyday walks, rather than the panoramic views he looks at with such mixed feelings at the beginning of the novel, begin to give real meaning to his experience of the city. In the terms proposed by de Certeau, the "imaginary totalizations" of the panorama make way for the less visible, but more tangible everyday practices of walking the city, with their own epistemological repercussions (de Certeau 1984: 93). In the last conversation Henrik has with the young woman he loves, the geography of the city has become infused with a comforting intimacy: "I have become so used to this city and to these familiar routes from your place to mine and from my place to yours", he tells her as he prepares to leave the city one last time (Järnefelt 1900: 541).[11]

Helsinki in Arvid Järnefelt's Veneh'ojalaiset *(1909)*

In Järnefelt's subsequent Helsinki novel, several of the themes that were taken up in *Veljekset* are further developed. *Veneh'ojalaiset* ("The Family Veneh'oja"; 1909) is a multifarious analysis of the social and historical events at the outset of the twentieth century, but also a kaleidoscopic panorama of an emerging metropolis. Following subsequent generations of the family Veneh'oja as they descend on the Finnish capital, *Veneh'ojalaiset* focuses, in particular, on the events of 1904–1906: the years of the Russian oppression, the murder of the Russian Governor-General Bobrikov, the Great Strike and the Viapori rebellion.[12] These eventful years are focalized mostly through one member of the family, Hannes, who is born in Helsinki. Järnefelt's novel recounts the coming-of-age and the inner struggles of this character, but it also tells the tale of a socially divided city. The narration moves through the city of the well-to-do, and descends into the urban districts of poor labourers, socialist agitators, working-class gang members and underground characters, resulting in a description of the city's development from below (cf. Häkli 1955: 373; Anttila 1956: 643). The way the city appears in this novel is not only given historical depth by situating Helsinki at the summit of a family history spanning numerous generations, it is also presented through different focalizations (male and female, middle class and lower class) and in relation to other imagined cities, particularly St. Petersburg. The narrated city, moreover, takes into consideration a much higher geographical portion of the city than earlier representations in literature, expanding into the suburbs and the islands in front of the Helsinki harbour.

In many respects, *Veneh'ojalaiset* is the kind of complex city novel V. A. Koskenniemi calls for in his 1914 collection of essays *Runon kaupunkeja* ("Literary Cities"), in which he claims that the Finnish capital as yet lacks a "synthetic literary work about Helsinki, a novel or an epic, in which this Northern capital would live in its totality with all those characteristics which nature, race and culture have bestowed upon her" (Koskenniemi 1914: 89).[13] *Veneh'ojalaiset* puts such claims in perspective. In this novel (as in a number of other literary texts from the first decades of the twentieth century which will be discussed below), Helsinki appears as a multi-layered space-in-motion: a city which changes; develops; which is threatened with destruction, and which undergoes radical modifications which have their direct and often far-reaching impact on the experiences of the protagonists. What makes this novel particularly interesting from the perspective of the literary experience of Helsinki is the way in which it combines radically different frames of reference pertaining to the city. Building on prevalent realist and naturalist discourse on the city, it infuses the experience of urban space with distinctly apocalyptic undertones, which culminate in the climactic events of 1906. The most striking aspect of the urban experience is the sense of intimacy which the protagonists, Hannes, in particular, gradually experience in their relationship with Helsinki.

A NOVEL ABOUT THE LAND QUESTION

Veneh'ojalaiset is a novel which is concerned throughout with experiences of the city and with the way in which characters react to and interact with the city they see growing and expanding around them, and yet it begins in a rural environment within an epic time frame. The temporal scale of the narration, which descends into a time before history, when a word for the city does not yet exist, is a first indication of the sweeping perspective Järnefelt wants to offer on the phenomenon of the city. The epic story at the beginning of *Veneh'ojalaiset* features an agrarian society before the introduction of property, there is an ancient king ruling over his far-away subjects, and a devil in human shape. The family Veneh'oja lives in a semi-paradisiacal state in the wilderness of southern Finland. In a plot reminiscent of the book of Job, the devil, angry at the well-ordered pastoral society, disperses the Veneh'oja, posing amongst others in the human shape of a land surveyor.[14] The partitioning of the land, possibly referring to the land enclosure started in 1757, when Finland was still part of the Swedish kingdom, is not dissimilar to the Fall of Man and the expulsion from paradise (see Molarius 1996a). The opening of the novel is couched in mythical and allegorical language, and it presents the history of the family Veneh'oja within a narrative structure that sets out in the time of the "absolute past" – the time of "fathers and founders of families" normally destined for the epic genre (cf. Bakhtin 1981: 13–14) – and that moves on to the historical past, to include events that are set apart in time only a few years from its first readers.

After the expulsion from their lands and through a series of adventures, a branch of the Veneh'oja – more a tribe than a family – descends on Helsinki. The voyage is recounted in terms of an epic struggle, including murder, banishment to Siberia, a contract with the devil and a fight with the god of the heavens himself. Throughout, the Veneh'oja long for a return to their lands. This longing, however, is profoundly contradictory, since they never were in the possession of any fixed lands, and their desire is hence for a return to a nomadic, pre-fall reality. It remains unclear throughout the novel whether Helsinki thus symbolizes the city of Cain, outside of paradise, or, regardless of everything, may bear some characteristics of a beckoning Promised Land.

In *Veneh'ojalaiset*, the question of land ownership takes on a central role, and the question is repeatedly associated with the problems posed by the city.[15] Since the city is the seat of government, rationalization and money-based economy, it is only logical that the primeval anger of the Veneh'oja is directed at the very idea of the city, and one of them, Heikki, concludes a pact with the devil to set fire to the "greatest village of all". In the way in which he describes the land question in a distinctly urban novel, Järnefelt follows international city literature. Richard Lehan has pointed out that writers such as Dickens, Balzac and Gogol, but also Joyce, Ibsen, Hauptmann and D'Annunzio were essentially "considering in literary terms what Marx and Engels had taken up in economic terms: the land question; the displacement of a peasant class; the entrapment of a commercial class in a new kind of city controlled by money and commodity relationships", and the whole commensurate breakdown of traditional social structures, culminating in the disorientating and alienating city experience (Lehan 1998: 107). In many ways, the land reform question was a crucial part of the urban question, and it is no mere smoke screen, then, that Järnefelt had originally claimed that *Veneh'ojalaiset* was going to be a book on the land question (see Kock 1916: 5).

CITY OF SIN: THE BROTHEL SCENE

Hannes and his nephew Hinkki are the first generation of the *Veneh'oja* who grow up in Helsinki, and they are also the first significant literary characters in Finnish prose born in the Finnish capital. They get to know the city from within, and from the very first scene in which they appear, they are described as negotiating the city's boundaries. Hannes and Hinkki appear into sight at the moment when the epic time frame from the beginning of the novel moves into the historical time of the late nineteenth century. This change is initiated first with a panoramic view of the city (Järnefelt 1909/1996: 49), which then zooms in on the group of boys to which Hannes and Hinkki belong (ibid.: 50–51). The introductory scene describes a fight in which different gangs of teenage boys compete for a stake in the capital's territory. The boys, from Finnish, Finland-Swedish and Russian backgrounds, repeat on the level of the city street the much more monumental struggles shaking Finnish society around the turn of the century. But for Hannes and Hinkki, this fight is not a political allegory; it is also about becoming acquainted with their immediate surroundings, the streets and parks of their home city.

Hannes grows up in the Finnish capital, but like many of the characters moving to Helsinki in this period, he will have to get to know the secrets of the city by way of an introduction into strange and alienating surroundings. A considerable number of the Finnish Young Man/Woman of the Provinces novels of this period feature the introduction of the protagonist in an unfamiliar space, where he or she will be confronted with the vices of the city, and where either he/she or the reader will shed his/her last doubts as to the real nature of the city. According to Robert Alter, the entrance of the protagonist into an unfamiliar space is a central topos in the realist novel, and particularly so, since "the realist novel is to such a large degree about the encounter with the new social and moral experience and how it reshapes the protagonist" (Alter 2005: 32). In Finnish literature, such pivotal spaces are more often than not the kind of spaces that Foucault has identified, in his "Of Other Spaces" (Foucault 1986) as "heterotopias", the kind of "other spaces" that not only carry their own manifold meanings, but that also have their ordering repercussions on the space at large they belong to.

Heterotopias, according to Foucault, are "something like counter-sites, a kind of effectively enacted utopia in which the real sites, all the other real sites that can be found within the culture, are simultaneously represented, contested, and inverted" (Foucault 1986: 24). Of the characters discussed in the previous chapters, Jaana Rönty is unwittingly introduced into a brothel (Leino 1907/1998: 195–210); Hilja Kahila is confined to a police gaol (Järnefelt 1919: 104), and students such as Antti in *Helsinkiin* ("Helsinkiin"; Aho 1889/2000: 83 ff.) and Eljas in *Hellaassa* ("In Hellas"; Ivalo 1890: 4 ff.) end up in the confusing maelstrom of crowded bars, all upon arrival in the capital. Almost invariably, these heterotopian localities symbolize an aborted initiation into one of the more disconcerting sides of the city.[16]

The heterotopian space in which Hannes is introduced in *Veneh'ojalaiset* is, again, a brothel (Järnefelt 1909/1996: 79 ff.), the spatial embodiment of the vices, but also of the double moral standards of modernizing urban society. In the late nineteenth century, literary representations of the brothel were informed by the vivid and complex discussion of prostitution that occupied sociologists from New York to Paris; the brothel became, in literary and other representations, "a metaphor for the whole new regime of nineteenth-century urbanism" (Wilson 1992: 105). In "Of Other Spaces", Foucault draws particular attention to brothels, denoting them as an "extreme type of heterotopias" (Foucault 1986: 27). The brothel is a heterotopia *par excellence*: it is set partly outside of the traditional set of moral values which upholds the social structure of society, a place in which social interaction is regulated according to a particular set of rules and habits. The brothel can be seen as an "institution" of sorts within society, mirroring and questioning sexual morals, ideas of family, femininity and masculinity.

Entrance into a brothel is generally restricted, a feature which Foucault saw as one of the typical characteristics of heterotopias (ibid.: 24).[17] In *Veneh'ojalaiset*, Hannes is led to the brothel passively, and he is guided by his nephew Hinkki, who has a more intimate knowledge of the city. The scene is seen through an extradiegetic narrator, something which is indicated, amongst others, by the way in which Hannes is continuously referred to by the nickname he hates, "captain". Hinkki claims that they are going to a farewell party organized in his honour; it is the day before he will leave the city. The party is supposedly taking place in the house of Hinkki's fiancée, Magda, but to the reader, it rapidly becomes clear that Hannes is introduced into a brothel. According to Saija Isomaa, the three central novels in Järnefelt's social commentary period (*Isänmaa* ["The Fatherland"; 1893], *Maaemon lapsia* ["Children of Mother Earth"; 1905] and *Veneh'ojalaiset* [1909]) all revolve around the moment of awakening of the protagonists, who, through various circumstances, "suddenly awaken to see the 'truth' about societal circumstances, and begin to act according to their new insight"; Isomaa speaks in this respect of a "poetics of awakening" (Isomaa 2009: 11). Hannes's awakening in this heterotopian space opens his eyes to urban problematics, but also to the vicious nature of society at large.

The initiation rite into the secrets of the city in *Veneh'ojalaiset* revolves around a gradual unmasking scene performed on Hannes by Hinkki, who wants Hannes to realize that his belief in the authorities (school, amongst others) is naïve. The space of the brothel contains a variety of elements of make-believe that are gradually revealed as deceptions. In the antechamber where Hannes is led, he is confronted with a subtle masquerade, which centres on the resemblances to normality and to the traditional bourgeois home. Similarly to other brothel scenes in Finnish literature, the women in this scene take a central role in the creation of a travesty of a bourgeois home: they are repeatedly described as occupied in an act of transformation in front of mirrors: combing their hair, changing clothes, putting on make-up, and the like (Järnefelt 1909/1996: 79; see also Leino's *Jaana Rönty* [1907/1998: 195 ff.]). In *Veneh'ojalaiset*, the element of dressing up is taken to unprecedented heights when Magda gets ready to see the clients, who are waiting in the room next door; she takes off her normal clothes and puts on a night gown (at least, this is how Hannes interprets her attire), as if to imitate an atmosphere of homely intimacy. It is at this point that recognition starts to dawn on Hannes (Järnefelt 1909/1996: 86).

A considerable part of the unfolding events gains its comic depth and suspense through the discrepancy between what the reader knows and what Hannes gradually starts to suspect: that he is not in the house of a respectable middle class family, after all. To maximize the effect of masquerade and impending unmasking, the description of Hannes's naivety is taken to extremes, and the brothel scene, in line with earlier comic undercurrents in the character description, is densely packed with comic and ironic narrative elements. Several words of modality ("probably", "apparently", "seemingly") serve as textual indications of the moments during which the narration slips into the point of view of Hannes, and all these cases underline Hannes's lack of understanding of the situation. When Hannes meets a number of intriguing creatures at Hinkki's "fiancée's" house, the narration continues: "probably they were Magda's sisters"; "apparently they really intended to have a party in Hinkki's honour" (Järnefelt 1909/1996: 79);[18] and when the matron arrives, "she was probably her [Magda's] mother or aunt" (ibid.: 82).[19] The misreading is carried to comic heights in a soliloquy by Hannes, in which he extolls the beauty of Hinkki's bride, and which reads like a farcical parody on Shakespeare's famous sonnet 130 ("My mistress' eyes are nothing like the sunne"), or the Song of Songs: "the skin of Hinkki's bride is white as the purest potato flour, and an indescribably sweet scent reeks from her clothes, but my girl is brown like a coffee bean and she certainly does not always reek well" (ibid.: 81).[20] The similes, making use of comparisons with everyday objects, enhance the comic effect: Hannes is presented as a simple and innocent boy, on the threshold of a profound and eye-opening shock.

Among the enigmatic elements experienced by the protagonist, sounds play a particular role. Gradually, Hannes starts to realize what is happening when "in the bigger room [next door] the noise of drunks can be heard" (Järnefelt 1909/1996: 84).[21] Lefebvre argues that "[s]pace is listened for, in fact, as much as seen, and heard before it comes into view" (Lefebvre 1974/1991: 199–200). In this case, the emphasis on the faculty of hearing in the brothel scene strengthens the focalizer's sense of passivity and insecurity.

Yi-Fu Tuan, in his influential work on environmental perception, states how the "effect of evanescence and fragility in this description of place is achieved by dwelling on the sounds. Compared with seeing, hearing is unfocused and passive." (Tuan 1974: 51) In *Venehojalaiset*, the sounds next door expand the spatial environments perceived by Hannes, who is confined to the enclosed space of the antechamber. Since he is in the brothel for the first time, however, he is unable to interpret the meaning of what he hears. Confused, he demands an explanation from Magda, who had warned him earlier that he should leave before the clock sounds midnight. Like an inverted Cinderella, the innocent girl will turn out to be a prostitute when the masks are taken off at midnight.

When Hannes hears the merry voices of men in the adjacent room, and distinguishes the voice of one of his teacher, a further sense of understanding dawns upon him – not only has the bourgeois home of his earlier illusion turned into a brothel, but he realizes that all of society is involved in upholding the vicious practices he detest.[22] In a Herculean rage, he throws everybody out of the building. The consequences of his actions are severe. The subsequent police enquiry results in his expulsion from school, and his possibilities of social advance thus diminished, he joins the armed forces and goes to the Military Academy at St. Petersburg, where his hate for prostitution and loose morals receives theoretical grounding through conversations with Russian revolutionaries. The urge to change society for the better and to dissolve prostitution will eventually lead him to join the revolutionaries and to draw up plans for the destruction of cities.

Tentacular City

In the brothel scene, the protagonist of *Venehojalaiset* comes to realize that prostitution lies at the heart of the city and its moral diseases. The city is not only the most explicit environment for loose morals, but their very cause. Hannes's uneasy feelings about the city's moral and social questions are later moulded into words by the revolutionary Natalja Federova he meets in St. Petersburg, who pities the human race, "builders of dead villages and rotten cities" (Järnefelt 1909/1996: 167), and who tells Hannes unequivocally that "prostitution is a disease produced by the city" (ibid.: 162–163).[23] Like the landlessness of the poor, and the exodus of the destitute to the major population centres, prostitution is caused by the city, and the injustice that has been done to the Venehoja can be compared with the injustice done to all poor men and women forced to sell the work of their body for money. Shocked by the vicious nature of society and by the role of the city and of his own actions within it, Hannes becomes ready to devote his life to a politics of radical change.

The image of the city which is constructed in *Venehojalaiset* from the epic time frame onwards, and which is reasserted in Hannes's experience in the Helsinki brothel and in the revealing conversations he has with the Russian revolutionaries, feeds into the discourse of the city as Minotaur, constantly yearning for new blood, draining and perverting the forces of the countryside. It is an image that becomes prominent in a number of late nineteenth-century writings on the city; London, for example, was described as expecting a yearly "maiden tribute of the New Babylon" (see Stead 1885)[24] and feeding on the countryside, like the "tentacular cities" described in the poetry of Émile Verhaeren (*Les Villes Tentaculaires*; 1895; see also Thum 1994: 246–281). In Finnish literature, Maila Talvio is one of the authors who repeatedly draw on such pessimistic discourse (see for example *Kultainen lyyra* ["The Golden Lyre"; 1916]). This dystopian imagery appears most tangible in descriptions of working-class conditions in Helsinki. Compelling examples can be found in the prose of L. Onerva: in "Pentti Korjus" ("Pentti Korjus"), published in the short story collection *Nousukkaita* ("Parvenus"; 1911), Helsinki is described as "this bright, clattering city" which every year "threw into the darkness hundreds of young people which it had used up, for which it did not have any use anymore, and every year it received new, uncorrupted blood from the countryside, new tender children's souls to eat" (Onerva 1911: 34–35).[25] In another passage in the same short story, which presents a prototypical description of a provincial character's degeneration in the capital, Helsinki is described both as a living being with tentacles, which throws up its slaves after a hard week's work, and as a technological construction which is composed of engine rooms peopled with "a dark people, that rarely sees the light" (ibid.: 30).[26] In Onerva's story "Jumalien hämärä" ("Twilight of the Gods"), a sketch published in the short story collection *Vangittuja sieluja* ("Imprisoned souls"; 1915), the working-class district Sörnäinen is likened to a Moloch's gaping mouth (Onerva 1915: 37–38). In her most famous novel, *Mirdja* ("Mirdja"; 1908), L. Onerva presents a similar image of Helsinki as a consuming force, but in this text, Helsinki appears not as an industrial city devouring the working classes, but as a city of light, leisure and (sensuous) pleasure that consumes the sensitive protagonist eager to experience the world. Seen from the protagonist's window, Helsinki is described in terms of a burning fire: "it is treacherous, it does not sleep, it is noisy and voluptuous, it burns. Mirdja knows it all too well. For many years, it has been burning Mirdja every day and every night." (Onerva 1908/2002: 84)[27]

Helsinki in Transformation

Behind the pessimistic realist and naturalist discourse on the city as "a diseased centre outside of nature" (Lehan 1998: 70) looms an awareness of the radical changes brought about in the modernizing and urbanizing society of the turn of the twentieth century. The city appears not only in the cloak of Biblical cesspit of vice it dons intermittently. In *Veneh'ojalaiset* and other early twentieth-century novels, it appears as the instigator of a radical commodification; first the commodification of space (see Harvey 1989b: 176–177), which in turn leads to a commodification of the landed labourers who are forced to sell their bodies in the city. It is ironical that for Hannes, who feels utterly repulsed by urban evil, there is no escape from the contaminating nature of the city and its vices, since he is both victim and beneficiary of urban developments. Hannes's education and his status in life are all grounded in the vices of the city, since they have been made possible by the money of his uncle Franssi, whose fortune, in turn, is based on the shrewd exploitation of urban evils. As a horse carriage driver, Franssi is familiar with the secrets of the city, and able to take his clients to brothels after bar closing time; his fortunes accumulate after he opens a brothel in addition to a liquor store (Järnefelt 1909/1996: 36–39). But it is the tremendous rise in real estate prices which forms the real basis of Franssi's fortunes: without having to raise a finger, he wakes up one morning almost ten times richer than he had thought he was. No wonder the city appears to Franssi like something out of a fairy tale: "A magical castle, a fairy tale wonderland was to him this golden city with its inexhaustible wells of fortune" (ibid.: 113).[28]

The city is a force transforming everything it comes into contact with, and in *Veneh'ojalaiset*, the development of Helsinki, the change from wooden houses to stone houses, speculation and the growth of the city – a metamorphosis that is also highlighted in the opening lines of *Veljekset* – accompany the protagonists' rise in society. References to the interaction between city growth and character development had featured only tangentially in Finnish novels from the late nineteenth century; in Santeri Ivalo's *Aikansa lapsipuoli* ("Stepchild of his Time"; 1895), for example, the description of the great building enthusiasm which sweeps the city in the early spring is juxtaposed only in passing with the desperate struggle of the protagonist to keep his financial situation from total collapse (Ivalo 1895: 132). In a number of 1910s novels and short stories, the city's whirlwind changes become increasingly central to the plot development, most prominently in Maila Talvio's *Niniven lapset* ("Children of Nineveh"; 1915), Eino Leino's *Pankkiherroja* ("Bank Lords"; 1914), and in the collections of short stories by Toivo Tarvas, published in the 1910s.

Maila Talvio's *Niniven lapset* is of particular interest, since it is arguably the first Finnish novel which thematizes urban planning and development. In this novel, the first effect of city growth, development and speculation is a moral one. *Niniven lapset* recounts a tale of speculation and fraud set in the worlds of publishing, finance, industry and urban development. One of the protagonists caught up in the corrupting scheming is Leo Teräs, the promising but gradually degenerating eldest son of the parvenu Ståhle family.[29] Towards the end of the novel, Leo is completely ruined and he becomes involved in one last scheme. Together with other leading speculators, he plans the construction of an enormous cultural temple that will transform the city, but that also constitutes an omen of the impending disaster threatening this world of speculation. The development project in question constitutes the climax of the novel, and within it, all different threads come together to seal the fate both of the city and the various protagonists. To build this cultural temple, which will be called "Nineveh", several wooden houses have to be razed to the ground, including the house of Old Man Säfstrand, an enigmatic and exceedingly rich recluse.[30] The old man in his dilapidated house grows to be a symbol of the repressed and distinctly uncanny conscience of the city; unheeded, he becomes a metaphor for a world overtaken by modernity, moved aside by the Faustian forces transforming the city. In his tragic quality, he resembles the figures of Philemon and Baucis, the old couple

Goethe's Faust has to dispossess in order to fulfil his plans as developer, and who are "the first embodiments in literature of a category of people that is going to be very large in modern history: people who are in the way – in the way of history, of progress, of development; people who are classified, and disposed of, as obsolete" (Berman 1982/1989: 67).

Finnish prose literature of this period contains a number of similar instances of the motif of the "mad old man in the back yard". In Järnefelt's *Veneh'ojalaiset*, the patriarch of the Veneh'oja, Heikki, lives hidden in Franssi's house after his escape from Siberia, first in a back room, later in a wooden shed in the yard of Franssi's brand-new stone building, babbling stories of past wrongdoing to which no-one listens. The motif of the old man in the wooden shed amidst the multiplying stone buildings emphasizes, both in Talvio's *Niniven lapset* and Järnefelt's *Veneh'ojalaiset*, a particular temporal rhythm in the relationship between the protagonist and the city. While the city can also be experienced as an unchanging background, contrasted with the rapid developments of a protagonist, this motif underlines the immobility of the characters in contrast with the changes in the urban landscape, and the experience of being left behind by one's own time (see Pike 1981: 16–17). From the early years of the twentieth century, urban prose on Helsinki increasingly draws on such dissonant rhythms between the development of literary characters and their urban surroundings.

In the decades following Finnish independence, Mika Waltari became one of the most important authors to document the fast-moving built environment. In his second Helsinki novel *Appelsiininsiemen* ("The Orange Seed"; 1931), perhaps more than in any other novel, Waltari shows Helsinki as a city with an ever-changing face; constantly new and highly symbolic buildings (the new, giant department store Stockmann, the Finnish Parliament) are being released from their scaffolds, and the effect is that the "face of the city has become more strange, more solemn" (Waltari 1931: 261–262).[31] In Mika Waltari's 1930s prose, the description of a changing and fluctuating Helsinki is mostly infused with an optimistic tone and by the thrill inherent to a sense of belonging to the vitality of a renewing world, but around the turn of the century, the dominant feeling was that of something being lost, and of being left behind by the fast changes of modernization which uncontrollably transformed the cityscape. In literature, Toivo Tarvas was the writer who most consistently took up the work of describing the disappearance of a bygone Helsinki in his collections of short stories. Amongst these, the aptly entitled *Häviävää Helsinkiä* ("Disappearing Helsinki"; 1917), is arguably the most interesting.[32]

Häviävää Helsinkiä starts out with a framing story which presents a panorama of the city seen from an island in front of the harbour. It is an "enchanting view" which opens up before the eyes of the protagonist: "the grand city glimmered in front him like a beautiful pearl thrown on the sea shore of the Baltic Gulf" (Tarvas 1917: 11).[33] The onlooker first rejoices in imagining the bustling life on the streets of Helsinki, but he is eventually overwhelmed by a desire to go down to the capital to experience the reality of the "city of his dreams"[34] – to leave the comprehensive panoramic view and to immerse himself into the fragmentary reality on ground level (ibid.: 15). The short stories which follow, sketches of life in the capital, can be considered as the results of the probing wanderings of the protagonist in the first story. The sketches guide the reader through working-class districts and through the lives of mostly elderly people who look with dismay at the transformation of their beloved environment through the creation of new streets and squares, and the replacement of wooden houses by stone buildings. In every sketch, the juxtaposition between the fast changes of the built environments and the inability of the characters and their lived places to keep up with the modernizing process are evoked. A labourer returning to his birth city notices "with a depressing feeling of melancholy in his heart" (Tarvas 1917: 60)[35] that the places he is looking for have gone for good ("Enkelten sävel" ["Angels' Melody"]); a wooden coffee kiosk has to be removed by the orders of the municipality to make way for a stone building ("Kahviputka" ["Coffee Shed"]); and a traditional sauna, situated in an overgrown inner yard amidst high stone walls, has to make way after a speculator has bought the ground ("Vanha sauna" ["The Old Sauna"]).

The motif of the elderly man or woman in an old dilapidated house waiting for imminent destruction returns repeatedly in Tarvas's sketches: there is a clear similarity between the fate of Old Man Säfstrand in *Niniven lapset*, for example, and that of Ottilia Silfverbäck, an old spinster who lives in a one-storey building, a "shrine protected by the Gods" in the middle of "the most noisy, most highly built part of Helsinki", which is "squeezed in between the shadows of high stone walls", and which will be expropriated by the city to make way for a new square (Tarvas 1917: 169; "Ottilia Silfverbäck").[36] The most tragic character in *Häviävää Helsinkiä* is the blind war veteran Antti Peltari, who keeps a cigarette kiosk at the southern side of the "Long Bridge" ("Pitkäsilta"). Antti Peltari has an intimate knowledge of the city which is based not on sight but on all other senses, but the changes in the built environment render his knowledge obsolete. Disoriented by the changes in the city's soundscape, evicted from his familiar place when the wooden bridge is replaced by a stone one, he becomes unable to read his immediate spatial environments, and is killed by a car on the new stone bridge ("Antti Peltari").

Figures resembling the Faustian Philemon and Baucis in the midst of a radically changing urban environment remain persistent in literature during the late 1920s and 1930s. In Joel Lehtonen's *Henkien taistelu* ("The Battle of the Spirits"; 1933), a novel that has strong Faustian undercurrents, the two elderly ladies living in a shed near the villa where the protagonist is housed clearly belong to this category (Lehtonen 1933: 123–124). The ladies are gradually chased out of their rightful home by the protagonist's vicious landlady. *Henkien taistelu* is for the most part set in the Helsinki suburbs (see Chapter 7); more urban examples of elderly people and houses in the middle of modernizing society can be found in the work of Unto Karri and Arvi Kivimaa. In the opening lines of Karri's 1929 novel *Sodoma*, the "clean and red-shining stone walls" of the new district Töölö are described to hide within themselves, "like a memory from times gone by", a dilapidated house in which one of the novel's protagonists, a young girl, is living together with her old stepfather (Karri 1929: 7).[37] Like Antti Peltari in Tarvas's *Häviävää*

Helsinkiä, the girl dies in a car accident at the end of the novel. Similarly, "Kaksi Äijää" ("Two Old Guys") a story in Arvi Kivimaa's collection *Katu nousee taivaaseen* ("The Street Rises to the Heavens"; 1931) evokes an urban world in the throes of developments which literally grow ahead of the city's inhabitants. Again, the urban transformations are reflected in a changing soundscape: "What a different melody it [the city] had taken on in a few years' time! First it had been peaceful, calm, familiar; now high-pitched, cold and taciturn!" (Kivimaa 1931: 127)[38] Like *Häviävää Helsinkiä*, Kivimaa's story describes a city in flux, in which a few remains of times past are still standing, wooden buildings inhabited by old men, embittered with the modernizing world around them, and bound to fade away. In Mika Waltari's 1931 Helsinki novel *Appelsiininsiemen* ("The Orange Seed"), the protagonist Irene's father, an elderly professor at the Helsinki university, is repeatedly referred to as being sidestepped by the rapid urban changes of his time, and is eventually run over by a car, the typical fate for a character out of tune with the rhythm of the city (Waltari 1931: 445–446, 453). Similarly, in Waltari's novel *Surun ja ilon kaupunki* ("City of Sorrow and Joy"; 1936), an elderly character is run over by a car, in this case immediately upon arrival in Helsinki.

Intimations of Apocalypse

As some of the titles of the novels discussed above indicate, turn-of-the-century Finnish literature drew on various strands of end-of-days rhetoric. Such strands included the apocalyptic undercurrents in decadent and symbolist literature in some of the work of Eino Leino, as well as (more indirectly) the profound pessimism experienced by people living through the carnage of the First World War, apparent, for example, in Talvio's *Niniven lapset*. The potent millenarian imagery attached to Biblical (and Classical) Cities was not lost on Finnish authors in this period. Large and prosperous cities reminded Koskenniemi inevitably of the ruins of Carthage and Nineveh (Koskenniemi 1914: 45–47), and in his letters to L. Onerva, Eino Leino explicitly refers to Helsinki as a Sodom and Gomorrah (Leino 1960: 145, 148); Maila Talvio identifies Helsinki with Sodom in her historical novel *Linnoituksen iloiset rouvat* ("The Merry Wives of the Fortress"; 1941). Following the Great War, the cultural pessimism of which Oswald Spengler (1918/1926) was one of the prophets continued to link the fate of Biblical cities with those of the perceived decay of the Western world. It is a feeling summed up by the protagonist of Unto Karri's Helsinki novel *Sodoma*, when he claims that "[s]imilar to Babel and Niniveh which lie in ruins, so will also this corrupted part of the world fall into ruins" (Karri 1929: 287).[39]

The Biblical end-of-time frame of reference which is visible in titles such as Maila Talvio's *Niniven lapset* (1915) and Karri's *Sodoma* (1929) permeates the experience of the city in a whole range of novels in the early twentieth century. In a novel such as *Sodoma*, the Biblical rhetoric was related to a moral threat in the first place; in several of the Helsinki novels that appeared in the 1910s, the Great War adds a new and acutely pessimist dimension to this rhetoric. In Toivo Tarvas's short story "The Old Sauna", the electric lights of a movie theatre are shining bright in the darkness, like "the fire writings at Belshazzar's feast" (Tarvas 1917: 141).[40] The same Biblical reference to the ominous letters spelling Babylon's impending doom is found in Tarvas's novel *Kohtalon tuulissa* ("The Winds of Fate"; Tarvas 1916b). A long description of a wartime Czarist festival depicts how the illuminated Russian battle ships in the Helsinki harbour, "those spectacular, grand vessels, rose and fell against a dark background like the giant fire letters painted by the hand at Belshazzar's feast" (Tarvas 1916b: 69).[41] The fiery letters spell out, in other words, the coming end of an Empire, as well as that of a whole age. In the same novel, the beautiful panoramic view of Helsinki seen from the top of the Fire Department Tower changes into a nightmarish scene when the longing for a lost home in the countryside overwhelms the protagonist Janne:

> [...] but the straight streets in the city below looked black and empty like the gaping abysses of eternity. He shuddered. The hundreds of metal stacks on the rooftops, with their moving, winged heads swinging back and forth in the spring wind, seemed like the black angels of the devil himself. And further away, the black smoke rising from the high factory chimneys blew like gruesome giant flags made from a mourning veil... (Tarvas 1916b: 76).[42]

The hellish features of the city at night are, in this passage, first and foremost the result of the projection of the protagonist's pessimistic feelings on the surrounding landscape – a way of reading the urban environment that will gain prominence in the inter-war period, as will be shown in the following chapter.

The nightmarish and apocalyptic experience of the city in the novels and short stories mentioned above is framed by the experience of the Great War, or, as in Leino's *Pankkiherroja*, by the culminating strain of foreign crisis and a domestic economic bubble about to burst. In Tarvas's *Eri tasoilta*, the Great War transforms the city into a frightening spectacle: the black tin roofs of Helsinki, bathing in the November moon light, resemble "extraordinarily large coffins" (Tarvas 1916a: 127),[43] and in the sequel *Kohtalon tuulissa*, the atmosphere of fear caused by the Great War is describe as "the dreadful scythe of sudden death" hanging over the city (Tarvas 1916b: 99).[44] At the end of *Niniven lapset*, the sense of unavoidable doom as the First World War approaches is mirrored by the vision of threatening clouds that take the shape of coffins (Talvio 1915: 303).

Nocturnal Outing to the Fortress

In Järnefelt's novel *Veneh'ojalaiset*, intimations of the Apocalypse add a crucial layer of meaning to the novel. The *basso continuo* of millenarian undercurrents is related to this novel's genre as a novel of revolution (see Isomaa 2009: 240–249; Freeborn 1982), but also attuned to the end-of-days rhetoric seeping into much of fin-de-siècle literature (see Lyytikäinen 1999). From the very opening pages onwards, there are elements present in

Veneh'ojalaiset that point to a potential cosmic battle and an end of times. As the novel reaches into historical times, revealing instances multiply in which the streets of Helsinki are transformed through the prism of a near-apocalyptic vision.

A particularly significant occurrence is a journey at night by stolen rowing boat to the fortress of Viapori, undertaken by Hinkki and Hannes. Similarly to the introduction into the heterotopian space of the brothel described earlier, this scene (which is set immediately preceding the brothel scene in the novel), is structured as a descent into liminal space in which boundaries are transgressed and in which a potent secret of the city is revealed. Various elements give the description of Hannes's and Hinkki's journey a tense and eerie feel: night is falling, and the two boys in their stolen rowing boat are on a border zone between the Finnish city and the Swedo-Russian fortress, between day and night. The atmosphere of suspense is enhanced by a rather rare instance in the novel of extensive metaphorical language. Here, as in Juhani Aho's novella *Helsinkiin*, the crossing of a border is indicated by an ever denser use of figurative language. Arvid Järnefelt generally uses similes and metaphors sparingly, but as Hannes's and Hinkki's boat leaves shore, the scene is described in vivid metaphoric language: "The sun had set and from behind the horizon of the sea, it glowingly transformed a long cloud into thousands of red swans, which, growing ever larger, rose unto the zenith" (Järnefelt 1909/1996: 58).[45] The figure of a cloud transformed into thousands of red swans flying up in the setting sun adds to the young boys' voyage the attributes of a descent into the netherworld: the swan is connected internationally to the journey to the next world, and in Finnish mythology and folk poetry, the swan is the mythical animal of the Netherworld, a taboo animal dwelling in the waters of "Tuonela", guarding the passages from this world to the next.

In this twilight zone, the familiar world has become distorted: "A new, strange world had appeared in front of him [Hannes] as if conjured up" (Järnefelt 1909/1996: 58).[46] The city, in particular, appears literally to have turned upside down: "When the waves [of the boat] had calmed down, the sea level became steady and the whole city was to be seen, turned upside down at the bottom of the bay" (ibid.: 59).[47] This strange vision affects Hannes strongly, and in an allegory of apocalyptic destruction, foreshadowing his future involvement with the revolution, he rocks the boat, bewildered at the miraculous effects of his childish actions upon the city he sees reflected in the water:

> The whole city burst in its junctures, the parks drifted apart from the ground, and the towers fell. The old customs magazines trembled, the multilayered stone walls shook, the banks, hotels, even the Emperor's palace burst into red flames and the church with its cupolas and golden crosses fell from its foundations. (Järnefelt 1909/1996: 59)[48]

Hannes's sudden crazed joy as he witnesses the destructive effect of his playful movements is reminiscent of the earlier visions of his ancestors, struggling with the gods and aiming at the destruction of cities (in the first, epic part of the novel), and a foreshadowing of Hannes's later inner struggles in a revolutionary context, both in St. Petersburg and when he will have returned to his home city Helsinki.[49] The description of the scene is almost Dickensian in the way it combines comic elements (two kids at play) with a frightening vision of utter destruction that will gradually take further shape as the plot evolves. Although concrete in its descriptions – even the flames seem realistic, since they could be simply reflections on the water of the last, red rays of the sun – the scene is also profoundly allegoric. The buildings are without exception allegories for functions within society Hannes will want to overturn later in life, during his time as a revolutionary: the Emperor's might, the churches' sway, the economic system of banks, the regulating forces of customs and the military. The highly stylized and archaic language used in the quote above gives the passage an enhanced solemnity, reminiscent of the language of the Biblical poetry of the psalms and the prophets. The effect in the Finnish original is enhanced by having three subsequent clauses begin with the verb rather than the subject, something which is not altogether impossible in the flexible Finnish language, but which carries an archaic and unnatural ring, and this stylistic device is continued anaphorically throughout the passage for further effect.

Prendergast, in his study of Paris in the nineteenth century, argues that the fin-de-siècle sense of things falling apart results in "two of our most powerful narratives of the contemporary metropolitan condition: stories of end-time and stories of playtime" (Prendergast 1992: 207). In stories of playtime, as opposed to apocalyptic stories, "the emphasis on accelerated falling apart remains but is redirected from the catastrophic to the aleatory […], from nightmare to fun, apocalypse to *bricolage*, ruins to waste, to the view of the city as playground and its debris as the material for a kind of urban *fort/da* game […]" (ibid.). In Järnefelt's *Veneh'ojalaiset*, the description of the outing carries images from this aleatory *fort/da* game, but there are undercurrents related to a very real and immediate threat. The fortress Hannes and Hinkki are approaching holds the key to the Finnish political and military situation, and functions as a threat to the Finnish capital as much as it constitutes an integral part of its defence. The deepening tension that accompanies the arrival of the two boys at the fortress unfolds in an unexpected and even playful manner: Hinkki steers the boat towards a threatening sentry, and in a swift exchange of goods, he gives the Russian soldier two boxes of cigarettes he has stolen earlier that day, and receives in return a bit of gunpowder. It turns out that the bored Russian soldiers scrape gunpowder from their grenades and exchange them for cigarettes and alcohol with Helsinki inhabitants brave enough to dare the trip. When Hannes realizes what is going on, he is suddenly overwhelmed with a feeling of being at ease amidst the walls: "In one blow, the solemn magic of the fortress shattered in the captain's [Hannes's] mind" (Järnefelt 1909/1996: 65).[50]

The passage marks the waterfront as a space of transition and transformation that will gain symbolic meaning as the plot unfolds. Hannes will later take a hill overlooking the fortress as his favourite spot to contemplate the possibility of conquering the fortress Viapori. The decisive events at the end of the novel will be played out on this very same hill. Hinkki's fate is equally bound up with this environment: he will drown fleeing from the rebelling fortress at the end of the novel. Helsinki, in this passage, takes the form of an enigmatic city, containing a number of thresholds and doors leading into a hidden secret. The scene gives a first indication of Hannes's future destructive powers, and of the city as a place that may be destroyed as a side-effect of seemingly innocent actions, something which is also intrinsically visible in the symbol of the gunpowder Hinkki barters from the Russian soldier – a potentially lethal weapon, turned over for a few cigarettes to a kid in order to make a bit of mischief at school.

"All culture is swaying, all forms are inverted"

The Finnish capital around the turn of the century is a growing and expanding city, and in literature, the experience of this changing urban world becomes infused with the dystopian rhetorics that are in vogue internationally. This end-of-days rhetoric gains an acute sense of urgency in the early years of the twentieth century when real, violent death and wholesale destruction become an all-too-real possibility. For a character such as Aarne Ruokoranta in Talvio's *Niniven lapset*, it is not much more than a frivolously expressed adherence to a decadent worldview when he quotes Baudelaire in a letter written to Otteli Ståhle, with whom he earlier had had an affair:

> All culture is swaying, all forms are inverted. Everything is in movement. "Je hais le movement qui déplace les lignes." (Talvio 1915: 172)[51]

Aarne is a disillusioned and degenerate character, and the quotation from Baudelaire's *Les fleurs du mal* (1857/1998) is firmly in tune with turn-of-the-century decadent sentiments. In the early twentieth century, the world is fast catching up with this kind of cosmopolitan decadence. Like his father, Old Man Säfstrand (see above), Aarne represents a world that belongs to the past. When the First World War breaks out, the first ship from abroad to reach Helsinki brings not only sad tidings, but a first corpse: that of Aarne, who, a relic of a bygone world, has died on the return journey home (Talvio 1915: 320–321).

Finnish literature drawing on decadent and symbolist currents tends to set images of the apocalypse in a mythical-historical context (Lyytikäinen 1999: 211), but the events of 1905 and 1906 as well as the outbreak of the First World War turns earlier apocalyptic visions into realities that had to be contended with. Starting from the Czar's issuing of the 1899 February Manifesto, which aimed at a far-reaching Russification of Finland and its institutions, an acute sense that "all forms are inverted" and that "everything is in movement" became endemic. In 1905 the Russian Empire, Finland included, came to a halt during the Great Strike, an event that constituted a real caesura to people living through these days (see Haapala et al. 2008). When in the following year the soldiers at the Russian fortress Viapori rebelled, the fate of the Empire was again in the balance and a potentially devastating shelling of the Finnish capital belonged to one of the possible scenarios. Several novels in addition to Järnefelt's *Veneh'ojalaiset* describe the events of these years: Eino Leino's *Jaana Rönty* (1907/1998), Kyösti Wilkuna's *Vaikea tie* (1915), amongst others.

In descriptions of the near-revolutionary events of 1904, 1905 and 1906, Helsinki appears no longer as a city that is merely in movement, but as a city that becomes fundamentally transformed. The first instance of acute apocalyptic sentiments in *Veneh'ojalaiset* appears when the news of Bobrikov's murder (June 16th, 1904) spreads through the city (Järnefelt 1909/1996: 268–269). After the death of the Governor-General, Kerttu, the wife of Hannes in *Veneh'ojalaiset*, believes the end of the world must be near: "Everything, everything started becoming confused, and she did believe what the old Kustaava [Hannes's mother] had whisperingly said, that all those novelties that had so suddenly filled people's thoughts, were nothing else than premonitions of the end of the world" (ibid. 276).[52] To Hannes, however, these events are not the end of the world, but the beginning of a new and better one, a feeling which he expresses in distinctly Biblical terms: "A miracle has occurred, Kerttu, in one year's time, a flowering city has come into existence in the desert!" (ibid.: 277)[53]

One of the elements that further enhance the sense of profound disorientation in this suddenly transformed Helsinki is the fog enveloping the city, into which Kerttu, afraid for her children and her husband, has ventured (ibid. 291–292):

> A dense fog hung on the street. It had begun to get dark. Here and there one could see people walking fast along the street or suddenly appearing from around the corners. The sound of clopping heels could be heard clearly, but no horses running. At the same time, however, the clatter of hoofs approaching at a dizzying pace began to be heard, and before Kerttu had the time to turn around, three Cossacks flew along the street past her so suddenly that her hands and face froze in horror. (ibid.: 292)[54]

The motif of the fog enveloping a city in turmoil is reminiscent of one of the founding texts of St. Petersburg's apocalyptic rhetoric: Pushkin's poem "Mednyĭ vsadnik" ("The Bronze Horseman"; 1833/1998), in which the equestrian statue of Peter the Great hunts a desperate and disorientated hero through the misty streets of the Russian capital (see Howlett 1985: 159-162).[55] The poem is arguably also referred to in Eino Leino's poem "Helsinki in the Mist" (1899), the first literary work to render the tense atmosphere in Helsinki after the publication of the February Manifesto, which heralded the beginning of the first period of Russian oppression. The apocalyptic rhetoric of St. Petersburg is vividly present in *Veneh'ojalaiset*: the first plan conceived by Hannes and his revolutionary friends calls for the flooding of St. Petersburg by opening the sluice gates of the Neva (Järnefelt 1909/1996: 175–176), which evokes an apocalyptic image from the mythology on St. Petersburg that was also strongly present in Pushkin's poem (see Pesonen 2003).

The image of fog enveloping a city has been used to manifold effects in urban literature; the fog shrouding Bruges in Georges Rodenbach's

Bruges-la-Morte ("Bruges the Dead"; 1892/2007) symbolized in part the melancholy of the protagonist, while in one of the most famous foggy openings in literature, Dickens's *Bleak House* (1852–1853/2003), the mist covering London could be interpreted as hiding from sight the capital's legal institutions (Keunen 2007: 282). In Helsinki novels, fog repeatedly occurs as a symbol of the disorientation of the protagonist, conveying the sense of a brooding atmosphere, but also, as in Leino's poem and the passage from *Veneh'ojalaiset*, as an image of political turmoil.[56] In *Veneh'ojalaiset* as in other novels, fog adds an eerie and profoundly disorientating dimension to urban scenes, and enhances the impression that sudden and momentous reversals can happen at any given moment.

On the day that Kerttu goes looking for her husband and children in the city, Helsinki is transformed on several occasions, giving Kerttu little certainty to hold onto. Almost immediately following the frightening scene in the fog, she finds herself on an overcrowded Esplanade. When rumours of an impending Cossack attack spread, the crowd panics and Kerttu is literally swept along, until she manages to get hold of an electricity pole (Järnefelt 1909/1996: 293–294). When she eventually returns home, she finds her children safe and sound, but she goes again in search of her husband in the dead of the night. The city is once more transformed:

> [...] a complete and dark emptiness reigned in the centre of the city. Here and there people were walking along the street, but in civilian clothes, with galoshes on their feet, stepping noiselessly. As if an invisible lion had suddenly stifled the whole city under its pawn, saying: silent, you little pups! The stone walls were gleaming like large, dark ghosts in the night, and here and there window lights were twinkling in the nocturnal fog. And the silence was so deep that you could have heard a pin fall. But not a single police officer could be seen who could have told Kerttu whether anything had been heard of anyone being imprisoned, or of any incidents. (Järnefelt 1909/1996: 297–298)[57]

Again, the fog gives the darkened city an eerie atmosphere, in which the walls are transformed into "large, dark ghosts", and in which the city is described through unusual light effects (the walls "gleam", the window lights "twinkle"). The apocalyptic experience of the city results in a specific kind of aestheticization of the urban environment. In the analysis of Juhani Aho's *Helsinkiin*, I noted the link between a particular kind of aestheticization of the city and the menacing undertones of a specific urban experience. In literary descriptions of the Great Strike and the Viapori Rebellion such as the one above, the urban environment is transformed by the use of particularly sensory description (with notable references to stark contrasts between darkness and sudden light) and the conspicuous use of figurative language. The "complete and dark emptiness" of the city centre is broken by twinkling lights and transformed by the fog, and the change of the environment is so total that it seems as if a giant, invisible force ("an invisible lion") has stifled the city.[58]

In almost all literary descriptions of the Great Strike and the Viapori Rebellion, changes concerning who is free to roam the city streets can be found.

Jaana Rönty, whose right to move through the city had been challenged with eventful consequences (see Chapter 4), lives the days of the Great Strike as "in a fever", and she joins the crowds of working-class people that throng the streets (Leino 1907/1998: 311).[59] Baron Manfelt, in the same novel, on the other hand, the man who, when challenged at the Esplanade, had shouted "I will go when I want to" (ibid.: 224),[60] experiences these days very differently. At first he, too, becomes enchanted by the changed city, he "walks the streets from morning to evening" and talks to total strangers (ibid.: 305).[61] For the first time, however, his freedom of movement is impeded, and he is ordered by a Russian sentry to turn back from the vicinity of a Russian barracks (ibid.: 306). At night, seeing the view of the blacked-out city from his window, his usual self-confidence is gone, and he asks himself: "Had time come to an end? Was this the beginning of eternity?" (ibid 307)[62]

Baron Manfelt's feeling that something of tremendous consequence is on the verge of happening, or has in fact already happened, is shared by several other literary characters. The events of 1905 and 1906 are experienced simultaneously as the apocalyptic end of the world, and the utopian beginnings of a new one. The simultaneous presence of utopian and dystopian impulses can be traced to a long tradition in writing on the city. Elizabeth Wilson has even argued that utopianism constitutes such a central theme in nineteenth- and twentieth-century (theoretical) texts on modernity, that, especially in Marxist texts, the "urban scene comes to represent utopia and dystopia *simultaneously*" (Wilson 1992: 108). Dystopian literary (and other) representations of the city can be argued to be animated by "an utopian desire" (Prakash 2010: 2), and this is certainly the case for the way characters such as Hannes in *Veneh'ojalaiset* and Jaana in *Jaana Rönty* experience the revolutionary city.[63] The sense that time is coming to an end, and that a new order is on the verge of being installed, is tangibly visible in the way Helsinki and its streets are transformed in these novels, and the contradictory implications this invokes are one of the reasons why the experience of the city during the Great Strike and the Viapori Rebellion is repeatedly described as a solemn, almost religious event. In Leino's *Jaana Rönty*, the scene describing Jaana, during the Viapori Rebellion, watching the rebellious fortress from Observatory Hill is compared to a near-religious experience, touching on the sublime:

> In the early morning, she was standing amongst a dense crowd on Observatory Hill. The sun was shining on the waters, still like a mirror, and on the straits, at both sides of which smoke puffs were rising up. Nature was enveloped in a deep silence. The cupolas of the temples of the main fortress glimmered under the cloudless sky [...]. At first, it seemed to Jaana as if children were playing at war, or as if a joyful workers' group was blowing incredibly large tobacco smoke spirals from its cheeks.
> But the incessant roar in the air soon filled her soul with a holy shudder. The children of God were at war there, and the Grim Reaper was collecting his harvest. She felt as if she was surrounded by higher powers, and instinctively she crossed her hands and silently she prayed to herself: "Our father, who art in heaven." (Leino 1907/1998: 320–321)[64]

The description of the rebellious fortress under siege accentuates the eerie calmness displayed by the natural elements, the sun, the waters and straits. There is the slightly surprising mention of the "deep silence" that "reigned in the nature" of the scene – a silence only interrupted by the roar of the canon. The presence of a higher power is first insinuated by the "cupolas of the temple of the main fortress", a reference to the Orthodox Church at Viapori. Similar to the nocturnal outing in *Veneh'ojalaiset* referred to above, the description of the fortress contains both elements of stories of end-time and those of playtime, in which, as Prendergast points out, one finds "the view of the city as playground and its debris as the material for a kind of urban *fort/da* game" (Prendergast 1992: 207; see above). Resembling the metaphor of the "invisible lion" in *Veneh'ojalaiset*, the smoke from the artillery guns looks to Jaana as if giant and invisible workers are blowing smoke rings. When Jaana recognizes, however, that she is not witnessing children at play, but "the children of God [...] at war", she is overwhelmed by a religious sentiment, and, regardless of her anarchist sympathies, she clutches to the Lord's Prayer. Similarly, Baron Manfelt turns to the national-romantic poems of Runeberg when staring into the frightening darkness of the revolutionary city (Leino 1907/1998: 309), and Kerttu and Kustaava in *Veneh'ojalaiset* turn to the Bible when oppressed by the thought of the confusion reigning in striking Helsinki (Järnefelt 1909/1996: 288–289). In *Jaana Rönty*, the effect of the view of the rebellious fortress on the other citizens standing silently around Jaana is experienced in equally religious terms:

> The crowd of people around her was standing silent as on a hill during church service. This view affected them as if it were Holy Mass. One had to be very silent in order not to disturb it.
> But in the evening, the nature of the landscape changed. The sky was clouded, and steel-grey waves were beating heavily on the shoreline. Large war ships had appeared on the horizon, their sides were shining in the sharp and bluish light, roaring and glistening, they came from under the dark clouds to the rebellious fortress. (Leino 1907/1998: 321)[65]

Similarly to the descriptions of the city during the Great Strike in *Veneh'ojalaiset*, the revolutionary city in *Jaana Rönty* is described as an environment subject to sudden and total changes: the sun and the stillness of the waters are transformed into darkness and stormy waves as Russian war ships, come to quell the rebellion, appear at the horizon.

The view of the fortress in *Jaana Rönty* literally affects the city crowd "as if it were Holy Mass". In Kyösti Wilkuna's novel *Vaikea tie* ("The Difficult Road"; 1915), the atmosphere in the city during the Great Strike is similarly described as that of a holy festival day, not in the least because all noise usually heard in the city has silenced:

> No whistles from factories or train engines, no squealing of the trams or rattling of carts could be heard. There was a feeling as of a great celebratory day in the air, and people had a festive expression of expectation on their faces, as they slowly passed by along the sidewalks [...]. (Wilkuna 1915: 200)[66]

The Great Strike lends the capital a particular solemnity, and to the focalizer, the view of the city is one of conspicuous beauty. When Markus, in *Vaikea tie*, sees the view of the city from Observatory Hill, he is overwhelmed by the experience, and exclaims: "What a beautiful capital we have, after all!" The peaceful and silent atmosphere appears to him, like to the narrator of *Jaana Rönty*, like that of a church festival in the countryside (ibid.: 205).[67] In Wilkuna's novel, the city is repeatedly described as transformed dramatically, if only through the expressions of its inhabitants and through their increasingly hurrying steps (ibid.: 186–187). The Great Strike, which had come "like a great Tsunami from the East", has thrown all of society into a "chaotic Urstate", and the inhabitants of Helsinki are described as awaiting the consequences of these events with frightful expectation (ibid.: 185).[68] The descriptions in *Vaikea tie* of the nocturnal city, bereft of its usual lighting, but lighted by spasmodic flashlights emanating from the Russian fortress, is particularly revealing:

> Hand-held gas lanterns were shimmering here and there like glow worms, and from time to time, the blinding beam from a Viapori searchlight swept over the city like the eye of fate, which restlessly followed the events in that city that had thrown off all its shackles, that had ended up in a bubbling state of fermentation and that was hiding all its possibilities, that city which had veiled itself in darkness like a woman in childbirth. (ibid 189)[69]

Similarly to the Great Strike descriptions in *Veneh'ojalaiset*, the eerie atmosphere enveloping the city is rendered in *Vaikea tie* by reference to suddenly appearing unusual light effects ("hand-held gas lanterns shimmering here and there like glow worms"; "the blinding beam from a Viapori searchlight"), and the extraordinary situation is described by using metaphors that describe the giant forces at work in the city. To Markus, the protagonist in *Vaikea tie*, the city appears as a personified being that has "thrown off all its shackles" and that "was hiding all its possibilities", and, perhaps the most striking simile to describe revolutionary Helsinki, as a city that "had veiled itself in darkness like a woman in childbirth". The passages reverberates with threatening and frightful references, but also with intimations of hope and promise.

As the quote from *Vaikea tie* illustrates, the apocalyptic intimations felt by several literary characters in turn-of-the-century Helsinki novels function as vehicles for specific aesthetic experiences. This aestheticization is expressed through an increased use of metaphorical language, as well as by striking light and colour imagery. Infused with a menacing, near-apocalyptic sense of threat, the urban landscape is given shape through sudden flashes of light, producing an effect of disorientation. Suddenly appearing and disappearing illumination and bright colour effects have been seen as central to the experience of the modernizing city. Robert Alter notes how Walter Benjamin, in "On Some Motifs in Baudelaire", had suggested that the invention of the match "contributed to the shaping of a new mode of staccato perception" (Alter 2005: 98; see Benjamin 2006: 190–191). Alter emphasizes the creative use of light effects in descriptions of urban scenes in early modern literature, arguing that the light in Flaubert's prose, for example, is often "stroboscopic, flaring for a moment and then going out, like the match of which Benjamin speaks" (Alter 2005: 26). Creative use of sudden light effects is also typical of Bely's (1916/1978) early modernist rendering of the city (ibid.: 98).

Sudden appearances of bright lights similar to the shimmering "handheld gas lanterns" and the "blinding beam from a Viapori searchlight" (Wilkuna 1915: 189) can also be found, for example, in the gloomy description of the Great Strike in *Veneh'ojalaiset* ("here and there window lights were twinkling in the nightly fog"; Järnefelt 1909/1996: 297–298; see above) and in the menacing view of war ships in the Helsinki harbour during the First World War, illuminated "against a dark background like the giant fire letters painted by the hand at Belshazzar's feast", in Toivo Tarvas's *Kohtalon tuulissa* (Tarvas 1916b: 69; see above). As these examples illustrate, the intense experience of a city under threat in literature of early twentieth-century Helsinki uses conspicuous use of light and colour effects to transform the way the cityscape is rendered. Such descriptions foreshadow the aestheticization of the city found in the Helsinki novels of Mika Waltari and others in the 1920s and 1930s. In such later representations, sudden light effects are typically used to render the view of the city at night, seen through the window of a speeding car; a motif that will be discussed in detail in the following chapter.

The Whore of Babylon

Different novels present different dissolutions to the apocalyptic tensions that held Helsinki in its thrall in 1905 and 1906. The most harmonious dénouement is found in *Vaikea tie*, in which the protagonist, in the course of the events of 1905, returns to his natural political position in the fold of the Finnish bourgeois forces without breaking off his relationship with the working-class girl Olga, and with undiminished emotional attachment to Helsinki. By comparison, the climactic scene in *Jaana Rönty*, which describes the clash between red guards and Russian sailors, on the one hand, and the civil guard, on the other, at Hakaniemi, confirms the worst apocalyptic fears of Baron Manfelt, who witnesses the scene:

> He saw a young woman with long plaits who was jumping in the street, and kicking dead Civil Guards, lying on the ground, in the face.
> It was Jaana. She had not been able to restrain herself anymore. She had become crazed by the smell of blood and gun powder, the ecstasy of revenge held her in thrall, she was jumping up and down, dancing in the middle of the steaming bodies, and kicking them in the face, in the chest, everywhere, shouting, arms flailing about, blazing like a flame in her red dress.
> There was something so frightening, something so primeval and beast-like in this sight that the old Baron Manfelt swaggered and was groping helplessly in the air with his hands. It felt as if he had seen in front of his eyes the Whore of Babylon herself and the dragon, dancing a triumphant, frolicking dance of death on the ruins of a world going up in ashes. (Leino 1907/1998: 325–326)[70]

Seen by Baron Manfelt, Jaana is described as the Whore of Babylon from the Book of Revelation, an image that linked age-old thinking concerning the evil nature of the city with one of the favourite symbols of turn-of-the-century decadent authors. Jaana appears as a Finnish version of Delacroix's painting "Liberty Leading the People" (1830), transformed into a raving woman trampling dead White Guard soldiers underfoot – an incarnation of both Gustave Le Bon's crowd psychology (1896/1983), and of the dormant, atavistic instincts of the uprooted common people in the city (see Knuuttila 1993). The vision amounts to a premonition of the end of times, and has been seen as symptomatic of the pessimistic view of the common people the Finnish intelligentsia started to harbour in this period (Lyytikäinen 1999: 212). The nightmarish sight so profoundly alarms Baron Manfelt that he has a heart attack. It is suggested that the Baron may well recover from the seizure, but for Jaana, the climactic events have fatal disruptive consequences. Immediately following the description of the Hakaniemi clashes, Jaana is described as broken:

> Jaana was now moving fast on a downward track.
> Her power of resistance was smashed. It was as if something in her was broken. (Leino 1907/1998: 328)[71]

This is the beginning of the end: the events at Hakaniemi seal the fate of Jaana, in whose personal history the downward, entropic dynamics typical of naturalism have run their course. At the end of the novel, she has become utterly numb and degenerate.

In *Veneh'ojalaiset*, the events of the Great Strike turn eventually into a euphoric revelation for Kerttu when she learns that Hannes is in charge of affairs. The whole city is transformed into a homely place: "The streets seemed to be like her home, and all the people, both those outside and inside their homes, felt like familiar loved-ones" (Järnefelt 1909/1996: 300).[72] The home of Kerttu, too, is transformed so totally that, together with Kustaava, Kerttu has to inspect all the rooms to see how they look after these great events (ibid.). In *Veneh'ojalaiset* the Great Strike constitutes not much more than the dress rehearsal for the truly pivotal events constituted by the Viapori rebellion, in which utopian urges and apocalyptic fear converge upon Hannes, who, as the leader of the rebels, is under pressure to shell the city as the ultimate means to safeguard the success of the revolution.

Towards a Sense of Belonging

In 1906, total destruction was avoided: the Viapori Rebellion lasted only 60 hours (Salomaa 1965). Seen through the perspective of the narration in *Veneh'ojalaiset*, the failure of the rebellion was in large part due to a feeling towards the city that is introduced in this novel for the first time with such far-reaching effects in literature written in Finnish on Helsinki: love. Crucial is the scene in which Hannes, at that moment the leader of the revolutionaries, looks down at the city and at the fortress lying below him, knowing that he has the power, at last, to guide the fate of both (Järnefelt 1909/1996: 336–339). The scene is reminiscent of the ending of Balzac's *Le père Goriot* (1835/1995), in which Rastignac looks down at Paris from Père Lachaise, challenging the French capital. In Järnefelt's *Veneh'ojalaiset*, the idea of conquering the city pervades the whole story from the first endeavours of forefather Heikki at setting fire to the "biggest village", and culminates in Hannes, who devotes years of his life to studying the art of besieging, explicitly equating it with conquering a woman (Järnefelt 1909/1996: 218). On the hill overlooking the city, Hannes, invested with extraordinary power, has the possibility of changing the course of his home city, and of the whole nation. Dystopian and utopian possibilities converge upon him: here is not a man who is being led passively through the city, and who is changed by it, but on the contrary a protagonist who is able to destroy the city and then recreate it. Hannes, however, refrains from giving the fateful order. In an inner monologue, he begs his revolutionary mentor, Vasili, for forgiveness: "Have pity, Vasili! This is my home city…" (ibid.: 338)[73]

Saija Isomaa argues that the feeling that keeps Hannes from carrying out his plans is pity, and that the scene on the Hill should be read first of all as a struggle between the Tolstoyan and Nietzschean world views that dominates much of the novel (Isomaa 2009: 210, 250–257). One of the most important reasons for Hannes's decision – or indecisiveness –, however, is the loving feelings he has for his home city. Throughout the novel, there are repeated references to the strong positive feelings Hannes, as well as his nephew Hinkki, have towards the capital. A loving attachment to Helsinki is present in *Veneh'ojalaiset* from the very beginning of the novel. When the narration shifts from the epic time frame to the historical present, there is a brief documentary passage, in which the narrator describes the city at some length, in particular the Observatory Hill ("Tähtitornivuori"; Järnefelt 1909/1996: 49–50). The narrator emphasizes the fact that it is a place loved by "a great many of the inhabitants of the golden capital" (ibid.).[74] It is the favourite place of harbour workers, idlers, and of the pupils at the new Finnish lyceum, among whom Hinkki and the "captain" Hannes. The first emotion that is mentioned in relation to Helsinki, then, is love.

Hannes is the first complex character in Finnish literature who is born in Helsinki and who successfully establishes a family there. Both Hannes and his double Hinkki are cut loose, for the better or the worse, from their family's mythic countryside past. They have no interest in the lost lands of the Veneh'oja: their loyalty lies with the city and the urban community they belong to. Both leave the city in the course of the novel, and both experience, upon returning to Helsinki, the most acute feelings of genuine homecoming and belonging. L. Onerva describes *Veneh'ojalaiset* as "the dark epic of a parvenu generation" (Onerva 1909: 397),[75] and other critics, too, have emphasized the pessimistic experience of the city inherent to Järnefelt's novel. This is to neglect the recurring passages in the novel in which Helsinki is referred to in a distinctly warm and loving tone, especially when focalized through the two protagonists. When Hannes returns from St. Petersburg to Helsinki, he walks "with joy in his heart […] along those streets of his home town along which he had run as a school boy and where every corner and every turn were well known to him and felt cosy" (Järnefelt 1909/1996: 125).[76] And when he later starts to develop plans to carry the revolution to Finland, he is described as thinking of the Viapori fortress islands opposite "the beloved shores of his home city" (Järnefelt 1909/1996: 201).[77]

Hannes's nephew, too, is described as having a profound love for his home city, although the consequences of this feeling are never as substantial. Like Hannes, Hinkki experiences an overwhelming feeling of homeliness when he returns to his home city, after long years at sea (Järnefelt 1909/1996: 237 ff.). In the sentiments expressed by Hinkki and Hannes upon arrival, there is a contradictory experience of being at once at home in the city and at odds with one's surroundings. Hinkki, for example, describes the streets of Helsinki as "homely, and yet become so strange" (ibid. 239),[78] before he lets himself be guided by an inner voice through the places he loves in the city.

Järnefelt's *Veneh'ojalaiset* can be considered as a novel that is trail-blazing in Helsinki novels written in Finnish for its description of clearly positive experiences of attachment, as opposed to the more typical dystopian tendencies found in literature of the turn of the century. Similar strong evocations of an experience of belonging to the city recur in a number of novels and short stories published during the decades following the appearance of *Veneh'ojalaiset*. Especially when characters return or leave the city, such strong feelings of attachment arise, although they are often mixed with a profound sense of loss. Urho in Toivo Tarvas's *Eri tasoilta* ("On Different Levels"; 1916a), frantically walks the streets of Helsinki when he realizes that he will have to leave "this city that had become dear to him" (Tarvas 1916a: 206).[79] His luck and his money have run out, but now, at last, he feels akin to his friend Albert Hagen, whose *flâneur* attitude has been discussed in the previous chapter.

An intriguing short story in Toivo Tarvas's short story collection *Helsinkiläisiä* ("Helsinkiers"; 1919), aptly entitled "Kaupungin rakkautta" ("Love for the city"), turns the more traditional city-countryside dichotomy of nineteenth-century Finnish literature upside down. In this story, the parvenu character Josef Kyllönen sings the praise of the city and feels "unusually nervous" when he has to spend a few days at a summer mansion in the countryside, exclaiming to a friend: "You really do not seem to have any idea what a sacrifice this trip to the countryside means to me. I literally feel like crying when I have to leave this beloved city." (Tarvas 1919: 21)[80] Josef Kyllönen is a comic character, and his love for the city is described satirically as a not very convincing pose, rather than as a genuine sense of belonging. A more sincere, if also more tragic, attachment to Helsinki is described in the short story "Lumottu" ("Enchanted") in the same collection, which has been noted as an exceptional example of strong belonging to the city (Laine 2011: 152 ff.). In this sketch, love for the city is felt so acutely by the protagonist that it causes his untimely death. Niilo is a sensitive and young man who decides to study forestry. On the eve of his departure from Helsinki, he is seized by a desire to say goodbye to all places he loves in the Finnish capital. In a frenzy he runs through the city's streets: "He hurried the one street up, the other one down. A secret fervour quickened his steps." (Tarvas 1919: 91)[81]

The prolonged stay in the wilderness of Lapland eventually drives him mad and he commits suicide at the end of a narrative that puts the more traditional plot structure of the young provincial descending into urban destruction on its head.

In Mika Waltari's 1936 novel *Surun ja ilon kaupunki* ("City of Sorrow and Joy"), it is again imminent departure that makes Aarne, a young man with a working-class background feel an acute sense of belonging:

> The Töölö bay glimmers like a pool of blood, and every one of the houses glowing like blood and gold is familiar to his eyes. A piercing feeling of loneliness and longing suddenly floods his mind, and intuitively he realizes for the first time in his life that he loves this great city. It is his home, it is his birthplace, its streets have been the background for his adventures and his disappointments, in the midst of it he has grown up, the city is what he knows, and he finds it difficult to leave. (Waltari 1936: 254)[82]

The view of a sundown over the Töölö bay carries menacing undertones: the bloody aspect of the water and the houses is inspired not only by the evening sun, but also by Aarne's gloomy thoughts about the turn his life is taking. Blended with these dystopian sentiments, and intricately related to them, is Aarne's sense of belonging and love for this city that is "his home, [...] his birthplace."

In many of the more protracted descriptions of a character's feelings of attachment to the city, Helsinki becomes personified: the city appears as a separate entity with its own attributes, and made comprehensible through a more or less panoramic view. In a crucial scene in *Veneh'ojalaiset*, Hannes weighs the fate of the city "which with its thousands glimmering lights was laying under a brightly lit star heaven" (Järnefelt 1909/1996: 337).[83] In other novels, too, Helsinki appears as an almost living organism, depicted as breathing, menacing, or waiting. This is the case most explicitly in several scenes from Toivo Tarvas's *Eri tasoilta*, in which Helsinki is seen through the eyes of Albert Hagen. At the end of a long nocturnal walk, Albert notices how the city gradually awakens to morning activities: "The silent city awoke from its dreams" (Tarvas 1916a: 57).[84] Albert is saddened by the spectacle: he had wanted to cultivate the silent understanding he has with the sleeping city, which is now disturbed: "Albert thought it was sad that the city's quiet peace was disturbed, but when a large city awakens, it yawns audibly like a fairy-tale giant" (ibid.: 58).[85] In a later conversation Albert has with his friend Urho, Albert's love for Helsinki is the subject, and Urho explicitly states that Albert's sentiments cause him to think of Helsinki as a living being:

> – No, Albert, try not to be dishonest, clearly your attachment to this city is the kind of admiration and adoration of the city that is out of the ordinary, because you have invented the city for yourself as if it were a living being, whose company you keep. (Tarvas 1916a: 74)[86]

Albert Hagen's attachment is indeed out of the ordinary, and rare in literature of Helsinki written in Finnish around the turn of the twentieth century. He enunciates a profound feeling of adoration in relation to the city, which runs counter to the continuous pessimistic undercurrents that inform the experience of the city both in *Eri tasoilta* ("On Different Levels"; 1916a) and its sequel *Kohtalon tuulissa* ("The Winds of Fate"; 1916b). In addition to this – and in this he is very different from Hannes and Hinkki in Järnefelt's *Veneh'ojalaiset* – Albert actively and in part consciously aestheticizes the urban spectacle surrounding him, turning the city into a poetic construct of his own making. The word used by Urho to describe Albert's aestheticizing attitude can be literally translated as poeticize ("runoilla"), to transform or conjure in a poetic manner. Here, we find already the creative, subjective and aestheticizing attitude to the city that arguably finds its most explicit emanation in *Suuri illusioni* ("The Great Illusion"; 1928) by Mika Waltari and in Helvi Hämäläinen's *Säädyllinen murhenäytelmä* ("A Respectable Tragedy"; 1941), novels that will be analysed in the following chapter.

A FULLY-FLEDGED HELSINKI NOVEL
In the literature of the early twentieth century, Helsinki appears as a multi-layered city in motion. The complexity evoked by this changing and expanding city is most clearly visible in Arvid Järnefelt's kaleidoscopic novel *Veneh'ojalaiset*, in which Helsinki appears as the catalyst of modernization. For Järnefelt, modernization is a force which, as Pertti Karkama points out, "results in alienation, which is not only a psychological phenomenon, but also an ethical one" (Karkama 2010: 14). The dystopian experience of Helsinki as a tentacular city feeding on the countryside is complemented with an experience that is relatively new in literary prose on Helsinki: a strong feeling of attachment that in some cases is described as outright love.

In all possible respects, Järnefelt's novel constitutes the kind of fully-fledged Helsinki novel V. A. Koskenniemi would call for five years later in *Runon kaupunkeja*: a novel that describes the various social layers of the city, a compelling narrative that gives an account of some of the most central characteristics of the Finnish capital, its geographical range and its history, as well as the people that inhabit it. If Koskenniemi and others did not read *Veneh'ojalaiset* as such, this was in part due to a blind spot when it comes to the genre of the city novel in Finnish literary critique. *Veneh'ojalaiset* has not been read predominantly as a Helsinki novel or as a city novel by most of the literary critics and scholars that have commented upon it during the century since its appearance. This includes also the reading by Saija Isomaa who, in her study of the genre of Järnefelt's social commentary novels, reads *Veneh'ojalaiset* as, inter alia, a novel of revolution and a novel of awakening, but not as a city novel (Isomaa 2009: 210–271). The same can be said of the other novels discussed in this chapter: Eino Leino's *Jaana Rönty*, *Olli Suurpää*, and *Pankkiherroja*, Toivo Tarvas's *Eri tasoilta* and *Kohtalon tuulissa*, Maila Talvio's *Niniven lapset* and *Kultainen lyyra* – they all have been predominantly read as representatives of other generic categories than the city novel.

As my readings above have demonstrated, many of these texts can be conceived as city novels in at least two respects: they thematize the city, and they construct the plot around the unfolding relationship between the protagonist(s) and the city. These novels can also be approached with the help of the city novel taxonomy proposed by Blanche Gelfant in her study of the American city novel. The three kinds of novels Gelfant discerns are the portrait novel, which centres on a single protagonist's development in the city; the synoptic novel, which aims at giving a kaleidoscopic view of the city, and the ecological novel, which looks at a particular environment within a city (Gelfant 1954: 11–14). The portrait novel closely resembles the Young Man/Woman from the Provinces novels (see Chapter 3); the ecological novel is most typical of neighbourhood-centred novels that start to appear in the inter-war period (in description of the working-class literature, for example). The synoptic novel is rare in Finnish literature of this period, although Mika Waltari's *Surun ja ilon kaupunki* ("City of Sorrow and Joy"; 1936) is a notable exception, and Tarvas's *Kohtalon tuulissa*, with its recurrent changes of perspective, is another possible candidate. *Veneh'ojalaiset* bears traits of all these categories. As a description of a family moving from the countryside to the capital, and also in the way it renders Hannes's coming-of-age, it resembles the portrait novel. As a novel moving from the well-to-do to the wooden shovels of working-class slums, from St. Petersburg to Helsinki, and from an epic past to a near-apocalyptic present, it also bears some traits of the synoptic novel. And as a depiction of a particular urban neighbourhood (Punavuori and its immediate surroundings), it also has some characteristics of the ecological novel.

Tentacular Cities

The concept of the "tentacular city" was developed by the Belgian socialist leader Émile Vandervelde, under whose influence it became well-known in socialist circles in France, as well as in Northern Europe (See Josefson 2003). In literature, the tentacular cities appeared in the poetry of the Belgian symbolist writer Émile Verhaeren, in which cities are described as vampires drinking the juice of the countryside. Cities in Verhaeren's poetry also hold, according to Jean Schlegel "regardless of their downsides, the element of redemption, because it is here that the spirit of reform and justice emerges" (Schlegel 1910: 465).

In Finland, the concept was referred to by the Finnish socialist leader N. R. af Ursin in a 1907 article in the socialist periodical Työmies (af Ursin 1907). While not explicitly drawing on Verhaeren or Vandervelde, Finnish turn-of-the-twentieth-century media exploited the idea of cities draining the countryside. One illustrative example is a newspaper article which appeared in 1900 in the periodical *Uusimaa* under the title "How the capital taxes the countryside" ("Maaseudun vero suurkaupungille"):

"Soon new flocks of inexperienced servants, young men and women, will begin to move from the countryside into the capital. Many of them do not even approximately suspect the dangers to which they expose themselves.

And before long, their luck might run out. Not much later, the countryside will receive back these people, broken in body and soul. That is what has happened – does it have to continue that way?" (Anon. 1900)[87]

The editor-in-chief of the periodical was, coincidentally, also a scion of the Järnefelt family, although not directly related to Arvid Järnefelt.

Disappearing Helsinki

Historically speaking, the late nineteenth and early twentieth century saw urban development and change in such rapid convulsions, that the spectacle of demolished buildings gave rise to a new kind of newspaper news section, headed "disappearing Helsinki" ("Häviävä Helsinki"). The sections on disappearing Helsinki also functioned as announcements of upcoming auctions in connection with the demolishing of wooden houses (see e.g. Anon. 1899a; Anon. 1899b; Anon. 1902; Anon. 1910a). The sections on the disappearing city were no complete novelty. In 1885, the Finland-Swedish author Zacharias Topelius had written a newspaper series under the title "Anteckningar från det Helsingfors, som gått" ("Notes regarding the Helsinki that has disappeared", see Topelius 1885/1986), but these consisted of more general, historical causeries on Helsinki's past. In the same period, Viktor Petterson published several collections of stories set in 1850s and 1860s Helsinki, focusing mostly on the district of Katajanokka/Skatudden (see Petterson 1881).

Alarmed by the disappearance of sections of the capital's buildings, the city municipality took notice and action, and a special board was founded to document this disappearing Helsinki. The work of the board and of the photographer Signe Brander on behalf of the board resulted in a valuable collection of early twentieth-century photographs of the city (see Alanco & Pakarinen 2005). On a similar interest in "disappearing Stockholm" in Swedish media and literature in the late nineteenth century, see Borg 2011: 90ff.

Belschazzar's Feast

Belschazzar's feast and the sudden appearance of the portentous "mene tekel" on the wall of the Babylonian palace was a popular theme in nineteenth-century apocalyptic discourse (see Dennis 2008: 49). Kaarlo Bergbom had already written a Finnish version of the story in 1864, and the topic became again popular in the early twentieth century. A play written on the subject by the Finland-Swedish author Hjalmar Procopé was staged in 1906–1907, with music composed by Jean Sibelius. The image was used also in political discussions in early twentieth century Finland, for example during a discussion of Russian infringements on Finland's autonomous status in the constitutional committee (see Anon. 1910b). The French movie called "Le Festin de Balthazar" (Feuillade 1910) toured the Finnish movie theatres in 1910. The popularity of a topic such as Belschazzar's feast is of course not only related to an interest in apocalyptic subjects, but can also be explained by the interest in the exotic and the oriental around the turn of the century.

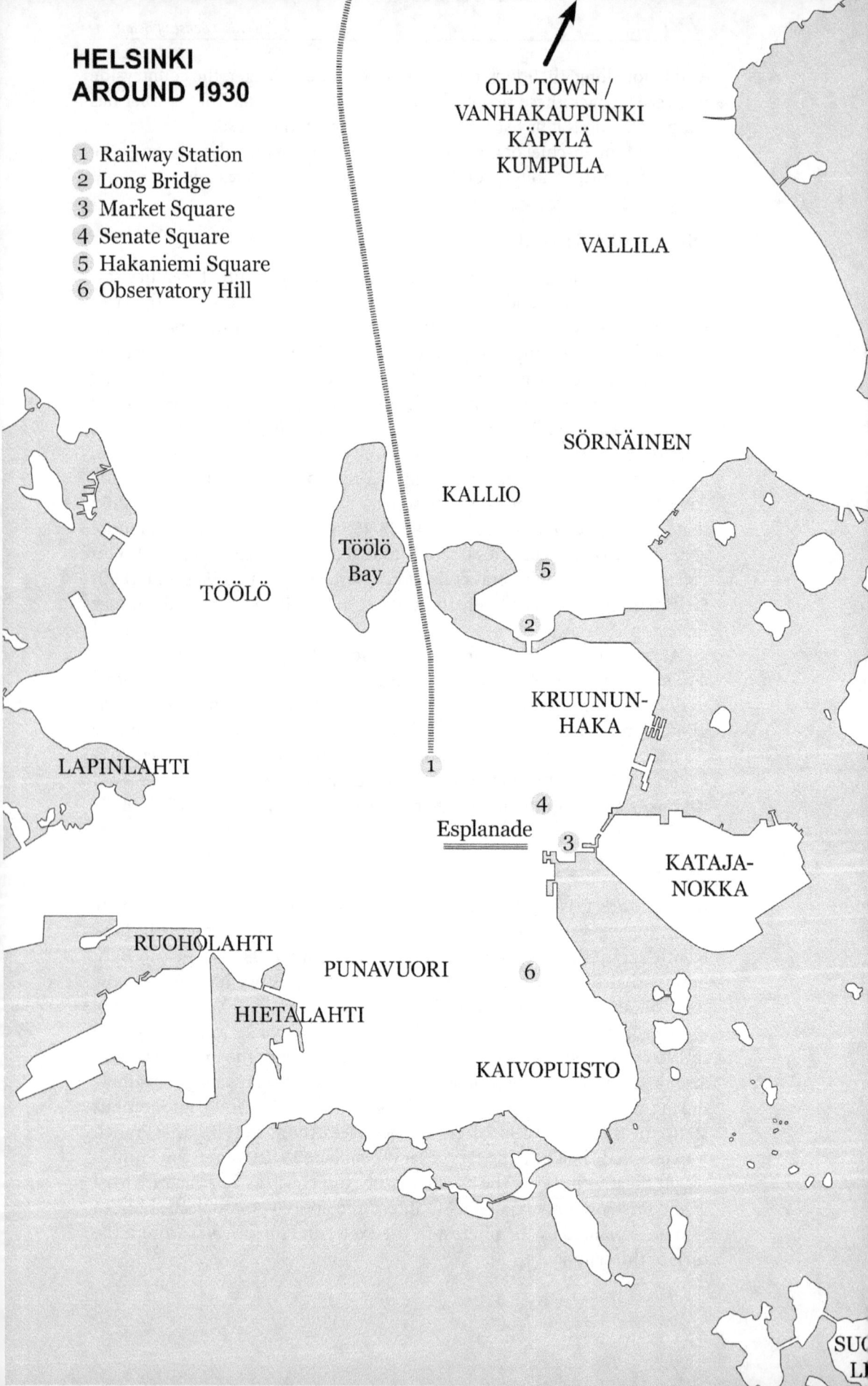

Helsinki 1917–1940: A Short History

After independence, Helsinki continued its growth and development as an industrial centre. In 1920, Helsinki had numbered more than 150,000 inhabitants; by 1930, the population had grown to 205,000, and in 1939, to 260,000 (City of Helsinki Urban Facts 2012: 6).[88] In fifty years' time, the population had multiplied five-fold. Helsinki also expanded in terms of geographical size and in built environment: new areas were added to the city, and new building blocks rose in the south of the Helsinki peninsula (Punavuori, Ullanlinna), in the north-west (Töölö), as well as in the expanding working-class districts to the north-east of the historical centre (Vallila, Käpylä) (Kervanto-Nevanlinna 2002: 140). The construction of the city district Töölö, in particular, can be considered as an architectural symbol of a new, independent Finland, and also as representative of a new class (the expanding middle classes), new aesthetics (from the 1930s on, functionalism) and a new urban lifestyle (see Saarikangas 2002: 166–201).[89] In the course of the 1920s and 1930s, the nature of the city centre changed, and the historical centre became more and more an administrative area with an increasing concentration of offices (Kervanto-Nevanlinna 2002: 140). Helsinki in the 1920s was also a capital gearing to new standards of velocity: the number of private cars almost trebled from 1,120 in 1925 to 3,299 in 1928 (Bell & Hietala 2002: 206).

One way to portray the developments within Helsinki during the decades following independence is to describe these years as a period of increasing homogenization. The ethnic and linguistic diversity that had characterized the city for centuries gradually disappeared, in part because of the continuous influx of Finnish speakers from inner Finland (see Bell & Hietala 2002: 141). In 1880, 12% of Helsinki's inhabitants had been born outside Finland (Tilastollinen päätoimisto 1909: 63); in 1910, the percentage of foreigners living in Helsinki had dropped to 6.5%, and steadily declined throughout the twentieth century. By the early 1990s, only 1% of the Helsinki population was foreign (Rönkkö 1992: 170).[90] Increasing homogenization was also visible in the cultural and literary field during the 1920s and 1930s, years that witnessed a "strong orientation towards nationalism and national culture" (Maironiemi 1992: 135). Only a small minority of Helsinki's population could uphold the attitude (or the pose) cultivated by the literary movement of the Torch Bearers, with their famous call to "open the windows to Europe" (see the following chapter).

In terms of national politics, the 1920s and 1930s were, as elsewhere in Europe, dominated by radicalization. From the very start, right-wing forces in independent Finland had their doubts about parliamentary democracy, and the Civil War had greatly exacerbated the existing divisions in Finnish society, although measures were taken to address the plight of the poor, crofters, in particular (see Hentilä 1995/1999: 121–125). The fact that many on the political right were oriented towards Germany during these years, and the understandable suspicion with which the political developments in the Soviet Union were eyed in Finland, did little to diffuse socio-political tensions. Towards the end of the 1920s, a radical right-wing faction emerged, the so-called Lapua movement, modelled on German and Italian examples. The radicalization associated with the Lapua movement resulted in a spike in political violence at the turn of the 1930s (Siipi 1962: 334). The year 1930 saw an increasingly tense political atmosphere in Helsinki when the Lapua movement staged the "Farmers' March" in Helsinki, modelled on the March on Rome that brought Mussolini into power (Lavery 2006: 98).

In terms of the experience of Helsinki's public space, one of the most significant legislative measures taken during these years was Prohibition. In Finland, Prohibition was inaugurated in 1919 and abolished in 1932. A substantial number of bars and restaurants were closed, and liquor runners and illegal distilleries held the public's imagination and kept the Helsinki police department busy (Peltonen 1992). During these years, the production, smuggling and consumption of illegal alcohol spiralled out of control, as did occurrences of alcohol-related crime (see Määttä 2007).

The 1930s was a decade of further radicalization, need and poverty, as Finland and its capital were hit by the Great Depression. Politically, however, the situation stabilized somewhat: the political right gained a victory when the Communist party was outlawed in 1930 (Carsten 1967/1982: 162), and not much later, after threatening to destabilize the country once more, the Lapua movement was outlawed without bloodshed (Hentilä 1995/1999: 163). The Great Depression hit Finland hardest in the early years of the 1930s, after which the economy recovered gradually. Helsinki continued building, expanding and modernizing, and an abundance of coffee table books, tourist guides and jubilant films (for Helsinki movies see Heiskanen & Santakari 2004: 11–61) appeared to advertise the beauty of the young nation's capital. In many respects, the 1940 Summer Olympics that were to be hosted by Helsinki were designed to be the crowning ceremony for the Finnish capital. Several elegant venues had been completed by late 1939. It was not to be: on 30 November 1939, the Soviet Union opened hostilities, and Helsinki was subjected to an air raid. The Finnish capital was at war.

6. Aestheticizing the City
The Internalization of a New Helsinki

The Helsinki which presents itself to the reader in most of the novels that appeared in the 1920s and 1930s is distinctly different from the Helsinki in turn-of-the-century novels. This is in part due to the drastically changed political context. Helsinki was no longer the provincial capital of an autonomous Grand-Duchy incorporated in the Russian Empire, but the proud political centre of a new nation, giving an added aura to the way in which the city is represented in literature. In terms of the built environment, too, Helsinki changed considerably in these decades, and it is indeed a physically "new Helsinki" which, in the form of the modern district of Töölö, is repeatedly foregrounded in the literature of this period. What is most striking is the extent to which many of these texts show an explicit interest in everything urban and modern: Helsinki is not necessarily presented as more complex or more multi-layered than before (indeed, in some cases rather the opposite), but the city as a subject matter, and more specifically, the experience of urbanity and modernity, become gradually more explicitly thematized.

The thematization of urbanity and the concomitant interest in modernity in the literature of this period are well attested, especially in relation to the work of the group of authors which became known as the Torch Bearers ("tulenkantajat").[1] In the context of this study, the inner circle of this literary movement, which debuted in the year 1924 in and around the magazine *Nuori Voima*, is of limited interest, since it was a group that consisted primarily of poets. In Finnish prose literature the city attains a more privileged position only slightly later, in the works of authors who published towards the end of the 1920s and in the early 1930s, and who partly drew on the work of the Torch Bearers. Apart from Mika Waltari, prose authors from this loosely interconnected generation include Arvi Kivimaa, and Unto Karri (see Paavolainen 1932: 14–15 ff.; Mauriala 2005: 239). The thematization of the city in the prose of these authors is a well-established fact. What this thematization entails for the way in which the experience of the city is given form in Finnish prose texts in these decades, however, has remained largely unstudied, and this will be the main research question addressed below.

This chapter examines one particular approach towards the city which is strikingly visible in a number of prose texts from the late 1920s on:

the internalization of the urban experience, and the related aestheticizing manner in which the narrator and/or literary characters experience Helsinki. The interiorized and aestheticizing experience of the city will be analysed by drawing on the work of Richard Lehan and Bart Keunen, in particular their thoughts concerning an "inward turn" (Lehan 1998: 72–73) and an "aestheticist turn" in urban imagery (Keunen 1995, 1999: 429). One particular *topos*, central to the experience of urbanity in literature of this period, will be analysed in detail: the nocturnal car drive through the deserted city, with its suggestions of geographical, temporal and moral boundary transgressions.

Mika Waltari's debut novel *Suuri illusioni* ("The Great Illusion"; 1928), which can be considered the cult novel of its age, will serve as a starting point and will be linked to relevant later novels and short stories.[2] In the second part of this chapter, a different although related way of experiencing the city in literature will be addressed: the aestheticization of Helsinki, in relation to the built environment as well as to specific natural elements within the city, which appears in Helvi Hämäläinen's *Säädyllinen murhenäytelmä* ("A Respectable Tragedy"; 1941). The landscape in Hämäläinen's complex novel is filtered through the awareness of highly sensitive protagonists who attach their powerful sense of loss and longing to the objects and localities surrounding them.

The new experiences of Helsinki in this period invite a number of contextualizations. In the background of the new discourse on the city, a whole new era comes into view: the gay twenties, with its jazz dance halls, its discussion concerning a new kind of woman, and the exciting nightlife of more than a decade of Prohibition (see Koskela 1999b). The pronounced interest in everything modern and urban and the accompanying enchanted view of the city is also in part related to an optimistic feeling that permeated (up to a certain extent) the 1920s in Finland, and which was related to the experience of belonging to a distinctly new generation, separated from the old world by the terrible caesura constituted by the Great War, and in the Finnish context, the Civil War of 1918.[3] In Finland, this experience was further enhanced by the knowledge that this new generation was also the first one growing up in the newly independent Republic. Much of the writing of the 1930s, in turn, is grounded in the pessimism of a world in the throes of economic depression, and dominated by a pessimistic climate further exacerbated by domestic and international threats of political radicalization.

The Internalized Urban Experience in Mika Waltari's Suuri illusioni *(1928)*

> The smell in the broad, dark staircase flew in our face. It was the smell of the city, – cold, washed stone; dust; fusty air and something else, something which you cannot explain, which you immediately become used to so that you don't even notice it, but which, if you return from the countryside, always has its own special effect.

> I had come to the city in the early days of August, because it was too hot in the countryside and because there were arguably some things that I could use as excuses for my return. In fact, I missed the city, the smell of asphalt, metal dust and gasoline, – that nervous longing that wanders the quiet streets in the darkening evenings (Waltari 1928: 7).[4]

In the much-quoted opening lines of Mika Waltari's debut novel *Suuri illusioni*, two important ways in which the city is described in this period are immediately visible: the thematization of the city, as well as the internalized and aestheticized way in which Helsinki is experienced.[5] The importance of the city in this novel is not only highlighted by placing the description of arrival in the city (or more specifically: the return to the city) at the very beginning of the narration, but the city is also presented as the instigator of the protagonist's decision to interrupt his holidays in the countryside. Longing for the city is the feeling which sets in motion the events unfolding in the first pages of the novel. In *Suuri illusioni*, the explicit foregrounding of the city can be linked to Waltari's ambition to break away from the perceived dominance of rural thematics in Finnish literature. A discussion at the beginning of the novel, in which one of the characters claims that he is "fed up with the smell of sweat and of the dunghill" (ibid.: 17) in Finnish literature can be seen as programmatic in this respect: using the city as subject matter was for Waltari and others a means of setting themselves apart from a perceived Finnish mainstream literature.[6]

In *Suuri illusioni*, the foregrounding of urban phenomena does not result in particularly rich descriptive references to the built environment or to the geographical features of the city.[7] Instead, the narration focuses on how the protagonist experiences the surrounding cityscape. What is described are personal sentiments and sensations, filtered through the highly subjective sensitive awareness of the protagonist. This is the case from the very first lines of the novel: *Suuri illusioni* begins *in medias res*, with the description of a specific smell.[8] The protagonist grapples to define the characteristics and meaning of this smell, and in the course of this introspective investigation, the reader is told how he (the journalist Hart; his name and profession are given only much later) has just returned from the countryside, and how he has coincidently met an old friend, Korte. Both men are now on their way to a private party at the mysterious Mrs. Spindel's apartment, where Hart will meet the two characters with whom he will form the fatal love triangle central to the plot's development: Hellas, a refined but mentally unstable author, and the unruly Caritas, the chain-smoking embodiment of the 1920s "new woman".[9]

The first pages of the novel, then, are for the most part an analysis of what a particular smell signifies for the protagonist. The choice to describe a smell, rather than outward features, puts added emphasis on the fact that the reader is not presented with an objectified or distanced description of space, but with a personal and highly intimate experience. As Henri Lefebvre argues, "if there is any sphere where [...] an intimacy occurs between 'subject' and 'object', it must surely be the world of smells and the places where they reside" (Lefebvre 1974/1991: 197). For the protagonist in *Suuri illusioni*, this certainly holds true: the smell which welcomes Hart and his friend as they enter the staircase leading to the apartment of the mysterious Mrs. Spindel's becomes a gateway to unfolding past and present worlds, not entirely unlike Proust's proverbial Madeleine cookie. It provides the olfactory background for the future meeting of the central characters of the novel, but to Hart, it is also brings to mind an experience from his past: "an unclear memory from my childhood, which the smell from the staircase had awakened from oblivion" (Waltari 1928: 8–9).[10] The smell reminds Hart of the day of his father's funeral, an experience to which, paradoxically, no sorrow or regret are linked, on the contrary: that smell "had been from that moment on [...] dear to me, for it symbolizes the city and everything unknown" (ibid.: 9).[11] Unlike so many Young Men/Women from the Provinces novels, in which the death of the father seals the protagonist's profound rootlessness, unrest and economic distress, for Hart his father's death symbolizes the city at its most enchanting: excitement, freedom – the promise of new possibilities. The late 1920's protagonist is not concerned with the past, but with the expanding and fragmentary time of a radical here and now.

The opening lines of *Suuri illusioni*, with their emphasis on personally experienced urban space, are indicative of a move in city representations towards a subjective and internalized urban experience, a move which Richard Lehan has called the "inward turn" in the literature of the city (Lehan 1998: 72–73). This subjective view of the city is characterized by the foregrounding of personally experienced impressions drawn from (public) urban space. It can already be found in the works of E. A. Poe and, of course, Charles Baudelaire, in whose texts an observer typically notices in the city streets or crowd "an object that triggers his imagination or memory and thus is internalized" (Lehan 1998: 72). As indicated above in relation to the opening pages of Waltari's debut, this subjective and interiorized manner in which the city is described entails a marginalization in *Suuri illusioni* of direct descriptions of the built environment. Most of the descriptions of the city are renderings of images or even after-images that are described as they are imprinted in the consciousness of the protagonist:

> I walked up the stairs, within my consciousness still the flickering image of the autumnal city evening: the bright rows of street lamps, the fire of the neon lights, the green electric flames of the tramcars, the screaming of the car horns. (Waltari 1928: 130)[12]

What is described above is not the moment when the protagonist sees the city, but the moment, occurring slightly later than the act of seeing, when the cityscape is being processed in his consciousness. As a consequence, the elements that are selected do not constitute the kind of totalizing, panoramic view that would result from a stable viewpoint (from a window, for example, such as in the opening passage in Arvid Järnefelt's *Veljekset* ["Brothers"; 1900]; see the previous chapter). Instead, they form a series of detached impressions, suggesting a viewpoint that is in motion rather than fixed.

What Richard Lehan describes as an "inward turn" in literary representations of the city is essentially a radical change in the perception of reality; "[a]s the mind moves inward, the physical world, including the city, becomes a subjective reality" (Lehan 1998: 121). Bart Keunen has described this inward turn in terms of an "aestheticist turn in spatial imagery" (Keunen 2001: 429), an attitude of the narrator which can be summed up in a quote from Charles Baudelaire's *Le Spleen de Paris*: "all these things think through me, or I think through them" (Baudelaire 1869/1989: 4; see Keunen 2001: 429). One narrative method identified by Keunen in relation to this "aestheticist turn" is the "correspondence method", in which an aestheticizing observer reads his own mood and consciousness into the city texture and vice versa. In his prose poetry, Baudelaire was a master in exploiting this technique.[13]

In *Suuri illusioni*, the city and the protagonist's mood are repeatedly described in unison, and it becomes increasingly unclear where to draw the border between the outward appearance of the city and the inner mood swings of the protagonist. Juxtaposing city and individual was, of course, nothing particularly new: in turn-of-the-century texts set in Helsinki, the cityscape had been contrasted with characters' inner feelings, but this had not entailed an invasion of the protagonist's consciousness by spatial experiences or vice versa.[14] In Waltari's debut novel, the description of gloomy morning light, a rainy autumn day or *l'heure bleue* tell the reader as much about the mental state of the characters as they tell about the physical aspects of the city. The mention of the "red fog of a frozen sun" outside a Helsinki café (Waltari 1928: 171), for example, relates as much to the wintery cityscape as to the protagonist's gloomy feelings of foreboding after his friend and adversary in love, Hellas, has left the city in search of the woman they both love.[15]

In later novels by Mika Waltari and some of his contemporaries, the experience of the city is often similarly described as profoundly in tune with the emotions of the characters, so much so that it becomes impossible to separate them from each other. More often than not, the effect of this "correspondence method" was to render a sense of melancholy or depression in and through the cityscape. In Waltari's Helsinki novel *Appelsiininsiemen* ("The Orange Seed"; 1931), the view of the crematorium from the window of Kurt Waldhof's home apartment, for example, resonates strongly with the feelings of transience experienced by this decadent character on the morning following a party (Waltari 1931: 51), while the feelings of loneliness overwhelming Ilmari, the protagonist Irene's fiancé in the same novel, are described as being in unison with the deserted city streets through which he wanders (ibid.: 145–148). Perhaps the clearest example of a synergetic city experience in this novel can be found in the following extract, which locates the growing erotic tension between Irene and Ilmari in the darkening cityscape:

> [...] evening came, one of those quickly darkening, heat-radiating evenings, when the whole city feels as if it is shuddering with a passionate anticipation, and when the street lamps shine more and more brightly above the burning streets (Waltari 1931: 271).[16]

Similar examples from novels and short stories from this period can be multiplied at will. Several revealing examples can be found in Arvi Kivimaa's novel *Epäjumala* ("Idol"; 1930), which is considered, together with *Suuri illusioni*, to give a particularly vivid reflection of the atmosphere of 1920s Helsinki (see Laitinen 1965: 459), and which was hailed by contemporary critic V. A. Koskenniemi as "the long-looked for Helsinki novel" Koskenniemi had already called for in 1914 (as quoted in Nieminen 1974: 118).[17] The protagonist of *Epäjumala* is the sensitive stage director Markus Saari, who cultivates a particular interest in modernity and urbanity, and who is an avid observer of the city spectacle, both in Helsinki and abroad. Markus's thoughts are repeatedly described as being intertwined with an interiorized view of the city, in particular when he feels most depressed:

> An enormous huddle of humid, bleak houses outside. The city. Grey sky. Desperate people. Work. (Kivimaa 1930: 129)[18]

In passages such as the one above, the manner in which the spatial description is rendered as a reflection of the character's inner feelings gives the narration characteristics of stream of consciousness. The highly elliptic clauses with their enumeration of successive nouns suggest that these are the almost unmediated thoughts of the protagonist who is simultaneously probing his own feelings and the view of the city outside. This narrative technique is in essence a further development of the "impressionist style" that had been pioneered in Finnish prose by Juhani Aho, in particular in renderings of modern and urban phenomena such as railway or tram movements.[19] In her study of urban space in Arvi Kivimaa's early works, Reetta Nieminen draws attention to the "impressionist glimpses" in Kivimaa's *Epäjumala* (Nieminen 1974: 119). The style of Mika Waltari's prose, *Suuri illusioni* in particular, has also repeatedly been referred to as impressionist, by contemporary critic Koskenniemi (1928: 500) as well as by later critics such as Aarne Laurila (Laurila 1982a: 76). In the French impressionist style, one of the most important characteristics had been a distinctive nominal structure: the domination of nouns over adjectives or verbs (see Scott 1976/1986: 219). Although the Finnish language and its sentence structure are highly different from Indo-European languages, nominal structures are one of the striking stylistic features in Helsinki novels drawing on the impressionist tradition, such as the texts by Kivimaa, Waltari and others discussed here.

Amongst 1930s Helsinki prose, Iris Uurto's texts take up a special position in the way they make effective use of the correspondence technique. In Uurto's debut novel *Ruumiin ikävä* ("The Longing of the Body"; 1930/1931), mathematics teacher Olli Lassila takes to walking the city at night after he has been deceived and left by his wife. The nocturnal city is described in terms that also reflect this character's loneliness and despondency. His walks are occasionally described in considerable geographical detail; one example is one long walk along the waterfront of the district Eira, which ends, by way of the street Punavuorenkatu, at the square Fredrikintori:

> A boundless gloominess lay reposing on the roofs. The desolate street felt as if it had sunk down into the ground from sheer fatigue. On the small square, a car was standing melancholically in the light of a lonely street lamp. (Uurto 1930/1931: 193–194)[20]

In this extract, the depressed sentiments of the protagonist transform the way in which the environment is rendered, and the gloominess of the focalizer is located in the urban landscape around him ("boundless gloominess"; "desolate street"; "a car standing melancholically"; "a lonely street lamp"). In Iris Uurto's following novel, *Kypsyminen* ("Maturing"; 1935), gloomy feelings again take shape in an almost synergetic link between the male protagonist, Lauri, and the city. In terms of genre, this novel is a 1930s version of the student novel, and it reuses prototypical elements from this turn-of-the-century genre, although infused with references to the economically dire conditions of the 1930s and concerned with the protagonist's psychology, rather than with the social or political consequences of his actions. Helsinki features extensively in this novel, and the cityscape is repeatedly described in unison with the mood of the main character. In a crucial scene, rendered in a long descriptive passage (of which only a fragment is included below), the protagonist Lauri, utterly depressed and lovesick, wanders the streets at night, and the deserted cityscape mirrors Lauri's inner despondency in the extreme:

> The city was empty as if it had died; the lamps were shining to themselves [...]. The streets were barren, without snow, the mighty stone buildings were lying along the street as if they were fallen and crouching, petrified sentries. (Uurto 1935: 222)[21]

In Iris Uurto's and Unto Karri's novels mentioned above, as in Waltari's later Helsinki novels, the closely felt bond between protagonist and city is only a secondary narrative strategy, but in *Suuri illusioni*, the unreal and strongly internalized nature of the city is linked to the overall thematics in the novel. As the title of Waltari's debut ("The Great Illusion") suggests, the literary characters in this novel consider life to be no more than an illusion, a succession of dream-like images and fantasies. This conception of reality fills the literary characters with a sense of profound insecurity, the unsettling symptoms of which are a blasé attitude and neurasthenia – typical diseases of modernity and the urban condition. Nevertheless, this insecurity also offers the appealing possibility of participating playfully in constructing and de-constructing the illusions that create the sensory world. Throughout the novel, the characters are continuously referred to as playing roles, as carrying masks, and they view the phenomenological world with suspicion. The protagonist Hart considers that his very being is not so much about conscious thoughts, but about illusory and fleeing impressions (Waltari 1928: 185–186).

City Archaeologies

The city in *Suuri illusioni* permeates everything, but it would be more exact to speak in this context of *cities* in the plural. *Suuri illusioni* is a novel which moves between two capitals, Helsinki and Paris, but numerous other cities, real and imagined, are present. On a first and most obvious level, this is the case for the mesmerizing existence of far-away cities acutely felt by all three protagonists in the novel. In Hellas's room, Hart notices a large map of Europe on the wall, and on the table he sees a Baedeker, which exerts an immediate and almost synesthetic effect on him: "in a flashing sensation, I felt in my ears the feverish clamour and honking of cars of the metropolis" (ibid.: 53).[22] As Paul Fussell notes in his study of inter-war British travel writing, the "very word *Baedeker* [...] is alone almost sufficient to connote the special travel atmosphere between the wars" (Fussell 1980: 62), an atmosphere that made a considerable mark on the literature of this period.

The importance of other European cities – Paris in particular – for the experience of modernity and urbanity in 1920s and 1930s Finnish prose literature thematizing Helsinki can hardly be exaggerated. These decades saw a growing interest in international travelling and a proliferation of travel literature, which extended its influence to fiction (see Juutila 1984; Lappalainen 1990: 79).[23] Finnish literature written in the wake of the Torch Bearers tended to include a trip to Paris as a means for the protagonist to come to grips with the problems he/she had left behind in Helsinki, a *topos* that followed an example that had been set by Juhani Aho in *Yksin* ("Alone"; 1890/2003; see Nummi 2002: 154). A typical example of such a journey can be found in Unto Karri's *Sodoma* (1929), a novel which can be considered symptomatic of Finnish prose written in the wake of the Torch Bearer movement. *Sodoma* is, like several other Helsinki novels of this period (Iris Uurto's *Kypsyminen* ["Maturing"; 1935]; Matti Kurjensaari's *Tie Helsinkiin* ["The Road to Helsinki"; 1937]), a text that bears considerable resemblances to the student novel. It is also, however, a novel concerned with dissecting the moral evils of the times, a Spengler-inspired vision of a modern Europe on the verge of collapse. In the novel, the protagonist goes on an extended visit to Paris, and there are descriptions, too, of a terrifying, "animalistic" Berlin (Karri 1929: 244).

Several other Finnish novels of this period align the experience of Helsinki with a journey to one or more European capitals. Joel Lehtonen's *Henkien taistelu* ("The Battle of the Spirits"; 1933), a novel which will be discussed in detail in the following chapter, shapes a literary Helsinki by juxtaposing it with Paris, and the novel sets out in the French capital. In Arvi Kivimaa's *Epäjumala* ("Idol"; 1930), the experiences of Helsinki are literally framed by visions of other cities, since the novel opens with the return of the protagonist from Europe (Berlin, amongst others), and ends with his return from the Soviet Union; in between, he has also had time to journey to the Netherlands.[24] In Elsa Soini's *Uni* ("Dream"; 1930), a considerable part of the novel is taken up by the European travels of the protagonist, which include a visit to Paris. Internationally, the 1930s has been considered the "golden age of travel writing" (Fussell 1980; see also Thacker 2003/2009: 193), and part of the fascinating spatiality in novels such as the ones above is related to the way these create a complex (and often jumbled) image of modernity by juxtaposing Helsinki with other European cities in novels that mix the superficial tourist observations typical of travel with fictional elements from more traditional genres.[25] In *Palava nuoruuus* ("Burning Youth"; 1935), the last part of his Helsinki trilogy, Mika Waltari describes, with the benefit of hindsight, the fascination for travelling to Europe and its cities during the 1920s. The protagonist of *Palava nuoruus*, Juhani, desires to travel abroad "to find modernity, of which life in Helsinki was no more than a lukewarm, Northern shadow" (Waltari 1935: 316)[26], and he finds it, like so many others, in Paris and its café Le Dôme.

One important generator of a sense of international urban simultaneity was the radio transistor, which literally enabled the people of the 1920s to tune into the everyday reality of far-off cities. Hart, in *Suuri illusioni*, notices how his little brother, a radio amateur, listens to the voices of far-away cities (Waltari 1928: 81), and in Iris Uurto's *Ruumiin ikävä* (1930/1931), it is the radio broadcasts from distant cities that give the first indication of Paula's profound longing towards a reality different from her conventional middle-class marriage. While listening to the radio broadcast, Paula dreams out loud of being in Berlin, walking along Broadway Boulevard, and seeing Kiki in Montmartre. When the rather conventional family friend Valjakka disagrees with Paula, the conversation turns to the contemporary interest in travel in Finnish literature:

> But literature – which is supposed to be the mirror of an era – literature is clearly seized by travel fever. One only reads about car trips, D-trains, Honolulu and eastern lands. (Uurto 1930/1931: 31)[27]

This statement, which refers back to a particular kind of literary programme, goes a long way in framing what is on the verge of happening in the novel. Paula is seduced by the architect Thorpe (also present at the conversation mentioned above) during exciting outings in his private automobile; she runs off with him and they consume their adulterous relation in a hotel room in London.

In *Suuri illusioni*, the synchronic existence of Europe's metropolises is but one layer of imagined cities through which the protagonists read their immediate Helsinki environments. In this novel, it is possible to find embryonic characteristics of the modernist view of the city, the idea that "one city leads to another in the distinctive aesthetic voyage into the metamorphosis of form" (Bradbury 1976/1986: 101). In *Suuri illusioni*, Hart and the other protagonists sound their environment using a much more diachronic way of reading urban space than a simple juxtaposition with existing and far-off foreign places. Seeing the exotic in the everyday has become a conscious endeavour for these characters, and also one of the incentives to use stimulants, as is illustrated by the following words, spoken by the journalist Korte to the protagonist:

> Have you ever tried cocaine? – No, you haven't. – Then a first-class experience has remained out of your grasp. – Do you want to feel you are smart, strong,

young, untiring, pure and innocent? Do you want to see, in the light of a street lamp, the shimmering gate of paradise? (Waltari 1928: 85)[28]

In *Suuri illusioni*, the literary characters are seen at work superimposing the everyday urban landscape around them with historical layers and fantastic mirages, and inventing imaginary geographic points of reference with which to read the city. The novel shares this tendency to read the urban landscape through imaginary and often diachronic layers of meaning with a number of international city novels, in which the city is increasingly seen as a conglomerate of overlapping and simultaneously present layers of time. In Charles Dickens's *Bleak House* (1852–1853/2003), the narrator relates how he would not be surprised to meet a Megalosauros in the thick London fog, and in the opening pages of Joseph Conrad's *Heart of Darkness* (1899/1994), the bygone presence of Roman legionaries adds a measure of uncanny brooding to the Thames riverscape. In high modernist texts such as T.S. Eliot's *The Waste Land* (1922/1971) and James Joyce's *Ulysses* (1922/1993), the overlaying of the contemporary cityscape with complex mythical layers becomes central to the composition. As Richard Lehan points out, it is a technique that amounts to "the literary complement to what was happening in archaeology – the discovery of layered cities, the realization that different cultures were superimposed upon each other in time" (Lehan 1998: 111; see also Alter 2005: 115–117; Gere 2009: 141–146). Seeing the city as a series of overlapping temporal frames, as "a kind of archaeological site", was one consequence of the way in which (early) modernist authors filtered the narration through the consciousness of the protagonist; a device which, as Robert Alter argues, "facilitates this archaeological perception of the city because the consciousness, though constantly impinged upon by present stimuli, can also exert great freedom in reverting to the cultural past" (Alter 2005: 115).

In *Suuri illusioni*, the simultaneous existence of different temporal layers in the city never takes on such a programmatic or complex form; the modernism of *Suuri illusioni* is only relative (see Karkama 1994: 200, 203). Several scenes in the novel, however, can be read in the light of an aestheticist poetics which draws attention to the city's imaginary layers, and amongst these, one scene set at the Helsinki waterfront is particularly revealing. In this scene, the transformation of the everyday cityscape through the fanciful way in which the characters comment upon it is taken to extremes. During a nocturnal outing, Caritas and Hart take a walk to Kaivopuisto, a park situated at the southern edge of the Helsinki peninsula. Caritas, who has invited Hart to accompany her, gives as her reason for the excursion "that we are going to make a nocturnal raid on the castle of the Emperor of Beijing, and you shall bring his head to me on a golden platter" (Waltari 1928: 50).[29] The playful addition of an Oriental map to Helsinki's geography can be read as a foreshadowing of the disturbing things to come – after all, Hart, Hellas and Caritas are becoming progressively more entangled in a triangle relationship that will end with Hellas's suicide, and the "Emperor of Beijing" is clearly identifiable with Hellas. Later on during the same evening, Hart takes up the playful suggestion of Caritas, reading the map of Helsinki as if it were a Silk Road oasis: "'I suggest that we go for a short walk to Kaivopuisto to look for the golden road to Samarkand,' I said. 'At the same time, I shall have the opportunity to cut off the head of the Emperor of Beijing and to offer it to the princess..."' (ibid.: 56)[30]

The mention of the "gold road to Samarkand" can be read as a revealing programmatic statement and as an intertextual reference to the 1925 collection of essays *Ny generation* ("The New Generation") by the Finland-Swedish author and literary critic Hagar Olsson. The first essay of the collection, entitled "Dikten och illusionen" ("Poetry and Illusion"), has as its motto the verse "we make the Golden Journey to Samarkand" from James Elroy Flecker's poem "The Golden Journey to Samarkand" (Flecker 1923: 144–145). Olsson's essay calls for a new kind of literature, driven by the notion of "illusion", and Olsson names the modernist authors subscribing to such a programme "Journeymen to Samarkand" ("Samarkandfararna"; Olsson 1925: 10). The fact that Waltari entitled his debut novel "The Great Illusion" serves as a first indication that the author wanted to follow the road indicated by Olsson. In Waltari's novel *Palava nuoruus* ("Burning Youth"; 1935), which is in part a commentary of the author's personal involvement in the 1920s literary scene, the protagonist, clearly modelled on the young Waltari, is described as being greatly affected by his reading of Olsson's *Ny generation* (Waltari 1935: 290).

In *Suuri illusioni*, the outing to Kaivopuisto does not end in Samarkand or Beijing, but in a nocturnal swim in the sea: Hart and Hellas (who has joined the other two) both go for a swim, while Caritas remains to guard their clothes. The scene, set on the border of night and day, city and sea, contains elements of a journey to the netherworld, in particular when it becomes clear that Hellas is contemplating suicide. There is much more to the scene, however: the Helsinki waterscape, the gleam of the city lights reflected onto the sky, and the roles of the protagonists receive added depth through the imaginary and historical layers of meaning that are attached to the cityscape. Caritas is left with Hellas's match box and is asked to light a match so that both men will be able to find their way back; a motif which is reminiscent of the internationally widespread tale of the *Schwimmersage*, which in turn can be traced to the classical love story of Hero and Leander (see Gillian 1957). And when Hellas and Hart return, Caritas calls them Vikings returning from seducing mermaids.

In this passage, the Helsinki waterfront at the Kaivopuisto park appears as multiple intersecting historical and imaginary layers: the road to Samarkand and the palace of the Emperor of Beijing become intertwined with the Dardanelles (the original setting of the myth of Hero and Leander) and with Nordic medieval history. Significant is also what is *not* visible amongst these various layers: the fortress of Suomenlinna, which is situated directly opposite the beach of Kaivopuisto, and which could have evoked clear political associations. Politics, however, plays no role in how the characters read their surroundings in *Suuri illusioni*. As Caritas exclaims at the beginning of the novel, political issues have no part in this world: "Silence! [...] Not a word about politics!" (Waltari 1928: 17)[31]

The aestheticizing way in which the protagonists try to read references to an imagined world in their immediate and everyday environments

(Kaivopuisto as a gateway to Samarkand, for example), is in part rooted in the turn-of-the-century symbolist movement. In *Suuri illusioni*, characters refer directly to G. K. Chesterton and (most probably) to his novel *The Ball and the Cross* (1910/1928). The same Chesterton, in his "A Defence of Detective Stories" (1902), had claimed that every element constituting the city is a sign, a deliberate symbol: "There is no stone in the street and no brick in the wall that is not actually a deliberate symbol – a message from some man, as if it were a telegram or a post card" (as quoted in Freeman 2007: 81). This vision was typical of the way the detective came to see the city, but also for a more widely-spread approach towards the city, found in decadent and symbolist poetics, which not only retreated "from the material world into realms of the imagination", but also went actively looking for the "signs, omens, messages that are delivered in queer ways and queer places" in the turn-of-the-century city (Arthur Machen [1924] as quoted in Freeman 2007: 168). This attitude – to look for signs "delivered in queer ways and queer places" – is in many respects a view that permeates the way in which the protagonists in *Suuri illusioni* look at the city: in search of traces of another, parallel universe. It is an approach to the urban environment that can be traced to the work of Baudelaire. Mika Waltari had read *Les paradis artificiels* (*Artificial Paradises*; 1860/1967) in 1927 (Waltari 1980: 191), and the journalist Korte's urge in *Suuri illusioni* to use cocaine to be able to see "in the light of a street lamp, the shimmering gate of paradise" (Waltari 1928: 85–86, see above) can be interpreted as a direct reference to *Les paradis artificiels*.

The complex superimposition of various layers onto everyday urban space performed by the characters in *Suuri illusioni* is relatively rare in Finnish Helsinki novels of this period, but similar scenes do occur. I mentioned earlier how, in Iris Uurto's novel *Ruumiin ikävä*, the female protagonist Paula imagines herself to be in Berlin, New York and Paris while listening to foreign radio broadcasts. In the same novel, Paula tries to imagine she is walking in Paris during a promenade through Helsinki; she looks at the Swedish theatre as if it were the Grand Opera in Paris (Uurto 1930/1931: 63). In Toivo Tarvas's short story "Yön mustat varjot" ("The Dark Shadows of the Night"; 1920), the protagonists belong to a youth gang in a working-class district in Helsinki. Profoundly impressed by a regular intake of popular movies, they refer to their everyday urban surroundings as a Wild West scene, identifying themselves with Indians whose hunting grounds are being encroached upon by the Whites (Tarvas 1920: 66–67).[32]

The way in which the Helsinki coastline is described in *Suuri illusioni* as a liminal environment with mythical dimensions bears relevance to the way this little-studied part of Helsinki – the waterfront – is constructed in literature. Helsinki is one of the few European capitals situated at the open sea, and it has an extensive coastline. One way in which this particular cityscape is given shape in Finnish literature is by recourse to pastoral imagery, but this is by no means the only mode in which the Helsinki waterfront appears in literature. The scene in *Suuri illusioni* in which all three protagonists go for an outing to Kaivopuisto is one in a whole range of passages in early twentieth-century literature which transform the shoreline of the Finnish capital into a liminal setting with mythical undercurrents, in which different frontiers of the city come together in order to be transgressed. This had been the case in Arvid Järnefelt's *Veneh'ojalaiset* ("The Family Veneh'oja"; 1909), in which a nocturnal journey by stolen rowing boat to the fortress of Viapori/Suomenlinna, undertaken by the two young protagonists, is structured as a descent into liminal space in which boundaries are crossed and in which a potent secret of the city is gradually revealed (see the previous chapter).

In several other novels from the first half of the twentieth century, the Helsinki sea shore carries connotations of a threshold, in which the menace of death looms large. In Helvi Hämäläinen's *Säädyllinen murhenäytelmä* (1941), one of the two protagonists, Tauno, is contemplating suicide on the ramparts of Kaivopuisto (Hämäläinen 1941b: 179–181). In the short prose and poetry collection *Tulta ja tuhkaa* by Iris Uurto (1930), several references to suicide by drowning in the sea can be found in relation to the Helsinki waterfront, amongst others in connection to a long urban walk that includes Kaivopuisto (Uurto 1930: 12, 32).[33] In Mika Waltari's Helsinki novel *Appelsiininsiemen* ("The Orange Seed"; 1931), which was written some years following *Suuri illusioni*, the waterfront at Kaivopuisto is again related to death, this time the death of a minor character – the brother of one of the protagonists – who died from pneumonia after playing around on thin ice in front of Kaivopuisto (Waltari 1931: 149). All three novels of Waltari's Helsinki trilogy include life-threatening storms situated on or near the Helsinki seashore, which take on increasing symbolic potential. The first novel of the trilogy, *Mies ja haave* ("A Man and his Dream"; 1933), features a scene of a storm over Helsinki, in which the protagonist's boys are at sea while the worried parents look on helplessly at the frightening scene from the safety of the Kruununhaka shore; the passage constitutes a turning point in the life of the protagonist, Elias, who turns to God (Waltari 1933: 320–325). In the subsequent *Sielu ja liekki* ("The Soul and the Flame"; 1934), the protagonist Toivo is surprised by a sudden storm while hunting birds on the islands in the vicinity of Helsinki (Waltari 1934: 268–271). The final novel, *Palava nuoruus* ("Burning Youth"; 1935) ends with an apocalyptic storm over Helsinki, which foreshadows the coming world fire.

Thoughts Breaking off in Mid-Sentence

As has become apparent when discussing the "correspondence method" and the "inward" or "aestheticist turn" above, the urban experience in *Suuri illusioni* and other Helsinki novels of its time is not only visible on the level of subject matter that is thematized, but also on the stylistic and formal level. In Waltari's debut novel, the city attains such a prominent position that it begins to exert a direct influence on the way in which the protagonist expresses his experiences.[34] The sentence structure repeatedly reflects the fragmentary spatial perception of the protagonist in the form of elliptic clauses, and the protagonist states explicitly that it is the city which is responsible for the fragmentary way in which he talks and thinks. The following fragment, in which Hart has just heard that Hellas has fallen severely ill after a nocturnal swim clearly modelled on their earlier, joint swim, deserves a closer look:

> Dark, autumnal night. The pale, fragile light of the street lamps. Black trees. Hellas. The thoughts in his utterly exhausted soul. His bitterness. Caritas. Dark, open sea. The lights of Suomenlinna receding far away in the darkness.
>
> We got a taxi, and the bustle in the street brought me back to my normal state of mind, that of a nervous inhabitant of the metropolis who is unable to think his thoughts to their end, and whose sentences are short and break off in the middle. (Waltari 1928: 122–123)[35]

The opening sentences of the quotation above render the fragmentary thoughts of the protagonist, who has just heard the news that Hellas is severely ill. These disconnected images relate to at least three separate, but intertwining time frames: they are images of what the protagonist remembers of earlier events (their joint swim in the sea), what Hart imagines to have happened during the night of Hellas's solitary swim, and the city images seen simultaneously by the protagonist while he considers these things. In this short fragment, the overlapping of images and experiences related to different moments in time is fairly complex, and rendered, moreover, in a narration that jumbles the chronological order of the narrative. The chronological order of the described events is as follows: Hart hears of Hellas's illness, after which he leaves his home and takes a taxi. In the taxi he returns again to his "normal state of mind, that of a nervous inhabitant of the metropolis" who thinks in fragmented sentences. At this point, images flash through his mind – things Hart simultaneously remembers, imagines and notices. In terms of the order of the narration, the chronology is disrupted. Firstly, the narrator gives a selection of disparate images in elliptic sentences ("Dark, autumnal night…"). In the following paragraph, the narrator recounts how he takes a taxi, and reflects on the way in which the city influences his thoughts and verbal capacities ("We got a taxi …"). It is in this second paragraph that the narrator partly explains the fragmentary images in the preceding paragraph: these are the impressions of an inhabitant of the city, thoughts that are unfinished, sentences that break off in the middle.

The quoted passage illustrates the point it makes: that the city has a disruptive influence on the capacity of the protagonist to place and voice his experiences. Moreover, it is a passage which is exemplary of the consequences of the "correspondence method", the narrative method used to describe the city through an interiorized consciousness. During the shortest possible moments of observation, a whole world of memories, images and descriptions is opened up, and the time experience becomes that of a Bergsonian "expanding internal time (*durée*)".[36]

The influence of the city is not only visible in the sentence structure, but also in the figural language used in the novel. The metaphors and similes used in *Suuri illusioni* draw repeatedly on the semantic fields of urban and technological concepts. In Finnish prose literature from the turn of the twentieth century the urban experience had been commonly expressed in metaphors drawn from a rural context: characters moving to the city are described as uprooted trees, and the confused environment of urban night life is rendered in terms of river rapids and a maelstrom. Even an author such as Toivo Tarvas, born in Helsinki and taking urban material as his subject, typically describes urban phenomena using figural language taken from nature, rather than the other way round. In Waltari's debut novel, however, the impression of a café enters the protagonist's consciousness "bitter like cocaine" (Waltari 1928: 194); a beloved woman is extolled as "the light of car lamps and the red eye of a watchtower over the dark sea" (ibid.: 66); a sudden new emotion is described as "a rhythm [that] began to resound in my soul like the jangle of metal hammers" (ibid.: 76), and the Helsinki city air is described as "a blend of raw spirits and lemon soda" (ibid.: 81).[37] When Hart and Caritas immerse themselves in Paris nightlife, they are pictured as being "taken along by the metropolitan night like particles of metal dust swept in the mouth of a giant vacuum cleaner under the arc lights of an industrial workshop" (ibid.: 225–226).[38]

According to Hart, the rumble of the metropolis "numbs all the senses and destroys thoughts, creating fragmentary clauses" (ibid.: 186),[39] and under the influence of the city, he literally begins to speak the language of the city, using figural language taken from the domain of urbanity and technology to express his feelings and observations. Similarly, in works written in the wake of *Suuri illusioni*, the urban reality is described using technological and urban metaphorical terms: in Kivimaa's *Epäjumala* ("Idol"; 1930), for example, the love of a woman is described as an airplane (Kivimaa 1930: 315–316).

The metaphors from the urban and technological field above are related to what has been called the "machine romantics" of the Torch Bearer generation, which has been discussed mostly in relation to poetry (see Lappalainen 1990: 95–97). The romanticizing vision of machinery in Finnish texts of the 1920s was mostly concerned with devices of locomotion, such as trains, cars and airplanes, and at least partly symptomatic of an optimistic view of society's progress and of a global humankind (Koskela 1999b: 270). A residue of the 1920s machine romantics can still be clearly seen in Waltari's *Appelsiininsiemen* (1931), for example in the excited associations evoked by cars (Waltari 1931: 8, 97), but in *Palava nuoruus* (1935), which in part is an autobiographical commentary on Waltari's own involvement with the 1920s literary movement, the narrator distances himself from the superficiality of the Torch Bearers' exoticism (Waltari 1935: 243–246).[40]

The Nocturnal Car Drive

As part of the new urban aesthetics expressed in the literature of this period, a new pivotal urban experience appears: that of the city at night seen from the window of a speeding car. In several novels and short stories, the nocturnal car drive serves as a node with various functions. As a liminal space, part private, part public, it performs the function of a space of transgression, with clear sensual and sexual undercurrents. In such scenes, the closed car takes on the function – similar to the city as a whole – of a transitory space of sexual possibilities. Characteristically, the automobile is described in Arvi Kivimaa's novel *Epäjumala* ("Idol"; 1930) as "the modern magnet", and the owner of a car is, by consequence, "always surrounded by girls" (Kivimaa 1930: 65).[41] Again in Karri's *Sodoma*, the car is seen as symptomatic of a new, modern relationship between men and women, for whom "the scene [for lovemaking] could be as easily a taxi as anything else" (Karri 1929: 102).[42]

The nocturnal car drive functions as a crucial symbol of speed and urbanity, through which the experience of the city is filtered. When the protagonists are transported by taxi through the dark city, the view of Helsinki becomes symbolic of modern urban life itself: defined by speed, and by the sudden appearance of disparate impressions that fade away as fast as they have appeared. The effect is one of disorientation, and the specific characteristics of this mode of transport affect the protagonist's capacity to read the urban environment. In Unto Karri's *Sodoma* ("Sodom"; 1929), for example, the speeding car has a drugging effect on the protagonist, who "felt that he was sinking down, as if in ether or in infinite space" (Karri 1929: 45).[43] The description of the city seen through the window of a speeding car tends to emphasize the experience of speed and the fragmentary and fleeting nature of the observations, and the resulting experience is repeatedly described in what can be called an "impressionist", elliptic and predominantly nominal style.

The nocturnal car drive in Finnish prose literature can be considered, like the walk along the Esplanade in earlier decades, as a highly programmed bourgeois ritual. The view seen from the car window tends to include particular geographical highlights, such as the scenery of the Töölö Bay and the clock of the central railway station. The events unfolding in the privacy of the car typically follow a more or less predictable order. From the moment a man and woman enter the car, the sense that moral borders are about to be transgressed, together with spatial and perhaps even social boundaries, becomes evident, and more often than not, they eventually embrace each other.

In Toivo Tarvas's 1916 novel *Eri tasoilta* ("On Different Levels"), all prototypical elements of the car drive are present. In a revealing scene, two of the protagonists, Martta and Albert, take a taxi through Helsinki at night. In the preceding passages, tension had been building up between the two of them; Martta is in love with Albert, while Albert is frustrated in his love for another girl, Ebba. Both know that Ebba is, at the very same moment, in a second taxi together with their common friend Urho, and the knowledge of what might be happening there adds extra suspense to the scene. The car's speed and the flashes of light seen through the window create a profound feeling of disorientation: "The street lamps flashed by as if they were fiery balls in space. He could not see anything else, because the speed was so high that everything else changed into a fuzzy chaos" (Tarvas 1916a: 101).[44] Amidst this disorientation, moral restraints fade, and Martta kisses Albert. Significantly, the journey ends in the private apartment of Martta at Museokatu, in Töölö, an apartment which exhibits an exotic atmosphere similar to the one found later, in *Suuri illusioni*, in Mrs. Spindel's apartment.

In *Suuri illusioni*, the nocturnal car drive constitutes the first intimate encounter between the protagonist Hart and the femme fatale Caritas. As the guests at Mrs. Spindel's party run out of alcohol, they take a taxi to a working-class district to buy illegal alcohol. The depiction of the nocturnal drive contains all the elements typical for such scenes. The drive entails a crossing of spatial divides, partly along the fault lines of the city's social geography: the street name mentioned is Vladimirinkatu (present-day Kalevankatu), but reference is made also to "a half-shaded row of lights at the other side of the Long Bridge" (Waltari 1928: 21).[45] Significantly, mention of the lower class districts in this context is not related to moral or social indignation: the lower class characters and interiors are pure scenery, serving the fantasy of the protagonists who look at their journey to the working-class district as if they were "slumming". The speed of the car, the sensuous atmosphere brought about by the suggestive light effect, the jostling movement the two people are subjected to, their physical closeness – Caritas is described as "becoming squeezed almost against me" (Waltari 1928: 21)[46] – all lead to the almost inevitable outcome, and they kiss. The way in which the journey is experienced highlights the illusory aspect of what is happening, and the extent to which it is created by the fragmentary impressions of the outside, nocturnal world, filtered through the window of the speeding car: "the light of a street lamp flashing by brought a strange gleam to her eyes" (ibid.: 24).[47]

A variety of novels appearing in the 1930s contain similar experiences. In Waltari's *Appelsiininsiemen* (1931), the protagonists Irene and Ilmari let themselves be driven aimlessly in a taxi through Helsinki by night. In a certain respect part of the drive is programmed – the tour around Eläintarha and the Töölö Bay can be found already in Leino's "Päivä Helsingissä" ("A Day in Helsinki"; 1905), which featured a nocturnal drive in a horse-drawn carriage through Helsinki. The experience of the city as seen through the perspective of the window of a moving car is rendered in a particular stylistic register, with elliptic clauses and an enumeration of successive nouns:

> The clock showed almost half past four; she could see it in the jolting corner of the street Kluuvikatu, the shiny black street, puddles, autumn lamps, like endless, terrifying balls, in the tossing and turning buzz of the car. (Waltari 1931: 332)[48]

Particular modes of transport can have considerable importance also for the literary techniques rendering the urban environment: the experience of the tram, most typically, has given rise to a particular, almost syncopated, description of the modern urban experience.[49] The same can be said of the experience of the nocturnal car drive. One of the interesting effects of the style Waltari uses to describe it is the dominance of nominal constructions ("black street, puddles, autumn lamps" etc.), which continues in the rest of the passage from Appelsiininsiemen, and recurs later in the novel. In the subsequent passage, which continues from the description of the car drive quoted above, the excitement felt by Irene, and the succession of her transitory impressions, are all expressed by an enumeration of nouns in a sentence that lacks a verb: "A car running wild in the street at night, the invisible autumn sky, lamps flashing by, the brightness of alcohol in her brains." (Waltari 1931: 333)[50]

Often, one of the few stable references to the physical surroundings is the mention of lighted public clocks in highly visible places, which offers a rare anchoring point in time and space. In *Suuri illusioni*, too, the protagonist Hart notices the clock of the railway station tower:

> The lighted clock dial of the railway square had flashed past us, and had imprinted upon the retina of my eye its yellowish after-image.
> "The moon of a modern landscape," I said. (Waltari 1928: 22)[51]

In the early decades of the twentieth century, the synchronized movement of the urban masses, directed by universally timed clocks, exerted a powerful influence on writers and filmmakers alike (see Prakash 2010: 3). In passages such as the one above, however, the clock would seem to function as a symbol of something different: it is an indication of the extent to which the protagonists, during the nocturnal car drive, are actually outside of the normally timed routines. Public clocks had functioned as important benchmarks in the life of the earliest *flâneurs*, too, and they had been indicative of the *flâneur's* interest in new technology and of the increasing importance of accurate time keeping (Wilson 1992: 94). In passages such as the one above, there is a further important dimension to the mention of the railway clock: what is highlighted is not so much the image of the clock itself, but that of the railway station and its tower, two of the penultimate images of urbanity and of the city's drive towards verticality and speed (see Laine 2011).

In a similar scene in the novel *Epäjumala* ("Idol"; 1930), the protagonist Markus takes a taxi together with Marcelle, the woman he has become infatuated with, and they drive aimlessly through the city. The female character is described as in charge of the situation: it is Marcelle who has given the order to the taxi driver to make a detour. In several novels discussed above, the woman seems as much, if not more, the instigator and seducer as the man; in Tarvas's *Eri tasoilta*, for example, Martta takes the active part. During the car drive in *Epäjumala*, furtive lights shine in through the window, and there is a vision of the railway station tower clock. Tension builds up, and they kiss (Kivimaa 1930: 81–87). Here, as in the other excerpts discussed, the scene is drenched in a sensuality that is in part rooted in the idea that the closed car presents a semi-public, semi-private environment which facilitates the transgression of moral borders.

In almost all cases (Ilmari and Irene in *Appelsiininsiemen* are the exception), the love between the man and woman involved is illicit; this is particularly true for Kivimaa's *Epäjumala*, in which Markus's beloved Marcelle is already committed.[52] Similarly, in Kivimaa's slightly later short story "Irja" ("Irja"; 1931), the taxi is the spatial environment in which the protagonist seduces Irja, the woman he has loved long ago, but who has since married another man. The passionate feelings of the protagonist are described in part through a description of the urban environment and the swinging movement of the car, and here, as in Kivimaa's *Epäjumala*, the sensuous atmosphere is juxtaposed with a dense fog as they drive near the Kaivopuisto waterfront (Kivimaa 1930: 116, 1931: 112).

There is another illicit dimension to the transitory bond created between man and woman in the confined space of a speeding car: in several texts, there is a considerable class difference between both. In *Appelsiininsiemen* the man, Ilmari, can be seen as something of a social riser, while the social divide is most explicit in *Eri tasoilta* ("On Different Levels"; Tarvas 1916a), which by its very title accentuates the inseparable differences of social class, imprinted in culture as well as in genetic outlook. In this novel, the intimacy between Martta and Albert is described as socially and culturally impossible, but in the illusory setting of the speeding car, such restraints can temporarily be put aside. In *Epäjumala*, the divide that is crossed in the taxi is the cultural and political abyss opening up between people from different nationalities. Especially for people who have no private spaces at their disposal, the taxi offers an opportunity to indulge in a rare intimacy. In Unto Karri's 1929 novel *Sodoma* ("Sodom"), the two protagonists Alli and Martti have no place to go, since they both share apartments with other people; for them, the car becomes a refuge, and within it, they become as if "outside of the whole society, people without home and without position" (Karri 1929: 121).[53] The car here becomes a surrogate for the home that is out of reach of the protagonists. Amidst the rocking movement and the feeling of rush brought about by the car, Alli and Martti fall asleep together (ibid.: 123).

The motif of illicit love performed in the closed confines of a carriage moving aimlessly through the city is, of course, much older than texts from the 1910s, 1920s and 1930s: one of the most famous instances can be found in Flaubert's *Madame Bovary* (1856/1996), and, as Angela Moorjani has pointed out in relation to this novel, the carriage as "a vehicle of seduction" has a long tradition as "one of the most persistent codes of erotic literature" (Moorjani 1980: 50). More generally, as Mieke Bal points out, events that are set in "vehicles of transportation, such as trains, boats, carriages, airplanes […] temporarily suspend the safe predictability and clarity of the social order" (Bal 2009: 222). Different kinds of vehicles convey, of course, different connotations: there are considerable differences between the images evoked by the kind of horse-drawn and typically closed carriage in nineteenth-century literature, and the speeding cars of the inter-war period, with their windows conspicuously opened to the outside urban world. In inter-war Helsinki novels, the sensuous atmosphere in a speeding car moving through the city at night entails a profound longing for a somewhere else, and an acute sense of being part of a new time frame. As he embraces Marcelle, Markus in *Epäjumala* feels that his world is set loose from that of an earlier generation: "Their world was dead, Markus's world was moving, flying; every moment it conquered something new and borderless" (Kivimaa 1930: 85).[54] In the image of the car speeding through the city night, two urges come together: the transgression of moral boundaries in a sensuous and illicit encounter, and the desire to embrace a world in relentless motion of which the city had become the symbol.

Little wonder that car outings were frowned upon by Helsinki citizens trying to uphold old-fashioned moral standards. More than a decade before Waltari's *Suuri illusioni*, Maila Talvio's novel *Niniven lapset* (1915) presents an image of private car outings as a symbol of moral evil. In the novel, Daniel, the youngest of the family Ståhle (see Chapter 6), imagines he is a present-day Jonah, who has been called upon to warn the citizens of modern Nineveh to renounce their sins. One of the ways in which Daniel carries out this mission is to try to prevent the inhabitants of "Metropolis" (the name given to Helsinki in this novel) from taking Sunday trips to the countryside; in his effort to stop their cars on the roads leading out of the city, he is almost run over (Talvio 1915: 284–287). Interestingly, Daniel is also concerned with the sensuous atmosphere that reigns in the crowded public-space-in-motion of the tram. When he sees what he interprets to be a young girl flirting with a ticket salesman on the tram, he tries to interfere in a dramatic attempt to ward of God's impending anger with the city (ibid.: 316). In Waltari's *Appelsiininsiemen* (1931), too, the tram is linked to loosening sexual morals. The novel's protagonist, young Irene, thinks of the nearness of the unknown people around her as arousing (Waltari 1931: 8). In the description of her awakening feelings of lust, the reader also learns that in the public and crowded space of public transport, even respectable-looking men give loose rein to their instincts: "And those men, often so old and looking so respectable, that you never would have believed that they are the kind that moved their hands around and touched her in a manner that disgusted and petrified her" (ibid.: 96).[55]

Aestheticizing "New Helsinki" and *Helvi Hämäläinen's* Säädyllinen murhenäytelmä *(1941)*

In Helsinki literature of the 1920s and 1930s the literary descriptions often focus not so much on Helsinki as on a limited and very specific part of the Finnish capital: the district of Töölö. This relatively new part of the city was widely seen as the quintessential scene of a triumphal architectural march towards modernity, in part since it was laid out on the basis of the very first urban planning competition in Finland (Bell & Hietala 2002: 163). Several narrators in this period feel it necessary to explicate (often repeatedly) that their characters live in Töölö. In Arvi Kivimaa's *Epäjumala*, for example, the narrator recounts even at a late stage in the novel that the protagonist Markus "left his Töölö apartment" (Kivimaa 1930: 252). Several novels of this period begin with a scene set in Töölö: at the beginning of the novel *Uni* ("Dream"; 1930), by Elsa Soini, the protagonist is introduced as an independent woman, living on her own in a two-room apartment in Töölö; Arvi Kivimaa's novel *Hetki ikuisen edessä* ("A Moment before Eternity; 1932) opens, after a prologue, with a description of the protagonist standing at a tram stop in Mechelininkatu in Töölö (Kivimaa 1932: 21). At the beginning of a later novel by the same author, *Viheriöivä risti* ("The Blooming Cross"; 1939), the protagonist, a young medical student, is living in a flat in Töölö.

Mika Waltari's Helsinki, in particular, is anchored in this new part of Helsinki.[56] Regardless of the fact that his characters journey through all parts of the capital, they almost invariably come home to Töölö. *Suuri illusioni*, of course, opens with the scene at Mrs. Spindel's salon, which most readers could be expected to situate in Töölö.[57] In Waltari's consecutive Helsinki novel, *Appelsiininsiemen* (1931), the protagonist Irene grows up in Töölö, and when she marries Ilmari, the young couple acquires a double-roomed flat in the northern part of Töölö, "exactly as they had planned" (Waltari 1931: 363).[58] In *Palava nuoruus*, the recently married couple Juhani and Kyllikki self-evidently move into an apartment in Töölö, in Mechelininkatu (Waltari 1935: 417), a street which is mentioned by Ilmari in *Appelsiininsiemen* as an example of successful modern architecture in Töölö, and along which, in the same novel, the apartment of the degenerate Kurt Waldhof is also situated. Aarni, the protagonist of Kivimaa's *Hetki ikuisen edessä*, also lives in Mechelininkatu, and he shares with Kurt Waldhof and Irene in *Appelsiininsiemen* a view of the Helsinki crematorium, which, like Töölö itself, was an architectural reminder of modernizing attitudes.

Töölö is repeatedly described as a new city, in tune with the modern age, and befitting a young nation. Literary descriptions of this part of the capital tend to focus on experiences of acute novelty, such as in Kivimaa's *Viheriöivä risti* (1939), set in the late 1920s, which describes Töölö as "full of white walls that had just risen up, full of scaffolding and the rattle of machines" (Kivimaa 1939: 24).[59] The experience of modern architecture and city planning was not unambiguously positive, however. In Kivimaa's *Hetki ikuisen edessä*, Töölö is also described as "cold and lifeless", and as "a messily created environment" – little wonder the main character, who considers the city "the murderer of real life", does not thrive there (Kivimaa 1932: 76–77).[60] An elderly character such as the professor in Waltari's *Appelsiininsiemen* sees Töölö as part of a whole litany of modernity, and as one of the many recent rationalizing processes that aim to make life more practical:

> Cars had come, and new, American trams, Töölö was born. Central heating, central kitchens, two-room apartments, the civil guard, conscription, compulsory education, small farmers, childless marriages, divorces, Prohibition, the black market, criminality, knife fights. All those things that one could endlessly enumerate. The socialization and rationalization of life. (Waltari 1931: 88)[61]

The list of the professor is surprisingly heterogeneous, but for an understanding of how Töölö was experienced, the first three concepts mentioned in immediate succession are of considerable interest: "Central heating, central kitchens, two-room apartments". The buildings of Töölö were designed for a new generation, for young couples who did not keep a maid (hence the central kitchen, from which all inhabitants could order their meals); they were smaller than the traditional bourgeois homes, but considerably better furnished and larger than the working-class homes. Töölö was indeed the architectural embodiment of the "socialization and rationalization of life", or as Olavi Paavolainen described it in the highly ironical poem

"Helsinki by Night", Töölö was as much as "the ideal-mechanic-machine-rational-city", the highlight of any touristic tour through Helsinki (Paavolainen 1929: 40–41).[62]

The specific nature of Töölö as a "New Helsinki", in the sense both of a new architectural totality and of a new living style, is evoked in detail in Helvi Hämäläinen's *Säädyllinen murhenäytelmä*. Töölö is literally described in the novel as the New Helsinki (Hämäläinen 1941a: 30–31), and its typical characteristics are given in a long passage, of which here only a fragment:

> New Helsinki is full of whims, but it is cheerful and funny in comparison to the old and heavy Helsinki of the last century, which [...] was grim, dark, unhealthy, and which made a sharp division between eight-room apartments and small apartments with only one or two rooms. [...] Old Helsinki does not in the least know those small and cheerful, clean and cosy apartments, which fill New Helsinki, but old Helsinki did not know that human breed that lives in them either: educated women providing for themselves and couples of which both man and woman work at an office outside their home. (Hämäläinen 1941a: 31–32)[63]

This new part of the city, where the female protagonist Naimi lives, is described later in the same passage as the "New Helsinki of the '30s, which has opened up like a garden flower, joyfully coloured, sunny, practical and impractical, in love with everything that is new this very moment, and with what it thinks to be surprising" (Hämäläinen 1941a: 32).[64] Töölö is described as a part of the city that has come into being together with the new generation whose lifestyle it makes possible. Young couples from the educated class, like Irene and Ilmari in *Appelsiininsiemen*, could move to small and comfortable apartments, and for the new generation of independent white-collar women working out of the home, Töölö provided better housing conditions than the oversized bourgeois houses in the centre, or the overcrowded houses in working-class districts.

Amongst the novels thematizing Helsinki in Finnish literature of this period, Helvi Hämäläinen's *Säädyllinen murhenäytelmä* (1941) occupies a special position.[65] The narrator describes Töölö in the passage quoted above, but it is suggested that at least part of the observations are filtered through the perspective of the female protagonist Naimi. The city is described from a perspective that is detached, and includes comments on the historical, aesthetical and social features of "New Helsinki", but as the narration evolves and gradually moves more firmly into Naimi's perspective, a personal and emotional attachment with the city becomes equally apparent. The city is conceived as the creation of, and in part a commentary upon, current socio-economic conditions (the buildings of Töölö as signs of a new kind of middle class), but also as a personally experienced, cherished environment. Throughout the novel, there is a constant play between a view of the city as seen through a filter of temporal and aestheticizing distance, and the more immediate and often intimate experience of everyday city walks.

Säädyllinen murhenäytelmä recounts the story of several reclusive characters, Naimi Saarinen and her brother Tauno, and their respective spouses, Artur and Elisabet. From the perspective of Helsinki experiences, Naimi and Tauno are the most interesting characters. Both are out of tune with their time, and they feel more connected with the values of an earlier era. This, however, does not keep them from indulging in an eagerness to aestheticize their immediate surroundings, which include the "New Helsinki" of the Töölö district they both inhabit. Naimi has never recovered from an intense love relationship which ended twenty years earlier, and which involved Artur, the man to whom she is still married.[66] The part of the narration told from Naimi's perspective can be read as the attempt of an aging woman to come to terms with her memories and to find ways in which she can reconcile the past, which she wants to conserve, with the present that imposes itself upon her. Naimi's brother Tauno is an archaeologist employed in a museum, whose respectable marriage gradually falls to pieces when he becomes infatuated with the neighbours' maid. The girl becomes pregnant and Tauno tries desperately to uphold a sense of respectability by attempting to separate the high-minded world of his senses from the reality posed by the formalities of his marriage, and the consequences of his extramarital affair. Both Naimi's and Tauno's quest is not only to live through the "respectable tragedy" of marital relationships running aground, but to weld together the radiant world of their vivid imagination and memories with prosaic and everyday realities.

To a large extent, the relationship between literary characters and the city is rendered in *Säädyllinen murhenäytelmä* by way of the "correspondence method", the mode of spatial emplotment discussed earlier in this chapter, by which the protagonist's inner mood is described through his/her spatial surroundings. In the opening pages of the novel, for example, the city street is described in terms that are attuned to the uncertain feelings of expectation experienced by Tauno, an elderly man with a doctorate in the arts, as he turns a corner with the aim to see the girl he has secretly fallen in love with. The street, which the doctor is well acquainted with, appears suddenly "strangely real", and "odd and slender shadows" are seen on the walls and the asphalt (Hämäläinen 1941a: 17).[67] In a more explicit passage, Tauno's wife Elisabet reflects on how her surroundings have changed after she received the news that Tauno's mistress is pregnant:

> Elisabet was afraid to look around [...] so that she did not have to feel the terrible wound in her heart [...], due to which the landscape of her soul had changed so much that her everyday surroundings, where she had until now happily moved about and onto which she had projected her inner self, had become painful, and incorporated with every step a terrible suffering, memories of her marriage and of love [...]." (Hämäläinen 1941b: 31–32)[68]

The everyday surroundings of Elisabet are explicitly described as environments onto which she projects her "inner self", a landscape that is intimately intertwined with the "landscape of her soul". Changes in her inner landscape radically transform her everyday surroundings, which become "with every step" an embodiment of the betrayal of her husband. In other scenes, too, the mood of particular characters in the novel is similarly reflected in the description of elements from the city's surroundings: Naimi, for example, thinks her brother's family life resembles the well-organized rose garden at the Helsinki Botanical Garden: "far too perfectly beautiful and silent" (Hämäläinen 1941a: 85).[69] Lauri Viljanen has pointed out that in Hämäläinen's novel, the voluptuous description of characters' surroundings functions as a technique similar to that of the stream of consciousness: "a highly sensuous and particularly visual artist, she [Hämäläinen] 'plucks' sensations from her characters' environment, from their rooms, streets, and from their gardens especially, and projects these unrelentingly and continuously onto their soul" (Viljanen 1959: 197).

The interaction between inner mood and outward space is not only invoked by the narrator, but also, and repeatedly so, by the characters themselves, in particular by Naimi. In *Säädyllinen murhenäytelmä*, the main characters consciously construct their spatial surroundings as repositories of their memory: the apartment Naimi inhabits is arranged as a personal museum landscape, reminiscent of her lost love, and the countryside home of Naimi's beloved Artur is a similar artificially conserved space. Most of the lengthy and meticulous spatial descriptions in the novel focus on elements that evoke the aging world of the protagonists, their bygone values, memories, stories and objects. The city is only one of the many elements that are aestheticized through the idealizing veil through which the protagonists view their surroundings: objects, plants, furniture, as well as the built and natural spaces of Helsinki are described in painstaking detail, half-imaginary spaces in which the protagonists wilfully retreat. "And everything that used to be feels precious" – the narrative comment when Naimi hears and sees her beloved Artur for the first time in twenty years – can be considered as one of the guiding principles in this novel (Hämäläinen 1941a: 166).[70] The undertone is that of a powerful sense of loss that is retained in the objects and landscapes surrounding the literary characters: "lost, forever lost, the golden polish of the sand beneath" (Hämäläinen 1941b: 214),[71] as Artur's aging mother thinks when considering how her life, which is nearing its end, has run its course.

Particular buildings, panoramas and parts of the city act as reminders of times gone by, while others are symbolic of the modern age which has in part swept past the protagonists, and in part taken them along. Töölö takes on a very special role in this novel, not only because it is the part of the city in which both protagonists live (Naimi and Tauno), but also due to its typical buildings, the style of living it represents, and its spatial planning. On the one hand, Töölö exemplifies a new and modern way of urban life (see, for example, the quote above, in which Töölö is described as a New Helsinki), while on the other hand it symbolizes bourgeois moral values, and the ideal of a particular kind of decent middle-class life with its strict moral boundaries, and the "respectability" of bourgeois marriage, despite the tragedies that are played out behind these façades.

Tauno's and Naimi's sense of urban space is formed according to daily walks in their immediate surroundings. In the case of Tauno, these give form to a limited geographical world, focused on the short daily walk in the little park in Topeliuksenkatu, a street situated in Töölö (Hämäläinen 1941a: 57); Naimi, on the other hand, is a more avid city walker, who exhibits a keen interest in her immediate surroundings, and who displays an intimate knowledge of the city. The walk around the Töölö Bay, in particular, constitutes one of her crucial spatial routines. Her relationship with the urban surroundings, and the way in which Naimi sees objects as referring to another time, is aptly summed up in the following passage, which describes the Karamzin Mansion, on the south-eastern edge of Töölö:

> She knew it [the mansion] in all of the variety brought about by changing weather or light. When passing by, she rejoiced if the moonlight caressed its yellow walls or rested on the black roof; the building was alive to her in rain and in sunshine. It was the only building in Helsinki which seemed to her filled with soulful shadows: she looked at it as if it were an object which the dead had left on the earth […]; the building enclosed, untouched, a life gone by, whose events and whose thread nobody possessed any longer. It was to her the box of life, which has to be lost. (Hämäläinen 1941a: 82)[72]

Naimi reads this old building as if it were "an object which the dead had left on earth"; a box for her to open, a world to rejoice in, but also something that will inevitably be lost. Naimi does not feel outright love for Helsinki – she describes Helsinki as lacking a soul, a city that seems "too barren and hard" (see above, Hämäläinen 1941a: 78)[73] – but she does find meaning in the city. The detailed description of Karamzin's mansion illustrates that her knowledge of the city is based on walks in every season, day and night, and in all weather conditions ("She knew it [the mansion] in all of the variety brought about by changing weather or light"). Naimi even occasionally acts as a guide to the city: she mentions in passing that she has shown a Romanian journalist around in the Finnish capital (ibid.: 168). Naimi Saarinen is one of the few characters in the literature of this period who combines a detached panoramic vision of the city with the kind of engaged and everyday view that is enacted on ground level, a double epistemological approach that is expressed in the following:

> There were no buildings in Helsinki which she would have loved – but she loved the profiles of Helsinki, the one in which the black needle of Töölö's church thrust its narrow spike up in the air, or the one which opened up above the playground at the end of Hesperiankatu, during a moment when the air was pregnant with blue and grey; profiles in which Helsinki showed her its face differently, and always uncovered new features. And then she loved Helsinki's trees, the parks at Observatory Hill and Kaivopuisto were a thing apart, but she loved the poplars in Hesperia park, the larches and bird-cherries, especially the one which was close to that only soulful building, the Karamzin Mansion. (Hämäläinen 1941a: 81)[74]

Although the narrator states that there are "no buildings in Helsinki which she would have loved", the experience of Helsinki's built environment is not lacking in positive emotions, as the mention of the Karamzin Mansion makes clear. It is not so much buildings with which Naimi experiences a strong bond, however: she does love what she calls the "profiles" of Helsinki, and what are in effect mini-panoramas in which she sees the ever-changing face of Helsinki. Naimi returns repeatedly to this idea of Helsinki as a face that shows different profiles she feels strongly attached to; and these again are mostly related to Töölö. Immediately preceding the passage above, she describes several Helsinki profiles in detail (ibid.: 80–81), and a reference to one of her favourite profiles across the Töölö Bay is made again later in the novel (ibid.: 145).

Helsinki as Urban Pastoral

One of the most striking features of the experience of the city in *Säädyllinen murhenäytelmä* is the strong attachment to particular, often individualized natural elements in the city, a literary experience of the city that can be described as "urban pastoral". The term "urban pastoral" has been used to describe a variety of approaches to the city in literature, referring, *inter alia*, to Wordsworth's poetry (Steinman 2012), to a movement of New York poetry (Gray 2010), and to the experience of London in Virginia Woolf's *Mrs. Dalloway* (Alter 2005: 103–121). Here, my use of the term urban pastoral closely resembles Robert Alter's use of the term in his reading of *Mrs. Dalloway* (1925), in which he notes that instances of urban pastoral appear when the "urban experience, seen quite vividly in its abundant particularities, can provide the sense of invigoration, harmony with one's surroundings, and enrapturing aesthetic revelation that is traditionally associated with the green world of pastoral" (Alter 2005: 105). In the context of Helsinki novels, urban pastoral provides a useful concept for describing the particular kind of experience of the city to which a sense of natural cyclicality is restored. In texts drawing on realism and naturalism, nature and the city had become separated from each other, and it was in part in this violent separation that the sense of alienation experienced by turn-of-the-century characters in the industrialized city was rooted. Disconnected from more traditional cyclical processes, characters were forced to surrender to a linear movement of progress, which in individual cases tended to entail an entropic and downward trajectory.

In a novel such as Mika Waltari's *Suuri illusioni* (1928), the aestheticizing experience of the city substitutes a new mode of temporality for the lost natural cyclicality. As Bart Keunen points out, in self-referential urban texts, space "often loses its 'natural' and cyclical character [...] to make way for an internal cyclicality of the recurrent and repeatable psychic processes of observing and remembering" (Keunen 2001: 428). In *Suuri illusioni*, a single moment of observation opens up a whole number of temporal dimensions, past and present, without, however, restoring the lost sense of attachment to natural cycles. As the urban experience in *Säädyllinen murhenäytelmä* illustrates, however, an aestheticizing approach to the city could also restore the kind of intimate relationship with one's surroundings typical of the pastoral.

In the glimpses of urban pastoral visible in *Säädyllinen murhenäytelmä* and a few other Finnish prose texts in this period, the retreat, on the part of the protagonist, from the exigencies of the linear time of modernity is commensurate with a strong attachment to the cyclical, pastoral elements in the city. For most of the characters in *Säädyllinen murhenäytelmä*, the predominant sense of time is one detached from the modern, accelerating space of the "New Helsinki" in which they live. The repeated reference to clock towers in Hämäläinen's novel is an explicit reminder of the temporal difference between Naimi's experience of time and the modern city's time: Naimi, who visualizes herself as a kind of "bell tower" (Hämäläinen 1941a: 78–87), tries to keep a bygone time from receding beyond memory, while simultaneously, "in the clocks of the railway station and the Main Church, time was adrift" (Hämäläinen 1941a: 140).[75] Similarly, for Tauno's wife Elisabet, who has become aware of her husband's infidelity, time is a dangerous element, and as she ponders their disintegrating lives, time in the city moves on relentlessly: "outside, the heavy soft thumping of cars' rubber tires on the street, and the shrieking of brakes could be heard – the twentieth century was speeding forward, walking, making wheels crackle" (ibid.: 229).[76] All characters, Naimi and Tauno, as well as Artur and Elisabet and Artur's mother, live mummified lives in which they try to keep time from flowing. But if they aim to be detached from the temporalities set by the industrializing and modernizing city, these characters, and Naimi, in particular, have found ways to attach themselves to another kind of cyclicality: that of nature within the city. Through her intimate knowledge of the natural components of the city – specific trees, parks – Naimi's experience of the city restores a measure of attachment to nature's cyclical processes that seems to have been irretrievably lost in the modern city. Henri Lefebvre suggests that city gardens and parks essentially function as "a utopia of nature [...] against which urban reality can situate and perceive itself" (Lefebvre 2003: 26; see also Steele 2012: 182), and nature and city can be and often have been understood as radical opposites. However, as Richard Lehan points out, the city is also, paradoxically, "the place where man and nature meet" (Lehan 1998: 13), and, as all city dwellers know, intimacy with the city is not only expressed in knowledge of its built environment, but also in a familiarity with its physical features and natural elements.

In *Säädyllinen murhenäytelmä*, the main characters are not at odds with the urban environment in which they live, in part because they connect with the cyclical, natural time underneath the city's asphalt and stone. To Naimi and Tauno, trees and parks are not anonymous or interchangeable; they become individualized and are linked to their own personal life stories. A particular group of birch trees in a small Helsinki park in Topeliuksenkatu constitutes a favourite place, a kind of "landscape of the soul" for Tauno, who compares it with a landscape by the symbolist Finnish painter Hugo Simberg (Hämäläinen 1941a: 64).[77] When Naimi walks along the Töölö Bay, her steps take her along a road with "a large, familiar poplar", whose "luminous form of its top and yellow light-green stem were well-known to her from many morning and evening walks" (ibid.: 80–81).[78] When she walks to Observatory Hill, the trees in the park are not just trees, but described with precision as "birch trees and maples" (ibid.: 146).[79]

The intimate and detailed knowledge literary characters have of their city environments, often in relation to the natural environment (flowers, trees, parks) is one of the many urban *topoi* (in addition to *flânerie*, and a strong sense of attachment to the city) that were pioneered in Helsinki literature by Toivo Tarvas, and subsequently taken up by authors such as Iris Uurto, to reach a climax in Helvi Hämäläinen's *Säädyllinen murhenäytelmä*. In Toivo Tarvas's 1916 novel *Kohtalon tuulissa*, the protagonist Albert and his daughter walk through an enchanting summery Helsinki, and the various parks, with their abundance of flowers and specific smells are described in rich detail: the chestnut trees in the yard of the University Library, amongst others, and the lilac bushes of Kaivopuisto (Tarvas 1916b: 314–316). The narrator compares the view with that of the gardens of countryside vicarages – one of the central pastoral environments in Finnish literature (see Schildt 1912), to which the Finnish capital is favourably compared here. When, in Tarvas's story "Lumottu" ("Enchanted"), the protagonist Niilo takes a long walk through Helsinki at night to say goodbye to all the places he loves, special mention is given to the birch tree in the yard of his former school (Tarvas 1919: 90–92).

Even trees and natural elements that are no longer physically present can add meaning to the spatial experiences of literary characters, such as in a short story by Elvi Sinervo, in which a working-class woman goes for a walk with her daughter to the centre of the city and shows her the place where they used to live, and where there once stood a large mountain ash; the daughter tells her that she still remembers the tree and its suffocating smell in the summer (Sinervo 1937: 168). Depictions of the attachment to urban nature from the perspective of working-class characters, such as those found in Sinervo's collection of short stories *Runo Söörnäisistä* ("Poem about Sörnäinen"; 1937) tend to function as counter-currents to an otherwise alienating experience of the city: through a personally known natural element, the city becomes a personally lived and experienced place regardless of its dystopian characteristics.

In the Helsinki prose of Iris Uurto, the aestheticized attitude towards the city and the strong sense of emotional attachment exhibited by the protagonists is similarly visible in the description of trees. In *Ruumiin ikävä* ("The Longing of the Body"; 1930/1931), the enumeration of disparate elements rendering the feeling of a beautiful spring evening in Helsinki is completed with the mention of a "girl and a boy beneath the first linden tree of Bulevardi" (Uurto 1930/1931: 241).[80] Trees in the novel are described as acting like human beings, "stretching their bodies, opening their eyes" and seeking each other's intimacy (ibid.: 348).[81] In Uurto's subsequent Helsinki novel *Kypsyminen* ("Maturing"; 1935), there is a long description of a particular tree well-known to the protagonist Lauri:

> He knew the large bird-cherry, which was leaning over the street and the passers-by; in the spring it would take pleasure in silently dangling its fruit clusters while trams and cars were speeding past and its strong smell wafted through their open windows. Now the surface of the bird-cherry was black, it looked barren; Lauri noticed how it was desperately swinging its stiff branches in the wind. (Uurto 1935: 139)[82]

The emotions Lauri attaches to the tree are symptomatic of his own inner misery ("black", "barren", "desperate"), and the way in which the individualized tree reflects the literary character's inner feelings is entirely similar to comparable instances in the same novel and in contemporary texts, in which the urban environment resonates with the protagonist's mood. The intimate attachment to the city in such scenes is one of the more striking urban experiences in Helsinki novels of this period, and also one of the least recognized. It is a sense of attachment that does not make characters immune to dystopian or pessimistic experiences of the city, but that is nevertheless symptomatic of the more involved relationship with the city experienced by natives to Helsinki in this period, and that seems to be out of reach to the newcomers that had dominated prose texts from the turn of the century.

Conclusion

In Finnish literature of the 1920s and 1930s, a "New Helsinki" is celebrated, evoking new architectural forms and new modes of living, but also new experiences of the urban environment. What is most striking in many of the Helsinki novels that appeared in the late 1920s and 1930s is the new stylistic and thematic paradigm in which these experiences of the modern city are couched. Mika Waltari's *Suuri illusioni* is in many respects prototypical: set for the most part in Töölö, reverberating with distant and ancient city images, it is also a novel that describes characters' emotions through impressions of their spatial surroundings. It evokes a modern urban world by way of a fragmentary sentence structure and metaphors drawn from the urban and modern realm. The innovative formal features with which the city is rendered aim to evoke the experience of modernity, which is typically characterized by the "transient and 'fugitive' nature of encounters and impressions made in the city" (Wolff 1985: 38). In Waltari's debut novel, Helsinki is experienced as a constantly shifting palimpsestic text consisting of both real and imagined layers, and symptomatic of conscious aestheticizing and internalizing approaches to the city. The result is a fragmentary and kaleidoscopic mindscape, in which the literary characters' memories, fantasies and sensitive experiences become entangled with the city's mythical, historical and imaginary layers of meaning.

It is worth reiterating that many of the new literary experiences of Helsinki in this period were initiated in the literature of the preceding decades. In Toivo Tarvas's *Eri tasoilta* (1916a), one finds the kind of erotically charged nocturnal car drives, as well as *flâneur*-like city walks that would become more typical for 1920s and 1930s Helsinki literature. Similarly, a kind of "thrill of arrival" related to the return of the protagonist to the Finnish capital, which was typical of Helsinki novels of the 1920s, was already present in the opening scene of Eino Leino's 1914 novel *Pankkiherroja* ("Bank Lords"). A second observation is that the fascination with the city in Finnish prose texts in the wake of the Torch Bearer Movement is far from identical with an optimistic experience of the city. Even *Suuri illusioni* can be and has been read as a particularly gloomy reflection on the city (Liuttu 1950: 79–80; Koskela 1999b: 275), and the work of Arvi Kivimaa and Unto Karri shows both optimistic and distinctly pessimistic experiences of Helsinki (see Korsberg 2008). The experience of Helsinki continues to be one that includes both positive views, as well as near-apocalyptic views of a "degenerate city threatened by a flood of sin", to quote one critic of Martti Merenmaa's 1926 Helsinki novel *Nousuvesi*, a novel that shares traits with *Suuri illusioni* and *Sodoma* ("High Tide"; 1926; see Nieminen 1927: 388–389). One distinct feature of the urban experience in the Finnish literature of this period, and in Helvi Hämäläinen's novel *Säädyllinen murhenäytelmä* in particular, is the evocation of a sense of urban pastoral. In this particular kind of aestheticizing and interiorizing experience, the protagonists are reconciled to natural cyclicality through a profound attachment to the city.

Mika Waltari and Archaeology

Mika Waltari had become fascinated by the image of ancient cities at an early age (see for example his poem "Kuolleet kaupungit" ["Dead Cities"], published in 1928, the same year as Suuri illusioni), and he had a particular interest in archaeological findings and in ancient history, as can be witnessed from his later highly successful historical novels. Mika Waltari was one of the two editors of the Finnish translation of J. A. Hammerton's overview of archaeological finds *Wonders of the Past* (1923; published in Finnish as *Muinaisajan ihmeet* in 1934 and 1935). An archaeological find also features in Waltari's short story "The New Construction Site" ("Uusi rakennusmaa"; 1943, but written in 1936), in which a construction crew finds a Viking grave on a building site in Töölö. Under pressure to complete the job, the crew almost completely destroys the find, and the stones of the grave are turned into gravel for the new roads. To one of the workers, however, the find triggers a feeling of insignificance, but also a realization of the temporal depth of the city in which he lives.

Interest in archaeology can, of course, be found in Finnish literature in earlier years, too. Maila Talvio's *Niniven lapset* ("Children of Nineveh"; 1915) refers already in its title to the idea that an ancient city is underlying present-day Helsinki, and one of the minor characters in the novel is, in fact, an amateur archaeologist, whose return from a journey in the Middle East is described in some detail.

7. Towards the Margins
Cumbersome Movement through the Urban Fringes

The novel *Rakastunut rampa* ("A Cripple in Love"; 1922) by Joel Lehtonen[1] begins with the description of a disconcerting view, bordering on the grotesque. On a road at the outskirts of the Finnish capital, an animal-like being is slowly progressing:

> A strange being is walking along the road. Walking… or rather, moving. Leaping on all fours… He is like a dog or a hare.
> The road, lined by sombre fir trees, is receding into Autumnal fog, so that from afar, it is not possible to see him clearly. The only thing you can see is that it is some kind of being… a being that is hopping clumsily. (Lehtonen 1922/2006: 3)[2]

Seen from a distant vantage point, the narrator describes the appearance of the novel's eponymous protagonist: the poor and crippled Bolshevik Sakris Kukkelman, whose romantic love and Nietzsche-inspired high-minded ideas of self-fulfilment are doomed to tragically fail. Written only a few years after the end of the Finnish Civil War, the image of the deformed Bolshevik, cumbersomely but stubbornly making his way forward, must have struck some readers as distinctly *unheimlich* – a reminder of something repressed which reappears out of a strangely familiar landscape. But as Irma Perttula points out, the novel is not only about a rupture in describing the common people – a thematic that Lehtonen addresses repeatedly in his works – but also about a "new kind of aesthetics" (Perttula 2010: 104). Irma Perttula, in her study of the grotesque in Finnish literature, has given an extensive analysis of the figure of Sakris Kukkelman as an example of the "subjective grotesque" (Perttula 2010), and other studies, too, have tended to concentrate on the novel's main character.[3] As contemporary critics noticed, this novel not only introduced a new kind of character to Finnish literature, but also a new kind of environment: the outskirts of the Finnish capital (Hellaakoski 1922/2006: 240). From the perspective of the experience of urban space, two elements in the description in the opening scene of *Rakastunut rampa* are of particular interest: the corresponding manner in which the unattractive physical features of both landscape and protagonist are described, and the cumbersome manner of the movement of the protagonist through the fringes of the city. Both are indicative of a new aesthetics in relation to descriptions of urban experiences – an aesthetics rooted in the grotesque, and profoundly determined by questions of class, but also bearing reflections on the moral state of society in this period.

This chapter will focus on experiences of Helsinki in the urban margins. The first part of this chapter will present an analysis of the dystopian landscape of Krokelby, an imaginary environment which was introduced by Joel Lehtonen in *Rakastunut rampa* and further developed in *Henkien taistelu* ("The Battle of the Spirits"; 1933), which would remain Lehtonen's final novel. With this imaginary environment, Joel Lehtonen has constructed a locality that is at once one of the most disturbing and one of the most original landscapes to be found in Finnish literature of the last century: a deformed landscape, made up of a disconcerting natural environment and crooked houses, and intertwined with the grotesque characters living there. One of the most interesting features of this imagined landscape, in particular in Joel Lehtonen's final novel, is that it appears as a spatial environment with universalist dimensions: an *imago mundi*, representative of all of Helsinki, and by extension, of society at large. The analysis of Krokelby will be supplemented with images of the urban margins from other relevant novels of the same period, amongst others Helvi Hämäläinen's *Katuojan vettä* ("Water in the Gutter"; 1935), Elvi Sinervo's collection of short stories *Runo Söörnäisistä* ("Poem about Sörnäinen"; 1937), as well as *Ruumiin ikävä* and *Kypsyminen* by Iris Uurto ("The Longing of the Body"; 1930/1931; "Maturing"; 1935).

Krokelby in Joel Lehtonen's Rakastunut rampa *(1922)*

In *Rakastunut rampa*, the novel with which Joel Lehtonen introduces the imaginary suburb of Krokelby, all the central characteristics of Krokelby that will be further developed in *Henkien taistelu* can already be found. The reader receives a fairly good idea of Krokelby's outward appearance, but also of where this suburban village is situated in relation to the Finnish capital: Krokelby lies to the north-east of Helsinki, near the mouth of the river Vantaa and the Vanhakaupunki area. Although Krokelby can be related to existing neighbourhoods, it is by definition a fictional area, and as a consequence, it can be considered as the *everyman* amongst the Helsinki suburbs: the imaginary and prototypical model through which all separate marginal areas of the Finnish capital are measured.

Like Sakris Kukkelman, the eponymous "Cripple in Love" who inhabits the suburban margins of the Finnish capital, Krokelby is described as a deformed amalgam of heterogeneous and contradictory elements. The most fundamental characteristic of the suburban landscape in *Rakastunut rampa* is that of deformity; of being unnatural, diseased, crooked, and crippled. The link between Krokelby and deformity is a semantic one to begin with: the name of this imaginary environment is made up of the suffix *-by*, a common Swedish suffix in toponyms, which today has the meaning "village",[4] added to the root *Krokel*. *Krokel* resembles the Swedish word *krokig*, meaning "bent", "crooked", "hooked".[5] The Swedish word *krokryggig* means "hunchbacked" and this relates the name to the literary character described in terms of near-symbiosis with his environment: Sakris Kukkelmann.

In *Rakastunut rampa*, deformity is described first of all in relation to the eponymous cripple, but also in the way the built environment is rendered in the narration. The buildings of Krokelby are portrayed as unsuccessful stylistic mishmashes that aim to represent social codes they are unable to fulfil. The deformity of the buildings is explicitly linked to the upward social drive of the parvenu inhabitants, and indicative of the unrealistic expectations lying behind this drive. The following extract is representative of many of the descriptions of the built environment found in *Rakastunut rampa*:

> Over there, someone had built a slender tower on top of the far end of a wooden shed: a little shelter balancing on top of four high pillars… as if it were the bell tower of a countryside mansion. But the anchoring of the pillars had been carried out badly and they were bent out of shape, and with them, so had the whole structure… (Lehtonen 1922/2006: 7–8)[6]

The deformed architectural structure is described as the result of the builder's ill-warranted attempt to mimic the building style of an upper class countryside mansion – a hubristic attempt at architectural verticality doomed to fail. The same can be said of the deformity of many things in Krokelby, of its inhabitants as well as of the landscape as a whole. Misshapen by their desire to rise socially, the characters and the environment they inhabit have turned into caricatures of both themselves and their professed examples. Significantly, like so many characters in Finnish literature from the 1910s on, Sakris is occasionally employed as a construction worker, and he is, in other words, actively involved in shaping the built environment.[7]

The natural landscape, too, is described in terms of deformity. From the opening lines of the novel, the protagonist and his surroundings are described in unison: in this gloomy environment, enveloped in "autumnal fog", with a path lined by "sombre fir trees" (see above), the approaching cripple seems markedly at home. The natural landscape is repeatedly described in despondent terms and in relation to descriptions of adverse climatic conditions (rain, fog, dirty smoke), and even a pine tree is described as "twisted and trimmed at the top" (Lehtonen 1922/2006: 47; see Perttula 2010: 104).[8] The landscape is also capable, however, of reflecting positive change in the protagonist's luck. When Sakris Kukkelman reaches the heights of happiness, after his beloved Nelma has moved in with him, the landscape, too, is transformed: "Everything is […] hazy like in a dream… similar to the air, too, which now covers the world" (Lehtonen 1922/2006: 145).[9] Smoke from far-away forest fires in Russia covers the land and the sea, giving the whole surroundings an unreal quality (ibid.).[10] Later in the novel, when Nelma has left Krokelby for good, leaving a desperate Kukkelman to fend for himself, the landscape changes again into a depressing and brooding environment. Fog rises from the sea and the waves of the river Vantaa are described as "cold and murky"; autumn comes, "[t]he world darkens… And it rains" (ibid.: 217–218).[11] The mist that covers the land "sucks the last warmth from the land… and freezes the remaining plants […]"; the fields smell of decaying plants, and a mist comes that "cuts through bones and marrows" (ibid.: 218).[12] As the cold fog, the darkness and the rain drive out the last bit of warmth from the landscape, Sakris's despair deepens. Death and decay affect first the landscape, and then the protagonist – not much later, Sakris is found dead: he has committed suicide by hanging himself.

Henkien taistelu *(1933):*
The Margins of the City as Testing Ground

Rakastunut rampa introduced a new kind of literary character, as well as a new kind of landscape and aesthetics, but it was still fairly modest in terms of plot, genre and the spatial scale within which the narrative was played out. The same cannot be said of Joel Lehtonen's final novel, in which the environment introduced in *Rakastunut rampa* takes on further universalist meaning as a testing ground of modern society. A novel set at the height of Prohibition, *Henkien taistelu* recounts the story of the pious Kleophas Leanteri Sampila, who is lured to the suburban fringes of the Finnish capital to be tempted by the devil. Krokelby appears relatively late, some 100 pages into the story, when the two main characters are approaching Helsinki by train on their journey home from Paris. They are an unlikely couple to say the least. Sampila is a naïve and good-humoured forester, who has taken a year's leave from his position in order to get to know the world. His companion Victor Sorsimo is a beer factory owner who is, in fact, a devil in disguise, a corporal in the army of Barbuel, general of demons. Sorsimo, also known as "the devil in the bottle" (Lehtonen 1933: 10),[13] has chosen as his task to bring his companion to destruction. As they approach the Finnish capital, Sorsimo persuades Sampila to come and spend some time in his home town, Krokelby.

The devil does not try to bring Kleophas to destruction in a truly large metropolis – he would have had the chance to do so in Paris, where they met, nor in a desert or god-forsaken wilderness, as tradition would have it. The environment of choice is Krokelby, and with good reason according to the devil: this is the environment that will function as the symbol of the world in all its ugly viciousness. In his discussion with Sampila, the devil argues that Krokelby will have an instructive function – suggesting overtly an optimistic and uplifting purpose: in Krokelby, too, "you can see and learn a thing or two, if you should wish to" (Lehtonen 1933: 102).[14] The explicit purpose of the extended stay of Sampila in Krokelby, then, is to explore a particular urban landscape in order to gain a better understanding of the world in all its ramifications. The Finnish capital and its suburb Krokelby take on the form of a specific kind of metaphorization of the city, that of an *imago mundi*, which, in Henri Lefebvre's words, constructs the citizens' "representation of space as a whole, of the earth, of the world" (Lefebvre 1974/1991: 243–244).[15]

The universalist nature of the spatial environment in *Henkien taistelu* is enhanced, first of all, by the fact that Krokelby is by definition an imagined space. The neighbourhood does not have any location in the physically and geographically identifiable city of Helsinki, which is one of the reasons why it has the capacity to take on such strong universalist overtones. Krokelby's universalist nature is also closely related to the novel's generic features, which draw on genres with clear moral dimensions, such as the medieval mystery play, the renaissance picaresque novel, and, in particular, the Menippean satire. Framed by such a genre, the landscape becomes quite literally a *symbolic* landscape, an allegorical spatial environment that functions as an "exemplum", a moral warning one should bear in mind. This is most explicitly the case if we choose to read *Henkien taistelu* as an exponent of the Menippean satire, a satirical genre that flourished in antiquity and that, as a quintessential protean genre, has left a considerable mark on the development of the novel.[16] As is typical of a novel belonging to the Menippea, the description of space – like all other elements of the narration – is profoundly carnivalized, and is presented in a way that turns familiar elements inside out: it is space which, in Bakthin's words, is "drawn out of its *usual* rut, ... to some extent 'life turned inside out,' 'the reverse side of the world' ('*monde à l'envers*')" (Bakhtin 1984b: 122). The satirical distortion of the world is described as a deliberate representational strategy at the very outset of the novel by the limping devil who guides both the protagonist and the narration in *Henkien taistelu*:

> I intend to show him [the protagonist, Kleophas Leanteri Sampila] what people, not without a kind of pride, call life, as if in a film visited by the scissors of the censor, only with the difference that I shall cut out the *harmless* parts, the quiet, nice people, and shall direct a blinding light from the projector on the corrupt sides of the average citizens and even the exemplary ones. I shall represent it all, intentionally, as largely disconnected episodes; the result, I hope, will be confused and imprecise, like the time in which the world is now living. (Lehtonen 1933: 22)[17]

The devil, in his prologue, states that the very manner of his representation will be distorted and fragmentary, and he stresses that he will describe *people* in a satirical light. The novel's subtitle, too ("A Story about Our Famous Citizens"), draws the reader's attention to the character description. But the devil's words can be equally applied to the carnivalesque description of the spatial surroundings in *Henkien taistelu*, whose "confused and imprecise" description is representative of the contemporary world in turmoil. The fragmentary description promised by the crippled devil is visible on a variety of levels. These include the narrative structure of the novel, which is constructed, as promised, as "largely disconnecting episodes", as well as the individual sentences, which are occasionally fragmented and in which even the conventions of punctuation are carnivalized. Not only are the landscape, characters and their movement described in this novel as deformed: the narration itself becomes infected.

Similar to the descriptions of the built environment found in *Rakastunut rampa*, deformity is first of all given shape by way of the distorted characteristics of buildings inhabited by parvenus and indicative of the unsuccessful desire to emulate the style of the more privileged social classes. The wooden villas and sheds that constitute the village of Krokelby are described as imitations of imitations, unsuccessful adaptations of foreign building styles which bring to mind comical objects (Lehtonen 1933: 115–118). Some buildings are described using the same similes – a Kirgizian tent and a helmet, for example – that can be found in *Rakastunut rampa* (Lehtonen 1922/2006: 143; Lehtonen 1933: 117). The built environment is portrayed as profoundly inauthentic, and various examples are given of how it displays ill-fitting influences, and of the ridiculous image which is the result. The built environment appears literally as a mirror of the preposterous aspirations of its inhabitants, as in the case of a house which resembles a Kirgizian yurt, but with a roof of galvanized sheet metal, of which the proud owner – one of the many bootleggers residing in Krokelby – boasts that "it shines, so that I can see my own image in it" (ibid.: 117).[18] Another roof, too, reflects the owner, but in a different way: the roof is of gilded sheet metal, because the owner is a tinsmith (ibid.).

The buildings in which many of the characters in Krokelby live can thus be seen as complex spatial metaphors for their inhabitants: presumptuous, preposterous, misshapen and haphazardly constructed buildings the aim of which is to give the impression of a higher social status. As a whole, the cityscape of Krokelby is symptomatic not only of the mentally and physically crippled characters appearing in the novel but of the society at large in which it is set. This is a world in which the parvenus from L. Onerva's 1911 collection of short stories *Nousukkaita* ("Parvenus") have risen to become the leading members of society. In Onerva's text, the degenerating in-between people who had only recently moved to the capital are depicted as the victims of a rapidly modernizing society. In Lehtonen's world, misshapenness – moral as well as physical – has become the standard: Krokelby is inhabited by degenerate former prostitutes, liquor runners, speculators, as well as working-class people on their way up on the social ladder, and members of the old bourgeoisie on their way down. Degradation and entropy have run their course, but to the dismay of the protagonist, Kleophas Sampila, he seems to be the only one disturbed by the resulting grotesque spectacle.

A Deformed Landscape
Krokelby can be characterized by the deformity of individual inhabitants and buildings, but on a larger scale it appears as a deformed version of the city itself, as is apparent from the long soliloquy with which the devil-in-the-bottle introduces Krokelby (Lehtonen 1933: 114–118); some extracts from this speech have been quoted above. Using a highly oxymoronic style, juxtaposing high and low, typical of satirical genres and the Menippean satire in particular (Bakhtin 1984b: 118), Sorsimo extols Krokelby, in the meantime, drawing Sampila's attention to the environment's flaws. Krokelby is described as an organically grown village, showing similarities to the aesthetic ideal of a naturally developed medieval town – its centre is compared to that of picturesque Siena, but the totality is simultaneously described as a jumble of ill-designed buildings (Lehtonen 1933: 115).[19] In another sense, too, Krokelby is described as an organically grown entity: the very first

thing the devil tells Sampila is that it resembles a disease-like extension to the body of Helsinki: it is a "village, which like a bump, has grown onto the side of Helsinki" (ibid.: 102).[20] Images of the grotesque tend to be related to transgressions of the boundaries of the body, and to what protrudes from the body (Perttula 2010: 108), and the image of a cancer-like extension of the city reads the suburb as a grotesque deformity of the normal urban fabric. It is an image which draws on the traditional imagery of the city-as-body – one of the most potent metaphors with which the city can be conceptualized, and a descriptive strategy which, according to Lefebvre, is made use of in particular when the city and its representatives feel threatened.[21] This metaphor of the body is used in a sense that equates the city with the body politic, attributing perceived diseases in society to the ailing body of the city. Raymond Williams has pointed out that the consequence of this image is a broader vision of society as rotten: if the city "was seen as monstrous, or as a diseased growth, this had logically to be traced back to the whole social order" (Williams 1974: 146). *Henkien taistelu* is indeed an analysis of a disease of the societal body, a "medical case history", as one critic calls it: a "merciless analysis of the disintegration and degeneration in a societal body infected by disease" (Ekelund 1937: 379). Lehtonen is one of the first authors to apply such thinking to the literary image of Helsinki and its suburbs, and in *Henkien taistelu*, the vision of the expanding suburban environment as a deformed, unhealthy, crippled landscape takes on stronger overtones as the novel proceeds.

The distorted features of Krokelby's landscape are signs of the moral failure of society, but they are also symptomatic of the far-reaching commodification that affects the landscape as well as its inhabitants. Krokelby is portrayed as a space distorted by the "struggle for life" (Lehtonen 1933: 266; see below), the rat race performed to the tune of money, greed and profit. Ironically, Sampila himself is part of the machinery that industrializes the idealized landscape of eastern Finland: he is a "forstmestari", a forester working for an industrial company.

FROM CARNIVALESQUE TO GROTESQUE LANDSCAPE
Until well into the first part of the novel, *Henkien taistelu* and the image it gives of the urban and suburban landscape may be described in terms of the comic and the satirical. This initial comic rendering of space is bound up with the perspective in the first part of the novel, which is largely guided by and through the bottled devil. Gradually, however, focalization shifts to Sampila, and with this change in perspective, the tone of the novel becomes ever more pessimistic. The satirical perspective of the devil is gradually adopted by his victim Sampila, and as the devil's vision of the surroundings, and, by extension, of society at large is interiorized by the protagonist, the tone shifts from the comic grotesque, which dominates the first part of the novel, towards an unsettling, terrifying mode of the grotesque. These two modes of the grotesque can be traced to the two main branches of this generic tradition: the comic grotesque has been related to Mikhail Bakhtin's account of low, carnivalistic culture (Bakhtin 1984a), while what has also been called the uncanny grotesque can be related to Wolfgang Kayser's

analysis of the concept (1957).[22] Typical of the latter mode of the grotesque is an inward turn and the expression of a subjective world view, which is the reason Irma Perttula has called this the "subjective grotesque" (Perttula 2010: 30). In *Henkien taistelu*, the vision of a grotesque landscape is gradually internalized and expressed from the perspective of the protagonist Sampila, which entails a shift towards the subjective grotesque. This shift is most clearly visible in two panoramic visions of Krokelby (see below), the first, which appears early in the novel, focalized by the devil (Lehtonen 1933: 117 ff.), the second, which appears much later, focalized by Sampila (ibid.: 558 ff.). It is arguably this subjective grotesque dimension of the novel which has resulted in the reading of *Henkien taistelu* as a "misanthropic satire" that "reflects pure despair" (Tarkka 1965: 92), as a profoundly pessimistic novel, and even as a "nightmare dream of society" (Kivimaa 1934: 292) despite its many comic passages.[23]

This shift in perspective is also visible in the overall structure of the novel, and in an often overlooked change in the character guiding Sampila. *Henkien taistelu* consists of two parts or volumes; the first volume concentrates mostly on Krokelby, whereas the second volume pays much more attention to Helsinki itself. At the end of the first volume, the devil recedes, and in his place a new figure appears: that of Oiva Tommola, who begins to guide Kleophas Sampila through Helsinki (Lehtonen 1933: 298–299). This change in guides is only minor, however, in comparison with the much more eventful change that takes places within the protagonist. Increasingly, Sampila begins to see society in terms earlier used by the devil in disguise, but without the ironical distance this character lends the narration. Sampila begins to describe Krokelby as a natural landscape corrupted by the vicinity of the capital (ibid.: 205), and he perceives it as a locality that resembles a mishmash "scrapped together with debris from the countryside and the refuse from Helsinki" (ibid.: 267).[24]

The question of who sees and frames the landscape in *Henkien taistelu* is of considerable importance for the interpretation of the experience of space. An urban landscape entails a panoramic view – a vision of the city which contains moral undertones, since framing it as a comprehensive totality gives the focalizing instance the possibility of passing judgment. As Sharon Zukin points out, landscape "connotes a contentious, compromised product of society" (Zukin 1991: 16). The grotesque, like the landscape, is something that can be argued to not exist *a priori*: it is not important what *is*, but how it is described (see Perttula 2010: 52, 53), and who sees (see Salmela 2012: 192). The grotesque, then, resides not in the landscape itself, but in the vision that frames it and gives it meaning. The gradual change of focalization to Sampila, and the pessimistic terms in which his vision of Helsinki's (sub)urban space is couched illustrate that the workings of the devil have started to have their effect on him. Sampila feels so upset by how his opinions of society and of the Finnish people have changed that he begins to feel repulsed by Krokelby:

> He really wanted to move away from this village, this half-city in the neighbourhood of Helsinki, which the struggle for life, as he called it in his thoughts, had certainly ruined, distorted, brutalized [...]. (Lehtonen 1933: 266)[25]

Sampila longs for the pond he left behind at the beginning of the novel, and when thinking of this Arcadian locality he explicitly considers that for him the idea of the pond implies a degree of devoutness and faith: "by that pond he meant something metaphorically, which was devoutness, *belief*..." (ibid.).[26] It becomes clear by implication that the landscape of Krokelby takes on exactly the opposite symbolic meaning: it becomes a symbol of Sampila's growing despair.

As Sampila increasingly becomes the focalizer, he moves up in the narrative hierarchy in another sense, too: he appears less and less as the naïve victim of the devil, and increasingly begins to analyse what is happening around him. He becomes obsessed with a story that he has remembered, in which a devil in a bottle is driving an innocent victim to destruction. In a thoroughly satirical conversation, Sorsimo, who is the bottled devil himself, discusses with him the literary antecedents of the story in which they are mixed up. The discussion contains an interesting, although almost untranslatable pun on Helsinki's dystopian character; Sampila considers that in similar earlier stories, the devil tries to drive his victim "to Helsinki" ("päin Helsinkiä") (ibid.). The intended pun lies in the similarities between Helsinki and the Finnish word for hell ("helvetti"), and the fact that "driving one to Helsinki" sounds very much like the Finnish saying to "drive someone to hell/to destruction" ("päin helvettiä").[27] Whereas at first it is the devil's mission to convince Sampila of society's vices and shortcomings, at this point Sampila himself becomes eager to look at the vices of society with his own eyes, and to "gather evidence" (ibid.: 375).[28] The testing of an idea, carried out by the devil through the figure of Sampila, starts to take its toll: amidst these distorted environments and people, Sampila is described as a man transformed both inwardly and outwardly (ibid.: 378).

"Like meat on a grill"

A crucial moment in Sampila's experience of the (sub)urban environment comes at a farewell party organized by the devil on the occasion of the latter's departure from Krokelby. From this moment on, Kleophas Leanteri Sampila will be decidedly on his own; his guide quite literally leaves the stage. The view seen from the upper floor of the villa in which the devil rented an apartment is similar to the panoramic view with which Krokelby was introduced much earlier in the novel (Lehtonen 1933: 115 ff.), but at this point (ibid.: 518 ff.), the focalization is entirely that of Sampila, and the dystopian terms in which the description is couched are indicative of the despair which has gradually taken hold of the protagonist. The long description is couched in visual, almost painterly language:

> It was a beautiful day at the end of June. From the upper floor of "Villa Kanisto" one could see the horizon like a wide and grand half-circle, arching to the right and the left, carrying the enormous vault of heaven, underneath which the world seemed to shrink in size and seemed to be flattened down. That horizon, black like the landscape backgrounds in the paintings by da Vinci, seemed like an artistic device, with the effect of making the glaring greenness of the valley seem even more intense than it would have been on its own. [...] There was

not a breath of wind, everything seemed to have come to a halt. The sea, of which a glimpse could be seen further away, at the grey mouth of the Vantaa River, hardly even rippled, but did not glimmer: it, too, had come to a halt, had dozed off, fallen asleep in the murky veil of the evening haze. – The freshness of spring had long since disappeared from the fields and meadows, – no longer the brightness of the marsh marigold, the brass of the buttercups, the blinding gold of the dandelions! Below, in the garden of Sorsimo's landlady – which used to be a whory, but was now a Christian person's garden, where the lilacs had just now opened their blue and white loveliness, the white roses were furrowing at the very same moment amidst the brazen grass. – Further away, on the top of a rock, where the whitewashed tower of a villa shimmered, small beings moved around: half-naked sun-bathers, – or they were lying motionless on the rock as if on a torrid stove or like meat on a grill. On the dusty railway track, between the shining rails, a few black labourers were slowly moving to or from their work. – A great silence. Not even a swallow enlivened with its flying circles the milky emptiness of the sky… (Lehtonen 1933: 518–519)[29]

The view from the upper floor of the villa is described as utterly overwhelming, a characteristic which is stressed by the repeated adjectives accentuating its hyperbolic enormity: the "*wide, grand* half-circle", and the "*enormous*" vault of heaven. The enormity of the heavens makes the world itself appear small and shrunken in size, and in relation to it, the human beings moving through the landscape are represented as further diminished in size. The description emphasizes the extent to which the panorama is an artificial, aestheticizing rendering; the horizon is similar to the backgrounds in paintings by da Vinci, and its wide expanse and dark aspect appear to be purposely designed to make the green colour of the valley appear even more garish. Describing the (sub)urban landscape in terms of a painting follows a well-established tradition in city literature, pioneered in French literature by the brothers Goncourt and Zola, and in Sweden by authors such as Oscar Levertin, and Hjalmar Söderberg (Borg 2011: 204). In the long description from *Henkien taistelu*, the painterly description provides the landscape not only with aesthetic qualities; it also results in an eerie, almost threatening atmosphere. The uncanny artificiality of the landscape is enhanced by the repeated emphasis on the immobility of its features: there is not "a breath of wind" and the river "hardly even rippled". The description contains several oxymorons and combinations of high and low to depict one and the same thing – the horizon is portrayed first as pitch black, the sky is the colour of milk – and since it is suggested that the focalization in this passage is that of Sampila, the effect is to convince the reader that the devil's teachings have had their effect, and that Sampila has started to see the environment in the pessimistic terms used by the devil. The very fact that the setting is a "beautiful day at the end of June" makes the enumeration of negative elements appear the more striking.

The references to natural splendour in this passage are in part that of a faded beauty, and more generally, too, the description focuses rather on what is absent, or what is no longer there: the opulence of the spring flowers, movement, and sounds. An idyllic setting is turned on its head, is "drawn out of its […] rut" and "turned inside out" (Bakhtin 1984b: 122; see above):

the positive elements of the landscape are described through negation, and the effect is one of utter desolation. In the case of the "Christian" garden of the landlady, the "whory" past of the landlady is erased to make way for a presumptuous and artificial construction. The garden is not an Eden but a transformed garden of a former prostitute. The tower of the neighbouring villa, which is "painted white", can be read as a reference to the whitewashed graves from Matthew 23:27, which are beautiful on the outside but on the inside "full of dead men's bones, and of all uncleanness". The intertextual reference to Matthew 23:27 resonates with the immediately consecutive view of half-naked sun-bathing people on the rocks beside the white tower – bodies not described in terms of bodily health, but of carnal transience. The comparison Sampila makes is revealing: to him, these people lie still on the rock "as if on a torrid stove or as meat on a grill".

The description of the Krokelby rock as a "torrid stove" on which to grill human flesh is one of a number of recurring and disturbing references to human beings in terms of flesh in the novel. Immediately preceding the panoramic description of the view from Villa Kanisto, the reader gets a revealing insight into the thoughts of Sampila concerning the culture of sunbathing and nudity which was practised on the Helsinki beach:

> There's also the kind of people who stroll in their bare shirts along the Helsinki streets, glowing in the summer heat, and who plod to the public beach, where Kleophas, too, once had strayed, as if this political turmoil did not concern them in the least. No, they are just lounging about there in the sand, or throw a somersault in the sunshine, those thousands, tens of thousands of people, almost naked, on their stomachs, on their backs, eyes in the glaring sand, – on their backs as if they are bronze statues cast down, black as mulattoes, on their stomachs like dough [...] while the loudspeaker is trumpeting wailing saxophone melodies. Healthiness: flirting, adventures! – And there are similar people all over the country... such – flesh! To Kleophas it is flesh! It seems as if he has started to feel strangely repulsed by flesh. (Lehtonen 1933: 515–516)[30]

The flirtatious mood of the age, and its interest in exercise and "body culture", sunbathing and loose clothing performed to the sound of jazz music, is sharply juxtaposed in Lehtonen's novel with a vision of mortal flesh. The feeling that the body culture on the Helsinki beach is practised against the backdrop of impending doom is made tangible by the reference to the "political turmoil" that is described as not affecting the sun-bathers. It is a reference, of course, to the deepening political divide in the country, and the rise, both in Finland and abroad, of extremist forces.

The pessimistic vision of society and of the people that inhabit the near-infernal landscape in *Henkien taistelu* is grounded in the cultural pessimism that held much of Europe in its thrall in the inter-war period and that found its expression in avant-garde movements like German expressionism, a movement to which Lehtonen's work is not unconnected. This cultural pessimism was exhibited in the work of a whole series of authors and thinkers commenting on a world in disarray, from Oswald Spengler's *Der Untergang des Abendlandes* (*The Decline of the West*; Spengler 1918/1926) and

Hermann Hesse's *Blick ins Chaos* (*In Sight of Chaos*; 1920/1922) to Freud's *Das Unbehagen in der Kultur* (*Civilization and Its Discontents*; 1930/2002) and Johan Huizinga's *In the Schaduwen van Morgen* (*In the Shadow of Tomorrow*; 1935), and in Finland, Tatu Vaaskivi's *Huomispäivän varjo* ("The Shadow of Tomorrow"; 1938). Joel Lehtonen's utterly pessimistic vision of modern and urban pleasure in the jazz age was shared by other Finnish contemporary authors, most notably by Unto Karri, whose novel *Sodoma* ("Sodom"; 1929) was perhaps the most Spengler-inspired prose work ever published in Finnish (and who was ridiculed for it by Olavi Paavolainen; see Paavolainen 1932: 78). Similar feelings as those expressed by Kleophas Sampila, above, are also felt by *Sodoma*'s main character Martti, who, after an aborted initiation rite into a worldwide Jewish conspiracy in a suburb of Paris, gets back to civilization only to be confronted with senseless partying in urban nightclubs. "'This is seething hell!' Martti thought. 'Flesh, flesh and sensuousness everywhere.'" (Karri 1929: 233)[31] Other novels set in Helsinki during this time exhibit a similar troubled image of humans as "mere flesh". In Mika Waltari's *Suuri illusioni* ("The Great Illusion"; 1928), too, there is a scene of grotesque carnality, set on a German ship in the harbour of Helsinki, in which one of the characters comments that "[t]his is flesh, and however hard you will try to find anything else, at this moment you will not find anything else here but flesh" (Waltari 1928: 90).[32] In a later Helsinki novel written by Waltari, *Surun ja ilon kaupunki* ("City of Sorrow and Joy"; 1936), the elderly director Sunnila is musing how human flesh can change into an image of death, as he watches a female dancer perform in the electric light of a night club (Waltari 1936: 291–292).

The example from *Surun ja ilon kaupunki* illustrates the era's interest in the human body as a mask behind which mortal flesh hides itself; an interest related to the image of the *dance macabre*, which rose again to prominence in the early twentieth century.[33] It is a motif which recurs repeatedly in *Henkien taistelu*, and which culminates in the most disturbing landscape of the novel, in one of the last chapters, aptly called "Tombs" ("Haudat"). In this chapter, Kleophas Leanteri Sampila has a dream in which he finds the idyllic countryside environment of his childhood suddenly transformed into a graveyard (Lehtonen 1933: 607–611).[34] Sampila experiences this infernal landscape as even worse than hell, since it contains no devils or dead souls, in fact nothing at all except filth and flesh. The transformation of a fertile and idyllic childhood landscape into the derelict wasteland of carnal refuse is compared in this passage with late medieval, plague-inspired paintings such as the dance of death at the St. Mary Church in Lübeck, and the "triumph of death" fresco in Pisa; but in comparison, Sampila experiences the nightmare as much more unsettling (Lehtonen 1933: 610). In the industrializing world, the link between humans and mortal flesh takes on an even more distressing meaning than the one found in the late medieval, plague-inspired millenarianism. Industrial warfare and the dehumanizing routines of grand-scale factory work have shown that human beings, too, can become part of a rationalized and devouring food chain, and at the end of the novel, a locality appears to embody this apocalyptic vision: the slaughterhouse.

The Slaughterhouse

In the chapter immediately following "Tombs", the nightmarish image of an infernal landscape is concretized in one particular building set in Krokelby: the slaughterhouse, conveniently situated next to a sausage factory. As Sampila walks past the slaughterhouse, he is again reminded of the Pisa triumph of death fresco, and he happens to look inside through the opening door. The disturbing view of the inside where Sampila sees, amongst others, a bull being stabbed and bleeding profusely, and the head of a pig being crushed with an axe-hammer, in addition to the deafening roar of the various animals, profoundly shakes his already fragile inner balance (Lehtonen 1933: 613 ff.). What is so disturbing about the image of the slaughterhouse at this point of the narration? The fact that most of the characters in *Henkien taistelu* have animal names and animal-like characteristics makes the prominent presence of a slaughterhouse, and the vision of "mass destruction" it presents all the more forbidding (Tarkka 1965: 92). But the slaughterhouse can also be seen here as a symbol of the unsettling consequences of modernizing society, especially in relation to earlier motifs of human bodies-as-flesh and the dance of death in the novel, references that culminate and become concrete in the slaughterhouse, and complete the gradual and relentless process of utter despair within the protagonist.[35]

There is a long tradition of seeing death in the everyday city, but the image of the slaughterhouse here amounts to a particular kind of symbol of modernity, since it links the fate of humankind with the accelerating process of modernization and commodification, of which the industrialized slaughterhouse provides one of the most disturbing images. In 1908, the Danish historian Gustav Bang, in his monumental work on modern times *Vor tid* ("Our time"; 1908), devotes a special chapter to the Chicago slaughterhouses and to Upton Sinclair's literary description of the phenomenon in the novel *The Jungle* (1906); both books were published in Finnish immediately upon appearance (*Chikago* 1906; *Nykyaika* 1908). Gustav Bang notes that the phenomenon of the slaughterhouse city, which Chicago had become, also has it consequences for the fate of the working class as well as the consuming class, since both are fleeced by modern techniques as effectively as the animals they produce and consume (Bang 1908: 32).[36] The 1920s and 1930s commentators of (American) modernization, such as Vladimir Mayakovsky (1925/2010) and Georges Bataille (1929/1997) were fascinated by the slaughterhouse. Part of this fascination must be understood in terms of the uneasiness with which the early decades of the twentieth century saw the advent of a modernizing society dominated by machines and rationalized processes of production, amongst which men and women were perceived to run the risk of being reduced to mere slaves (see, for example, Spengler 1918/1926: 504–505). Several examples from literature and movies of the 1920s and 1930s depicted modern urbanites being passively led to slaughter in the machine-city.

When Sampila looks through the open door of the slaughterhouse, he reads his own despair and his own fears in the eyes of the frightened animals. The desperation felt by Sampila is not so much related to a fear of death, I would argue; rather, it is the fear that the "struggle for life" which has infected and distorted the (sub)urban landscape and its inhabitants, has erased the last possibilities of believing in humanity. Part of Sampila's desperate attempt to distance himself from the dystopian world he sees is to become a vegetarian – one last futile endeavour to remain outside of the processes he sees at work in society.[37] It is a strategy which, in the ironical words of the narrator (words that could, at this point, be identified with the devil), seals the fate of Sampila. Strangely enough, it is one of the reasons why he should die: "Let him die, since he does not understand how good a stroganoff-steak tastes […]!" (Lehtonen 1933: 618)[38] With the view of the slaughterhouse, immediately following Sampila's nightmare in which his childhood landscape is transformed into a dismal landscape of carnal refuse, the dystopian vision of the city has come to a culmination point. Sampila's excursions into Krokelby and Helsinki have gradually shattered his optimistic view of the world, and the "struggle for life" starts to weigh down on him – the extended sojourn in this depressing suburban landscape leads to his ruin. At the side of some nondescript forest road in the vicinity of Krokelby, Sampila, disillusioned and resigned to his fate, is killed by a tramp for no particular reason or purpose.

Mapping a Socially Divided City: Place Names

Many of the most disturbing spatial elements in the distorted landscape of Lehtonen's Krokelby novels not only construct an image of the moral failure of the inter-war society, but are also indicative of the desperate struggle between competing social classes to be king of the dunghill. The ridiculously deformed houses in Krokelby are symptomatic of a satirized upward social drive, and in *Henkien taistelu*, the "struggle for life" is what has "ruined, distorted, brutalized" the landscape and the people living in Krokelby (Lehtonen 1933: 266; see above). The whole of Krokelby is infused with a sense of class: it is an in-between landscape (or even "No man's land"; see Olsson 1925: 133–134) inhabited by a class of in-between, parvenu people; an environment whose very existence is proof of a society that is on the move. In Lehtonen's novels, and more generally, in Helsinki novels from the 1920s and 1930s, geographical location is permeated by a sense of social class. In the carnivalesque environment of Krokelby, social identity is fluid and constantly re-negotiated, a condition which constitutes one reason for the anxiety that spurs on its inhabitants. In literary representations of more central districts of Helsinki and in a number of clearly-defined working-class districts, social class appears as much more fixed. When literary characters move from the one locality to the other, their social class changes accordingly. Characters' trajectories through the urban landscape are thus symbolic of their social rise and fall. In *Henkien taistelu*, the formerly successful Myyrimö, for example, has moved downward in society, and has been forced to take up residence in a gloomy cellar in the environment of the working-class districts of Sörnäinen and Vallila, a "terrible place",[39] which Sampila imagines to be inhabited by dangerous gang members looking like Apaches from Western movies, and people planning their shady business in the shadows and the fog (Lehtonen 1933: 359–360). The trajectory of another minor character in the novel, the successful art dealer and swindler Mikael Reineck (a reference to Goethe's Reineke Fuchs; see Tarkka 1965: 89), has gone in a different direction, ending up in a large private palace in the up-market Kaivopuisto neighbourhood (Lehtonen 1933: 367). And when Sampila takes a tram to leave the centre of the city, he meets yet another of his acquaintances, the architect Maimanen, formerly successful but now an impoverished drunkard living in the area around the street Hämeentie, a locality which constitutes, again, a clear marker of the character's downward social mobility (ibid.: 439).

The ebb and flow of people's social trajectories through Helsinki's space is already depicted in late nineteenth-century literature. In Santeri Ivalo's *Aikansa lapsipuoli* ("A Stepchild of his Time"; 1895), a student novel which is also, in part, the story of the protagonist's unsuccessful endeavours to rise in society, there is a compelling description of the bustle of people moving on the first of June. This specific date, according to the narrator, is "some kind of yearly adjustment day, which more or less organizes and places the various layers and elements of society according to the events of that year, each to the place where he belongs" (Ivalo 1895: 273).[40] Some of the Helsinki citizens move to a better locality, but many, like the protagonist Juuso himself, have to move to more modest localities – the examples given are "down in Vladimirinkatu [present-day Kalevankatu] or in Sörnäinen or in the villas of Eläintarha" (ibid.: 274).[41]

As these examples indicate, a place name is often enough to breathe social meaning into the surroundings. From the very beginning of Helsinki descriptions in Finnish literature, the literary city is shaped according to particular proper names that function as clear markers of social boundaries. In literary representations, a single geographical proper name may amount to a momentous process of world-making, in the sense proposed by Nelson Goodman (Goodman 1978: 13 ff.). In such a radical condensation of meaning, which leaves only the proper name, a whole social-geographical construct is put in place. This is already the case in the prototypical Helsinki text discussed in Chapter 3, Juhani Aho's novella *Helsinkiin* ("To Helsinki"; 1889), which ends with a reference to a brothel, a locality suggested by the mere mention of a particular address.

Place names guide the movement of people through the city by evoking a complex social geography (de Certeau 1984: 104), but also by providing boundaries and thresholds, indicating the crossing of implicit social (and other) boundaries. De Certeau, in his treatment of spatial stories, argues that frontiers and bridges are "essential narrative figures" of stories, and hence, crucial to stories' capacities to found spaces and establish spatial demarcations (ibid.: 123). One of the most prominent Helsinki thresholds, which has received considerable attention in writing on Helsinki since the beginning of the twentieth century, is the Long Bridge ("Pitkäsilta"), which connected the centre of the city with the rapidly expanding working-class districts to the immediate north-east. It functions as a border as well as a bridge between two distinct environments. In early twentieth-century writing on Helsinki in literature, the Long Bridge has a prominent position:

Runar Schildt (1912), as well as V. A. Koskenniemi (1914) and Mikko Saarenheimo (1916a), in their essays on Helsinki in literature, saw not one Helsinki, but two different cities, divided and connected by the Long Bridge. Schildt ponders what future writer would become the interpreter of the "swarming masses there, north of the Long Bridge, and their dark psychology" (Schildt 1912: 13). Other literary commentators followed Schildt in looking forward to descriptions from across this social divide. Saarenheimo remarks that "the strongly willing world, which looms large on the other side of the Long Bridge, and which encircles Helsinki on other sides as well, has had to be content with crumbs in the allocation of literary attention" (Saarenheimo 1916: 206–207). Koskenniemi envisions the possibility of a future socially inspired Helsinki novel, which will pit the bank directors of central Helsinki against socialist agitators from which they were separated – and to whom they were connected – by way of the Long Bridge (Koskenniemi 1914: 89–96). One of the most important works to describe the working-class conditions north of the Long Bridge is Heikki Waris's academic dissertation *Työläisyhteiskunnan syntyminen Helsingin Pitkänsillan pohjoispuolelle* ("The Birth of a Working-Class Community North of the Helsinki Long Bridge"; 1932/1973), which was drawn upon by Mika Waltari when he was writing his Helsinki trilogy (Waltari 1980: 231–232).[42]

Several novels thematize the Long Bridge as an important spatial benchmark in Helsinki. In Arvid Järnefelt's *Veneh'ojalaiset* ("The Family Veneh'oja"; 1909), the Long Bridge is mentioned repeatedly as a symbolic threshold which also has a strategic function, since by blocking its traffic, an important entry road to the city could be blocked (Järnefelt 1909/1996: 240–241, 304–305, 329, 367). In the short story "Antti Peltari" ("Antti Peltari"), in Toivo Tarvas's collection *Häviävää Helsinkiä* ("Disappearing Helsinki"; 1917), the Long Bridge is not only the great divider between the working-class districts where the eponymous protagonist feels at home and the estranging city centre, but also a threshold between old and new, and even life and death. In the novel *Eri tasoilta* ("On Different Levels"; 1916a), again by Toivo Tarvas, there is one particularly revealing reference to the Long Bridge, in which the protagonist, Albert, after a long stay in the hospital, is at last again walking through his beloved home city. The spring evenings are enchanting:

> During those evenings he sometimes has the habit of walking against the stream, as it were, along the street Unioninkatu. The labourers have already changed their dress and they come in a dark queue together with their brides, wives and children to the centre of the city, across that gently curving stone bridge, which […] connects the city of labour and tears with the beautiful city of affluence and joy. (Tarvas 1916a: 249–250)[43]

The Long Bridge appears literally as a bridge between two different cities – the working-class "city of labour and tears" and the "beautiful city of affluence and joy". The position of the protagonist Albert in this social geography is clear: as a privileged member of the upper class, on a beautiful spring evening he walks "against the stream, as it were", across the bridge to the working-class districts, while "a dark queue" of labourers moves into the centre in the evening. Albert is one of the few natural *flâneurs* in the literature of this period, which may be one explanation why he ventures with such exceptional passion into the working-class areas north of the Long Bridge. One of the other rare *flâneurs* in Finnish Helsinki novels in the first half of the twentieth century, Lauri Pallas in Iris Uurto's novel *Kypsyminen* ("Maturing"; 1935), sees his nightly walks repeatedly punctuated by the Long Bridge, which more often than not functions as a mental barrier. Lauri, a student, lives in the working-class district north of Sörnäinen, and it is never made explicit what makes him stop at this threshold – not social background, since his father is relatively wealthy and lives in the very centre of Helsinki. Lauri sees the Helsinki centre across the Long Bridge repeatedly as a mirage of lights "as if [seen] through a heavy veil" (Uurto 1935: 163)[44] – a vision that could be interpreted as representative of Lauri's unaccomplished dreams of self-fulfilment, both in relation to the woman he loves and with respect to his unsuccessful social advancement. In most prose texts, however, the Long Bridge carries clear connotations of social meaning, and functions as a radical geographical divide between centre and periphery. In Elvi Sinervo's collection of short stories, *Runo Söörnäisistä* ("Poem about Sörnäinen"; 1937), the very title indicates its focalization of one of Helsinki's most (in)famous working-class districts north of this spatial benchmark.

The repeated focus on the Long Bridge, however, has obscured the fact that the social geography of Helsinki, in literature as in reality, was much more complex than a simple north-south dichotomy separated by the Long Bridge suggests. The division in literary representations of Helsinki is more often a juxtaposition between the areas at either side of the railway station running along a north-south axis to the Helsinki central station. In the east, the working-class areas of Kallio, Sörnäinen, Vallila, Kumpula, Toukola and Hermanni. In the west, the "New Helsinki" of Töölö. Such a dichotomy is explicitly visible in Helvi Hämäläinen's novel *Säädyllinen murhenäytelmä* ("A Respectable Tragedy"; 1941), in which the New Helsinki is set apart from the older Helsinki centre of the previous century, but also from working-class Helsinki:

> Old Helsinki does not know this human breed [the new generation living in Töölö] any better than the present 1930s New Helsinki knows the working class, whose Helsinki is still situated in the wooden houses of Vallila and the shacks of [...] Toukola, or in the unhealthy and wretched stone houses of Kallio and Sörnäinen. The Helsinki of the early twentieth century which built them sent its inhabitants from the very beginning into unhomeliness and communal living, which nurtures criminality and which spreads venereal diseases and breeds prostitution and rears their children [...] into human material which is unhealthy in body and soul [...]. (Hämäläinen 1941a: 32)[45]

The description of the diseased city in this passage from *Säädyllinen murhenäytelmä* is reminiscent of the "tentacular city" in texts by Järnefelt and Onerva. It is the centripetal city centre which is responsible for society's ills by the very urban structures it imposes on its surroundings. Most readers of Hämäläinen's novel could be expected to know that Hämäläinen's preceding Helsinki novel *Katuojan vettä* ("Water in the Gutter"; 1935), which had been widely reviewed (Lappalainen 1984: 47–48), was set in Vallila, one of those working-class areas which the "New Helsinki" of *Säädyllinen murhenäytelmä* was said to ignore. A further layer of meaning is added to the juxtaposition between a working-class and middle-class Helsinki in this passage from *Säädyllinen murhenäytelmä*, especially when considering that Hämäläinen and her works had been drawn into a bitter polemic concerning perceived leftist and rightist preferences of style and content, a polemic in which the "Literature Polemic" of 1936 was but one part.

The idea that Helsinki consisted of three separate cities – "old", "new" and "working class" – was also explicitly visible in Arvi Kivimaa's *Hetki ikuisen edessä* ("A Moment before Eternity"; 1932), in a passage that is prototypical for a vision that can be found more generally in literature of this period:

> Here was Töölö – a part of the city that was artificially lifted on rocks and their hollows; across the Bay were Sörnäinen and Hermanni, and further away, grey Katajanokka and Kruununhaka in their eternal sleep, a piece of a bygone century. (Kivimaa 1932: 24–25)[46]

The protagonist Aarni, whose thoughts are conveyed here, is lost in thought at a tram stop in Töölö, and is saying goodbye to the city he intends to leave. He tries to visualize the city both diachronically, as the sum of his experiences in Helsinki, and synchronically, and it is at this point that he visualizes Helsinki as a city divided into three parts: the middle class Helsinki of Töölö, the working-class Helsinki north-east of the centre, and the old centre, enveloped in "eternal sleep", something from a past era. But even a division in three clearly separable parts with their clear symbolic and social connotations, such as presented in these quotes from Hämäläinen and Kivimaa, does not do justice to the more complex reality, both in historical Helsinki in the 1920s and 1930s, and in the experiences of Helsinki in the literature of this period.

An illustrative example of the complex distribution of working-class areas is provided in the passage in Ivalo's *Aikansa lapsipuoli* mentioned earlier, in which, on a set day of the year, people whose luck have run out are forced to take up residence in less-desirable areas: "down in Vladimirinkatu or in Sörnäinen or in the villas of Eläintarha" (Ivalo 1895: 274). Vladimirinkatu, present-day Kalevankatu, is situated south-west of the centre, while the villas of Eläintarha (at the Töölö bay) are situated in the west, and Sörnäinen to the north-east of the Centre. The district of Punavuori, situated in the south of the Helsinki peninsula, is repeatedly referred to as a seedy working-class area, for example, in the reference at the end of Juhani Aho's *Helsinkiin*. The working-class area to the south-west of the Helsinki centre, in particular, with which also parts of present-day Kamppi and Ruoholahti are identified, repeatedly provides the setting for particularly dismal working-class conditions in literature, in fact almost more so than depictions of "north of the Long Bridge" do. In Waltari's *Sielu ja liekki*, it is referred to as "the wretched district of Lapinlahti" (Waltari 1934: 137).[47] In Eino Leino's

Frost Year Novel *Jaana Rönty* ("Jaana Rönty"; 1907), the social conditions of the protagonist Jaana are defined in part by the simple mention that her lodgings were "somewhere near the Cemetery",[48] words that evoked the working-class area to the south-west of the Helsinki centre. This is also where the mistress of Olli Suurpää, in *Olli Suurpää* (1908) is mentioned as living, and the words used are identical to the ones used in *Jaana Rönty*. This geographical information is all the reader learns about her (Leino 1907/1998: 190, Leino 1908/1998: 380). Other literary characters with a dubious background are similarly placed in the south-western working-class districts of Helsinki: the prostitute girl who acts as Hinkki's fiancée in *Veneh'ojalaiset*, for example, lives on the street "Hietalahden rantakatu" (Järnefelt 1909/1996: 78), and the prostitute Sandra, in Kyösti Wilkuna's *Vaikea tie*, lives in the direction of Hietalahti (Wilkuna 1915: 86–87). Names of streets situated in the very same south-western working-class part of the city reappear in literature of the 1920s and 1930s: the back-street abortionist visited by Nelma in *Rakastunut rampa* (1922/2006: 203) lives in Lapinlahti; Hart and Caritas go to Vladimirinkatu to procure illegal alcohol in Waltari's *Suuri illusioni* (1928: 21); the working-class mistress of Artur, in *Säädyllinen murhenäytelmä* ("A Respectable Tragedy"; 1941) lives in Lapinlahdenkatu (Hämäläinen 1941b: 13).[49]

The boundaries between such socially defined neighbourhoods are rarely crossed unthinkingly. When, in Järnefelt's *Veneh'ojalaiset* (1909), Hannes returns to Helsinki from St. Petersburg, he hesitates to go straight to his mother's and uncle's home in Punavuori, since his appearance in broad daylight in officer's uniform "in these disreputable streets on the outskirts of the city would draw unnecessary attention" (Järnefelt 1909/1996: 125).[50] Toivo, the protagonist in Mika Waltari's novel *Sielu ja liekki* ("The Soul and the Flame"; 1934), realizes that his bourgeois attire attracts unwanted attention when his wanderings take him north of the Long Bridge: his white student cap, symbol of his class, is frowned upon, and in subsequent journeys, he masks himself with the help of his old labourer's cap when "wandering far to the 'Lines' or along the new main road all the way to Hermanni" (Waltari 1934: 137; see also Palmgren 1989: 118).[51] The most cynical of such bourgeois characters feeling ill at ease in working-class environments is arguably the doctor in Helvi Hämäläinen's *Säädyllinen murhenäytelmä*, who is so concerned about his impeccable reputation that, when visiting his former working-class mistress, who is pregnant, he demands that his wife accompany him, because as a couple, they will arouse less suspicion (Hämäläinen 1941b: 37). The doctor's wife Elisabet experiences it as a "terrible walk, to which her societal instincts had forced her to protect the reputation of her husband and family" (ibid.: 43–44).[52]

In addition to the wide range of socially divided residential areas, the literature also contains a number of areas of leisure that are just as radically divided socially. In the summer months, the island of Lammassaari and the beach of Mustikkamaa are frequented by the working class (see for example Lehtonen 1922/2006: 171–177; Sinervo 1937: 6), while the better-off go to the island of Kulosaari (see Waltari 1931: 178). Parks, too, are part of a social geography: "The poor paid taxes from their wages, so that the state could buy weapons and the city could construct parks for the rich and plant flowers around statues", as Aarni, the young labourer in Waltari's *Surun ja ilon kaupunki* ("City of Sorrow and Joy"; 1936: 27) thinks bitterly at the beginning of the novel.[53] Even death separates the privileged and the underprivileged: the poor have a resting place for twenty years, after which period the earth is opened up and a new body buried in the same place, while the rich buy a resting place for eternity – a possible reference to the two main graveyards in Helsinki at the time, the more exclusive graveyard of Hietaniemi, and the newer graveyard of Malmi (Uurto 1936: 289–289; see Sallamaa 1995: 63).

The Loss of the Centre

Helsinki, then, appears as a divided city, but not in the dualistic manner that has often been suggested by the image of the Long Bridge as a central benchmark of social divisions. If two parts of Helsinki are directly juxtaposed with each other in 1920s and 1930s literature, it is not Sörnäinen and the centre of Helsinki, but Sörnäinen and Töölö, in addition to a number of proliferating socially-defined areas at the fringes. The increasing importance of these new parts of the city in Finnish literature entails a gradual diminishing of the importance of the centre of the city, a centre that is described as a dormant remainder of a bygone age. Around the turn of the century, the Esplanade had still functioned as a focal point for all classes and for all the inhabitants of the Finnish capital, even though cohabitation in this synecdoche environment was never without its friction, as the analysis of uneasy encounters at the Esplanade in Chapter 4 illustrates. In addition to the Esplanade, particular vantage points, such as the Observatory Hill, and large squares, such as the Railway Square and the Senate Square, had acted as congregators of the most diverse citizens during the major upheavals that shook the city during the early years of the twentieth century. Such centrally located focal points gradually lose their meaning in literature of the 1920s and 1930s. The image of the gravitational urban centre begins to recede, and in some of the most prominent Helsinki novels of the late 1920s and the 1930s, it is largely left empty: bereft of symbolic meaning, literary protagonists merely pass it by on the move from one part of the periphery to the other. We still find protagonists arriving at the Helsinki railway station, or bumping into acquaintances in the Esplanade. But increasingly, if the city centre is referred to, it is as a world of commodities, and less and less as representative of the traditional symbols of the city as a meeting place, a market place, or as a potent symbol of community.

In Mika Waltari's *Suuri illusioni* (1928), mention is made of the Esplanade and of the street Aleksanterinkatu, the two main arteries of the city, but the characters' interest in the asphalt of the Esplanade is limited, and when Hart and Hellas meet in one of the legendary cafés in the Esplanade, they are bored by their surroundings (Waltari 1928: 82 ff.). An interesting example of the diminishing importance of the centre is present in one of the key scenes in *Suuri illusioni* discussed above (see Chapter 6), in which the protagonist goes on a car trip from Töölö to Vladimirinkatu to buy illegal liquor. The scene is set at night and the centre of Helsinki is quickly passed by and only tangentially observed by means of the lights that fall through the window of the speeding car. The only thing that is visible is the clock of the railway station, which immediately assumes symbolic power as "the moon of modern times" (ibid.: 22).[54] No real interaction is possible between such a literary exalted symbol and the protagonist speeding by.

If the diminished importance of the centre is clearly visible in some of the novels and texts focusing on Töölö discussed in the previous chapter, this change is even more apparent when looking at novels describing the life of the working classes in Helsinki. A particularly poignant example is offered by Helvi Hämäläinen's novel *Katuojan vettä* ("Water in the Gutter"; 1935), which is set in a working-class district immediately adjacent to Sörnäinen, to the north-east of the centre. In this novel, the centre of the city almost completely recedes out of sight, and it is a locality which is visited only for very specific purposes, for example, to go to the hospital (located at Unioninkatu) to give birth. Various Utopias outside of the city (the Soviet Union, America) exert a far greater fascination on this working-class area's inhabitants, and when the neighbours of the protagonist Kirsti compare their own environment with that of the better-off, they do not refer to the centre, but, predictably, to the new district of Töölö (Hämäläinen 1935: 224).

THE SHOP WINDOW AND THE CITY AS A "BORDELLO OF CONSUMPTION"

In novels depicting the working class, such as Hämäläinen's *Katuojan vettä*, it is not the tower that is mentioned first when characters visit the centre, but the shop window, which appears as an embodiment of social difference, and is representative of the transformation of the city centre into a repository of commodity culture. In *Katuojan vettä*, the shop window is quite literally the only element of the city centre that is referred to. To the poor working-class mother Kirsti, the shop window does not embody the "women's paradise"[55] of the shopping centre in any positive sense, but instead, the impossibility of the protagonist of partaking in the feast of consumption. The narrator describes in detail the opulence displayed in front of the protagonist: the beautiful shoes and clothes, the warm children's clothes, the books, the fruits: oranges, apples, grapes, the beautifully made pastries – all things she is utterly unable to procure (Hämäläinen 1935: 34). In the 1930s, Helsinki, like much of the Western world, was in the throes of a severe depression, and the mention of the riches on display in shop windows becomes an important symbol of unattainable happiness. This topos is also present in the work of authors such as Iris Uurto and Elvi Sinervo (Juutila-Purokoski 2006: 121; see also Koskela 1999c: 332). The shop window is one of the images in which the city shows itself to be what David Harvey has called in his discussion of Dreiser's *Sister Carrie* (1900) a "veritable bordello of consumer temptation" in which "money (or the lack of it) becomes itself the measure of distance" (Harvey 1989b: 176).

In Joel Lehtonen's novel *Rakastunut rampa*, too, in addition to the mention of beckoning images of lights and towers, the centre of Helsinki is featured almost exclusively by a shop window. Similarly to the use of this image in *Katuojan vettä*, the shop window in *Rakastunut rampa* functions as an image for the riches of the city which are unattainable to the working-class woman Nelma as she walks through the centre. It provides the immediate background for the act of seduction which will lead to her moral downfall:

> There was no money, no hope… It was evening. The sky was black … rainy snow fell on the street … It would be nice to go into the centre of town, where the lights shone more densely. Nelma walked in thoughts… she stopped in front of the window of some shop. And there a gentleman approached her, young, good-looking, and polite… (Lehtonen 1922/2006: 121–122)[56]

The gloomy environment where Nelma lives is juxtaposed with the "bright lights" of the city centre, to which she feels attracted. While standing in front of a shop window, and gazing at the out-of-reach commodities it displays, Nelma is approached by a man from a higher social class as if she were a commodity – she is seduced and eventually becomes pregnant, after which a descent into prostitution seems certain.

The Centrifugal City

The experience of a city in which the centre has become largely stripped of its symbolic meaning, and in which movement to and from areas on the urban fringes attains ever greater importance, give literary Helsinki in this period the appearance of a centrifugal city, defined by movements and representations increasingly fleeing the centre. Several elements contribute to this experience of the city in literature of the 1920s and 1930s. It is enhanced, first of all, by the physical and material layout of the Finnish capital, and by the way this guides Helsinki's urban development during these years. Situated on a peninsula projecting southwards into the sea, the suburbs expanded out of necessity in the north-eastern and north-western directions once the southern tip of the peninsula had become occupied. As a consequence, both the north-eastern and north-western main roads, and several of the tram lines connecting the various parts of the city, converged upon the centre. Notorious was a traffic node in front of the Student House and the Stockmann department store (the new Stockmann department store was erected in 1930), referred to repeatedly in *Henkien taistelu* as "the madhouse" ("hullunmylly" or literally "mad mill") or "merry-go-round" ("karuselli"), which was "the knot of tram lines in front of the Student House that was hard to get across or around on account of the swarming vehicles" (Lehtonen 1933: 549; see also ibid.: 347).[57] Traffic problems were further enhanced by the fact that movement on an east-west axis was mostly blocked by the railway. These specific features of the capital exert a profound influence on the way the city is experienced by Lauri, the protagonist in Iris Uurto's *Kypsyminen* ("Maturing"; 1935), who earns his money giving private classes to pupils in different parts of the city:

> Helsinki is like a slightly irregular five-pointed star, and he had a pupil at every point; and to get to every tip of the star, he had to pass through the centre. These days, he was always in a hurry and he was leaping those long trips like a madman. (Uurto 1935: 126)[58]

The centrifugal dynamics guiding the experience of literary Helsinki in these years were also informed by developments within literary paradigms and genres. Literary representations of the Finnish capital were not only literally fleeing the centre and becoming more interested in the urban fringes, they were also doing so in a more metaphorical sense. In this respect, they resembled international developments in city literature. Richard Lehan, in *The City in Literature* (1998), uses the concept of the centrifugal city to describe the paradigm shift from naturalism to literary modernism in terms of a move from the centripetal city to the centrifugal city.[59] Lehan refers first of all to a change in narratorial perspective: "The naturalistic narrator observes forces at work from a centre; the modernist narrator finds the centre becoming more complex and opaque, his or her own vision more subjective" (Lehan 1998: 70). Similar observations can be made about the aestheticizing and interiorizing terms in which experiences of Helsinki were couched in novels discussed in the previous chapter, but also the works of Lehtonen, Uurto, and Hämäläinen can be read as part of an increasing interest in subjective experiences (see Laitinen 1991: 413–416; Perttula 2010: 104). The interest in the urban fringes and in experiences of urban dynamics that flee the centre is concomitant with an increasing reluctance to present a comprehensible, totalizing panoramic view of the city, focusing instead on subjective urban experiences, on the fragmentary and the peripheral.

The centrifugal dynamics and the symbolic emptying of the centre in Finnish literature in the 1920s and 1930s can be seen as emanations of what Henri Lefebvre has called "abstract space", the dominant space in capitalist and post-capitalist society. Lefebvre argues that "around 1910 a certain space was shattered" (Lefebvre 1974/1991: 25), and new spatial modes appeared: "abstract spaces", that can be seen at work in "the disappearance of trees, [...] the receding of nature; [...] the great empty spaces of the state and the military – plazas that resemble parade grounds; [...] commercial centres packed tight with commodities, money and cars" (Lefebvre 1974/1991: 50; see also ibid.: 53, 285).[60] Abstract space levels and homogenizes the complex layers of historical space, and reduces differences. In the way it dominates space, it draws all elements of space into a process of commodification.[61] The emptying of the centre found in Finnish Helsinki novels from the 1930s is an instructive example of how literature posits urban forces at work that have managed to "force worrisome groups, the workers among others, out towards the periphery" and "to organize the centre as locus of decision, wealth, power and information" (Lefebvre 1974/1991: 375). In this constellation, the city centre no longer functions as a natural meeting place. Emptied of its symbolic meaning, it becomes filled with consumerism and with politically inspired spectacle.

One highly interesting and eventful attribution of symbolic meaning to the historical centre in this period – as described in Helsinki literature –

is the "Farmers' March" (1930), the extreme-right Lapua movement's display of power. Significantly, it was a spectacle organized and performed primarily by outsiders to the city: one of the aims of the march was to show the moderate and leftist forces in the Finnish capital what the Finnish heartland (or more specifically, the province Ostrobothnia) thought and felt. The description of the Farmers' March in specific novels goes a long way in telling the narrator's political leanings, as well as his/her stance on the question whether it would be the city or the country that would have the decisive voice in choosing political directions in 1930s Finland. In Lehtonen's *Henkien taistelu*, Kleophas Sampila is a detached observer as the farmers march through the city which is not his (Lehtonen 1933: 509–523), but the description is couched, as is the novel as a whole, in profoundly satirical terms. In Arvi Kivimaa's novel *Viheriöivä risti* ("The Blooming Cross"; 1939), the march is juxtaposed with the protagonist's confused thoughts following the birth of his child, but it is tempting to interpret the juxtaposition in this novel of a new birth and the Farmers' March as an indication that the narrator welcomes the countryside's call to action. No dissonant voices in the "jubilant crowd" are recorded (Kivimaa 1939: 259),[62] and not much later, the protagonist turns his back on the city to take up the position of a doctor in a small countryside parish. Juhani, in Mika Waltari's *Palava nuoruus* (1935: 385 ff.), looks at the marching farmers with detachment, certain only of the fact that he is living a historical moment (ibid.: 386), but although he voices some doubts about the Lapua movement's methods, nothing in the description indicates that a large part of the Helsinki population would not have been waving their handkerchiefs and hats at those "men of the countryside with their tanned and hardened faces" (ibid.).

The Farmers' March is a revealing example of how spectacles endeavour to control and dominate urban public space, not in the least since it was modelled on the parade through Helsinki organized by the victorious white army in 1918. This parade, too, was organized in part as a celebration of the victory of a particular kind of rural (and in part Ostrobothnian) Finland over what to a certain degree was a particular kind of urban Finland, and it features in several Finnish novels and short stories written in the 1920s and 1930s.[63] In Waltari's *Palava nuoruus*, it features in relation to a third parade: the celebratory parade that was organized to commemorate the fifteenth anniversary of the Victory Parade in 1933. The sight has a profound effect on the protagonist Juhani, and while looking at the passing army regiments, he remembers his feelings as a child when watching the same men marching through the capital for the first time. Again, the description shows a unified picture of the 1918 celebration: "he remembered the sunny picture of the first great parade of the Finnish army, resplendent with flowers, flying flags and delirious, thoughtless delight from his childhood" (Waltari 1935: 452).[64] Similarly to Leo in *Viheriöivä risti*, his experience is swiftly followed by what could be understood as a response to the call of what is described as the "farmers' army" (ibid.), in a clear echo of the "Farmers' March" Juhani witnessed in 1930. Not much later, he feels "an overwhelming desire to go there, where all of their power had come from originally" (ibid.: 455), and he travels back to the farm where his family originally started out from on their journey to Helsinki.[65]

Dissenting voices about how rightist endeavours to dominate the capital's public space, such as the 1918 parade and the 1930 Farmers' March, were experienced can be found in a number of prose texts from this period. The description of the Victory Parade in the final passage of Joel Lehtonen's novel *Punainen mies* ("Red Man"), for example, gives a profoundly satirical view of the events (Lehtonen 1925/2008: 649–651; see also Palmgren 1989: 103) that resonates with the description of the Farmers' March in *Henkien taistelu*. And the working class, in turn, took occasional possession of the symbolic potential of the city centre, as in, for example, a short story in Sinervo's *Runo Söörnäisistä* ("Poem about Sörnäinen"; 1937), in which a girl remembers a triumphant May Day march (Sinervo 1937: 38).

Hampered Mobility

The transformation of the city into a "bordello of consumer temptation" was, according to David Harvey, also commensurate with the extent to which "money (or the lack of it) becomes itself the measure of distance" (Harvey 1989b: 176). In Finnish literature of this period there is a striking correlation between belonging to the less privileged social classes and experiences of hampered physical mobility in the capital. In the Torch Bearer -inspired literature of the late 1920s and 1930s, heightened speed and mobility were symptomatic of the inner drive of the characters, of their interest in modernity, urbanity, and the exotic, but also indicative of their social class. The exceptionally large range of mobility and described urban geography, for example, in Waltari's novel *Appelsiininsiemen* ("The Orange Seed"; 1931), especially from the perspective of the female protagonist Irene, is indicative of the literary characters' desires and dreams, but also of their social class and the possibilities engendered by membership in the upper social strata. Running parallel to texts inspired by Torch Bearer aesthetics, however, a whole literature of the urban margins comes into view during these same years; a literature which is more concerned with the extending horizontal plane of urban sprawl, and with experiences of cumbersome movement and severely hampered mobility.

A case in point is the description of the young woman Kirsti in Helvi Hämäläinen's *Katuojan vettä* ("Water in the Gutter"; 1935). In the very beginning of this novel, there is a description of severely impinged mobility, in which the protagonist Kirsti is described while she is dragging her cumbersome belongings through the snow on her way to the railway station from where she will take the train to Helsinki. She has only recently been fired from her white-collar job because she is pregnant. With an absent husband and no savings or financially supportive family, she finds herself fast on a downward social track. Throughout the novel, images of cumbersome movement reappear at crucial stages. When, in the latest phase of her pregnancy, she goes to the maternity institution (at the centrally located Unioninkatu), she walks with great difficulty through dark and snowy Helsinki.

Rather than spending the little money she has on a tram ticket, she decides to walk the distance, and her difficulty of movement is described at considerable length (Hämäläinen 1935: 33–35). Legally, too, Kirsti's mobility is restricted: her husband has left her, but as long as they are married, Kirsti falls under the authorities of her husband's home town, and it is this place she is supposed to go to if she wants poor relief. The difficulty of movement in *Katuojan vettä* is related, in particular, to movement from the periphery to the centre, not so much because extensive distances have to be crossed, but because Kirsti lacks the money to spend on public transport. There are also material reasons why Kirsti feels ill at ease moving in the centre: her clothes and shoes are in a poor state, and as a result, "while moving in the centre of the city, she received the kind of glances reserved for suspicious and badly-dressed creatures" (Hämäläinen 1935: 138).[66] Physically, too, she begins to change through the hard manual work, and her body becomes deformed (ibid.: 158).

Apart from Kirsti in *Katuojan vettä* and Sakris Kukkelman in *Rakastunut rampa*, there is a whole range of literary characters who, due to a variety of causes, exhibit a degree of deformity which has its effect on the way they move through their urban environment. In most prose texts, social class takes on a central role in the factors leading to hampered mobility. This is the case, for example, in the short story "Lentolehtiset" ("Pamflets"), in Elvi Sinervo's *Runo Söörnäisistä*, in which a communist agitator is literally crippled by a police horse during a demonstration (Sinervo 1937: 66). A sense of restricted mobility, however, is not only felt by this individual character, but also by the girl Anna in the same story, and by the working class as a whole, which was "in a way in the same state as Anna, crippled by what had hit it, didn't dare to do anything, didn't want anything" (ibid.: 71).[67] In this story, the debilitating effects of the losses incurred during the Civil War are still felt by the unprivileged. Other examples of crippled characters are the blind war veteran of the Crimean War, who is eventually run over by a car on the Long Bridge, in a 1917 short story by Toivo Tarvas (see Chapter 5), and the old man, crippled by sorrow, who is hit by a car in front of the Helsinki railway station where he has just arrived, in Waltari's *Surun ja ilon kaupunki* (1936). Both of these working-class characters are overtaken by modernizing society. A particular case is Kalle, in Matti Kurjensaari's 1930s student novel *Tie Helsinkiin* ("The Road to Helsinki"; 1937). This sickly student is repeatedly described as having difficulties to walk the streets of Helsinki because of a medical condition, but he is also sexually frustrated and crippled by poverty. His plight is that of a generation of Finnish young men and women trying to move upwards in society in the decades between the wars (Laitinen 1963: 7). Kalle's friend, the novel's protagonist, expresses their predicament as follows: "All our ability to act was broken by an appalling and incessant lack of money. We were like cripples watching from the sidelines how others moved." (Kurjensaari 1937: 45)[68]

In a number of texts by Iris Uurto, too, questions of class find their expression in the crippled mobility of the protagonists. This is the case on a very material level for the protagonist Lauri, in *Kypsyminen* ("Maturing"; 1935), the student mentioned above. A part-time *flâneur*, not all his city walks are performed voluntarily. Because of lack of money, he rarely takes the tram but instead covers the considerable distances he has to cross in the capital on foot (Uurto 1935: 154). In between lessons, he rarely has time to return home to his peripherally located rented room, which means he is forced to spend his time idling around, a situation which angers him and gives him the feeling that his life is out of joint: "How disjointed is my life, an hour here, another one there, and always running around through the city" (Uurto 1935: 49).[69] Lauri's difficulties in terms of mobility, however, run much deeper. He is repeatedly described as unable to move, and lying on his bed in a state of utter lethargy (ibid.: 192, 231, 314, 387). This immobility is in part brought about by feelings of depression due to his unhappy love, but also related to Lauri's in-between position in society: educated, he is unable to work with his hands, but he does not have the possibility of turning his knowledge into financial profit, either, and he explicitly states that this social position is at the root of his unsuccessful love (ibid.: 349). Lauri is not the only character in the novel who displays a "lethargic passivity" that enraged some readers (Väre 1946: 26). Lauri's friend Niilo is also an in-between character, but one who has made the reverse social journey: as an educated member of the working class, he feels pulled in two opposing directions, with lethargy as the result: Niilo confides to Lauri that he dreams of spending his life lying down, but regrets it is impossible (Uurto 1935: 72). In the sequel to the novel, *Rakkaus ja pelko* ("Love and Fear"; 1936), the same characters again take central stage (this time Lauri's sister Kaari is the focal point of the narration), and their difficulties in taking their lives in their own hands is repeatedly juxtaposed with descriptions of how they are lying in bed or lounging on couches (Uurto 1936: 34, 51, 61). Again, the characters' passivity is related to the difficulties they encounter in fulfilling themselves – difficulties that stem, in part, from sexual and moral conventions of the society in which they live, but also from class-related conditions.

A Divided City: Class and Gender

Movement through the city is also, of course, closely related to the gender of the city walker. The analysis of the experiences of female city walkers in Helsinki around the turn of the century, in Chapter 4, demonstrates how literary instances of women being harassed in the capital's public space during these years typically carried a clear message of social, moral or even political indignation. In literature of the 1920s and 1930s, unpleasant encounters in urban public space are framed within a rather different discourse, and more often than not, they are used as illustrations of an unbridgeable moral or social divide. The evil that befalls women in Helsinki's public space does not function, in this context, as a wake-up call to change social injustice, but as a reminder of perceived social realities.

A socially divided city is repeatedly visible in the encounters by women in the Helsinki of Mika Waltari's 1920s and 1930s novels. In almost all of these novels, there are descriptions of women being harassed and, in some cases, raped in a public or semi-public space, but little in the way of moral indignation is expressed by the narrator. A symptomatic example can be found in Waltari's debut novel *Suuri illusioni* ("The Great Illusion"; 1928). When Hart and Caritas go by taxi to a working-class home to buy illegal liquor, the working-class woman they meet tells them that her little daughter sells liquor on the streets, and that she is sometimes harassed by upper-class men. She insinuates that one of them has tried to rape the girl (Waltari 1928: 23). To Hart and Caritas, the whole scene is merely interesting as an example of urban working-class conditions, not as a reminder that anything should or could be done: "This is kind of an adventure. And such a cute little girl!"[70] Caritas exclaims when they are back in the car (ibid.).

In Waltari's subsequent Helsinki novel, *Appelsiininsiemen* ("The Orange Seed"; 1931), there are again repeated instances in which references are made to women being harassed in Helsinki's public space. The threat of gendered violence is repeatedly related to transgressions of class boundaries. At the beginning of the novel, the charm of the April evening is compared by the middle class protagonist Irene to the exciting moment when she is approached by a working-class man on the streets – dangerous, but also arousing (Waltari 1931: 20). Towards the end of the novel, a shocking case of gang rape is recounted, which involves one of the students of Irene's father, a university professor, who has secretly and platonically fallen in love with an innocent-looking student. During an intermission at a concert at the University, the professor overhears people telling the story in question. At first he is hardly moved, and revealingly, the reason for his indifference is that he considers the event to be not more than "a sign of all those things, of which he was already certain: that they lived in times that were brutal and pitiless" (ibid: 451).[71] The only reason why he is moved slightly more than usually is that "it concerned an educated girl, a student" (ibid.).[72] To the professor, violence against working-class women is not something by which he is moved, let alone something which would lead him to consider taking measures. When someone from the educated class is involved, however, his interest is awakened.

The description in *Appelsiininsiemen* of the terrible events which had befallen the female student, who turns out to be the object of the professor's idealized love, revolves again around class and the perception of class. On the fateful night, the girl had been visiting acquaintances in the district of Munkkiniemi – to the north-west of the Helsinki centre – and was walking back late in the evening to a tram stop. A group of men forced her into a car, raped her, and subsequently left her in the working-class district of Sörnäinen. Interestingly, the reason, as proposed by the gossiping people standing near the professor, why the men had picked this particular girl, was that the men had "perhaps thought that she was some sort of servant girl or a normal [sic] fallen woman" (ibid.).[73] It is a trail of thought which reveals the speakers' world view: shocking is not so much what had happened in itself, but that the person involved was from the educated class, and had apparently been mistaken for a working-class girl. The events themselves are considered normal by the speakers, and would not have been the subject of conversation if the victim had been a "servant girl or a normal fallen woman". The conversation, moreover, strengthens a sense of social geography, in which the working-class district of Sörnäinen appears as a particularly dangerous area; in the same conversation, a story is told of a "bloke with a venereal disease who had tried to rape an eight-year-old" girl in Sörnäinen (ibid.).[74]

In *Sielu ja liekki* ("The Soul and the Flame"; 1934), the second part of Waltari's Helsinki trilogy, a mini-story recounts how a country girl comes to Helsinki, is seduced and raped. The story, set in the years of the Great Strike and the Viapori rebellion, is recounted from the point of view of the protagonist Toivo, a vicar. It is remarkably similar to the tales of seduction found in literature from the turn of the century – a young girl moves to the city, is seduced and/or raped and becomes pregnant – but the conclusion drawn by the narrator is very different from these earlier stories. The case "gave Toivo a deeper insight into life on the city's fringes than ever before" (Waltari 1934: 323).[75] Toivo does not blame the man who had seduced the girl, then made her drink alcohol, and raped her, nor does he fundamentally consider how the structures of society underlying such events could be changed, as Henrik in Järnefelt's *Veljekset* ("Brothers"; 1900), Hannes in *Veneh'ojalaiset* ("The Family Veneh'ojalaiset"; 1909), or Markus in Kyösti Wilkuna's *Vaikea tie* ("The Difficult Road"; 1915) would do. Instead, he ponders the motives of the girl. He is not sure whether her tale is an expression of innocence or stupidity; eventually he decides "that the strange, fabulous city life had drugged the senses of the girl, so that she didn't know what she did" (Waltari 1934: 324).[76]

The way in which rape and the harassment of women in urban public space is represented in Waltari's oeuvre in the 1920s and 1930s is interesting also from the perspective of a discourse on the "new woman" and a new kind of relationship between men and women based on equality and comradeship, which authors such as Waltari and other contemporary authors such as Arvi Kivimaa have been claimed to represent.[77] In Waltari's 1920s and 1930s Helsinki novels, women such as Caritas, as well as the girlfriend of the protagonist's little brother in *Suuri illusioni*, Irene in *Appelsiininsiemen*, and Sisar Sunnila in *Surun ja ilon kaupunki* have all attained a measure of independence, and in their relationships, men and women pay lip service to equality. Behind a new and relative independence and a new kind of relationship based on being soul mates, however, lies a radical class-divide. This is something Aarne, in *Surun ja ilon kaupunki*, the working-class man who is in love with the upper class girl Sisar, learns to his dismay. To Aarne, the centre of Helsinki constitutes a place where he, as a member of the working class, is not at ease: when going to the main library in the centre "he always went walking fast, slipping past passers-by, with his hands deep in his pockets and his hat over his eyes" (Waltari 1936: 75).[78] The library itself appears as a more or less class-neutral environment, in which Aarne is able to cross the social divide and become acquainted with Sisar Sunnila, the daughter of a factory director. Outside the library, however, there is a divided world order. Whereas Aarne feels uncomfortable in the centre of the city, the presence of Sisar is not accepted in the working-class cafés Aarne frequents, and they can only meet in secret in places on the urban fringes, such as the waterfront (ibid.: 79–80). In a final meeting in Kaisaniemi Park, the situation comes to a head when, consumed by his impossible love, Aarne tries to forcibly embrace the girl. Sisar slaps him in the face, and their ways part. To Aarne, Helsinki has no future to offer, and he leaves the city.

A Home in the Margins?

Henri Lefebvre suggest that all cities have "an underground and repressed life, and hence an 'unconscious' of its own" (Lefebvre 1974/1991: 36). In several novels and short stories that appeared in the 1920s and 1930s and thematized Helsinki, this urban unconscious appears as often distinctly uncanny images of crippled figures, landscapes and buildings, through which characters are cumbersomely making their way. Helsinki novels and short stories in these decades are not only concerned with speed and with accelerating mobility; on the contrary. During these years, a whole range of city novels and short stories come into being that depict the impeded mobility – both concrete, and socially – of marginalized characters.

In all the novels discussed in this chapter, the experience of the capital is permeated by a sense of class, and it is class or class struggle that looms large in the background of the trajectories taken by characters such as Sakris in Joel Lehtonen's *Rakastunut rampa*, Kirsti in Helvi Hämäläinen's *Katuojan vettä* and Lauri in Iris Uurto's *Kypsyminen*. The cumbersome movement of these characters through the city, and their often downward social trajectories in the city, would seem to warrant the conclusion that for lower-class characters, the experience of Helsinki is a distinctly pessimistic one. Not only are the urban fringes described – like the people that inhabit them – in terms of deformity, poverty and disease, they are also repeatedly portrayed as generic and nondescript. The street where Kirsti lives in *Katuojan vettä*, for example, is described by a visiting doctor as indistinguishable from other similar streets: "Is it here? [...] These small streets on the outskirts of the city are so hard to distinguish from each other" (Hämäläinen 1935: 228).[79] Similarly, in the opening story of the collection of stories in Sinervo's *Runo Söörnäisistä* ("Poem about Sörnäinen"; 1937), the narrator describes the wooden houses in one working-class street as "all the same" (Sinervo 1937: 5).[80] These suburban fringes are portrayed as a generic environment, displaying characteristics of what Edward Relph has described with the term "placelessness" (Relph 1976: 79–121); Relph uses the term to denote (mostly industrialized) environments that lack "diverse landscapes and significant places" and that are defined by "[c]ultural and geographical uniformity" and by inauthenticity (ibid.: 79, 80–89).

If one were to give the final word, however, to the extradiegetic narrators in Sinervo's *Runo Söörnäisistä* or in Lehtonen's *Rakastunut rampa*, or to the outsider perspective of the doctor in Hämäläinen's *Katuojan vettä*, this would be to miss an important point concerning the experience of the city in these novels. The urban fringes that are repeatedly portrayed by outsiders as generic and nondescript are also portrayed as homely and infused with individual stories and emotions. Even the most dystopian environment can be experienced as a home for the people who inhabit it. Krokelby is a case in point. For all its terrible defects, Krokelby in *Rakastunut rampa*

("A Cripple in Love"; 1922) is repeatedly described lovingly. In the summer, even the houses in Krokelby are described as beautiful and homely (Lehtonen 1922/2006: 144) and the natural beauty is repeatedly portrayed without the downgrading tone of irony or satire. Tellingly, Sakris does not want to move away from these surroundings: he dreams of a place for him and his beloved Nelma not far from Krokelby, near the Vantaa River rapids (Lehtonen 1922/2006: 131).

The sense of attachment to everyday urban environments visible in several of the above novels is in part related to their genre. Several of these prose texts are, in terms of genre, close to what Blanche Gelfant has called the "ecological novel", a novel that "focuses upon one small spatial unit such as a neighbourhood or city block and explores in detail the manner of life identified with this place" (Gelfant 1954: 11). Helvi Hämäläinen's *Katuojan vettä*, Joel Lehtonen's *Rakastunut rampa* and several of the texts by Elvi Sinervo in *Runo Söörnäisistä*, with their limited perspective and focus on a very limited area in the city – sometimes as small as one house, street, or block of houses – bear many traits of the ecological novel. In ecological novels, the dystopian characteristics of the city as a whole tend to be offset or at least temporarily suspended by the sense of place that everyday and often communal experiences of dwelling and making-do is able to confer to the bleakest of environments. As Relph points out, "superficial expressions of placelessness are far from being an infallible guide to deeper attitudes; being lived-in confers some authenticity on even the most trivial and unrelentingly uniform landscapes" (Relph 1976: 80). In all of the examples above, the view of the environment as typified by "placelessness" is not shared by the people inhabiting these districts. Kirsti, in *Katuojan vettä*, becomes a member of a closely-knit society with a strong sense of communal solidarity. Similarly, in *Runo Söörnäisistä*, the inhabitants of the outskirts of the city are described as having an intimate knowledge of the secrets of that particular area, especially from the viewpoint of children: young Veera, for example, introduces her friend, the I-narrator of the story "Veera", to the "secrets of the outskirts of the city" (Sinervo 1937: 31).[81]

For a native of Helsinki, the city is able to offer some consolation even in conditions of poverty and unemployment. Lauri, the protagonist in Iris Uurto's *Kypsyminen* ("Maturing"; 1935), considers with a sting of self-irony when he wanders the city in search of a job: "I also still have one particular right in this birth city of mine: I am allowed to walk on the shady part of the street" (Uurto 1935: 335).[82] This statement may at first sight seem purely ironical, but regardless of his difficulties in Helsinki, Lauri feels a profound sense of attachment to his home city, which surfaces occasionally during the narrative. The most explicit passage occurs when Lauri returns home after some time in the countryside, which he experienced as particularly depressing. When watching the urban panorama from the threshold of the railway station, he feels joy and almost gratitude, and when he starts to walk, the experience is described as "real pleasure from the city" (ibid.: 393).[83] In part, this happiness is related to the fact that what Lauri sees around him in the city are things he desires but has not (yet) attained, and which for him are embodied in the tram: "speed, easy velocity, collectivity" (ibid.).[84]

Situating Krokelby on the Map

The imaginary Krokelby is situated to the north-east of Helsinki, close to the Vanhakaupunki area, the location of the original Helsinki settlement of 1640. Krokelby has been identified on various grounds with a number of existing Helsinki suburbs, notably with Oulunkylä, Kumpula and the western Helsinki area of Haaga-Huopalahti (see Laurila 1967: 105; Pulkkinen 2004; Kallinen 2011; Tarkka 2012: 208–209; see, however, Hellaakoski 1950: 96). The desire to locate Krokelby on the map is in part rooted in a wish to read Lehtonen's own life into his writings: the author had moved to Haaga/Huopalahti, a community at the western fringes of Helsinki in the 1910s, and continued spending time there until his death. Although both *Rakastunut rampa* and *Henkien taistelu* unequivocally place Krokelby at the *eastern* fringes of the Helsinki peninsula, several critics have identified Krokelby with Huopalahti (Ahokas 1973: 200; Palmgren 1989: 103). Ironically, over the past few years, different parts of the Finnish capital have claimed a stake on the dubious legacy of Krokelby: both Oulunkylä and Kumpula, two districts in eastern Helsinki, claim they are depicted in literature as Krokelby (see Pulkkinen 2004; Kallinen 2011).

The Future of Mankind: Athleticism or Deformity?

In the collection of essays *Nykyaikaa etsimässä* ("In Search of Modern Times"; 1929/2002), Olavi Paavolainen expressed uncertainty as to whether the modern age, with its interest in machine and body culture, would lead to a healthy or, on the contrary, a crippled future human. Clearly, the possibility that the modern age would deform and distort the human body was for him one of the possible options:

"What is going to be the emblem of the future generation? Is it going to be the naked, tanned youngster in the sparkling sunlight, with underneath his feet the sand and slack of a sports stadium, with an enormous concrete wall in the background? Or is it going to be a freak, degenerated by pleasure and by automatized comfort, with an unnaturally developed skull, a decrepit body, and with arms and legs that have become atrophied by the use of circuit breakers and elevators?" (Paavolainen 1929/2002: 452)

Conclusion

Helsinki literature written in Finnish in 1890–1940 contains a range of urban experiences that is much more complex than contemporary critics have claimed, or than would appear from the limited attention that has been given to literary Helsinki during most of the twentieth century. Contrary to the depreciative idea of literary Helsinki as an eternal Cinderella, an idea which occurs repeatedly during these decades, Finnish prose literature set in Helsinki in this period is conspicuously rich, both in quantitative terms and in the range of experiences it covers. Several novels published during this period can aspire to the title of a fully-fledged Helsinki novel, with Arvid Järnefelt's *Veneh'ojalaiset* ("The Family Veneh'oja"; 1909) as arguably the first candidate for the title of a Great Helsinki Novel. In the 1910s, several more texts that could be read predominantly as city novels appear in quick succession: Eino Leino's *Pankkiherroja* ("Bank Lords"; 1914), Maila Talvio's *Niniven lapset* ("Children of Nineveh"; 1915); Toivo Tarvas's *Eri tasoilta* ("On Different Levels"; 1916) and *Kohtalon tuulissa* ("The Winds of Fate"; 1916). What these novels have in common is that most literary critics have not read them predominantly as city novels, although the plot in all cases revolves around the ways in which the protagonists come to grip with the city. In the 1920s and 1930s, again, a number of prose texts appear that can be considered as city novels: Joel Lehtonen's *Henkien taistelu* ("Battle of the Spirits"; 1933), several of the novels written by Iris Uurto, as well as novels by Unto Karri, Arvi Kivimaa and Mika Waltari. The only works that have been read mostly as Helsinki novels are those by Mika Waltari and other authors associated with the Torch Bearer movement, such as Karri and Kivimaa.

The foundational urban experience in Finnish prose literature written around the turn of the twentieth century is that of the shock induced by arrival in the disorientating city. Juhani Aho's novella *Helsinkiin* (1889) can be considered as a prototypical text in this respect. The disorientating and in part paralyzing shock of arrival experienced by Antti Ljungberg, the protagonist in *Helsinkiin*, reverberates with the collision of different spatial and temporal dimensions: a cyclical, agrarian society running head-on into the more linear spatial experience of the modern city. In the context of international literature of the city, the experiences of Antti and similar characters in Finnish prose fiction of the nineteenth and early twentieth centuries fit into the pattern of the "Young Man/Woman of the Provinces" novels (following Chanda 1981), which describe the move of ambitious provincials to the metropolis. The shock of arrival must also be understood as rooted in the dystopian and entropic visions of naturalist and decadent literature, in which the city is experienced as an alienating and degenerating environment.

The everyday experiences of urban public space in literary texts depend largely on the class, gender, and even on the political and linguistic background of the literary character in question. The centrally located Esplanade is crucial for an understanding of how differently Helsinki's public space was experienced by people from various backgrounds. In literature, the Esplanade constitutes a microcosm of all of Helsinki and appears as a "shorthand expression" of the city (following Wohl & Strauss 1958). For the bourgeoisie, a walk along the Esplanade at the appropriate moment amounts to a ritual that affirms one's status and position in society. The fact that this environment is, in particular around the turn of the century, also the main area in which Helsinki's street prostitution was carried out, leads to a number of revealing misunderstandings concerning the unwritten rules governing the use of public space. In Eino Leino's novel *Jaana Rönty*, one further dimension of the experience of Helsinki's public space in this period becomes evident: the tense political situation in the Finnish capital during these years.

In the first decades of the twentieth century, Helsinki is experienced as a space in motion. The Finnish capital is depicted as an expanding and transforming city, with new streets being laid out and stone houses replacing dilapidated wooden sheds. In texts such Toivo Tarvas's *Häviävää Helsinkiä* ("Disappearing Helsinki"; 1917), Helsinki is also described as a disappearing city, and inhabitants of the city see beloved places being swept away by the forces of modernity. The accelerating transformations visible in Helsinki are intimately bound up with the strained socio-political situation. Arvid Järnefelt's novel *Veneh'ojalaiset* (1909) presents a kaleidoscopic panorama of the various experiences evoked by Helsinki during these volatile years. In the early twentieth century, the political tension of the "Frost Years", the first period of Russian oppression, transforms the experience of Helsinki into something that borders on the ecstatic, but also on the apocalyptic. In several prose texts, Järnefelt's *Veneh'ojalaiset*, in particular, the sense of an urban world falling to pieces is not entirely pessimistic, but exists side by side with feelings of a strong attachment to characters' urban surroundings.

Helsinki literature of the 1920s and 1930s further develops the defining traits that take form around the turn of the century, and adds a number of new thematic and stylistic nuances. In novels by authors such as Mika Waltari, Iris Uurto and Arvi Kivimaa, the city experience is explicitly thematized, and, more importantly, the urban experience is increasingly aestheticized and internalized. The internalization of the urban experience and the appearance of particular motifs, such as the nocturnal car drive through the city, give rise to specific narrative techniques through which the innermost emotions of the literary characters are rendered. In Mika Waltari's debut novel *Suuri illusioni* ("The Great Illusion"; 1928), in particular, the city appears as a catalyst of plot developments, and functions as the privileged subject matter of the characters' discussions and imagination. As a lived environment, it becomes intimately intertwined with the protagonists' consciousness.

During these decades, a rupture in the way the Finnish capital is experienced in literature becomes visible. This rupture is not, as often ascertained, primarily situated in the works of the Torch Bearers or prose authors writing in their wake. Rather, the new literary approaches to the Finnish capital can be found in literary works that explore a two-fold periphery: on the one hand, novels that describe marginalized city dwellers and city spaces, and on the other hand, texts that make use of literary genres that until then had been fairly marginal. Joel Lehtonen's novel *Henkien taistelu* can be considered as a key novel in the way it explores new, hitherto peripheral terrain on the outer edges of Helsinki, and particularly in the way it makes innovative use of an unusual literary genre, the Menippean satire.

As the description of the city moves inwards, the experience of Helsinki becomes increasingly dominated by a sense of centrifugal dynamics, moving from the centre outwards towards the fringes. The analysis of literary descriptions of spatial movement reveals to what extent Helsinki in 1930s literature is described in terms of relations, directions and thresholds. New city districts assume the role of central environments in the city novels and prose stories during these decades, and the importance of the city centre gradually diminishes. The district Töölö becomes the symbol of a New Helsinki and of a new, middle class urban experience. In addition to literature centred on Töölö and middle class experiences of Helsinki, the 1920s and 1930s witness an increasing number of texts exploring working class areas such as Vallila, Sörnäinen and Punavuori, as well as the expanding suburban edges of the city. Several of the characters in the prose texts describing these social and/or geographical margins of the city display difficulties in their movement through urban public space. In texts such as Joel Lehtonen's *Rakastunut rampa* ("A Cripple in Love"; 1922), Helvi Hämäläinen's *Katuojan vettä* ("Water in the Gutter"; 1935) and Iris Uurto's *Kypsyminen* ("Maturing"; 1935), hampered mobility becomes the symbol of the difficulties characters experience in rising above the limitations imposed by class or by the moral boundaries set by society.

One final conclusion to be drawn is the profound sense of attachment to the city which permeates many of the Helsinki prose texts written during this whole period. Even in the most pessimistic Young Man/Woman from the Provinces novels, an optimistic view of the city is present at least in the form of a potential future in the capital. The distinctly negative experiences of many turn-of-the-twentieth-century characters, whose environments are forcibly transformed by modernization and industrialization, are also, paradoxically, rooted in a profound sense of attachment to environments that are experienced as intimately known and even beloved.

Many of the central characteristics of how Helsinki is experienced in the literature published during this period (1890–1940) remain part of the ongoing discourse on literary Helsinki: Helsinki as a city of leisure and light, inviting dreamy wanderings; the experience of a city divided along the fault lines of gender, class and language; the city as a disorientating and paralyzing cesspit of vice; the city as an *imago mundi*, symbolic of the body politic; the city of everyday and often very mundane experiences, and the city that invites a profound sense of attachment – an environment onto which characters project their innermost sentiments.

Notes

INTRODUCTION

1   "[...] kaupunki hengähtää kivisenä ja armottomana, avoimen meren ja vaalean taivaan syleilemänä karulla niemekkeellään [...]"
    All translations are mine unless mentioned otherwise.
2   See Zacharias Topelius, who states that in comparison with Turku, Helsinki "does not have any history" (Topelius 1845/2003: 11), and the foreword to *Helsinki, a Literary Companion*, which begins with the words "Helsinki is a young city" (Hawkins & Lehtonen 2000: 6). See also Marja-Liisa Rönkkö on the myth of Helsinki's youth (1992: 160).
3   Tunturi 1996: 160.
4   "Tukholmalla on Strindberginsä, Pietarilla Dostojevskinsa, Berlinillä Kretzerinsä, Hampurilla Frensseninsä, Oululla Pakkalansa ja Raumalla Nortamonsa – kuka on Helsingin runoilija? Kuka on Helsingille lunastanut lupakirjan runon kaupunkien yhdyskuntaan?"
    It is noteworthy that Koskenniemi debuted with a collection of poetry in which urban images dominated (1906); in his later lyrical works, however, urban material gradually disappeared from sight (see Kupiainen 1941: 368).
5   "[...] synteettistä runoelmaa Helsingistä, romaania tai eeposta, jossa tämä pohjoinen pääkaupunki eläisi kokonaisuudessaan kaikkine niine ominaisuuksineen, joita luonto, rotu ja kulttuuri ovat sille määränneet."
6   Maila Talvio draws a direct comparison between Helsinki and Cinderella in a short essayistic text "Pieni puhe meidän Helsingille" ("A Small Talk with Our Helsinki"; 1936/1951), which is clearly in dialogue with Koskenniemi's *Runon kaupunkeja* (see also Talvio 1936: 9). In 1929, a column in the magazine *Aitta* refers again to the ongoing discussion concerning the lack of a real Helsinki novel (Ahonen 1929). Ahonen gives as one of the reasons the fact that many Finnish authors were not born in the capital. In 1931, Yrjö Kivimies returns to the same thematics in the causerie "Öistä Helsinkiä" ("Helsinki at Night"), regretting the lack of a novel with Helsinki as its main character (1931).
7   This exclusion does not want to suggest that these genres are without interest for the development of urban literature – on the contrary. In many respects, the modern city was thematized most clearly in the light literature of "office girl books", detective novels and youth novels (see Tunturi 1996; Koskela 1999b: 266, 279; Malmio 1999: 291–292, 2005: 77–110). The popular fiction written by Kersti Bergroth, in particular, contains innovative and fascinating experiences of Helsinki from an unusual perspective (that of young, upper middle class girls).
    Historical novels include Maila Talvio's Helsinki trilogy *Itämeren tytär* ("Daughter of the Baltic"; 1929, 1931, 1936; see Suolahti 1948/1981, 1960/1981), set in the 18th century.

9   The most important reason for excluding literature in Swedish is that there are arguably two different literary traditions on Helsinki: one written in Swedish by Finland-Swedish authors, the other written by authors writing in Finnish. The rich tradition of writing on the city in Finland-Swedish literature has already received considerable academic attention, and recent academic monographs on the subject serve as reminders of the continuing interest in city images in Finland-Swedish literature (see Ciaravolo 2000, and in particular, Toftegaard Pedersen 2007). In contrast, little progress has been made in mapping the experiences evoked by Helsinki in literature written in Finnish.
10 At least two 2012 publications do refer to Helsinki's literature. *Helsingfors i ord och bild* ("Helsinki in words and images"; Assmuth et al. 2012) presents photographs of Helsinki from the turn of the twentieth century side by side with literary excerpts in a volume aimed at the general public. There is, however, little or no contextualization or analysis of the literary examples. And Eino Leino's (no relation to the famous author) *Kirjailijoiden Helsinki* ("Writers' Helsinki"; 2012) gives a popular history of anecdotes related to Helsinki and its literary authors.
11 General overviews of Helsinki literature, aimed at a broad audience, include Kalajoki 1993; Hasu & Peltonen 2000; Hawkins & Lehtonen 2000; Larmola 2005. Ismo Loivamaa has drafted a useful list of representations of Helsinki in Finnish literature (1993).
12 My gratitude goes out to Jarmo Wideman, who created, with painstaking attention to detail, the maps of Helsinki used in this study.

Ways of Writing and Reading the City

1   See Bradbury 1976/1986; Williams 1985; Wilson 1995: 153; Hirsh 2004; Brooks 2005: 131.
2   See Klotz 1969; Pike 1981; Lehan 1998; Keunen 2000.
3   For examples of studies on the city in the work of a particular author, see for example Goode 1978/1979; for particular cities, see for example Citron 1961 and Stierle 1993/2001 (Paris); Pesonen 1987 (St. Petersburg); Patell & Waterman 2010 (New York). For studies of city literature in historical or literary periods, see for example Nolda 1980; Prendergast 1992; Den Tandt 1998; Nead 2000; Hirsh 2004; Freeman 2007; Philips 2007. For studies of city literature structured around a thematically, periodically or geographically defined selected corpus, see Jaye & Watts 1981; Wirth-Nesher 1996; Rotella 1998; Laplace & Tabuteau 2003.
4   See Madsen 2001; Resina 2003; Sintobin & Rymenants 2007; Borg 2011.
5   For the oscillation between enchantment and disenchantment, see Keunen 2011. Overviews of city representations in literature are informed by a whole range of dichotomies: Peter Keating, for example, in his article "The Metropolis in Literature" (1984) structures literary representations of the city with the help of two competing traditions, the one defined by a comprehensive, the other by an internalized view.
6   There are, of course, many more worldly cities to which Jerusalem is opposed in Biblical thought (and Western thought in general): Sodom, Gomorrah, Nineveh, Rome, Babel, Troy may be considered most prominent (see also Pike 1981: 6–7).
7   In his second century AD *Description of Greece*, Pausanias gives a short list of institutions that should not be lacking in a city. A temple is not mentioned, which reflects that in antiquity, the presence of a temple would be so self-evident as to be unnecessary to mention (Pausanias 1918; see also Lendering & Bosman 2010: 181). The list features government offices, a market place, but also water facilities, and significantly, sport facilities (a gymnasium) and a theatre.
8   With its disorientating abundance of choices, its chance encounters and its sudden shifts in individual and collective fortunes, the city is by definition too complex,

fleeting and fragmentary to be fully comprehensible. As a consequence, it forces upon its citizens on a daily basis the urge to make sense of the totalities, to read the city text and to compose their experiences into a readable whole. It may well be the case that it is also this fundamental urban condition, the city's inherent challenge to comprehensibility, which is the reason why the city has been taken up with such vigour in literature (and other representations). Composing a sense-making story out of the fragments of urban life is indeed what every city dweller is doing on a daily basis, as Hana Wirth-Nesher argues (see Wirth-Nesher 1996: 10).

9   I prefer the term "metaphorization" rather than "metaphor" to stress that what is denoted here is a continuous and unfinished process.
10 See also Lindner 2006: 36 ff.; Borg 2011: 34 ff.
11 For a highly relevant enumerations of motifs related to the city in Western literature, see Daemmrich & Daemmrich 1987: 64–67; Tonsor 1988.
12 This is one of the most potent metaphors used to experience, describe and study cities, both in literary studies, urban studies, and urban planning. Studies like Jane Jacobs's *Life and Death of Great American Cities* (1961) or Peter Ackroyd's *London: The Biography* (2001) bear witness to the continuous appeal of its rhetoric.
13 Lewis Mumford points out that the very first surviving image of the city depicts, in fact, its destruction (Mumford 1961: 51).
14 For more on the heated debate surrounding the statute, see Kalha 2008.
15 The image recurs also in Arvi Kivimaa's novel *Hetki ikuisen edessä* ("A Moment before Eternity"; 1932: 73), and in much more recent novel, Kjell Westö's *Lang* (Westö 2002: 35).
16 The metaphor of the city (polis or city-state) as body is, of course, age-old, and was already prominent in antiquity (see Osborne 2011: 104–105).
17 Both the metaphor of city-as-body in a more literal (often economic) sense and in a moral (social critical) sense have been used to approach the literary city in academic research (see Altnöder 2009).
18 As Raymond Williams points out, quoting a source dating from 1783, London was, time and again "looked upon to be no better than a wen or excrescence upon the body-politic" (Tucker 1783, as quoted in Williams 1973: 146).
19 Lewis Mumford has traced the feminine nature of the city to ancient Greek and Egyptian sources (Mumford 1961: 13), and the conceptualization of the city as feminine has found its way in a number of (Indo-European) languages in which the gender of the word for city is feminine (*die Stadt, la ville*). Throughout the centuries, various European cities have acquired feminine names, symbols or attributes.
20 Illustrative examples are respectively the notion of "the rape of Troy", and the famous 1968 Parisian situationist graffiti "I came in the cobblestones" (see Sadler 1998: 80). See also Parsons, who argues that "[w]oman are rarely present in the city of myth; rather, they are personified as the mythic city itself, a landscape for the hero to explore and conquer" (Parsons 2000: 222).
21 On the city as Moloch in late nineteenth-century city novels, see also Keunen et al. 2006: 250. The city as Moloch and Minotaur comes close to the metaphor of the city as machine or magnet – in Dreiser's *Sister Carrie* (1900), for example, the city is "described as a magnet, possessing a compelling attraction that draws people to it with pulsating energy" (Lehan 1998: 199), but it has also "become more and more like a machine" (ibid.: 201). In Swedish literature at the turn of the twentieth century, the image of the "man-eating city" appears in particular in descriptions of American cities (Borg 2011: 205–206). In Finnish literature of this period, one of the most explicit renderings of this concept is "Hell's Den" ("Hornan luola"), an industrial complex in Irmari Rantamala's St. Petersburg novel *Harhama* (1909; see Kurikka 1998: 130; Timonen 2011: 43–44)

22 See Prendergast 1992: 212–213; Benjamin 2006: 85.
23 The city is frequently compared in literature with a tomb or with a graveyard (see Mumford 1961: 6–7; Lehan 1998: 5). The city as a metaphor of life itself follows Samuel Johnson's famous saying "when a man is tired of London he is tired of life" (quoted in Wall 2011: 117; see also Pike 1981: 7).
24 Representational space can be understood as the emanation (for example in buildings or in art work) of representations (or conceptions) of space and spatial practices – the two other categories in Lefebvre's triad.
25 The "spatial turn" (one amongst many closely-related "turns", see Gunn 2001), is a "turn" which has been long in the making, as is evident when considering that some of the most important works such as Henri Lefebvre's *The Production of Space* (1974), Yi-Fu Tuan's *Topophilia* (1974) and Edward Relph's *Place and Placelessness* (1976), were already written in the 1970s. As early as 1967, the French philosopher, Michel Foucault, in a talk given to architects, had famously proclaimed that "[t]he present epoch will perhaps be above all the epoch of space" (Foucault 1986: 22). The appearance of a number of seminal works in 1989, David Harvey's *The Urban Experience*, Edward Soja's *Postmodern Geographies*, and Peter Jackson's *Maps of Meaning*, amongst others, can be taken as particularly pivotal.
26 See Friedman 2005: 192–197; Phelan 2007: 106–107; Bal 2009: 134; Finch 2011: 30–33.
27 This is not to say that there was not a long tradition of interest in spatial matters well before the spatial turn, an interest that is linked to the names of Ernst Cassirer, Yuri Lotman and Mikhail Bakhtin, and that studies aesthetics of space (see Hallet & Neumann 2009: 16–18; Nünning 2009).
28 Zoran 1984: 313–314; Hallet & Neumann 2009: 20–21; Nünning 2009: 47.
29 See Benjamin 2006; Keunen 2000: 185–189; Frisby 2001: 27–51.
30 The *flâneur* is in many respects a figure outside of class and outside of the production processes, but he is clearly not a member of the working class (Wilson 1992: 95).
31 Note that in humanistic geography, the conceptual pair place-space is used in a very different way: humanistic geographers use place to denote personally lived and experienced place, as opposed to more abstract and impersonal space. To add to the conceptual confusion, the pair place-space is used differently also by some narratologists. Mieke Bal explicitly differentiates her own use of place-space from that of other uses, defining place as "location" in narrative, and space as the specific use that is made of that location (Bal 2009: 178).
32 See also see also Harvey 1989a: 67; de Certeau 1984: 219, note 12.

The Shock of Arrival: Expectations and
First Impressions of the City

1 Two stories by Juhani Aho (1889, 1892), as well as stories by Maila Talvio (1896), Ilmari Kianto (1911), and Hilda Tihlä (1911), all carried the same title "To Helsinki" ("Helsinkiin").
Juhani Aho's second short story entitled "Helsinkiin" describes a provincial character's longing for the country's capital, described by way of his desire to see the renovated restaurant of Kappeli (Aho 1892).
2 In the middle of the nineteenth century, Helsinki was still mostly a Swedish-speaking town; by 1900, Finnish-speakers comprized half of the population (see Suolahti 1949: 270–272). The experience of Helsinki as an alien environment for Finns from inner Finland is poignantly summed up in Juhani Aho's short story "Maan sydämmeen" ("Into the Heartland"; 1891b), in which the Finnish capital instils someone from inner Finland with a sense of insecurity, "as if one were not really at home, as if one was surrounded more by strange people than by people

of one's own race" (Aho 1889 1b: 90) ("[...] niinkuin ei olisi oikein kotonaan, niinkuin olisi ympärillä enemmän vierasta väkeä kuin omaa sukulaista rotua.")

3   Apart from the title of Juhani Aho's *Helsinkiin*, we can find the image of the road to the capital in Matti Kurjensaari's *Tie Helsinkiin* ("The Road to Helsinki"; 1937) and Kyösti Wilkuna's *Vaikea tie* ("The Difficult Road"; 1915). In all these novels (as, indeed, in most student novels), and most explicitly in *Vaikea tie*, the advancement to the capital is seen as a road towards fulfilment in society, in the service of the fatherland. The link between a patriotic programme and the personal development in the student novel is explicitly developed in Järnefelt's classic *Isänmaa* ("The Fatherland"; 1893).

4   Juhani Aho (1861–1921) was the first professional author writing in Finnish, and one of the first Finnish writers to gain considerable attention in Europe through swift translations (amongst others in German, Swedish and Dutch). Today, he is probably best remembered for his classical novels *Rautatie* (*The Railroad*; 1884) and *Juha* (*Juha*; 1911); the latter was made into two operas and four movies, including an acclaimed black-and-white mute adaptation by Aki Kaurismäki. Juhani Aho is considered a ground-breaking writer of short prose, of which the collections of *Lastuja* ("Chips from the Block"; 1891, 1892, 1896) bears proof. Much of his work is still in print and receives considerable academic and popular attention up to this date (see a.o. Nummi 2002; Nummi et al. 2011). *Helsinkiin* was adapted into an opera as recently as 2005.

5   For an early study of the Finnish student novel, see Söderhjelm (1916/1920); for an exhaustive overview of the student novel in Finland, see Molarius (1991, 1993, 1996a, b). Claes Ahlund has provided a detailed study of the Scandinavian student novel (excluding, however, Finnish literature) in his dissertation *Den skandinaviska universitetsromanen 1877–1890* (1990).

6   The shift in the Finnish student novel has been seen as reflecting a change in the Finnish national-romantic project, the "Fennoman" movement. When this movement entered into a crisis, the student, initially a positive figure reflecting the hopes of Finnish national-romantics, became increasingly a subject of satire and irony (see Lappalainen 1999a: 51–53). It should be noted that Finnish student novels differed in a number of respects considerably from their Scandinavian counterparts, if only because the role of the students in Finland differed politically and socially from that in other Northern European countries (see Nummi 2003b: 100).

7   For a comparison between Aho and Tavaststjerna and their similar roles as innovators in Finnish literature, see Nummi 2007. The theme of doubles can be traced to examples from (amongst others) French novels of disillusionment, such as Gustave Flaubert's *L'Éducation sentimentale* (*Sentimental Education*; 1869) and *Illusions perdues* (*Lost Illusions*; 1837–1843); see Rossi 2007: 123–133 for a comparison between Tavaststjerna's *Barndomsvänner* and *Illusions perdues*.

8   "...tuohon huimaavaan, hupaisaan Helsinkiin, joka vuosi vuodelta kuului tulevan yhä suuremmoisemmaksi, yhä iloisemmaksi."

9   In his 1884 short story "Kello" ("The Watch"), Juhani Aho had already juxtaposed a naïve provincial and the dangers of the capital in profoundly ironic terms. In this short story, an inexperienced countryside boy is relieved of his brand-new watch at the Esplanade (Aho 1884/1918; see also Anttila 1956: 641).

10 See also the discussion of the metaphorization of the city as female figure in Chapter 2. In Aho's novella *Yksin* ("Alone"; 1890/2003), the metaphorization of the city – in this case Paris – as woman is much more explicit (see Rojola 1993: 170).

11 The Swedish words of the song Kalle is singing in the quotation can be roughly translated as follows: "lalala, the night is fine!"
"Helsinki rupesi kangastamaan hänen edessään tummanpunaisena, samettisohvaisena huoneena, josta lähti hurmaava parfyymi, jossa oli salainen puolihämärä, jos-

sa liikkui väljävaatteisia olennoita, mitkä ihan lähelle tunkivat, istuutuivat polvelle, kietoivat käden kaulaan ja toisella soittivat pianoa, johon lauloivat kevyttä, hehkuvata säveltä, tuota samaa, jota Kallekin hyrähteli: 'frallallalla, natten ä' bra!' [...] Hän oli käynyt kasvoiltaan kalpeaksi ja lasia ottaessa vapisi käsi tuntuvasti."

12 A comprehensive analysis of the changing experience of time and space in the period 1880–1918 is provided by Stephen Kern in *The Culture of Time and Space, 1880–1918* (1983) and, for the specific case of the railway, by Wolfgang Schivelbusch in *The Railway Journey* (1979/1986).

13 "Ja lupaus siitä oli jo jokaisessa veturin kiihkeässä vihellyksessä ja junan kiivaassa kulussa ja nopeasti jälelle jäävissä asemissa, joka kaikki tiesi sen, että matka lyhenee joka hetki ja sen määrä Helsinki lähenemistään lähenee. Helsinki! johon kiidetään yhä kiihtyvän virran vauhdilla ja joka odottaa kuin kuplia kiehuva suvanto ja aina vaan ahnaammin itseänsä kohti nielee."

The use of the Finnish word "suvanto" in the original is enigmatic, not to say oxymoronic, in the context of the full passage. The word, here translated as "quiet pool" (based on the translation offered by Herbert Lomas; see Aho 1889/2000: 74), denotes the part of a river immediately following or preceding rapids, and thus, while suggesting immobility, it presupposes the idea of a violent stream of water.

14 In his translation of excerpts of *Helsinkiin*, Herbert Lomas translates this as "aglow as if from a bonfire" (Aho 1889/2000: 74), which substitutes a sense of festivity for the clear menacing undertones present in the original.

15 This translation, and the following translations of Aho's *Helsinkiin*, are based on the translation by Herbert Lomas (Aho 1889/2000: 74).

"Kun juna seisottui lasisen katoksen alle ja piti astua ulos vaunusta, ei hän ollut päästä paikaltaan. Polvinivelet olivat niin vetreät, ett'eivät tahtoneet kantaa." (Aho 1889/1997: 80)

16 The translation follows that by Lomas (Aho 1889/2000: 77). Note that the Finnish word "pyörre" can be translated by a number of words, including "maelstrom"; other words are, amongst others, "whirl", "whirlpool", "vortex" (Wuolle 1979/1981: 288). Herbert Lomas has translated "pyörre" in this fragment as "whirlpool" (Aho 1889/2000: 74).

"Huumauksissaan kuin kosken kuohusta alas tullut istui Antti hetken päästä pehmosella sohvalla, vihreässä huoneessa, jonka katossa paloi monivaloinen kristallikruunu ja jonka seinällä oli maalauksia ja suuri peili. Se oli kuin sihisevä suvanto, johon hän oli seisottunut. Mutta ei levon suvanto, vaan vaahtoisen pyörteen, joka hetken päästä heittää uuteen koskeen, yhä alemma, eikä tietoakaan pysähtymisestä. Se tuntui pyörittävän ja sen tuntui pyöryttävän, se nosti veren päähän ja haihdutti silmistä oikean suunnan. Eikä Antti muutamaan hetkeen oikein käsittänyt, mistä oli tullut ja minne oli menevä."

17 The white student hat is a reappearing symbol of education, aspirations and class in Finnish literature. The golden lyre symbol in the coat of arms of the hat has inspired the title for Maila Talvio's student novel *Kultainen lyyra* ("The Golden Lyre"; 1916), in which a female student degenerates and becomes mad after she takes up studies in Helsinki (see also Söderhjelm 1916/1920).

18 For the presence of brothels at Tarkk'ampujankatu, see Häkkinen 1995: 38–42.

19 The following Finnish novels discussed here, and published in the period 1889–1920, can be considered as student novels: Juhani Aho's *Helsinkiin* ("To Helsinki"; 1889); Santeri Ivalo's *Hellaassa* ("In Hellas"; 1890) and *Aikansa lapsipuoli* ("Stepchild of his Time"; 1895); Arvid Järnefelt's *Isänmaa* ("The Fatherland"; 1893) and *Veljekset* ("Brothers"; 1900); Maila Talvio's *Tähtien alla* ("Under the Stars"; 1910) and *Kultainen lyyra* ("The Golden Lyre"; 1916); Toivo Tarvas's *Eri tasoilta* ("On Different Levels"; 1916a); Kyösti Wilkuna's *Vaikea tie* ("The Difficult Road"; 1915). Several novels, such as Maila Talvio's *Aili* ("Aili"; 1897) and *Niniven lapset*

("Children of Nineveh"; 1915) bear traces of the student novel. In the period 1920–1940, a number of novels appeared that continue the tradition of the student novel: Unto Karri's *Sodoma* ("Sodom"; 1929); Arvi Kivimaa's *Saari tuulten sylissä* ("Island in the Winds"; 1938); Matti Kurjensaari's *Tie Helsinkiin* ("The Road to Helsinki"; 1937); Iris Uurto's *Kypsyminen* ("Maturing"; 1935); Mika Waltari's *Sielu ja liekki* ("The Soul and the Flame"; 1934); Erkki Kivijärvi's *Tiimalasissa valuu hiekka* ("Sand through the Hourglass"; 1935).

20 In the following, I use the capitalized Young Man and Young Man from the Provinces as referring to the character typology proposed here. A close relative of the Young Man is the "overdetermined individual", a term used to describe the young protagonist "typical of the naturalist-realist novel" (Keunen 2001: 426).

21 If such grand-scale upheavals and sudden reversals of fortune are depicted in Finnish turn-of-the-century literature, such as in Eino Leino's novel *Pankkiherroja* ("Bank Lords"; 1914), they were criticized for being unrealistic in the Finnish context (see Saarenheimo 1916: 202).

22 Examples of such characters are Eljas (Ivalo's *Hellaassa* ["In Hellas"]; 1890), Juuso (Ivalo's *Aikansa lapsipuoli* ["Stepchild of his Time"]; 1895), Henrik (Järnefelt's *Veljekset* ["Brothers"]; 1900), Markus (Wilkuna's *Vaikea tie* ["The Difficult Road"]; 1915), and Hilja – one of the few female provincials moving to the capital in Finnish prose of this period (Talvio's *Tähtien alla* ["Under the Stars"]; 1910).

23 *Helsinkiin* is not the only text by Aho which carries undertones of medieval romance; Jyrki Nummi has analysed one of the short prose extracts by Aho, "Kosteikko" ("Wetlands"; 1890), as a story which can be read from the perspective of the mythical search for the Grail (Nummi 2002: 119–121).

24 Just as the Man from the Provinces has a male double to put his rise and fall in perspective, the choice in life (between ambition and family) of the Young Man is embodied in two types of women: the upper class/city girl, and the lower class/provincial woman (Chanda 1981: 354–355). In the case of *Helsinkiin*, this is covertly present in the juxtaposition between the pure, but unattainable Alma, who stays behind in Kuopio, and the rather more attainable girls at the ship buffet. Such doubles as the object of romantic feelings occur frequently in novels of this period: in Järnefelt's *Isänmaa* (Liisa and Fanny) and *Veneh'ojalaiset* (Kerttu and the daughters of the colonel), Leino's *Jaana Rönty* (Heikki and the secret policeman), and Ivalo's *Hellaassa* (Anni and Sylvia).

25 Helsinki is also referred to as a city of churches in Tarvas's novel *Kohtalon tuulissa* (Tarvas 1916b: 74).

26 "[…] että Anna-Kaisa tulee olemaan täydellinen kaunotar, kun hän saa oikeat vaatteet päälleen, että kaikki tulevat hänestä pitämään, hän pääsee pääkaupungin tansseihin ja huveihin, niin paljon kuin hän ikinä tahtoo […]."

27 "[…] Helsingissä löytyy kauniita kirkkoja, joissa jokikinen päivä on jumalanpalvelus ja niin hyviä pappeja…"

28 "[…] oli nyt astumaisillaan sen lumottuun piiriin."
Quite similarly, the young girl Aili, in Maila Talvio's novel *Aili* (1897), feels as if she has entered "the circle of wondrous fairy tale events" when she arrives in Helsinki (Talvio 1897: 143) ("Hän oli siirtynyt ikäänkuin satumaailman ihmeellisten tapahtumain piiriin").

29 "Äitimuori sitä jo oli sureskellut hänen näin nuorena lähtöä tuohon Babeliin, kuten sanoi, jossa jo niin monta kunnon poikaa oli pilalle mennyt. – Hm… Ainahan niitä vaaroja, varsinkin löyhille luonteille, jotka heittäytyvät arvelematta virtaan. Pahempikin se henki on, joka siellä kuuluu vallitsevan, mädännyt henki."

30 Several of the Young Men in turn-of-the-century Finnish prose carry names with Biblical or Christian connotations. In Eino Leino's short story "Päivä Helsingissä" ("A Day in Helsinki"; 1905) the main character Teofilius Malakias Tavela carries

his Biblical name Malakias (quite fittingly a second-rate prophet) with pride when he arrives in Helsinki with the ambition to settle the internecine party strife in the capital. Markus, the protagonist in Wilkuna's *Vaikea tie* (1915) carries the Finnish name for the evangelist Mark, while Henrik, in Järnefelt's *Veljekset* (1900), is named after the catholic bishop who, according to legend, christened Finland.

31 "[...] mustaan, syvään, pimeään lokaviemäriin."
The motif of the city as a sewer or cesspool, into which the young people of the nation are gathered, was widespread in the late nineteenth century. In Conan Doyle's *A Study in Scarlet* (1887), London is described as the "great cesspool into which all the loungers and idlers of the Empire are irresistibly drained" (as quoted in Lehan 1998: 86). See also the earlier description of anticipation of Helsinki in Aho's *Helsinkiin*, in which the capital appeared as "a quiet pool, boiling with bubbles, ever more greedily swallowing up the waters" (Aho 1889/1997: 76–77). In Santeri Ivalo's subsequent student novel *Aikansa lapsipuoli* ("Stepchild of His Time"; 1895), the degenerating development of the protagonist, the provincial student Juuso, is described repeatedly in terms of sinking and drowning.

32 "Tornikellon viisarit lähenivät kahta päivällä, kun ylioppilas Markus Kaarlela Nikolainkatua kävellen saapui Säätytalon kohdalle. Huomatessaan puistikon penkeistä yhden olevan tyhjänä ja suojassa auringonpaahteelta, läheni hän sitä ja vaipui huoahtaen istumaan.
[...] Hän tunsi hermoissaan epämääräistä levottomuutta ja outoa kiihottuneisuutta kuten ainakin se, joka maaelämän rauhasta juuri on joutunut keskelle pääkaupungin melua ja kirjavata hyörinää. Kuormarattaiden räminä, sanomalehtipoikien kimeät huudot ja raitiovaunujen ilkeästi vihlova vonkuna katukäänteissä vaivasi hermoja epämieluisasti, samalla kuin kaikkialla eteen kohoava kivinen suorasärmäisyys ja ahtaiden puistojen tyylitelty kauneus painostivat luonnon vapaisiin muotoihin tottunutta mieltä."

33 For time-space compression, see Harvey 1989a: 260–283, 2003: 37; Massey 1994/2008; Thacker 2003/2009: 38–40; Warf 2008.

34 "Pääkaupungin elämään jouduttuaan oli hän ollut kuin juuriltaan temmattu puu, vailla varmaa tukikohtaa ja alttiina jokaiselle tuulenpuuskalle."
Similar metaphors can be found in other student novels. In Ivalo's *Aikansa lapsipuoli*, the protagonist Juuso, after an extended and unhappy stay in Helsinki, feels as if he is a young fir tree, half-broken and struggling on hopelessly; or like some kind of tumor, which has to be cut away (Ivalo 1895: 234, 276).

35 "Parin lähimmän toverin seurassa oli hän viettänyt apaattista ja vegeteeraavaa elämää."
"[...] missä alkoholi ja musiikki ympäröivät lamautuneen mielen kuin pehmeillä untuvilla."

36 "Ihmiset tottuivat elämään ilman aurinkoa, kuuta ja korkeita tähtiä. He täyttivät kahvilat, teatterit, ravintolat ja kokoushuoneet ja antautuivat kokonaan niihin töihin ja huvituksiin, joita Helsinki niin runsaasti varaa syksyn osalle."

37 "[...] olivat ilmat jo muuttuneet hyvin kolkoiksi. Kylmät ankarat syystuulet puuskuivat pitkin katuja, nostattivat pölypilviä ilmaan ja tanssittivat kellastuneita lehmuksenlehtiä käytävillä."

38 "[...] ihmiset rientelivät kehenkään katsahtamatta sinne tänne asioillaan [...]"

39 "Ei ollut enää kysymystäkään siitä mahtavuudesta, jolla varustettuna hän oli tullut kaupunkiin. Kaikki uudet mielialat unohtuivat ja kesken raukasevaa, levotonta kuumetta hän yhtäkkiä oli taas entinen turvaton Henrik. Ei hän voinut mitään muuta ajatella, kuin vaan tuskalla kortteeriasioitaan."

40 For Olli Suurpää's rather bizarre dreams of a lost imaginary home, see Kunnas 1972: 66; Ameel 2006: 42–74.

41 The topos recurs in later Helsinki novels. One example can be found in Mika

Waltari's novel *Mies ja haave* ("A Man and his Dream"; 1933), the first part of the trilogy *Isästä poikaan* (1933, 1934, 1935).

42 While the sense of rootlessness and the lack of a home in the country is almost universal amongst the Finnish Young Men/Women from the Provinces, these characters come from various backgrounds. Important in this respect is that very few of the protagonists in prose from this period come from the kind of idyllic, idealized countryside environment that was still typical of the national-romantic literature of the national poet Runeberg. In Järnefelt's *Isänmaa*, for example, the countryside around the protagonist's homestead becomes gradually corrupted by an ironworks factory ("ruukki"). In Juhani Aho's *Helsinkiin*, the protagonist sets out from the small provincial town Kuopio, which was a centre of Finnish culture of national importance. In *Hellaassa*, the provincial town in which the protagonist went to school is described as being already affected by the lethal venom of the era, and in *Jaana Rönty*, the countryside is described as profoundly degenerate.

43 See Baguley 1990: 204–223; Molarius 1998a, 2003; Lyytikäinen 1998; Rossi 2003, 2007: 92–117. Richard Lehan argues that naturalism was not entirely pessimistic, since it posited individual failures side by side with the upward evolution of the species as a whole (Lehan 1998: 53). Exemplary of such a naturalist optimism are Albert Hagen's words, in Toivo Tarvas's *Eri tasoilta* ("On Different Levels"; 1916a), concerning the great amount of first generation students who fail: "I believe that it [our nation] has a great future indeed, even though in building its future, several construction accidents will happen, which will demand human sacrifice…" (Tarvas 1916a: 246) ("Uskon, että sillä [kansallamme] on suurikin tulevaisuus, vaikka sen tulevaisuutta rakentaessa sattuu useita rakennusonnettomuuksia, jotka kysyvät ihmisuhreja…")

44 "[…] tuo siirto ruumiillista työtä tekevästä luokasta henkisen työn luokkaan ei suinkaan aina asianomaisille itselleenkään ole mitään leikintekoa. Se voi olla suorastaan vaarallista sekä sielulle että ruumiille. Se siirto, se siirto ja se uusi maaperä – kaikki taimet eivät sitä kestä."

45 In the much earlier novel *Aili*, a similar positive image of Helsinki as bodily part of the country is voiced, when young Aili, recently arrived in the capital, ponders that Helsinki is "after all the heart, whose beats feed life into the whole country, the focal point, where everything that was grand and beautiful in Finland came together." (Talvio 1897: 128) ("Helsinki oli sittenkin sydän, jonka lyönnistä eli koko maa, polttopiste, johon yhtyi kaikki mitä oli suurta, kaunista Suomessa.")

46 "Katsokaa nyt, hän ei kestänyt siirtoa. Puutkin käyvät läpi koulun, ennen kuin tottuvat. Hän ei kestänyt."

47 The characters most clearly and explicitly described as tragic first generation students are arguably Urho Koskula, in Toivo Tarvas's *Eri tasoilta* ("On Different Levels"; 1916a; see, in particular, Tarvas 1916a: 89–90), and Pentti Korjus in L. Onerva's *Nousukkaita* ("Parvenus"; 1911).

48 For more on the authorship question concerning Hilja Kahila, see Oja 2007 (and, more generally, Karkama 2010: 516).

49 "[…] taikamainen sekoitus talvesta ja kesästä, yöstä ja päivästä, auringosta ja valkoisista lampuista […]."

50 "Junamatkalla olin ensikertaa elämässäni. Outo kolina ja hirmuinen vilinä ikkunoissa oli saattaa aivoni sekaisin, kun päässäni jo ennestään olivat kaikki asiat mullin mallin: tuntematon tulevaisuus, etenevä koti, lähestyvä kaupungin kummitus. […] Lopulta en ymmärtänyt enää mitään, en muistanut minne minua vietiin, en käsittänyt hurjaa kolinaa allani, ylläni ja sivuillani, enkä osannut ajatella mitään."

51 "Juna päätti hänen puolestaan."

52 "[…] humisevan kaupungin suurta ovea kohden."

53 "Hänen itseluottamuksensa oli kokonaan mennyt."

54 In later literature, too, the countryside appears as both literally the father's land and the fatherland; see Arvi Kivimaa's *Hetki ikuisen edessä* ("A Moment before Eternity"; 1932: 181).
55 "Nyt hän kävelee asemasiltaa pitkin yhtenä parinsadan muun tulijan kiireisessä sekasorrossa. Katoksen varjo lannistaa häntä, silmänräpäyksen ajan hän tuntee lohduttomasti kaiken ponnistuksensa tarkoituksettomuuden, voima hylkää hänet, hän sammuu ja lyyhistyy seuraten matkustajajoukkoa leveille graniittiportaille. Tori leviää hänen eteensä, hän pysähtyy jättiläispylvään juurelle, aurinko paistaa hänen silmiinsä sokaisevana tulena, hän on neuvoton ja arka. [...]
Neljännesmiljoona ihmistä on tuntemattoman miehen ympärillä muutaman kilometrin piirissä hänen nojatessaan aseman graniittipylvääseen sammuneena, voimansa hylkäämänä ja toivottomana."
56 For examples of disorientating experiences of arrival in movies, see Tani 1995: 108–116.
57 ("Tähän mädätyksen maailmaan, tähän saastaisten intohimojen pohjattomaan kuiluun ja pyörteeseen syöksyi Antti nyt [...]")
58 ("He olivat kodittomia ja joutuivat huvituksista rikkaan kaupungin hukuttaviin pyörteisiin")
59 The fortress was known under the Swedish name "Sveaborg" (literally "fortress of Sweden"), which in Finnish was known as "Viapori". In 1918, the name was changed to Suomenlinna ("fortress of Finland").

The Fateful Esplanade

1 "Me putoamme molemmat kuin kaksi kypsää omenaa yhteissuomalaisesta sukupuusta. Minne? Maailmankulttuuriin! Siellä on meidän paikkamme eikä Esplanaadin asfaltilla."
2 Eino Leino (1878–1926) is today remembered as one of the most significant poets in Finnish literary history. His birthday (6th of June) is celebrated as the festive day of Finnish poetry (and summer). Leino's poems are still widely read and frequently adapted to music. His two collections of *Helkavirsiä* (*Whitsongs*; 1903, 1912), in particular, have been canonized as ingenious syntheses of Finnish national-romantic material and international symbolist movements. His work as a journalist, columnist and prose author, however, has traditionally attracted less attention. Critics of Leino's prose have condemned his novels' lack of coherence, their overcrowded plots and their seemingly random turns of events. As a prose author, Leino has been seen as a clumsy dragoon, fallen of his horse, however gracefully he might have managed to ride proud Pegasus in his lyrical output (Palmgren 1950: 23; Molarius 1998c: vii). Recent decades, however, have seen a modest increase in the academic interest in Leino's prose output.
3 For an architectural and cultural-historical approach to the Esplanade, see Lilius 1984 and Kervanto-Nevanlinna 2003b, respectively.
4 The oldest public monument in Helsinki is the Empress' Stone (1835), located at the Market Square. Quite fittingly, Eino Leino, too, is eternalized in a statue at the Esplanade, erected in 1953; this statue is situated next to that of the writer Topelius (erected in 1932). In the year 2005, the absence of female authors in the monumental space of the Esplanade was put into question by a temporary statue of L. Onerva. One of Helsinki's other famous monuments situated close to the Esplanade is the statue of Czar Alexander II on the Senate Square, erected in 1894.
5 "Mutta nyt oli kesä päättynyt. Huomenna olisivat nämä hiljaiset seudut jo jätetyt ja puhaltamassa levoton kaupunkilaistuuli. Syys-toaletit, hatut, hansikkaat, esplanaadi kappelineen ja sähkövaloineen – – !"
6 In Finnish literature of the time, such juxtapositions abound. In Juhani Aho's

Yksin, the lonely protagonist feels repulsed by the spectacle of the Esplanade (Aho 1890/2003: 15). Towards the end of Järnefelt's *Isänmaa*, Heikki walks along the Esplanade during the first bright spring days of the year, but feels acutely out of tune with the happiness and youth of the other people at the Esplanade (Järnefelt 1893/1997: 182–186). In L. Onerva's novel *Mirdja* ("Mirdja"; 1908), the protagonist senses alienation and loneliness when walking through the celebrating Esplanade crowd on May Day (Onerva 1908: 105). In the much later novel *Hetki ikuisen edessä* ("A Moment before Eternity"; 1932), written by Arvi Kivimaa, the character Walter, who has just realized he has amassed enormous debts, looks out of the window of a hotel restaurant, from which he sees the carefree people at the Esplanade, and he hears the music playing at Kappeli (Kivimaa 1932: 56). The juxtaposition between protagonist and Esplanade crowd could also be a device to enhance the social divisions separating a literary character from his/her surroundings. The first lines of Alpo Noponen's 1894 newspaper sketch "Leikkikentältä asti" ("It Starts at the Playground") juxtapose the unhappy protagonist Ms. Virtanen with the noisy crowd at the Esplanade. In Maila Talvio's short story "Hämähäkki" ("Spider"; 1912), which is, like "Leikkikentältä asti", a story concerning social inequality, the opening setting finds the two protagonists amidst a scene of May Day joy at the Esplanade.

7   "Tuossa hän taas istua käyrötti 'Kappeli esplanaatin' soittopaviljongin kupeella tavallisella paikallaan. Ilma ei juuri ollut suotuisimpia … hiljainen tihkusade vihmoi näet ehtimiseen taivaalta. Senpä tähden ei ihmisiäkään tänä iltana paljo näkynyt soittoa kuuntelemassa ja nekin, jotka tulivat, toimittausivat kiireen vilkkaan katon alle, tilasivat lasin lämmintä 'tuutinkia', kuumennettua punssia tai muuta sellaista, että ollenkaan tarkenisivat. Eivätkä vielä siihenkään tyytyneet, vaan käskivät […] viinurin tuoda jonkun noita tavallisia raanuja, joita Kappelissa istujat kolkolla säällä kääreivät sääriensä suojaksi.
Mutta tuo pitkään ja kuluneeseen mustaan päällysnuttuun kääreytynyt olento se vain istui hyypeyksissään kovalla ja märällä penkillänsä."

8   One of the most influential early Helsinki novels in Swedish, published in 1907 by Richard Malmberg (pseudonym Gustav Alm), is significantly entitled "Autumn Days" (*Höstdagar*; the subtitle was "en Helsingforshistoria", a story of Helsinki; see Toftegaard Pedersen 2007: 154–157).

9   "Jäinen viima puhalsi läpi Helsingin puistokatujen. Talvi oli, mutta lumi oli sulanut moneen kertaan ja lopuksi kokonaan unohtunut pilvien tuolle puolen. Ajurien kärryt vierivät viluisina kylmillä katukivillä.
Ihmisiä ei näkynyt monta liikkeellä, vaikka oli tavallinen iltakävelyn tunti, hetki ennen teatterien ja konserttien alkamista. Perheet pysyivät mieluimmin kotonaan. Poikamiehet pujahtivat nopeasti kapakan ovesta sisälle.
Varatuomari Olli Suurpää purjehti laajassa pietarilaisessa turkissaan turvallisesti pitkin Pohjois-Esplanaadia. Hän oli varannut maallisen majansa jotakuinkin täydellisesti kaikilta kylmän ja lämmön vaihteluilta. Kuitenkin tähtäsivät hänenkin silmänsä sangen kiinteästi kahta Kämpin edessä palavaa sähkölamppua, jotka hän jo kaukaa erotti suurten myymäläin lähettämistä valokimpuista. Hän oli matkalla pieneen, salaiseen puoluekokoukseen."

10 In a letter to L. Onerva, Leino recounts how he identifies, up to a certain degree, with Olli Suurpää's protagonist (Leino 1961: 35).

11 "[…] kehitellä sieluaan vaihtelevilla ja sisältörikkailla keskusteluilla kaupungin ylevimpien koirien kanssa, joiden seurassa minä puolestani astun joka päivä Pohjois-Esplanaadin päästä päähän yhtä juhlallisena kuin konsanaan minun isäntäni salkku kainalossa."

12 "Mutta minun myötätunteeni ovat tässä asiassa kokonaan sen laillisen esivallan puolella, jota näen niin monen vertaiseni Helsingin esplanaadilla edustavan. Niin

kauan kuin virkakunnat toimivat, lain koura tekee työnsä säännöllisesti ja kansa on keisarille ynnä isänmaalle järkähtämättömästi uskollinen, ei mielestäni rauhallisella kansalaisella ole vähintäkään järjellistä syytä kapinalliseen huolenpitoon kansan ja yhteiskunnan kohtalosta."

13 For Eino Leino's involvement with the party struggles around the turn of the twentieth century, see Kunnas 1973; Vattulainen 1998.

14 The importance of the daily routine at the Esplanade is reiterated in a second short story by Aho featuring Mauritz Ahlfelt, "Hätääkärsivien hyväksi" ("For the Benefit of the Needy") in which the narrator states that we "all know Mauritz because of his office [...] and from the Esplanade, where he habitually walks with his briefcase under his arm between two and three" (Aho 1891a).
("[...] jonka me kaikki tunnemme hänen virastostaan [...]; ja Esplanadilta, missä hän salkku kainalossaan säännöllisesti kävelee kello kahden ja kolmen välillä [...]")

15 "[...] iso prosentti pääkaupungin piikoja ja renkejä seisoi tiukalle ahdetussa läjässä soittokomeron edustalla ja ympärillä."

16 "[...] kaupungin sydämeen"; "Joku laitakaupungin pimeä kaunotarkin uskaltaa joskus eksyä jokkoon [sic]. Hän herättää kiusallista huomiota, pysyisi poissa - - -!"

17 "[...] hän pian kiirehtää pois, laidemmalle missä jälleen voi vapaasti hengittää."

18 See for a number of treatments of the gendered gaze in relation to the *flâneur* Pollock 1988; Mulvey 1989; Hapuli et al. 1992: 102; Gleber 1999: 184–185; Warhol 2005: 194; Leslie 2006: 90; Ameel 2013b.

19 See Sarajas 1962: 135–154; Lyytikäinen 1999: 213; Ojajärvi 2008: 210, 2009: 205–224; Rojola 2008. It should be stressed that the narrator's occasional ironical attitude towards Jaana (and other characters) in *Jaana Rönty* cannot be interpreted as a straightforward bias against the lower classes, since all three protagonists of the Frost Year Trilogy are described in profoundly satirical terms.

20 The most important of these eruptions are the Great Strike (1905) and the Viapori Rebellion (1906), followed in 1918 by the Civil War.

21 "Ulkona oli lämmin kevät-ilta. Soitto kuului Kappelista. Jaanan askeleet tuntuivat niin keveiltä, että hänen kengänkantansa pyrkivät aina koholle maasta hypähtelemään. Hänen huulensa hymyilivät ja hänen silmänsä sädehtivät."

22 The above-mentioned passage in Ivalo's novel is also the very first known appearance of old Helsinki slang in writing. The full passage reads (freely translated): "When I returned yesterday from the laboratory, I met the sub at the University's Anatomy department, and then when came here to the Esplanade, where there was a terribly good maids' parade." ("Kun minä eilen illalla palasin labbiksesta, tapasin Aasiksen kohdalla Supiksen, ja niin me laskeusimme tänne espikselle, jossa oli mahdoton hyvä piikis.")
The quote presents a combination of Helsinki slang and academic jargon.

23 "[...] kutu kävi kuumimmillaan".

24 In old Helsinki slang we find some of the following synonyms for prostitute: "Esplanade angel" ("espisenkeli"), "Esplanade bird" ("espislintu") and "Esplanade butterfly" ("epsisperhonen"). The earliest references to the "Espis" given by the Helsinki slang dictionary are telling, for example: "if the seamstresses think they're not paid well enough, let them go to the Esplanade [i.e., to prostitute themselves]!" (Paunonen 2000: 177).

25 "Kapakoista tulleisiin miehiin liittyivät katunymfit, jotka kuin yöperhoset olivat lähteneet liikkeelle laitakaupunkikätköistään ja keskiyön varjojen suojassa uskaltautuneet kaupungin hienoimpaan osaan saalistamaan. Julkeata kaupanhierontaa säestivät äänekkäät naurunkikatukset ja rivot sukkeluudet. Kaapuihinsa kääriytyneet poliisikonstaapelit mittelivät hiljalleen keskikatua kuin elävät patsaat."

26 Minna Canth, in an article entitled "Naiskysymyksestä" ("On the Woman Ques-

tion"; 1884), condemned the fact that Helsinki women did not dare to go to the Kaisaniemi park at night for fear of being considered not respectable – something no man would be concerned with (see also Häkkinen 1995: 30). Similar articles, condemning the common idea that women were not supposed to be in the city without a chaperon in the evening, appeared in the decades to come (see for example Räsänen 1903).

27 In the Esplanade scene in *Nuoruuteni muistelmia*, Hilja has dressed particularly carefully because she has gone searching for the boy she loves. Eino Leino's *Jaana Rönty* presents a similar case: Jaana, too, had dressed carefully, and she was on the way to meet a boy she claims to be her "fiancé" on the fateful evening. When a working-class girl in literary texts dresses too luxuriously at an early age, this is seen as a foreboding of her future fall, for example in Kasimir Leino's short story "Emmalan Elli" ("Elli from Emmala"; 1884) and Pakkala's *Elsa* ("Elsa"; 1894) (see Lappalainen 1998a: 112–113, 2008), or in the case of Maila Talvio's "Helsinkiin" ("To Helsinki"; 1896).

28 "– Mitä te sitten kävelette niin hitaasti! tiuskasi herra oikeutetun suuttumuksen vallassa ja jättäytyi jälelle."

29 "[…] sipsuttivat niin sievästi ja soreasti, ottivat lyhempiä askelia kuin muut ja kantoivat toisella tavalla hamettaan." "[…] rupesi kahta pahemmin jäljittelemään, tällä kertaa tahallisesti ja itsetietoisesti."

30 "Poliisikonstaapeli, joka seisoi kadunkulmassa, oli jo jonkun aikaa seurannut silmillään Jaanan askeleita. Nyt lähti hän päättävästi hänen jälkeensä ja tarttui erään pimeän porttikäytävän kohdalla tytön käsipuoleen.
– Mitä sinä tässä kävelet? hän kysyi."

31 In Helsinki around the turn of the century, the police did not usually interfere with street prostitution, as long as a prostitute was in the possession of a booklet with information on her medical condition, and as long as she acted discreetly, was sober and did not dress in any inappropriate way (Häkkinen 1995: 166, 30).

32 For the concept of the geography of fear, see Asikainen & Koskela 1992.

33 Notable examples of allegorical texts from the years of Russian oppression can also be found in Arvid Järnefelt's oeuvre (see Karkama 2010: 217).

34 "[…] ryssäpiruksi […]"

35 "Mitäs te tässä aina kävelette?"
The only substantial difference with the question asked to Jaana by the police officer is the use of the polite verb form in Jaana's question.

36 "– Minä menen silloin kuin minä tahdon, ärjäsi vanha herra."

37 "– Minä olen parooni Manfelt, kenraalimajuri, virasta eronnut, oikeudella kantaa univormua. Asuva tässä kaupungissa."

38 "Tapahtuihan joka päivä samallaista ja paljon pahempaa."

39 "[…] vähäpätöisestä katukohtauksesta."

40 "[…] huikentelevainen, Helsingin turmelema tyttö raukka."

41 "Hanna parka, hän ei ymmärtänyt mihin vaaroihin sellainen elämä voi johtaa […]"
In another sketch, published in the women periodical *Koti ja yhteiskunta* ("Home and Society"), entitled "Hanna Toivosen ystävät" ("The Friends of Hanna Toivonen"; 1893), two female ideals are juxtaposed in a way similar to the story of the Ant and the Grasshopper. The pleasure-loving working-class girl is described as loving big wages and little work, nice clothes, and walks along the Northern Esplanade (e 1893: 81).

42 "Voi lapsi parka. Varo sinä tyttöpaha illalla kävelemistä, se voi tulla tavaksi, josta ei pääse eroon vaikka kuinka tahtoisi. Katuja riittää tässä kaupungissa niin, ettei niitä yhdessä ihmisiässä saa loppuun käytyä […]."
Similar scenes can be found in later literature, too. In Iris Uurto's novel *Ruumiin ikävä* ("The Longing of the Body"; 1930), the young working-class woman Ester

gets the advice from her elderly landlady not to end up on the street. When Ester proudly answers "Everyone walks the street", the old woman warns her: "Yes, but at different times." (Uurto 1930/1931: 337) ("Katujahan kulkevat kaikki. [...] Kulkevat eri aikoina.")

43 "[...] katujen saasta vetää heitä jättiläismagneetin tavoin puoleensa [...]"
"[...] Alli tunsi kadun huudon sielussaan [...]"

44 Several articles concerning the prostitution question appeared in this period, particularly in working-class newspapers (see for example Willman 1906; J. S. 1909).

45 In a sense, *Venehöjalaiset* consists of a succession of recognition scenes, and there are repeated instances in which Hannes recognizes, often to his dismal surprise, Kerttu. For the importance of a "poetics of awakening" as central to Järnefelt's prose see Isomaa 2009: 11. For a discussion of one particular awakening scene, the brothel scene in *Venehöjalaiset*, see the following chapter.

46 "[...] jotka tämän kaupungin lapsista enin sitä tarvitsevat."

47 "Jos minun täytyisi jokaista tuommoista naista kohdella niinkuin sisartani, niin enhän sitten joutaisi muuta tekemäänkään, – en pääsisi kaduilla kulkemaankaan."

48 The theme of a man trying to save a working-class girl from prostitution recurs continuously in prose of the turn of the century, in Finnish literature as well as in international prose. Tolstoy's final novel was built around these thematics (*Resurrection*; 1899); Järnefelt translated the novel into Finnish, and it was published the very next year (1900) (see Isomaa 2008: 211, 237). The novel is referred to in Tihlä's *Leeni* (1907), in which we find, again, a young idealistic student (who has read *Resurrection*) and a young country girl hastening towards damnation.

49 *Vaikea tie* is to a considerable degree an autobiographical novel. Kyösti Wilkuna did write for *Työmies* in August 1904, and one of his articles carried the same title as the article Markus Kaarlela writes on the basis of the encounter in the Old Church Park (see Railo 1930: 86– 88).

50 The entry for "flâneur" in the nineteenth-century *Encyclopaedia Larousse* concluded that only a true metropolis could act as the scene for *flânerie* (Wilson 1992: 93–94). Walter Benjamin locates the *flâneur* in a limited period of time and in a particular city – Paris during part of the nineteenth century (Benjamin 2006).

51 "Kyllä tämä rakas Helsinki sentään on pieni, – sanoi Albert. – Tuskin on päässyt menemisen alkuun, niin silloin meri taikka metsä jo on vastassa."

52 Helsinki is called the "Daughter of the Baltic", which is also the title of a historical novel on Helsinki by Maila Talvio.

53 "Otto siirtyi keskustelemaan parin uuden toverin kanssa ja Juuso pujahti sillävälin ulos. Hän käveli rantaan, laskeusi jäälle ja retkeili kauas selälle, jossa päivä kimallutti kirkkaaksi lumista tannerta ja raitis merituuli vapaasti puhalteli. Siellä hän koetti koota ja järjestellä ajatuksiaan."

54 "Pääkaupungin asukkaat, niin nuoret kuin vanhat, olivat tänään liikkeellä lumisessa luonnossa, mikä jalkaisin, mikä hevosella, monet, nuoremmat varsinkin, suksilla. Heitä hiihti pieniä ryhmiä ulos kaupungin joka laidasta ja joka tullista, toiset haarausivat selälle saaria kohden, toiset metsiin ja mäkilöille."

55 "[...] tänä talvena ja keväänä oli hänestä näet tullut ahkera kävelijä, ulkoilmassa liikkuminen ikäänkuin rauhoitti hänen mieltään ja viihdytti hänen ajatuksiaan."

56 "Hän kulki tavallisesti pitkät matkat ulos kaupungista [...]"

57 "[...] saa liikkua ihmisvilinässä ja tuntea kuuluvansa siihen [...]"; "Suloista on olla ihmisjoukossa ja kuvitella, että ne tuntevat samoin kuin itse..."

58 "Minä rakastan tätä kaupunkia erikoisesti. Rakastan sen katuja, ikkunoita, taloja, liikettä. Parhainta ajanvietettäni, puhdasta iloa, on minulle kuljeksia pitkin katuja, varsinkin iltaisin. [...] Vain siitä, että saan siirtää jalan toisen eteen, hitaasti, huolettomasti. Ja samalla kiinnittää katseeni kasvoihin, ihmisiin, kaikkeen."

59 "Olen koditon ja kadun vilinässä koetan unohtaa itseni. Tämä kuljeksiminen on

tosi kuva itsestäni. Vieraana kaikille, katselijana, vailla mitään johtotähteä. Levoton ikävä rinnassa."
60 "Nyt oli hän yksi vanhan puolueen johtajia ja käveli puolituntisensa finspongilla niinkuin muutkin miehet"
61 "– Elähän, vai tässä se on se mainio ... niinpä niin, tässähän se on ... vai tässä ne kävelevät ja tapaavat toisensa ja ratkaisevat maan ja kansan asioita."
Hänen teki mieli kävellä finspongilla, hän tahtoi nähdä, miltä 'ne' näyttävät."

EXPERIENCES OF A METROPOLIS IN MOTION

1 Arvid Järnefelt (1861–1932) was one of the most colourful and prolific Finnish writers of the late nineteenth and early twentieth centuries. Descendent from a family belonging to the nobility, his father was a high-ranking officer in the Russian army, later a Finnish senator, while his mother Elisabeth kept one of the most important literary salons of Finland. His brother-in-law was Jean Sibelius, and his brothers Armas and Eero belonged to the artistic elite of his time. The most well-known Tolstoyan in Finland, he at one point renounced his position at law court to become a farmer. Järnefelt was influenced not only by Tolstoy, but directly and indirectly by a whole range of nineteenth-century Russian authors, such as Pushkin, Gogol and Dostoevsky (for a study of the influence of Russian realism on Finnish late nineteenth-century literature, see Sarajas 1968). His most canonized writings today are his debut novel *Isänmaa* ("The Fatherland"; 1893) and the biography of his parents *Vanhempieni romaani* ("The Book of My Parents"; 1928–1930). Several monographs have been written about Arvid Järnefelt's works and life (see Häkli 1955; Niemi 2005; Isomaa 2009; Karkama 2010); amongst these, Saija Isomaa's analysis of the generic complexities of three novels by Järnefelt, including *Veneh'ojalaiset*, bears the most immediate relevance to my study.
2 See de Certeau 1984: 91–95; Prendergast 1992: 210–211; Berg 2011: 189.
3 The brothers of the title live in different parts of Finland and are representative of different layers of society: the ambitious civil servant (Uuno); the labourer (Gabriel); the parson (Johannes); and the undecided student (Henrik).
4 "Henrik asui pääkaupungin äärimmäisellä laidalla, missä kallioiden vuoksi ei enää ollut säännöllisiä katuja tai oli vastasuunniteltuja tulevaisuuden linjoja keskellä rikkiammuttujen kivien röykkiöitä; – näiden takaa muutamien paljaiden aallon nuolemien karien perästä avautui meri aavaksi ulapaksi maan näkymättä taivaanrannassa, ja alituisesti pauhasi. Ikkunasta näkyi oikealle eräs turvalaitos langenneita naisia varten ja suunnattoman korkea tiilitorni, josta aina tuprusi paksu musta savupilvi, tuulen suuntaa osoittaen. Se oli sähkövalaistuksen voimankeskus, jonka ansiosta kaupungin puodeissa, julkisissa laitoksissa, juhlasaleissa, kaduilla kirkkaat valot leimahtivat vaan pientä nappulaa siirtämällä. Vasemmalla näkyi lähinnä lapsensynnytyslaitos, enemmän merelle päin kaivopuiston vallit, maallepäin katolisen kirkon viheriäinen huippu ja sitten alkavan kaupungin säännöllisemmät piirteet."
5 "Oli todella jotakin säteilevää ja sähköittävää tuossa valkoisessa kaupungissa, jonka taloryhmien lomiin meri soudatti ystävällisiä sinisiä lahdelmiaan. Kolmannesta kerroksesta katsoen, missä kunnallisneuvoksen huoneusto sijaitsi, lepäsi kaupunki lauhana ja hymyilevänä jalkojen juuressa, näyttäen ojentelevan iloja oikealle ja vasemmalle, iloja kaikille niille sadoille ja tuhansille, jotka niitä kaupungiltaan pyysivät. Rakennukset olivat ryhmittyneet valkoisen kirkon ympäri ylpeissä, säännöllisissä ryhmissä. Tomun, asfaltinhajun ja katumelun täyttämä ilma oli kuin kyllästytetty ärsyttävällä elämällä. Puissa, jotka muodostivat rykelmiä siellä täällä kaupungissa ja pitkin sen laitoja, hehkui se oudon tumma vihanta, mikä kokoon-

tuu kasviin ennen lakastumista."
6 For a similarly threatening panoramic opening in the same period, see Eino Leino's *Pankkiherroja* ("Bank Lords"; 1914).
7 "[...] että hän itse vapautuu niistä varsinaisista kaupunkilaistoimista, jotka juuri tekivät hänen olonsa niin mukavaksi, kuten enimmät ja välttämättömimmät ruumiilliset kaupunkityöt: katujen lakaseminen, kasteleminen, rakentaminen, ajurina oleminen ja niin edespäin."
What Henrik is concerned with in this passage is what Marx has called the "fetishism of commodities" (Marx 1867/2005), the masking operation that hides from sight the production processes and workers involved in producing commodities (see also Harvey 1989b: 8)
8 "[...] suuren hävityksen näky."
9 "[...] sydämmestä se juuri noin revittiin kuin tämäkin."
10 "Kotipappila ja hänen entinen kuvansa elämästä oli vaan niinkuin rikkinakutettu munankuori, josta hän oli tullut ulos. Ja tuon ahtaan asumuksen jättäminen, joka ensin suretti, muuttui riemuksi, kun uuden kodin katto taivaan laeksi väljeni ja seinät eteni siniautereeksi."
11 "Olen niin tottunut tähän kaupunkiin ja näihin tuttuihin välimatkoihin teiltä meille ja meiltä teille [...]"
12 As a historical document, the novel is particularly interesting, since the main character Hannes was modelled on Johan Kock, a prominent historical figure Arvid Järnefelt was well acquainted with. Captain Kock was one of the most important actors during the Great Strike and the Viapori Rebellion; the leader of the Red Guard in Helsinki during these years. The accuracy with which Järnefelt has described the events of 1905–1906 can be gleaned from the fact that in a long open letter to Järnefelt, posthumously published in 1916, Kock accused the author of publishing confidential information and of presenting events in a way which was so convincing and so recognizable, that it made it almost impossible for the general audience to see it as a work of fiction; Kock consequently accused Järnefelt of libel (Kock 1916; see also Isomaa 2009: 210–213). Apart from the interest caused by the accusation of libel, the novel received relatively little attention at the time of appearance.
13 "Meillä ei ole [...] synteettistä runoelmaa Helsingistä, romaania tai eeposta, jossa tämä pohjoinen pääkaupunki eläisi kokonaisuudessaan kaikkine niine ominaisuuksineen, joita luonto, rotu ja kulttuuri ovat sille määränneet."
14 On the intertextual relation of the novel with the Biblical story of Job, and with Faust, elements which bear relatively little relevance to the literary city, see Isomaa 2009: 218–232. Isomaa shows that many of the characters in the novel bear traits of Faust, but that these Faust figures are complex and thoroughly ambiguous characters.
15 Järnefelt was particularly preoccupied with the land reform question, and he wrote on the subject the novel *Maaemon lapsia* ("Children of Mother Earth"; 1905) and the pamphlet *Maa kuuluu kaikille; Matkoiltani Laukon lakkomailla* ("The Land Belongs to Everyone; From My Journeys to the Strike-Torn Region of Laukko"; 1907 [for the English translations of these Finnish titles, I am indebted to Ahokas 1973: 177]). Some literary historians have been keen on seeing in the novel direct references to contemporary events, going so far as to identify the Veneh'oja directly with the thousands of tenant farmers notoriously evicted from their homes at Laukko during the winter of 1906–1907 (see Ahokas 1973: 107), and situating the legendary lands of the Veneh'oja at Laukko (Niemi 2005: 168).
16 In Järnefelt's debut novel *Isänmaa*, there is a brothel scene which has some similarities to the one in *Veneh'ojalaiset*. The scene was deleted from some of the later editions of the novel (Niemi 2005: 87). The protagonist in *Isänmaa* is certainly

aware of what kind of place he finds himself in, and any sense of sudden awakening or initiation in his case is out of the question (Järnefelt 1893/1997: 172–175).

17 The other "principles" of the heterotopia singled out by Foucault are that all world cultures constitute heterotopias, that the function of a specific heterotopia can change over time within a society, that a heterotopia "is capable of juxtaposing in a single real place several spaces [...] that are in themselves incompatible", that heterotopias tend to be linked to significant turning points in people's lives, and, lastly, that they "have a function in relation to all the space that remains" (Foucault 1986: 24–27). See Ameel 2012 for a detailed examination of the brothel and the literary salon as heterotopian spaces.

18 "[...] arvatenkin ne olivat Magdan sisaria." "Nähtävästi oli tässä aikomus viettää todella juhlaa Hinkin kunniaksi [...]."

19 "[...] oli kaiketi tämän äiti taikka täti."

20 "Hinkin morsiamen iho on valkea kuin hienoin perunajauho ja sanomattoman ihana tuoksu lähtee hänen vaatteistaan, mutta se minun tyttöni on ruskea kuin kahvipapu eikä suinkaan aina hyvältä tuoksu."
The reference to the smell of Magda's clothes may also be read as a parody on the Song of Songs 4:11; "the smell of thy garments is like the smell of Lebanon" (in the King James Bible Translation). A reference on dark skin is also present in the Song of Songs (1:5; "I am black ... / as the tents of Kedar / as the curtains of Solomo").

21 "[...] rupesi sen ison huoneen puolelta kuulumaan humalaisten melua [...]"

22 One important detail which further enrages Hannes is that Hinkki claims he can see Hannes's illegitimate father through the key hole (Järnefelt 1909/1996: 88); he thus links the brothel with Hannes's traumatic background and the shame about being a child fathered in unclear circumstances (see also Isomaa 2009: 235).

23 "Voi teitä kuolleiden kylien ja mätien kaupunkien rakentajia [...]"
"Prostitutsioni on kaupungin tuottama tauti."
Natalja's verdict on prostitution and the city has immediate relevance to Hannes, since the place where he meets Natalja is a St. Petersburg orphanage where he has gone searching for the illegitimate child Kerttu has borne him (see also Isomaa 2009: 211).

24 Henry James, in 1888, described London as a "strangely mingled monster", an "ogress who devours human flesh to keep herself alive to do her tremendous work" (as quoted in Walkowitz 1992: 15). In the late nineteenth century, London was repeatedly described as a devouring monster and a heathen god. As Freeman points out, this association "employed Christian rhetoric in demonizing the metropolis, admitting both the city's spiritual failings and the continuing totemic power of religious language in describing its realities" (Freeman 2007: 202).

25 "Joka vuosi syöksi tämä valoisa, helisevä pääkaupunki pimentoihin satoja nuoria ihmisiä, jotka se oli käyttänyt loppuun, joilla se ei tehnyt enää mitään, joka vuosi sai se uutta turmeltumatonta verta maaseudulta, uusia herkkiä lapsensieluja syödäkseen."

26 "Ja suurkaupunki syöksi onkaloistaan ilmoille kaikki raskaan työviikkonsa mustat orjat. Se purki taivasalle maan-alaisista konehuoneistaan hämärän kansaa, joka harvoin näki aurinkoa [...]."

27 "[...] se on petollinen, se ei nuku, se hälisee ja hekumoi, se palaa. Sen tietää kyllä Mirdja. Jo monen vuoden ajan on se häntä polttanut joka päivä ja joka yö."

28 "Taikalinna, satujen ihmemaa oli hänelle tämä kultainen kaupunki ehtymättömine rikkaudenlähteineen."

29 Like so many families in early twentieth-century Finnish prose literature, the elder generation still has the traditional Swedish name, while the son has changed his last name into the Finnish equivalent. In *Niniven lapset*, Old Man Säfstrand's son Aarne has changed the family's surname to Ruokoranta. In Toivo Tarvas's *Eri ta-*

soilta ("On Different Levels"; 1916a) and *Kohtalon tuulissa* ("The Winds of Fate"; 1916b), Albert Hagen changes his surname to Hakala (Tarvas 1916b: 32–33). In Maila Talvio's *Niniven lapset*, the children of the Ståhle ("steel") family use different translations: the son Leo changes his name into Teräs (literally "steel"), while his sister Gisela uses different pseudonyms derived from her name: her tango pseudonym is Gisela Acero, while her pen name is Cela Rauta (Cela Iron). In the case of Gisela, the name changes can be considered representative of the masquerading and self-fashioning strategies typical of newcomers to the city, and in particular of upwardly socially mobile women (for examples in American fiction see Geyh 2006: 428; Simpson 2011: 503)

30 Old Man Säfstrand is referred to as the nation's Diogenes, but also compared explicitly to Balzac's Père Grandet (Talvio 1915: 180).

31 "Kaupungin kasvot muuttuivat vieraammiksi, ylhäisemmiksi."

32 Toivo Tarvas is the first author writing about Helsinki in Finnish who is also a native of the Finnish capital. In the 1910s, he wrote several novels and short stories in which Helsinki features prominently, and in which the literary characters' intimate knowledge of the city and its codes is expressed also by a vivid use of Helsinki slang. He is mentioned in all of the lengthy studies concerning Helsinki in Finnish literature (Liuttu 1950: 49; Anttila 1956: 645; Liuttu 1963; Palmgren 1989: 45; Laine 2011: 150–155), but otherwise, Tarvas has been almost completely forgotten by posterity (see also Laine 2011: 150). Lea Rojola does look at Tarvas's novel *Eri tasoilta* (1916a), but links the thematics in the novel to earlier, turn-of-the-century novels, rather than as seeing Tarvas's prose as a predecessor of 1920s and 1930 thematics (Rojola 1999: 166–172).

33 "Hänen eteensä avautuu hurmaava näköala. Ikäänkuin Suomenlahden merenrannalle heittämä kaunis helmi hohtaa hänen edessään suuri kaupunki."

34 "[...] unelmiensa kaupunkiin [...]"

35 "[...] alakuloisen haikea tunne rinnassaan [...]"

36 "[...] jumalien suojelema pyhättö"; "[...] keskellä meluavinta, korkearakenteisinta Helsinkiä"; "[...] korkeitten kivimuurien pimentoisessa puristuksessa."

37 "Töölön siistien, punaisenhohtavien kivimuurien keskellä [...]"; "kuin muistona entisiltä ajoilta [...]"

38 "Kaupunki muuttui.
Kuinka toisen sävyn se olikaan saanut muutamassa vuodessa! Ennen leppeä, tyyni, tutunomainen; nyt korkea, kylmä ja vaitelias!"

39 "Niinkuin on raunioina Babel, Ninive, niin raunioituu tämäkin turmeltunut osa maailmaa."

40 "[...] niinkuin Belsazarin pitojen tulikirjoitus."

41 "[...] nuo tummaa taustaa vasten loistavat suuret alukset nousivat ja laskivat juhlallisesti niinkuin Belsazarin pitojen käden piirtämät jättiläistulikirjaimet."

42 "[...] mutta alla olevan kaupungin suorat kadut näyttivät mustilta ja tyhjiltä kuin iankaikkisuuden ammottavat kuilut. Häntä puistatti. Kattojen päällä olevat sadat metalliset savutorvet, joiden liikkuvia, siivekkäitä päitä kevättuuli heilutteli edestakaisin, tuntuivat itse pahan mustilta enkeleiltä. Ja etäämmällä korkeista tehtaitten piipuista nouseva musta savu liehui kuin hirvittävän suuret suruharsosta tehdyt liput..."

43 "[...] tavattoman suuria ruumisarkkuja." In *Eri tasoilta*, the view is not so much related to an external threat, but rather inspired by the pessimistic feelings of the protagonist.

44 "[...] äkkikuoleman kammottava viikate."

45 "Laskenut aurinko paistoi meren takaa pitkän pilven tuhansiksi punajoutseniksi, jotka yhä surenevina kohosivat taivaan laelle asti."

46 "Uusi, merkillinen maailma oli kuin loihtimalla noussut hänen eteensä."

47 "Kun sen laineetkin tyyntyivät, silisi merenpinta ja koko kaupunki näkyi ylösalaisin kääntyneenä lahden pohjasta."
A similar image appears later in the novel, when Hinkki watches Helsinki from the rebellious fortress (Järnefelt 1909/1996: 345).

48 "Hajosi liitoksistaan koko kaupunki, puistot maasta erkanivat ja tornit kaatuivat. Horjuivat vanhat tullimakasiinit, vavahtelivat monikertaiset kivimuurit, pankit, hotellit, itse keisaripalatsikin syttyi punaliekkeihin ja kirkko kupuineen ja kultaristineen perustuksiltaan sortui."

49 Saija Isomaa has drawn the connection between such violent, visionary scenes and one particular scene from the Finnish national epic: the arrival out of the sea of a little man with an axe, who cuts down the majestic world tree which has grown so large as to block the rays of the sun (Isomaa 2009: 227). It should be noted, in the light of the presence of a comic touch in the passage quoted above, that the scene from the national epic (Lönnrot 1849/1999: 6–7), combines distinctly comic dialogue and description with what in effect is an instance of cosmic destruction.

50 "Ja yhdellä iskulla hajosi linnoituksen jylhä taika kapteenin mielessä."

51 "Kaikki kulttuuri huojuu, kaikki muodot käännetään nurin. Kaikki on liikkeessä. 'Je hais le mouvement qui déplace les lignes.'"

52 "Kaikki, kaikki alkoi mennä sekaisin, ja hän uskoi hyvin vanhan Kustaavan hiljaa lausuman arvelun, että kaikki tuo uusi, mikä nyt niin äkkiä oli täyttänyt ihmisten ajatukset, ei ollut muuta kuin lähestyvän maailmanlopun enteitä."

53 "– On tapahtunut ihme, Kerttu, erämaasta on yhdessä vuodessa syntynyt kukkiva kaupunki!"

54 "Kadulla oli sakea sumu. Oli jo alkanut hämärtää. Siellä täällä näkyi vaan joitakin ihmisiä nopeasti kulkevan kadulla tai vilkkuvan kulmauksissa. Askelien kopina kuului selvästi, mutta ei missään ajoa. Samassa kuitenkin alkoi kuulua huimaavaa vauhtia lähestyvä kavioiden kopse, ja ennenkuin Kerttu ehti ympärilleen katsahtaa, lensi kolme kasakkaa pitkin katua hänen ohitsensa, että oikein hänen kätensä ja kasvonsa kauhusta kylmenivät."

55 Järnefelt was intimately acquainted with St. Petersburg and Russian literature; he was born in St. Petersburg, studied at the University of Moscow (see Isomaa 2009: 28–36; Karkama 2010: 34), and his mother belonged to Russian (Baltic German) nobility; moreover, Järnefelt was not only a dedicated reader of Russian literature, but also a translator into Finnish of Tolstoy, amongst others.

56 In *Appelsiininsiemen* ("The Orange Seed"; see Chapter 6), a much later Helsinki novel by Mika Waltari, fog covers the Helsinki streets when the political crisis related to the Lapua movement deepens (Waltari 1931: 351–357). Eros and Thanatos are both present in this fog scene, in which the newly engaged protagonists Irene and Ilmari are visiting Irene's dying aunt, and in which the city, fearing possible clashes between the army and extreme-right elements, is enveloped in fog (1931: 357).

57 "[...] keskikaupungilla vallitsikin täysi ja pimeä tyhjyys. Siellä täällä kulki katuja myöten jotain henkilöitä rivissä, mutta sivilipuvussa, kalossit jaloissa, kuulumattomasti astellen. Niinkuin jokin näkymätön leijona olisi äkkiä tukahuttanut tassunsa alle koko kaupungin, sanoen: hiljaa nulikat! Kivimuurit kumottivat kuin suuret pimeät haamut yössä, siellä täällä tuikahteli yösumussa himmeät ikkunavalot. Ja hiljaisuus oli niin syvä, että olisi kuullut nuppineulan putoamisen. Mutta ei ainoatakaan polisia näkynyt, jolta Kerttu olisi voinut kysyä oliko mitään vangitsemista tai tapausta kuulunut."

58 The lion can be interpreted as a reference to the lion in the Finnish flag.

59 "[...] kuin kuumeessa [...]"

60 "Minä menen silloin kuin minä tahdon [...]"

61 "[...] pitkin katuja aamusta iltaan [...]"

62 "Oliko aika loppunut? Oliko iankaikkisuus alkamassa?"
63 As Saija Isomaa points, out, Hannes's obsession with his visions of the future is profoundly at odds with the practicalities of his everyday life: "he causes the evil that he wants to erase" (Isomaa 2009: 237).
64 "Hän seisoi varhaisena aamuna Tähtitornin mäellä tiheässä kansanjoukossa. Päivä paistoi päälle peilityynten vetten ja salmien, joiden kahden puolen valkeat savupilvet tuprahtelivat. Luonnosa vallitsi syvä hiljaisuus. Päälinnoituksen temppelien kupoolit kimmelsivät pilvettömän taivaan alla [...]. Jaanasta oli ensin kuin olisivat lapset käyneet leikkisotaa taikka iloinen talkooväki puhaltanut poskistaan summattoman suuria tupakkakiehkuroita.

Mutta yhtämittainen jyrinä ilmassa täytti pian hänen sielunsa pyhällä vavistuksella. Jumalan lapset siellä kävivät sotaa, kuolon viikatemies siellä teki korjuutaan. Ja hänestä tuntui kuin hän olisi seisonut korkeampien voimien ympäröimänä, vaistomaisesti hän risti kätensä ja rukoili äänettömästi itsekseen: 'Isä meidän, joka olet taivaassa.'"
65 "Kansanjoukko hänen ympärillään seisoi mykkänä kuin kirkkomäellä. Tämä näky vaikutti heihin kuin jumalanpalvelus. Täytyi olla hyvin hiljaa, ettei häiritsisi sitä. Mutta illalla muutti maisema luontoaan. Taivas oli pilvessä, teräsharmaat aallot löivät raskaasti rantamiin. Oli ilmestynyt ulapalle suuria sotalaivoja, joiden sivut välkkyivät väkevässä, sinertävässä valossa, jyristen ja salamoiden synkän pilven alta kohti kapinoitsevaa linnoitusta."
66 "Kaikki tavallinen suurkaupungin melu oli kokonaan vaiennut. Ei kuulunut tehtaiden ja veturien vihellyksiä, raitiotievaunujen vonkunaa tai rattaiden räminää. Ilmassa oli tuntu kuin suurena juhlapäivänä ja odottava juhlailme oli ihmisten kasvoilla, heidän hiljalleen soljuessaan pitkin katukäytäviä [...]."
67 "Kuinka kaunis pääkaupunki meillä sentään onkaan! [...] Kaikkialla on niin rauhallista ja hiljaista kuin maalla jonakin suurena kirkkojuhlana."
68 "[...] kuin mahtava hyökyaalto idästä [...]"; "[...] yhteiskunnan kaaokselliseen alkutilaansa [...]"
69 "Kuin kiiltomatoja vilkkui tuolla ja täällä käsilyhtyjä ja välistä hulmahti kaupungin yli Viaporista suunnatun valonheittäjän häikäisevä sädekimppu kuin kohtalonsilmä, joka levottona seurasi tapahtumia tuossa kaikki siteensä katkoneessa, poreilevaan käymistilaan joutuneessa ja kaikkia mahdollisuuksia kätkevässä kaupungissa, mikä oli verhonnut itsensä pimeydellä kuin synnyttävä vaimo."
70 "Hän näki nuoren, pitkä-palmikkoisen naisen hyppelevän kadulla ja potkivan kuolleita, maassa makaavia kunnalliskaartilaisia kasvoihin.

Se oli Jaana. Hän ei ollut voinut hillitä itseään enempää. Hän oli hullaantunut veren ja ruudin hajusta, koston hekkuma oli hänet haltioittanut, hän hyppeli, hän tanssi höyryävien ruumiiden kesken ja potki niitä kasvoihin, rintaan, kaikkialle, huutaen, huitoen, leimuten kuin lieska punaisessa puvussaan.

Oli jotakin niin peljättävää, jotakin niin alkuaikaista ja metsänpetomaista tässä näyssä, että vanha parooni Manfelt horjahti ja tapasi avuttomana käsillään ilmaa. Hänestä oli kuin olisi hän nähnyt silmiensä edessä ilmi elävänä itse Baabelin porton ja lohikäärmeen, joka karkeloi riemuitsevaa kuolemantanssiaan tomuksi menevän maailman raunioilla."
71 "Jaana meni nyt nopeasti alaspäin.

Hänen vastustusvoimansa oli murtunut. Oli kuin olisi hänessä mennyt rikki jotakin."
72 "Kadut muuttuivat ikäänkuin hänen kodikseen, ihmiset kaikki, sekä ulkona että sisällä olevaiset, tutuiksi omaisiksi."
73 "Armoa, Vasili! Tämä on kotikaupunkini..."
74 "[...] suuri joukko kultaisen pääkaupungin asukkaista jo silloin rakasti vuorta lempipaikkanansa."

75 "[...] nousukaspolven pimeä eepos [...]"
76 "[...] Riemu sydämmessä [...] hän asteli niitä kotikaupunkinsa katuja [...] joista joka soppi ja käänne oli hänelle tuttua ja kodikasta [...]."
77 "[...] vastapäätä kotikaupungin rakkaita rantoja."
78 "[...] kotoiset ja sittenkin niin vieraiksi käyneet kadut."
79 "[...] hänelle rakkaaksi käyneessä kaupungissa [...]"
80 "[...] tavattoman hermostunut [...]"; "Niin, et sinä taida tietääkään minkälainen uhri tämä maalletulo minun puoleltani on. Oikein itkettää kun täytyy jättää tämä rakas kaupunki [...]."
81 "Hän riensi edelleen katuja ylös toisia alas. Salainen kiihko joudutti hänen askeleitaan."
82 "Töölönlahti loistaa verilammikkona ja kultaa ja verta hehkuvien talojen jokainen ääriviiva on tuttu hänen katseelleen. Repivä yksinäisyyden tunto ja ikävä vuotaa äkkiä hänen mieleensä, vaistomaisesti hän tajuaa ensimmäisen kerran elämässään rakastavansa tätä suurta kaupunkia. Se on hänen kotinsa, se on hänen synnyinpaikkansa, sen kadut ovat olleet hänen lapsuutensa seikkailujen ja pettymysten taustana, sen keskellä hän on kasvanut, sen hän tuntee, hänen on vaikea sitä jättää."
83 "[...] joka tuhansine tuikkivine valoineen lepäsi kirkkaan tähtitaivaan alla."
84 "Hiljainen kaupunki heräsi unestaan."
85 "Albertista tuntui ikävältä, että kaupungin hiljainen rauha tuli häirityksi, mutta kun suuri kaupunki herää, niin se haukottelee kuuluvasti kuin sadun jättiläinen..."
86 "– Ei, Albert, älä koeta nyt olla epärehellinen, kyllä sinun kiintymyksesi tähän kaupunkiin on tavallisuudesta poikkeavaa kaupungin ihailua ja sen palvomista, sillä sinä olet runoillut kaupungin itsellesi ikäänkuin eläväksi olennoksi, jonka kanssa sinä seurustelet."
87 "Piakkoin taas hankkii pääkaupunkiin muuttoa uuden parvet kokemattomia maalaispalvelijoita, nuoria miehiä ja naisia. Moni heistä ei osapuillekaan aavista sitä waaraa, minkä alaiseksi antautuvat. Ja ennen pitkää saattaa heidän onnensa tähti laskeutua. Maaseutu saa jonkun ajan kuluttua noita takaisin ruumiin ja sielun puolesta sortuneina. Niin on ennen käynyt – ja niinkö edelleenkin täytyy käydä? [...]"
88 In the beginning of 2012, Helsinki numbered close to 600,000 inhabitants (City of Helsinki Urban Facts 2012: 5).
89 The architectural innovations visible during the 1920s and 1930s in the district of Töölö, but also in working-class districts such Vallila and Käpylä, were to a considerable degree rooted in the desire to modernize the Finnish home, which was in turn related to the changing role of women in an urbanizing society (see Bell & Hietala 2002: 208; Saarikangas 2002). For the ideals and aims behind architectural practices in Töölö and Vallila, see also Nikula 1981: 166–277.
90 During the 1990s and the 2000s, the number of non-Finnish residents increased considerably: in 2011, 8% of the population of Helsinki did not have Finnish nationality (City of Helsinki Urban Facts 2012: 13)

AESTHETICIZING THE CITY

1 The cultural impact of the Torch Bearer movement has been discussed extensively (see Saarenheimo 1966, 1969; Laitinen 1965; Lassila 1985, 1996; Hapuli 1995; Mauriala 2005). This literary movement, a group of young authors with a particular interest in everything exotic, modern, speedy and international, wanted to "open the windows to Europe". Most research has focused on the Torch Bearer authors and on the way their work (poetry, in particular) reflects the age. Little research has been carried out, in comparison, on the prose literature written in

the 1920s and 1930s in the wake of the Torch Bearer movement, and on the way this literature renders the experience of the city.

2 See Koskenniemi 1928: 496; Laitinen 1965: 459, 1982: 336; Koskela 1999b: 275.

3 It would be problematic to imply a shared and common experience of the 1920s in Finland, since the Civil War of 1918 had created a sharply divided nation. The victors of the war dominated the cultural institutions and the media during the following decades, and the triumphant tone of their rhetoric was not necessarily shared by the less visible working-class authors and intellectuals (see Maironiemi 1992; Koskela 1999b; Roininen 1999).

Many of the authors discussed in this chapter and in the following one were drawn into the political polarization of the 1920s and 1930s. One of the central literary polemics of the 1930s was the so-called "Literature Polemic" ("kirjallisuustaistelu") of 1936, in which the first shot was fired by Mika Waltari's suggestion that left-leaning authors (Helvi Hämäläinen, Iris Uurto, Toivo Pekkanen) had received positive reviews not because of the artistic value of their work, but for ideological reasons (see Lappalainen 1984, 1999b). In the political field, Mika Waltari can be clearly situated right of centre, while authors such as Helvi Hämäläinen and Iris Uurto were considered more left of centre; Uurto's novels following her debut, in particular, were seen by contemporaries as politically engaged (see Koivisto 1999: 321–322).

4 "Leveän, pimeän rappukäytävän tuoksu löi meitä vastaan. Se oli kaupungin tuoksu, – kylmää, huuhdeltua kiveä, tomua, ummehtunutta ilmaa ja jotakin muuta, jota ei osaa selittää, johon tottuu aivan heti, niin ettei sitä huomaakaan, mutta maalta tullessa on sillä aina oma erikoinen voimansa.

Olin tullut kaupunkiin elokuun alkupäivinä, koska maalla oli liian kuuma ja koska oli olevinaan joitakin asioita, jotka kykenivät olemaan tekosyynä. Tosiasioissa ikävöin kaupunkia, asfaltin, metallitomun ja bentsiinin tuoksua, – sitä hermostunutta kaipausta, joka pimenevinä iltoina kiertää hiljaisia katuja."

5 Mika Waltari (1908–1979) was only 20 in 1928, when his debut novel *Suuri illusioni* appeared, and in the following years, he established himself as one of the most popular Finnish authors. He wrote a large number of Helsinki novels and short stories, many of them still in print, and also made his mark as an author of detective stories, drama, and even movie scripts. He achieved lasting fame as the author of highly successful historical novels, amongst which *Sinuhe* ("The Egyptian"; 1945) is the most well-known. He is the second literary author writing about Helsinki in Finnish who was also born in the Finnish capital, and he is, incidentally, distantly related to Toivo Tarvas, who was the first in this category (see Waltari 1980: 5; Laine 2011: 151).

6 "Minä ainakin olen kyllästynyt hien ja tunkionhajuun [...]."

7 Silja Laine notes that *Suuri illusioni* has fewer detailed descriptions of the built environment than Waltari's later Helsinki novels (Laine 2011: 147; see also Laurila 1965: 450).

8 Waltari can be considered one of the pioneers of the first person narrator in Finnish prose (see Valkama 1960/1983: 261).

9 "Spindel", of course, is the Swedish word for spider; like a spider in her web, Mrs. Spindel is the sphinx-like character lurking at the centre of the urban labyrinth. The names of the protagonists are all more or less symbolic. "Hart" would seem to refer to the "hard" and matter-of-fact allure the young journalist wants to exhibit; "Caritas" is a somewhat ironic reference to the mothering nature the novel's femme fatale seems to lack, and which both male, boyish protagonists seem to be in dire need of. The name "Hellas" seems to underscore Hellas's old-fashioned sense of beauty and art; fascinated by modernity, Hellas nevertheless seems to belong more to an earlier time frame. In many ways he resembles oversensitive and/or decadent secondary characters in Finnish literature of this (and the immediately preceding)

period, characters such as Aarne Ruokoranta in Talvio's *Niniven lapset* ("Children of Nineveh"; 1915), Ruudi Winkler in Talvio's *Kultainen lyyra* ("The Golden Lyre"; 1916), Kurt Waldhof in Waltari's *Appelsiininsiemen* ("The Orange Seed"; 1931), Armas Aarni in Waltari's *Palava nuoruus* ("Burning Youth"; 1935), amongst others. Waltari himself claims that the title of Ivalo's novel *Hellas* may have been one of the unconscious reasons why he chose this name, but he also states that Hellas was modelled on Olavi Paavolainen, while Hart has been seen as modelled on Arvi Kivimaa (Waltari 1980: 185–186). The name Hellas can also be related to the character's feminine, perhaps even bisexual nature – again, a feature shared with some of the oversensitive characters mentioned above. Armas Aarni, in Waltari's *Palava Nuoruus*, for example, is said to have been modelled on the author Toivo Tarvas, who was homosexual (see Waltari 1980: 262–263; Rajala 2008: 53; Laine 2011: 152).

10 "[...] epäselvä muisto lapsuudestani, jonka kivikäytävän tuoksu oli herättänyt unhoituksista"
11 "[...] joka siitä hetkestä lähtien on ollut minulle rakas, sillä se symbolisoi kaupunkia ja kaikkea tuntematonta."
12 "Astuin portaita ylös tajunnassa vielä välähtelevä kuva kaupungin syksyillasta: katulyhtyjen kirkkaat jonot, reklaamien palo, raitiotievaunujen vihreät sähköliekit, autotorvien huuto."
13 See Keunen 1999: 365–366; see also Scott 1976/1986: 210–211.
14 Interesting early examples can be found, for example, in Juhani Aho's *Yksin* (1890/2003). When the protagonist walks through Helsinki in a mood of extreme despondency, the trees of Bulevardi are described as a "gloomy vault" ("synkkänä holvina"; Aho 1890/2003: 4). The following day, however, the protagonist feels more cheerful, and watching the view of the Helsinki harbour, he notes that "[t]he landscape seems purified like after a rain, and me, I feel as if I am inwardly brightened up." ("Maisema on kuin sateen jälkeen puhdistunut ja minä itse ikäänkuin sisällisesti kirkastunut" [Aho 1890/2003: 33]).
15 "[...] pakkasauringon punainen usva [...]."
16 "Kunnes ilta tuli, tuollainen nopeasti hämärtävä, lämmintä huokuva ilta, jolloin koko kaupunki tuntuu vavahtelevan kiihkeää odotusta, ja lyhdyt palavat yhä kirkastuvampina polttavien katujen yläpuolella."
17 For Koskenniemi's call for a great Helsinki novel, see Introduction. Koskenniemi's review of Kivimaa's novel in 1930 can be considered as indicative of how much the critic had become out of touch with his material, given the fact that several great Helsinki novels had appeared in the early twentieth century (see also the conclusion to Chapter 5).
18 "Vetisiä, koleita taloja ulkona suunnaton rykelmä. Kaupunki. Harmaa taivas. Toivottomia ihmisiä. Työtä."
19 See Nummi 2002: 142–143, 2003a: xv–xvi; Riikonen 2007: 847.
20 "Rajaton harmaus lepäsi kattojen päällä. Autio katu tuntui uponneen alas maan sisään väsymyksestä. Pienellä aukiolla seisoi eräs auto haikeana yksinäisen lyhtypatsaan valossa."
21 "Kaupunki oli yhtä tyhjä kuin olisi se kuollut, lamput loistivat itsekseen [...]. Kadut olivat paljaat, lumettomat, mahtavat kivitalot makasivat niiden varrella kuin kyykkyyn pudonneet, jähmettyneet vartiosotilaat."
22 "Pöydällä oli Baedeker, ja ohivilahtavana aistimuksena tunsin korvissani suurkaupungin kuumeisen hälinän ja autojen huudot."
23 This is not to say that Paris had not exerted a great influence in Finnish literature of the turn of the century, as K. A. Tavaststjerna's *Barndomsvänner* ("Childhood Friends"; 1886), Juhani Aho's *Yksin* ("Alone"; 1890; Nummi 2002: 129ff.), L. Onerva's *Mirdja* ("Mirdja"; 1908) and *Inari* ("Inari"; 1913), and Joel Lehtonen's

Punainen mylly ("Moulin Rouge"; 1913; see Perttula 2010: 97–100) show. In the 1910s, a character (in this case, in a novel by Kersti Bergroth, *Aptit* [1914]) could exclaim: "We are no longer Swedish, we do not want to become Russian, let us become Parisians" (as quoted in Toftegaard Pedersen 2007: 208) – echoing the famous, early nineteenth-century saying attributed to A. I. Arwidsson ("We are no longer Swedish, we do not want to become Russian, let us be Finns").

24 The travel descriptions in the novels by Karri and Kivimaa have been criticized in some of the most sarcastic comments in Paavolainen's *Suursiivous* ("Cleaning out the House"; 1932). To Paavolainen, the trip abroad by so many Finnish protagonists in the late 1920s and early 1930s novels had become no more than a superficial and staple motif (Paavolainen 1932: 78). Several Finnish authors writing in the 1920s and 1930s, Mika Waltari and Olavi Paavolainen among them, published travel books in addition to literary works. A particularly interesting case is Waltari's *Yksinäisen miehen juna* ("A Lonely Man on the Train"; 1929), a non-fiction travel report of Waltari's journey to Constantinople and back, which draws on a range of motifs and literary techniques that can also be found in *Suuri illusioni*.

25 The mixing of the literary genre of the city novel with passages that look reminiscent of international city guides, in inter-war Finnish Helsinki novels, is not only indebted to the popularity of 1920s and 1930s travel narrations, but also to a growing number of Helsinki tourist guides, history books and coffee-table books on Helsinki (see Lindberg 1931; Rancken 1932). One of these publications, *Hyvä Helsinkimme* ("Our Good Helsinki"; Janson & Kivijärvi 1926), written by two authors who were also producing fiction featuring Helsinki, was described by a contemporary reviewer as providing a "totally European" image of Helsinki (Finck 1927), something which was clearly perceived as desirable. Mika Waltari wrote several non-fiction books on Helsinki (Waltari 1937; Waltari & Blomberg 1941).

26 "Hän tahtoi [...] löytää nykyajan, josta Helsingin elämä oli vain laimea pohjoinen varjo."

27 "Mutta kirjallisuus, jonka pitäisi olla aikakauden kuvastin – se on ainakin matkakuumeessa. Ei saa lukea muuta kuin automatkoista, D-junasta, Honolulusta ja itämaista."

28 "Oletteko koskaan ottanut kokaiinia? – Ette. – Silloin teiltä on jäänyt ensiluokkainen vaikutelma saamatta. – Tahdotteko tuntea olevanne älykäs, voimakas, nuori, väsymätön, puhdas ja viaton? Tahdotteko nähdä katulyhdyn valon paratiisin säkenöivänä porttina?"

29 "[...] teemme yöllisen ryöstöretken Pekingin keisarin linnaan, ja te tuotte hänen päänsä minulle kultaisessa vadissa."

30 "'Minä ehdotan, että lähdemme pienelle kävelyretkelle Kaivopuistoon etsimään kultaista tietä Samarkandiin,' sanoin minä. 'Samalla on minulla tilaisuus katkaista Pekingin keisarin pää ja luovuttaa se prinsessalle...'"

31 "Hiljaa! [...] Ei mitään politiikkaa!"

32 The identification of urban gangs with "Apaches" has, of course, a tradition extending into late nineteenth-century Paris, and Helsinki slang, too, knows the word "apassi" ("apache") to refer to gang members (Paunonen 2000: 61). The reference to the "Apaches" of the Sörnäinen district is also made, amongst others, in Joel Lehtonen's novel *Henkien taistelu* (Lehtonen 1933: 360).

33 The motif of a girl committing suicide by drowning in the sea has its roots in Finnish folk poetry and the *Kalevala* (Lönnrot 1849/1999). In the Finnish epic, young Aino escapes the arranged marriage with Väinämöinen, the warrior-shaman hero of the *Kalevala*, by drowning in the sea. It is a story which could be considered as an intertext for Iris Uurto's "Gretan päiväkirjasta" ("From Greta's diary"; 1930: 5–18), in which an unmarried woman, pondering society's expectations of women, considers suicide by drowning as she wanders along the Helsinki waterfront. The

motif of the drowning maiden is a recurrent one in Finnish literature, and appears, for example, in Minna Canth's short story "Ompelija" ("The Seamstress"; 1894).

34 In fragments which evoke the daily work of the modern journalist, the experience of a fragmentary reality is reflected most explicitly in elliptic clauses (see Waltari 1928: 67). More generally, the newsroom, with its hectic atmosphere and the reference to elliptic sentences, becomes a new motif in urban literature from this period. For staccato descriptions see the publishing-house scene in Talvio's *Niniven lapset* ["Children of Nineveh"]; 1915: 148–156), and the newsroom scene in Kivimaa's *Epäjumala* ["Idol"]; 1930: 168)

35 "Pimeä, syksyinen yö. Katulyhtyjen kalpean hauras valo. Mustat puut. Hellas. Ajatukset hänen loppuun väsyneessä sielussaan. Hänen katkeruutensa. Caritas. Pimeä ulappa. Kaukana pimeään häipyvän Suomenlinnan valot.
Saimme auton, ja katujen vilinä sai minut jälleen tavalliseen mielentilaani, suurkaupungin hermostuneeksi asukkaaksi, joka ei kykene ajattelemaan ajatuksiaan loppuun asti, jonka lauseet ovat lyhyitä ja kesken katkeavia."

36 See Keunen 1999: 365–366; cf. Bergson 1889/1910: 100–139; see also Lehan 1998: 80, 134.

37 "Kirpeänä kuin kokaiini [...]"
"Sinä olet autolyhtyjen valo ja majakan punainen silmä pimeän meren yllä."
"Jokin rytmi alkoi soida sielussani niinkuin teräsvasarain kalke."
"Ilma oli kuin sekoitus raakaa spriitä ja sitruunasoodaa."

38 "Suurkaupungin yö vei meidät mukanaan niinkuin konepajan kaarilamppujen alla jättiläisimuri tempaa kitaansa metallihiukkaset."
The difference between these images in *Suuri illusioni* and earlier descriptions of the city in Finnish literature can be illustrated by a comparison with Juhani Aho's *Yksin*, in which Paris is also described as having a gaping mouth that swallows people (in this case, arriving at the railway station), but in which the mouth is compared to the bottle neck of river rapids – a traditional image from Finnish nature (Aho 1890/2003: 43).

39 "[...] suurkaupungin pauhu, joka turruttaa kaikki aistimet ja hävittää ajatukset, tehden lauseet katkonaisiksi."
In this instance, Hart is speaking of Paris.

40 In many other respects, too, the trilogy *Isästä poikaan* is critical of the city and of modernity; as Kai Laitinen points out, it was written in the years 1933–1935, "when the earlier ideals of the Torch Bearers made way for more robust, national-traditional values" (Laitinen 1982: 336).

41 "Hänen ympärillään pyörii tyttöjä, koska nykyaikaisen magneetin nimi on auto."

42 "Näyttämöksi kelpaa yhtä hyvin taksa-auto [...]"

43 "[...] hän tunsi vaipuvansa syvälle – niinkuin eetteriin tai äärettömään avaruuteen."

44 "Katulyhdyt vilahtelivat ohimennessä niinkuin tuliset pallot avaruudessa. Muuta ei hän nähnytkään, sillä vauhti oli siksi kova, että kaikki muuttui epämääräiseksi kaaokseksi."

45 "Pitkänsillan tuolla puolen välkähti näkyviin himmeä, puolivaloinen lyhytrivi."

46 "Caritas puristui melkein kiinni minuun autossa."

47 "[...] ohivilahtavan katulyhdyn valo loi hänen silmiinsä kummallisen kiillon."

48 "Kello alkoi olla puoli viisi, hän näki sen Kluuvikadun heilahtavassa kulmassa, kiiltävää, mustaa katua, lätäkköjä, syksyisiä lyhtyjä, loppumattomina, hurjina palloina, auton heittelehtivä surina."

49 See Thacker 2003/2009: 7–8, Alter 2005: 127–128; Freeman 2007: 145.

50 "Hullaantunut auto yöllisellä kadulla, syksyn näkymätön taivas, vilisevät lyhdyt, alkoholin kirkkaus aivoissa."

51 "Asematorin valaistu kellotaulu oli vilahtanut ohitsemme ja painanut silmän verkkokalvoon kellertävän jälkikuvansa.

'Modernin maiseman kuu,' sanoin minä."
52 In Arvi Kivimaa's *Epäjumala*, there are in fact several separate scenes in which Markus and Marcelle take a taxi together. In a final scene, the enclosed chamber of the taxi functions as a liminal space that frames their inevitable separation, and when Marcelle has gone, Markus imagines he will throw himself in front of the cars driving behind his taxi (Kivimaa 1930: 227–228).
53 "He olivat kuin koko yhteiskunnan ulkopuolella olevia, joilla ei ollut kotia eikä mitään asemaa."
54 "Heillä oli kuollut maailma, Markuksen maailma liikkui, lensi, voitti joka hetki uutta ja rajatonta."
55 "Ja ne herrat, monta kertaa niin vanhat ja arvokkaan näköiset, ettei mitenkään olisi voinut uskoa heistä sellaista, jotka liikuttivat käsiään ja koskettelivat vastenmielisellä, jäykistyttävällä tavalla."
56 See also Laurila 1982a: 80–81, 1982b: 42–43. There was a strong autobiographical element to this symbiotic relation between Töölö and Waltari's Helsinki novels: like the writer character in *Surun ja ilon kaupunki* ("City of Sorrow and Joy"), Waltari lived in Töölö (see Envall 1992).
57 Concerning Spindel's salon and the factual salon of Mrs. Craucher, see Waltari 1980: 159–167; Rajala 2008: 130–135; Selén 2010: 87 ff.
58 "[...] niinkuin olivat suunnitelleetkin."
59 "[...] täynnä juuri kohonneita valkeita seiniä, rakennustelineitä ja työkoneiden räminää."
60 "[...] eloton ja kylmä [...]"; "[...] tähän hutiloiden luotuun kaupunginosaan [...]"; "[...] oikean elämän surmana [...]".
61 "Autot olivat tulleet, uudet, amerikkalaiset raitiotievaunut, Töölö oli syntynyt. Keskuslämmitykset, keskuskeittiöt, dublettijärjestelmä, suojeluskunnat, asevelvollisuus, oppivelvollisuus, pienviljelijät, lapsettomat avioliitot, avioerot, kieltolaki, salakauppa, rikollisuus, puukotukset... Kaikki tuo, jota saattoi luetella äärettömiin. Elämän yhteiskunnallistaminen ja käytännöllistäminen."
62 "Ihanne-mekaanis-koneellis-asiallinen kaupunki." The full reference to Töölö in the poem, which is structured as a touristic tour through Helsinki, reads as follows:
"And now, the highlight of our trip – do you hear the symphony of our century: the ringing of automatic telephones, the news from divorce agencies, the rich rumble of water closets, the wheeze of radios, the scratch of nightly needles on gramophones... This is Töölö. The ideal-mechanic-machine-rational-city. Deus ex machina. The only reminders of ancient times: kids and bedbugs." (Paavolainen 1929: 40–41: "Ja nyt retkemme clou – / kuuletteko vuosisatamme / sinfonian: / automaattipuhelimien soi- / ton, uutiset avioerotoi- /mistoista / WC:iden vuolaan kohinan, / radiotorvien korahtelun, / yöneulojen kitinän gramo-/foneista... / Se on Töölö. / Ihanne-me- / kaanis- / koneellis- / asiallinen / kaupunki / Deus ex ma- / china. / Ainoat mui - / naismuis- / tot: / lapset ja lutikat.")
63 "Uusi Helsinki on täynnä päähänpistoja, mutta se on iloinen ja hauska vanhan raskaan viime vuosisadan lopun Helsingin rinnalla, joka [...] oli synkkä, pimeä, epäterveellinen, teki jyrkän eron suurten kahdeksan huoneen ja pienten yhden tai kahden huoneen huoneistojen välillä. [...] Vanha Helsinki ei lainkaan tunne näitä pieniä iloisia, puhtaita ja mukavia huoneistoja, jotka täyttävät uuden Helsingin, mutta vanha Helsinki ei tuntenut sitä ihmislajiakaan, joka niissä elää, itsensä elättäviä sivistyneistönnaisia tai aviopareja, jotka molemmat työskentelevät jossakin virassa kodin ulkopuolella."
64 "[...] Mutta tuossa kolmikymmenluvun uudessa Helsingissä, joka on auennut kuin puutarhakukka iloisen värikkäänä, aurinkoisena, käytännöllisenä ja epäkäytännöllisenä, rakastuneena kaikkeen tämän hetken uuteen, jota se pitää yllät-

tävänä [...]."
65 Controversies surrounding the novel delayed its appearance, scheduled for 1939, until 1941. The adulterous relationship at the heart of the plot, which was based on a real-life story involving easily recognizable people of Helsinki society, was considered particularly problematic. Parts of the manuscript were censored, including a critique on Hitler (see Juutila 1989: 427; Vaittinen 1995; Schoolfield 1998: 171). The sensuous and baroque-like style was criticized by some, although others, notably Tatu Vaaskivi, extolled Hämäläinen's novel and her "copiously flowing imagery" (Vaaskivi 1941: 326).
66 This aspect of the plot has been repeatedly read in the light of autobiographical information concerning the relationship between Helvi Hämäläinen and Olavi Paavolainen (see Palmgren 1989: 154; Mauriala 2005: 104).
67 "[...] oudon todellisena [...]" "talojen seinämillä ja kadun asfaltilla oli kummallisen hentoja varjoja [...]"
68 "Elisabet pelkäsi katsoa ympärilleen [...], jottei olisi tuntenut sydämessään kauheata iskua [...] jonka vuoksi hänen sielunmaisemansa oli niin muuttunut, että jokapäiväinen ympäristö, jossa hän tähän asti oli onnellisena liikkunut ja heijastellut sisäistä itseään, oli tullut hänelle tuskalliseksi ja sisälsi joka askeleella kauheata kärsimystä – muistoja avioelämästä ja rakkaudesta [...]."
69 "[...] liian kokonaan kaunista ja hiljaista."
70 "[...] kaikki entinen tuntuu kallisarvoiselta."
71 "Poissa, ainiaaksi poissa, tuo pohjahiekan kultahohto [...]."
72 "Hän tunsi sen kaikkien säiden ja valojen vaihteluissa. Mennessään ohi hän iloitsi, jos kuutamo hyväili sen keltaisia seiniä tai lepäsi mustalla katolla; se eli hänelle sateessa ja auringonpaisteessa. Se oli Helsingin ainoa rakennus, joka täyttyi hänelle lihattomilla varjoilla; hän katseli sitä kuin esinettä, jonka vainajat olivat jättäneet maan päälle [...]; se rakennus sulki koskemattomana menneen, elämän, jonka tapahtumia, jonka nauhaa ei enää kukaan omistanut. Se oli hänelle elämän lipas, joka on kadotettava."
Aurora Karamzin (1808–1902) was one of the most famous women of nineteenth-century Helsinki, and a celebrated philanthropist. The Karamzin Mansion, better known as Hakasalmi Villa (Hakasalmen huvila), is today one of the localities of the Helsinki city museum.
73 "Helsinki, joka hänen mielestään muuten tuntui sieluttomalta, ikään kuin liian paljaalta ja kovalta [...]."
74 "Helsingissä ei ollut rakennuksia, joita hän olisi rakastanut – mutta hän rakasti sen profiileja, sitä, jossa Töölön kirkon musta neula pisti ohuen piikkinsä ilmaan, tai sitä, joka aukeni leikkikentän ylitse Hesperiankadun päässä, hetkenä, jolloin ilma tihkui sineä ja hämärää, profiileja, joissa Helsinki näytti hänelle kasvonsa erilaisina ja paljasti niitä aina uusia. Ja sitten hän rakasti Helsingin puita – Tähtitorninmäki ja Kaivopuisto olivat asia erikseen, mutta hän rakasti Hesperian puiston poppeleita, lehtikuusia ja tuomia, erityisesti sitä, joka oli likellä tuota ainoaa henkevää rakennusta, Karamsinin huvilaa."
75 "[...] aseman ja Suurkirkon kellossa vaelsi aika [...]"
76 "[...] kadulla kuului autojen raskaiden pehmeiden kumipyörien massahtelu katuun ja jarrujen vinkuna – kahdeskymmenes vuosisata kiiti eteenpäin, käveli, ratisutti pyöriä [...]."
77 "[...] jotakin sielunmaisemaa [...]"
78 "[...] tutun suuren poppelin [...]"; "Töölönlahden rannalla kasvavan poppelin valoisan latvan muoto ja keltaisen vaaleanvihreä runko oli hänelle monilta kävelyiltä aamuisin ja iltaisin tuttu."
79 "[...] Tähtitornin koivuja ja vaahteroita [...]"
80 "Tyttö ja poika Bulevardin ensimmäisen lehmuksen juurella."

81 "[...] puut venähyttelevät vartaloaan, raoittavat silmiään [...]"
82 "Hän tunsi suuren tuomen, joka kumartuu pitkälle yli kadun ja kävelevien ihmisten, keväisin se hiljaisesti hekumoiden riiputti terttujaan raitiovaunujen ja autojen kiitäessä ohi ja niiden avoimiin ikkunoihin lemahti sen voimakas tuoksu. Nyt oli tuomi mustapintainen, paljas, Lauri huomasi sen epätoivoisesti huiskivan jäykkiä oksiaan tuulessa.".

Towards the Margins

1 Joel Lehtonen's (1881–1934) oeuvre started out in the early twentieth century within a symbolist frame of reference (also referred to as neo-romanticist; see Schoolfield 1998: 133), but his work written in the 1920s and 1930s is much harder to categorize. Most famous for *Putkinotko* ("Putkinotko"; 1919–1920), a novel that firmly belongs to the Finnish canon, and which is set in the countryside, he has also written travel stories and he was a prolific translator. Perhaps more than any other Finnish author in the inter-war period, Lehtonen was oriented towards a carnivalesque and profoundly pan-European literary tradition.

2 "Tietä pitkin kulkee omituinen olento. Kulkee… tai paremminkin liikkuu. Loikkii nelinkontin… Hän on niinkuin koira tai jänis.
Synkkäin kuusien reunustama tie hukkuu syksyiseen sumuun, niin ettei häntä kauempaa tarkasti eroita. Huomaa ainoastaan, että jokin olento se on … olento, joka hyppii kömpelösti."

3 See, for example, Hellaakoski 1950; Hannula 1998; Turunen 2006; Perttula 2006.

4 The same suffix is, of course, visible in English toponyms with Nordic roots.

5 The Swedish krok, from which krokig is derived, means "hook". It has also been argued that Krokelby is derived from the Swedish avkrok, which means "remote district" (Niklander 2003: 14).

6 "Tuossa on hoikka torni rakennettu ylhäälle mökin päätyyn: pikku katos neljän korkean pylvään varaan… ikäänkuin maalaiskartanoitten ruokakellotapuli. Mutta pylväitten kiinnitys on ollut huono, ne ovat kallistuneet vinoon, ja niiden keralla koko kattolaitos…"

7 Protagonists working in building construction can be found, amongst others, in Toivo Tarvas's short story collection *Häviävää Helsinkiä* ("Disappearing Helsinki"; 1917), Helvi Hämäläinen's *Katuojan vettä* ("Water in the Gutter"; 1935), and in Mika Waltari's *Mies ja haave* ("A Man and his Dream"; 1933), amongst others.

8 "[...] väärä ja latvasta typistetty [..]."

9 "Kaikki on [...] sellaista hämärää kuin uni… samanlaista kuin ilmakin, joka nyt peittää maailmaa."

10 The smoke from Russian forest fires covering the city is also described in some detail in Helvi Hämäläinen's *Säädyllinen murhenäytelmä* ("A Respectable Tragedy"; 1941), in which the resulting eerie atmosphere has a profound effect on the protagonist Naimi (Hämäläinen 1941a: 79).

11 "Kylmänä ja sameana [...]"; "Maailma pimenee… Ja sataa."

12 "Usva [...] imee maata… imee siltä viimeisen lämmön… palelluttaa loputkin kasvit." "[...] usva, joka viiltää läpi luiden ja ytimien."

13 "[...] piru pullossa [...]"

14 "Krokelbyssäkin voi nähdä ja oppia, jos sellaista nyt tahtoo, yhtä ja toista [...]."

15 Such a symbolic vision of the city was also present in one of the many literary texts that function as an inspiration for *Henkien taistelu*: Alain-René Lesage's satirical novel *Le Diable Boiteux* ("The Devil in the Bottle"; 1707), which in its turn is based on the text *El Diablo Cojuelo* ("The Devil in the Bottle"; 1641) by the Spanish author Luis Vélez de Guevara (see Klotz 1969: 22 ff.).

16 Bakhtin 1984b: 114–119; Riikonen 1985; Käkelä-Puumala 2007. As H. Riikonen has pointed out, *Henkien taistelu* can be considered a typical example of a Menippean satire (Riikonen 2007).

17 The translation is by Jaakko Ahokas (1973: 201–202), but here slightly modified ("censor" instead of the original "censure").
"Tarkoitukseni on näytellä hänelle sitä, jota ihmiset eräällä tavalla ylpeillen sanovat elämäksi, ikäänkuin filmissä, jossa sensuurin sakset ovat käyneet, se vain erona, että minä leikkaan pois vaarattomat kohdat, hiljaiset, siivot ihmiset, ja sinkautan heijastimesta räikeän valon keskolaisten ja mallikelpoistenkin viallisiin puoliin, – esitän kaiken harkitusti episodeina, joilla ei ole liioin yhteyttä; tuloksesta toivon hajanaista, ääriviivatonta niinkuin aika, jota maapallo nykyään elää [...]."
18 "Se kiiltää, jotta voin nähdä siitä kuvani [...]"
19 Other Italian cities, too, provide reference points for the urban space in the novel: the new student house in Helsinki is compared to the leaning tower of Pisa (Lehtonen 1933: 550).
20 "Se ikäänkuin pattina Helsingin kylkeen kasvanut kylä [...]."
21 Lefebvre 1974/1991: 274; see Grosz 1992.
22 See Barasch 1993: 88–89; Swain 2004: 11; Perttula 2010: 27.
23 Sarajas 1965: 63; Hellaakoski 1950: 90; Viljanen 1959: 164–165.
24 "[...] joka oli hänestä ikäänkuin maaseudun jätteistä ja joistakin Helsingin varisemista kokoonraapustettu [...]."
25 "Hän tahtoi todellakin jonnekin pois tästä kylästä, tästä Helsingin lähistön puolikaupungista, jonka elämänkilvoittelu, kuten hän sitä ajatuksissaan nimitti, oli varmaankin pilannut, vääristänyt, raaistanut [...]."
26 "No, hän tarkoitti tällä lammella nyt vertauskuvallisesti jotakin sellaista, joka oli hartautta, *uskoa*..."
27 James Joyce used the same pun in *Finnegans Wake* (see Finnegans Wake 326.12; Joyce 1939/2013).
28 "[...] lisäilee todistusaineistoaan."
29 "Se oli kaunis päivä kesäkuun lopulla. 'Villa Kaniston' yläkertaan näkyi horisontti laajana, suurena, kaartuen puoliympyränä oikealle ja vasemmalle, kantaen valtavaa taivaankupua, jonka alla maa ikäänkuin supistui pieneksi, painautui matalaksi. Se horisontti, musta kuin Vincin taulujen maisemataustoissa, oli ikäänkuin taiteellinen keino, jolla laakson räikeä vihreys oli saatu vaikuttamaan voimakkaampana kuin se yksinään olisi ollut. [...] Ei tuulenhenkäystä, kaikki tuntui pysähtyneeltä. Meri, josta näkyi pilkahdus kaukaa, harmaan Vantaan suusta, tuskin väreili, mutta ei kimaltanut: sekin oli pysähtynyt, torkahtanut, nukkunut autereen sameaan harsoon. – Kevään raikkaus niityiltä ja pelloilta kauan sitten kadonnut, – ei rentukkain kirkkautta, leinikköjen messinkiä, voikukkien sokaisevaa kultaa! Alhaalla Sorsimon asuntorouvan, entisen porttomaisen, nyt kristillisen ihmisen puutarhassa, jossa syreenit äskettäin olivat avanneet sinisen ja valkean ihanuutensa, rypistyivät valkoruusutkin parhaallaan kulottavan nurmikon keskellä. – Etäällä kallionhuipulla, josta hohti jokin valkeaksi laastittu huvilan torni, liikkui pikku olioita: auringonkylpijöitä puolialastomina, – tai he makasivat liikkumattomina kalliolla kuin tulisella hellalla tai liha halstarilla. – Pölyisellä rautatieradalla, kiiltävien kiskojen välissä, mateli pari mustaa työläistä työhön ja työstä pois. – Suuri hiljaisuus. Ei pääskynenkään elävöittänyt lentopiirilläään taivaan maidonväristä tyhjyyttä..."
Note that in the original text, the "K" in the name of the "Villa Kanisto" is printed as a mirrored letter, in reference to the distorted way in which the name is written on the actual villa in the novel. The distorted features of Krokelby's physical environment find their way into the very layout of the text of *Henkien taistelu*.
30 "On niitäkin, jotka kuljeskelevat Helsingissä kesän hellettä huokuvilla kaduilla paitahihasillaan, tallustelevat yleiselle hiekkarannalle, jonne Kleophaskin kerran eksyi, niinkuin tämä poliittinen kiihtymys ei koskisi heihin laisinkaan. Ei, siellä hiekassa ne vain loikovat, tai heittelevät kuperkeikkaa auringonpaisteessa, nuo

tuhannet, kymmenettuhannet, melkein alastomina, vatsallaan, selällään, silmiä häikäisevässä hiekassa, – selällään kuin siihen kaadetut pronssikuvat, mustina kuin mulatit, vatsallaan kuin taikina [...] kovaäänisen toitottaessa ulahtelevaa saksofoninsäveltä. Terveyttä: flirttiä, seikkailuita! – Ja sellaisia on pitkin maata... tuollaista – lihaa! Se on Kleophaasta lihaa! Hänelle tuntuu tulevan omituinen vastenmielisyys lihaa kohtaan."

31 "Tämä on kiehuva helvetti! ajatteli Martti. – Lihaa, lihaa ja aistillisuutta kaikkialla."
32 "Tämä on lihaa, ja vaikka kuinka tarkkaan hakisitte, niin ette ainakaan tällä hetkellä löytäisi täältä muuta kuin lihaa."
33 In ballet, the *dance macabre* was famously restaged in the 1932 ballet piece *The Green Table* by Kurt Jooss (see Vaaskivi 1938: 333); on the cinema screen, Fritz Lang's *Metropolis* (1927) features scenes reminiscent of the dance of death (see Prakash 2010: 25).
34 A visit in hell is a typical episode in Menippean satires (see Käkelä-Puumala 2007: 184–188), as is the "crisis dream" (see Bakhtin 1984b: 152–153). The profoundly misanthropic view expressed in Sampila's dream, however, and the disconcerting effect the hellish vision has on the protagonist, run counter to the satirical and comic tone of the Menippea, and are indicative of the shift of genre away from satire, towards the subjective grotesque.
35 The link between flesh and the slaughterhouse might have been received with added disgust by contemporary readers, since only a few years before the appearance of *Henkien taistelu*, in 1931, Helsinki had been shocked by the findings of human body parts on the outskirts of the capital (not that far, in fact, from the Old Town area), and a widely mediatized rumour claimed that human flesh had been mixed into food at a local meat grinding factory (Häkkinen & Similä 2010).
36 The mechanized processes of slaughter in the industrialized slaughterhouse were direct precursors of the assembly line (Hodson 2001: 120).
37 The protagonist in *Rakastunut rampa*, Sakris Kukkelman, is also a vegetarian.
38 "Kuolkoon, koska ei ymmärrä, miten hyvä on stroganoff-pihvi [...]."
39 "[...] kamala paikka [...]"
40 "[...] jonkinlainen vuotuinen tasauspäivä, joka ikäänkuin järjestelee ja sioittaa yhteiskunnan eri kerrokset ja ainekset vuoden tapausten mukaan kunkin hänelle kuuluvaan paikkaan [...]"
41 "[...] alhaalta Vladimirinkadulta tai Sörnäisistä, tai Eläintarhan huviloista..."
42 Waltari also mentions as sources for his trilogy Järnefelt's *Veneh'ojalaiset* (1909) and Dreiser's Chicago novel *The Titan* (1914) (Waltari 1980: 230–232).
43 "Silloin on hänellä tapana toisinaan kävellä ikäänkuin vastavirrassa pitkin suurta Unioninkatua. Työmiehet ovat jo muuttaneet pukuansa ja tulevat tummana jonona morsiamineen, vaimoineen ja lapsineen kohti keskikaupunkia yli tuon loivakaarisen kivisillan, joka [...] yhdistää työn ja kyynelten kaupungin kauniiseen varallisuuden ja ilon kaupunkiin."
44 "[...] paksun harson takaa [...]".
45 "Vanha Helsinki ei tuntenut tätä ihmisluokkaa enempää kuin nykyinen kolmekymmenluvun uusi Helsinki tuntee työväkeä, jonka asuma Helsinki on yhä Vallilan puutaloissa tai Toukolan [...] puurähjissä tai Linjojen ja Sörnäisten epäterveellisissä, kurjuuden täyttämissä kivitaloissa. Se vuosisadan alun Helsinki, joka ne rakensi, syöksi niiden asukkaat jo heti alusta epäkodikkuuteen ja yhteisasumiseen, joka edistää rikollisuutta ja levittää veneerisiä tauteja, synnyttää prostituutiota ja kasvattaa niistä jälkeläisistä [...] ruumiiltaan ja sielultaan epäterveen ihmisaineksen [...]".
46 "Tässä oli Töölö – kallioille ja niiden notkoihin keinotekoisesti nostettu kaupunginosa; lahden takana oli Sörnäinen ja Hermanni, kauempana harmaa Katajanokka ja Kruunuhaka ikuisessa unessaan, kappale paennutta vuosisataa."

47 "[...] Lapinlahden ilottoman kaupunginosan [...]"
48 "[...] jossakin hautuumaan puolella [...]"
49 This is also an area in which *Kultakutri* ("Goldilocks") grows up to a life of prostitution in Waltari's novella of the same name (Waltari 1946/1961: 250).
50 "[...] hänen liikkumisensa niillä kaupungin huonomaineisilla laitakaduilla olisi tarpeettoman julkista."
51 "[...] eteni kauas linjoille tai uutta viertotietä pitkin Hermannin seuduille asti."
52 "[...] tuolta hirvittävältä kävelyltä, jolle hänen yhteiskunnalliset vaistonsa olivat hänet pakottaneet miehen ja perheen maineen suojelemiseksi [...]"
53 "Köyhä maksoi veron palkastaan, jotta valtio saisi aseita ja kaupunki raivaisi puistoja rikkaille ja istuttaisi kukkia patsaiden ympärille."
A poem by the poetess Katri Vala, who belonged to the Torch Bearer movement, regrets that the working-class district Sörnäinen has no parks (Vala 1934/1947). Today, a small park in Sörnäinen named after Katri Vala is proof that some things have changed since the 1930s.
54 "Modernin maiseman kuu [...]"
55 Zola's *Au Bonheur des Dames* (*The Ladies' Paradise*; 1883) was published in Finnish for the first time in 1912 under the title *Naisten aarreaitta* (literally, the "Treasure trove of women"), and later as *Naisten paratiisi* (literally, "Women's paradise"), in 1974 (see Kortelainen 2005: 98). The name "women's paradise" had already been used to describe Stockmann in 1937 (see Hapuli et al. 1992: 107–108).
56 "Ei ollut rahaa, ei toivoa... Oli ilta. Taivas musta... Kadulla satoi lumiräntää... Teki mieli keskemmälle kaupunkia, jossa valot kiiltelivät sakeammassa. Nelma käveli ajatuksissaan... pysähtyi jonkin liikkeen ikkunan eteen. Siihen tuli herrasmies, nuori, miellyttävä ja kohtelias."
57 "[...] 'hullunmyllyyn' eli 'karuselliin', Ylioppilastalon edustalla olevaan raitiolinjain solmuun, josta ei aivan päässyt yli eikä ympäri viliseven ajoneuvojen."
58 "Helsinki on kuin hiukan epäsäännöllinen viisihaarainen tähti ja hänellä oli jokaisessa haarassa oppilas; kuhunkin kärkeen piti kiertää keskustan kautta. Nykyään hänellä oli kiire aina ja hän harppaili noita pitkiä matkia kuin hullu."
59 Robert Alter argues that in the course of the nineteenth century, the city had acquired a new, centrifugal character, which what he calls "experiental realism", pioneered by Flaubert, managed to convey in an innovative manner: "Flaubert [...] had succeeded in fashioning an innovative language that could register the compelling, disturbing, and essentially centrifugal character of the new urban realm" (Alter 2005: 42).
The term "centrifugal city" has also been used in urban studies, most prominently perhaps in relation to Los Angeles and to that city's dispersed urban character (Steiner 1981). It is a notion that has more generally been related to a typical Northern American urban phenomenon, and to the emptying of downtown areas. It will be clear that the Finnish context in the inter-war period is very different. The term has also been used in other contexts; in a collection of urban studies essays, for example, the concept of the centrifugal city is used to approach a particular example of urban planning in nineteenth-century Berlin (Meuwissen 2006).
60 Lefebvre is not the first, nor the last, thinker who has positioned a radical shift in spatial experience in the years of his childhood; Raymond Williams traces similar thinking throughout centuries of writing on the loss of an idealized countryside (Williams 1973: 9–12). This does not, however, completely disqualify Lefebvre's observation that radical spatial changes were indeed taking place during the early twentieth century.
61 The homogenizing process involved in abstract space can be considered as a more radical expansion of the "levelling" brought about by the force of money in the Metropolis, as described by Simmel (1903/1969). The effects of the accelerating

expansion of what Lefebvre calls "abstract space" also bear some similarities to the more recent notions of non-places, places set apart from history and contrasted with "places of identity, of relations and of history"; a concept developed by Marc Augé (Augé 1992/1995: 43), and to Edward Relph's notion of placelessness (1976).

62 "[...] riemuitsevasta ihmisjoukosta [...]"
63 In the work of popular novelist Elsa Soini, both parades are featured: in her debut novel *Oli kerran nuori tyttö* ("Once there was a young girl"; 1923), there is an ecstatic description of the 1918 parade (Soini 1923: 265–270), and in the novel *Rouva johtaja* ("Mrs. Director") an equally euphoric experience of the 1930 Farmers' March (Soini 1932: 289) (see Liuttu 1950: 72–73; Palmgren 1989: 102, 132). For a revealingly positive description of the parade, see also Eino Railo's *Koti virran rannalla* (Railo 1937 III: 376–380).
64 "[...] mieleen kohosi lapsuuden aurinkoinen, kukkia, hulmuavia lippuja ja haltioitunutta, ajatuksetonta riemua säteilevä kuva Suomen armeijan ensimmäisestä suuresta paraatista."
65 "[...] valtavan kaipuun sinne, mistä heidän kaikkien voimansa oli alkuaan lähtenyt [...]"

The solutions offered in Kivimaa's *Viheriöivä risti* and Waltari's trilogy have been seen as part of a more general development in the 1930s, when authors that had earlier thematized the city turned increasingly to countryside thematics, a move that can be rooted in the patriotic and rightist atmosphere (see Koskela 1999c: 332).

An interesting postscript to the experience of the 1918 parade was written by Waltari in the educational booklet *Helsinki kautta vuosisatojen* ("Helsinki through the centuries"; 1937). In describing the events of the first decades of the twentieth century, Waltari reused material and characters from his Helsinki trilogy, but the description of the 1918 parade is not as unequivocally positive: the protagonist's grandfather tells the boy Juhani that, regardless of the joyous atmosphere, he feels sad, since "there are thousands, for whom this day is a disconsolate day of disillusion" (Waltari 1937: 90). For his primary school audience, Waltari seems to have consciously tried to construct a past in which both the winners and losers of the Civil War have their place.

66 "[...] hän keskikaupungilla liikkuessaan sai osakseen sellaisia silmäyksiä, jollaisia kohdistetaan epäilyttävän näköisiin, huonoissa pukeissa oleviin olentoihin."
67 "[...] koko työväenluokka oli jollakin lailla samassa tilassa kuin Anna, halvautunut saamastaan iskusta, ei uskaltanut mitään, ei tahtonut mitään [...]"
68 "Meidän kaiken aloitekykymme mursi kaamea ja alituinen rahattomuus. Me olimme kuin rampoja, jotka katselivat sivusta muitten liikkumista."
69 "Onpa minun elämäni hajallista, tunti silloin, toinen taas erikseen, aina harppailla yli kaupungin."
70 "Tämä on seikkailua tavallaan. Ja niin suloinen pikku tyttö."
71 "[...] vain merkki kaikesta tuosta, mistä hän jo aikaisemmin oli varma, että aika oli raaka ja armoton [...]."
72 "[...] kysymyksessä oli sivistynyt tyttö, ylioppilas."
73 "[...] olivat ehkä luulleet joksikin palvelustytöksi tai tavalliseksi huonoksi naiseksi [...]."
74 "[...] sukupuolitautinen jätkä, joka yritti raiskata kahdeksanvuotiasta tyttöä [...]."
75 "Tämä kohtaus antoi Toivon silmätä syvemmälle laitakaupungin elämään kuin koskaan aikaisemmin."
76 "[...] että vieras, komea kaupunkilaiselämä oli huumannut tytön aistit, niin ettei hän tiennyt, mitä teki."
77 In one of the few doctoral dissertations devoted to Waltari's work to date, Taru Tapioharju focuses on the discourse concerning the "new woman" in Mika

Waltari's 1920s and 1930s Helsinki novels (Tapioharju 2010). Tapioharju only tangentially refers to class differences, and focuses mostly on the middle class experiences of the novels' protagonist. This approach obscures the extent to which the gendered geography of fear in 1920s and 1930s Helsinki was defined by class – as well as the lack of narratorial concern in relation to the harassment of women in Helsinki's public space. A more recent dissertation concerning Waltari's early works, Juha Järvelä's *Waltari ja sukupuolten maailmat* ("Waltari and gendered worlds"; 2013), focuses on gender questions and masculinity, discussing questions of urban representations in literature only in passing.

78 "[…] sinne hän meni aina nopeasti kävellen, livahdellen vastaantulijain ohitse, kädet syvällä taskuissa ja hattu silmillä."
79 "Täälläkö se on? […] Näistä laitakaupungin pikkukaduista ei tahdo saada selvää."
80 "Kaikki puutalot ovat samanlaisia […]"
81 "[…] laitakaupungin salaisuudet."
82 "Onpa minulla vielä myöskin eräs oikeus tässä syntymäkaupungissani, voin kulkea varjonpuolella katua."
83 "[…] tunsi suorastaan nautintoa kaupungista […]"
84 "[…] nopeus, vaivaton vauhti, yhteisyys […]."

References

Primary Sources

Aho, Juhani 1884: *Rautatie*. Porvoo: Werner Söderström.
Aho, Juhani 1884/1918: "Kello." In Aho, Juhani: *Kootut teokset I*. Porvoo: Werner Söderström, 32–47.
Aho, Juhani 1889/1997: *Helsinkiin*. Helsinki: SKS.
Aho, Juhani 1889/2000: *To Helsinki*. Translated by Herbert Lomas. In Hawkins, Hildi & Lehtonen, Soila (eds.): *Helsinki. A Literary Companion*. Helsinki: SKS, 73–81.
Aho, Juhani 1890/2003: *Yksin*. Helsinki: SKS.
Aho, Juhani 1890: "Mallikelpoinen." In *Päivälehti* 25.10.1890, 3–4.
Aho, Juhani 1891a: "Hätääkärsivien hyväksi." In *Uusi kuvalehti* 1891/12, 94.
Aho, Juhani 1891b: "Maan sydämmeen." In Aho, Juhani: *Lastuja. Kertomuksia ja kuvauksia*. Porvoo: Werner Söderström, 87–94.
Aho, Juhani 1892: "Helsinkiin." In Aho, Juhani: *Uusia lastuja. Kertomuksia ja kuvauksia*. Porvoo: Werner Söderström, 123–128.
Aho, Juhani 1893/2000: *Papin rouva*. In Aho, Juhani: *Papin tytär. Papin rouva*. Helsinki: SKS, 121–350.
Aho, Juhani 1896: "Kaunis sielu." In Aho, Juhani: *Lastuja. Kertomuksia ja kuvauksia III*. Helsinki: Weilin & Göös, 106–120.
Balzac, Honoré de 1835/1995: *Le père Goriot*. Paris: Librairie Générale Française.
Baudelaire, Charles 1857/1998: *The Flowers of Evil*. Translated by James McGowan. Oxford: Oxford University Press.
Baudelaire, Charles 1860/1967: *Les Paradis Artificiels*. Paris: Livre de Poche.
Baudelaire, Charles 1861: "À une passante." In Baudelaire, Charles: *Les Fleurs du Mal*. http://fleursdumal.org/poem/224 14.5.2013
Baudelaire, Charles 1869/1989: *The Parisian Prowler. Le Spleen de Paris, Petits Poèmes en Prose*. Translated by Edward K. Kaplan. Athens, GA: University of Georgia Press.
Bely, Andrei 1916/1978: *Petersburg*. Translated by Robert A. Maguire and John E. Malmstad. Hassocks: Harvester Press.
Bergbom, Kaarlo 1864/1907–1908: "Belsazarin pidot." In Bergbom, Kaarlo: *Kaarlo Bergbomin kirjoitukset*. Helsinki: SKS, 221–228.
Bible. King James Bible 1611/2012. http://www.kingjamesbibleonline.org/ 14.5.2013
Calvino, Italo 1972/1997: *The Invisible Cities*. Translated by William Weaver. London: Vintage.
Canth, Minna 1894: "Ompelija." In *Suomen Kuvalehti* 1894/1–2, 8–11, 19–24.
Chesterton, G. K. 1910/1928: *The Ball and the Cross*. London: Welss Gardner, Darton & Co.
Conrad, Joseph 1899/1994: *Heart of Darkness*. London: Penguin.
Dickens, Charles 1852–1853/2003: *Bleak House*. London: Penguin.
e. 1893: "Hanna Toivosen ystävät." In *Koti ja yhteiskunta* 1893/6–7, 80–82.

Eliot, T. S. 1922/1971: *The Waste Land*. London: Faber & Faber.
Flaubert, Gustave 1856/1996: *Madame Bovary*. Translated by Eleanor Marx Aveling. Mineola, N. Y.: Dover Publications.
Flecker, James Elroy 1923: *The Collected Poems of James Elroy Flecker*. London: Martin Secker.
Hämäläinen, Helvi 1935: *Katuojan vettä*. Jyväskylä: Gummerus.
Hämäläinen, Helvi 1941a: *Säädyllinen murhenäytelmä I*. Porvoo: Werner Söderström.
Hämäläinen, Helvi 1941b: *Säädyllinen murhenäytelmä II*. Porvoo: Werner Söderström.
Ivalo, Santeri [Santeri] 1890: *Hellaassa. Novelli*. Helsinki: Otava.
Ivalo, Santeri [Ingman, Santeri] 1895: *Aikansa lapsipuoli*. Porvoo: Werner Söderström.
Joyce, James 1922/1993: *Ulysses*. Oxford: Oxford University Press.
Joyce, James 1939: *Finnegans Wake*. London: Faber & Faber.
http://www.trentu.ca/faculty/jjoyce/F1-1.htm 15.9.2013
Järnefelt, Arvid 1893/1997: *Isänmaa*. Helsinki: SKS.
Järnefelt, Arvid 1900: *Veljekset*. Helsinki: Otava.
Järnefelt, Arvid 1905: *Maaemon lapsia*. Helsinki: Otava.
Järnefelt, Arvid 1909/1996: *Veneh'ojalaiset*. Helsinki: SKS.
Järnefelt, Arvid [Kahila, Hilja] 1919: *Nuoruuteni muistelmia*. Helsinki: Kirja.
Järnefelt, Arvid 1928–1930/1944: *Vanhempieni romaani*. Porvoo: Werner Söderström.
Karri, Unto 1929: *Sodoma. Romaani*. Helsinki: Otava.
Kivijärvi, Erkki 1935: *Tiimalasissa valuu hiekka. Romaani vuosisadan alun Helsingistä*. Helsinki: Otava.
Kivimaa, Arvi 1930: *Epäjumala. Romaani*. Helsinki: Otava.
Kivimaa, Arvi 1931: *Katu nousee taivaaseen. Novelleja*. Helsinki: Otava.
Kivimaa, Arvi 1932: *Hetki ikuisen edessä*. Helsinki: Otava
Kivimaa, Arvi 1938. *Saari tuulten sylissä. Romaani*. Helsinki: Otava.
Kivimaa, Arvi 1939: *Viheriöivä risti. Romaani*. Helsinki: Otava.
Kivimies, Yrjö 1931: *Sentaattorin sankarityö*. Jyväskylä: Gummerus.
Koskenniemi, V. A. 1906: *Runoja*. Porvoo: Werner Söderström.
Kurjensaari, Matti 1937: *Tie Helsinkiin*. Jyväskylä: Gummerus.
Lehtonen, Joel 1913: *Punainen mylly*. Helsinki: Otava.
Lehtonen, Joel 1922/2006: *Rakastunut rampa, eli Sakris Kukkelman, köyhä polseviikki*. Helsinki: SKS.
Lehtonen, Joel 1925/2008: *Punainen mies*. In Lehtonen, Joel: *Sorron lapset. Punainen mies*. Helsinki: SKS, 337–652.
Lehtonen, Joel 1933: *Henkien taistelu. Kertomus tunnetuista kansalaisistamme*. Helsinki: Otava.
Leino, Eino 1899: "Helsinki sumussa." *Päivälehti* 18.2.1899, 3.
Leino, Eino 1905: *Päivä Helsingissä. Pilakuva*. Helsinki: Otava.
Leino, Eino 1906/1998: *Tuomas Vitikka*. In Leino, Eino: *Routavuositrilogia*. Helsinki: SKS, 3–182.
Leino, Eino 1907/1998: *Jaana Rönty*. In Leino, Eino: *Routavuositrilogia*. Helsinki: SKS, 183–332.
Leino, Eino 1908/1998: *Olli Suurpää*. In Leino, Eino: *Routavuositrilogia*. Helsinki: SKS, 333–508.
Leino, Eino 1908: "Meren kaupunki." In Leino, Eino: *Halla*. Helsinki: Otava, 121–136.
Leino, Eino 1914: *Pankkiherroja. Kuvaus nykyaikaisesta suomalaisesta liike-elämästä*. Helsinki: Kirja.
Leino, Kasimir 1884: *Runokokeita. Emmalan Elli*. Porvoo: Werner Söderström.
Leino, Kasimir 1889: "Neron tähteet. Kuvaus pääkaupungista." In Leino, Kasimir: *Elämästä. Pienempiä kertomuksia*. Porvoo: Werner Söderström, 29–46.
Lönnrot, Elias 1849/1999: *Kalevala*. Helsinki: SKS.
Maija 1902: "Elämän todellisuudesta." In *Kodin ystävä* 1905/5, 4–5.

Merenmaa, Martti 1926: *Nousuvesi*. Helsinki: Otava.
Noponen, Alpo 1894: "Leikkikentältä asti." In *Uuden Suomettaren juttu-tupa* 1894/37, 147–148.
Onerva, L. 1908/2002: *Mirdja*. Helsinki: SKS.
Onerva, L. 1911: *Nousukkaita. Luonnekuvia*. Helsinki: Weilin & Kumpp.
Onerva, L. 1913: *Inari. Romaani*. Helsinki: Kirja.
Onerva, L. 1915: *Vangittuja sieluja. Novelleja*. Helsinki: Kirja.
Paavolainen, Olavi 1929: "Helsinki by Night. Psykodraama v:lta 1929." In *Aitta* 12: 34–43.
Petterson, Viktor 1881: *Bilder ur Skatuddslifvet i forma dagar*. Helsinki: Hufvudstadsbladet.
Poe, Edgar Allan 1840/1912: "The Man of the Crowd." In Poe, Edgar Allan: *Tales of Mystery and Imagination*. London: J. M. Dent & Sons, 101–109.
http://etext.virginia.edu/toc/modeng/public/PoeCrow.html 14.5.2013
Procopé, Hjalmar 1905: *Belsazars gästabud. Skådespel i 4 akter*. Helsinki: Helios.
Pushkin, Alexander Sergeyevich 1833/1998: "The Bronze Horseman: A St. Petersbrug Story." Translated by John Dewey. In *Translation and Literature* 7/1, 59–71.
Railo, Eino 1937: *Koti virran rannalla I-III*. Porvoo: WSOY.
Rimminen, Mikko 2004: *Pussikaljaromaani*. Helsinki: Teos.
Rimminen, Mikko 2007: *Pölkky*. Helsinki: Teos.
Rodenbach, Georges 1892/2007: *Bruges-la-Morte*. Translated by Philip Mosley. Chicago: University of Scranton Press.
Shakespeare, William 1994: "Sonnet 130." In Shakespeare, William: *The Poems & Sonnets of William Shakespeare*. Ware: Wordsworth Editions, 67.
Sinervo, Elvi 1937: *Runo Söörnäisistä*. Jyväskylä: Gummerus.
Soini, Elsa 1923: *Oli kerran nuori tyttö. Romaani*. Helsinki: Otava.
Soini, Elsa 1930: *Uni. Romaani*. Helsinki: Otava.
Soini, Elsa 1932: *Rouva johtaja. Romaani*. Helsinki: Otava.
Talvio, Maila 1896: "Helsinkiin." In Talvio, Maila: *Nähtyä ja tunnettua. Kertoelmia ja kuvauksia*. Porvoo: Werner Söderström, 169–180.
Talvio, Maila 1897: *Aili. Kertomus*. Porvoo: Werner Söderström.
Talvio, Maila 1910: *Tähtien alla. Romaani*. Porvoo: Werner Söderström.
Talvio, Maila 1912: "Hämähäkki." In Talvio, Maila: *Hämähäkki ja muita kertomuksia*. Porvoo: Werner Söderström, 55–93.
Talvio, Maila 1915: *Niniven lapset. Romaani*. Porvoo: Werner Söderström.
Talvio, Maila 1916: *Kultainen lyyra. Katkelmia naisylioppilaan elämästä*. Porvoo: Werner Söderström.
Talvio, Maila 1929: *Kaukaa tullut. Itämeren tytär – romaani vanhasta Helsingistä*. Porvoo: Werner Söderström.
Talvio, Maila 1931: *Hed-Ulla ja hänen kosijansa. Romaani vanhasta Helsingistä*. Porvoo: Werner Söderström.
Talvio, Maila 1936: *Hopealaiva. Romaani vanhasta Helsingistä*. Porvoo: Werner Söderström.
Talvio, Maila 1941: *Linnoituksen iloiset rouvat. Romaani vanhan Viaporin ajoilta*. Porvoo: Werner Söderström.
Tarvas, Toivo 1916a: *Eri tasoilta. Nykyaikainen romaani*. Helsinki: Otava.
Tarvas, Toivo 1916b: *Kohtalon tuulissa. Nykyajan romaani*. Helsinki: Otava.
Tarvas, Toivo 1917: *Häviävää Helsinkiä. Novelleja*. Helsinki: Otava.
Tarvas, Toivo 1919: *Helsinkiläisiä. Piirroksia pääkaupungin elämästä*. Helsinki: Ahjo.
Tarvas, Toivo 1920: *Kadun lapsia. Novelleja*. Helsinki: Ahjo.
Tavaststjerna, K. A. 1886: *Barndomsvänner. Ett nutidsöde*. Porvoo: Werner Söderström.
Tihlä, Hilda 1907: *Leeni*. Helsinki: Yrjö Weilin.
Topelius, Zacharias [Zachris] 1845/2003: "Nuori pääkaupunki." In Martinsen, Rolf

(ed.): *Sydän on hyvä. Zachris Topeliuksen kirjoituksia Helsingistä.* Helsinki: Helsinki-Seura, 11–13.
Topelius, Zacharias [Zachris] 1881/1882: *Vinterqvällar. Första Cyckeln.* Stockholm: Alb. Bonniers Boktryckeri.
Topelius, Zacharias 1885/1986: *Muistiinpanoja vanhasta Helsingistä.* Helsinki: Helsinki-seura.
Uurto, Iris 1930: *Tulta ja tuhkaa. Novelleja ja runoja.* Helsinki: Otava.
Uurto, Iris 1930/1931: *Ruumiin ikävä. Romaani.* Helsinki: Otava.
Uurto, Iris 1935: *Kypsyminen. Romaani.* Helsinki: Otava.
Uurto, Iris 1936: *Rakkaus ja pelko. Romaani.* Helsinki: Otava.
Vala, Katri 1934/1947: "Summer in Sörnäs/Kesä Sörnäisissä." Translated by Cid Erik Tallqvist. In Tompuri, Elli (ed.): *Voices From Finland.* Helsinki: Sanoma, 161–162.
Verhaeren, Émile 1895: *Les Villes Tentaculaires.* Brussels: Deman.
Waltari, Mika 1928: *Suuri illusioni. Romaani.* Porvoo: WSOY.
Waltari, Mika 1928/2004: "Kuolleet kaupungit." In Vartio, Eero (ed.): *Illusioni 2004.* Helsinki: Mika Waltari -seura, 45.
Waltari, Mika 1929: *Yksinäisen miehen juna.* Porvoo: WSOY.
Waltari, Mika 1931: *Appelsiininsiemen. Romaani.* Porvoo: WSOY.
Waltari, Mika 1933: *Mies ja haave. Romaani.* Porvoo: WSOY.
Waltari, Mika 1934: *Sielu ja liekki. Romaani.* Porvoo: WSOY.
Waltari, Mika 1935: *Palava nuoruus. Romaani.* Porvoo:WSOY.
Waltari, Mika 1936: *Surun ja ilon kaupunki. Romaani.* Porvoo: WSOY.
Waltari, Mika 1942: *Isästä poikaan. Romaani kolmen sukupolven Helsingistä.* Porvoo: WSOY.
Waltari, Mika 1943: "Uusi rakennusmaa." In Waltari, Mika: *Novelleja.* Porvoo: WSOY, 239–256.
Waltari, Mika 1946/1961: "Kultakutri." In Waltari, Mika: *Koiranheisipuu ja neljä muuta pienoisromaania.* Porvoo: Helsinki, 231–307.
Westö, Kjell 2002: *Lang.* Stockholm: Norstedts.
Westö, Kjell 2006: *Där vi en gång gått. En roman om en stad och om vår vilja att bli högre än gräset.* Stockholm: Norstedts.
Wilkuna, Kyösti 1915: *Vaikea tie. Romaani nykyajalta.* Helsinki: Kirja.

Non-Literary Sources

Feuillade, Louis 1910: *Le Festin de Balthazar.* France: Société des Etablissements L. Gaumont.

Secondary Sources

Aalto, Minna 2000: *Vapauden ja velvollisuuden ristiriita. Kehitysromaanin mahdollisuudet 1890-luvun lopun ja 1900-luvun alun naiskirjallisuudessa.* Helsinki: SKS.
Ackroyd, Peter 2001: *London. The Biography.* New York: Nan A. Talese.
af Ursin, N. R. 1907: "Kaupunkien laajeneminen." In *Työmies* 22.02.1907, 3.
Ahlund, Claes 1990: *Den skandinaviska universitetsromanen 1877–1890.* Stockholm: Almqvist & Wiksell.
Ahokas, Jaakko 1973: *A History of Finnish Literature.* Bloomington: Indiana University Publications.
Ahonen, Albin 1929: "Siitä oikeasta Helsinkiläisromaanista, jota ei vieläkään syntynyt ole." In *Aitta* 1929/11: 52–53.
Alanco, Jan & Pakarinen, Riitta 2005: *Signe Brander 1869–1942. Helsingin valokuvaaja.* Helsinki: Helsinki kaupunkimuseo.

Alhoniemi, Pirkko 1972: *Idylli särkyy. Kansallisromanttisten ideaalien mureneminen jälkiromantiikan ja realismin kauden kirjallisuudessamme.* Helsinki: SKS.

Alkio, Santeri [S. A.] 1909: "Kirjavia kuvia Helsingistä I. Iltasella Espiksellä." In *Pyrkijä* 1909/17, 264–265.

Alter, Robert 2005: *Imagined Cities. Urban Experience and the Language of the Novel.* New Haven: Yale University Press.

Altnöder, Sonja 2009: "Die Stadt als Körper: Materialität und Diskursivität in zwei London-Romanen." In Hallet, Wolfgang & Neumann, Birgit (eds.) 2009: *Raum und Bewegung in der Literatur. Die Literaturwissenschaften und der Spatial Turn.* Bielefeld: Transcript, 229–318.

Ameel, Lieven 2010: "Walking the Streets of Helsinki. Traces of the Flâneur in Early Finnish Prose Literature." In Broomans, Petra and Ronne, Marta (eds.): *In the Vanguard of Cultural Transfer. Cultural Transmitters and Authors in Peripheral Literary Fields.* Barkhuis: Groningen, 119–134.

Ameel, Lieven 2012: "On the Threshold. The Brothel and the Literary Salon as Heterotopia in Finnish Urban novels." In Nünning, Ansgar & Sicks Kai (eds): *Turning Points. Concepts and Narratives of Change in Literature and Other Media.* Berlin: De Gruyter, 125–144.

Ameel, Lieven 2013a: *Moved by the City. Experiences of Helsinki in Finnish Prose Literature 1889–1941.* Helsinki: Unigrafia.
https://helda.helsinki.fi/bitstream/handle/10138/39407/ameel_dissertation.pdf?sequence=1

Ameel, Lieven 2013b: "'Mitä sinä tässä kävelet?' Naisiin kohdistettu katse Helsingin julkisissa tiloissa 1900-luvun vaihteen kirjallisuudessa." In Rossi, Riikka & Isomaa, Saija (eds.): *Kirjallisuuden naiset. Naisten esityksiä 1840-luvulta 2000-luvulle.* Helsinki: SKS, 141–164.

Anonymus 1899a: "Häviävä Helsinki." In *Isänmaan Ystävä* 1899/3, 3.

Anonymus 1899b: "Häviävä Helsinki." In *Uusi Suometar* 16.2.1899, 2.

Anonymus 1900: "Maaseudun vero suurkaupungille." In *Uusimaa* 1900/99, 1–2.

Anonymus 1902: "Häviävä Helsinki." In *Päivälehti* 18.5.1902, 3.

Anonymus 1903a: "Hermojen kuluminen ja niiden suojeleminen." In *Aamulehti* 14.8.1903, 4.

Anonymus 1903b: "Hermostuminen ja kaupungin elämä." In *Päivälehti* 08.10.1903, 3.

Anonymus 1907: "Jaana Rönty englantilaisen arvostelemana." In *Tampereen sanomat* 6.16.1907, 3.

Anonymus 1910a: "Häviävä Helsinki." In *Työväenliitto* 19.04.1910, 3.

Anonymus 1910b: "Valtakunnan lainsäädäntökysymys eduskunnassa." In *Viipurin Sanomat* 9.5.1910, 2.

Anttila, Aarne 1956: "Helsinki kaunokirjallisuuden kuvastimessa." In Rosén, Ragnar; Hornborg, Eirik; Waris, Heikki & Jutikkala, Eino (eds.): *Helsingin kaupungin historia* IV: 2. Helsinki: Helsinki City, 639–649.

Asikainen, Annamari & Koskela, Hille 1992: "Naisen pelon maantieteestä maaseudun naisen arkeen: feministisen maantieteen haasteita." In *Naistutkimus* 5/1, 5–13, 80.

Aspelin-Haapkylä, Eliel 1980: *Kirovuosien kronikka. Eliel Aspelin-Haapkylän päiväkirja v. 1905–1917.* Helsinki: SKS.

Assmuth, Lari; Berger, Anne-May; Ervalahti, Nora & Rosenström, Marika (eds.) 2012: *Helsingfors i ord och bild. Huvudstaden kring sekelskiftet 1900.* Helsinki: Svenska litteratursällskapet i Finland.

Augé, Marc 1992/1995: *Non-Places. Introduction to an Anthropology of Supermodernity.* Translated by John Howe. London: Verso.

Augustine, Saint 2001: *Expositions of the Psalms, 51–72.* Translated by Maria Boulding. Hyde Park, New York: New City Press.
http://pm.nlx.com/xtf/view?docId=augustine/augustine.23.xml;chunk.id=div.aug.

psalms.v3.204;toc.depth=1;toc.id=div.aug.psalms.v3.204;brand=default 14.5.2013

Augustine, Saint [Augustinus, Aurelius] 2007: *De Stad van God.* Translated by Gerard Wijdeveld. Amsterdam: Ambo.

Baguley, David 1990: *Naturalist Fiction. The Entropic Vision.* Cambridge: Cambridge University Press.

Bakhtin, Mikhail 1981: *The Dialogic Imagination.* Translated by Caryl Emerson and Michael Holquist. Austin: University of Texas Press.

Bakhtin, Mikhail 1984a: *Rabelais and His World.* Translated by Helene Iswolsky. Bloomington: Indiana University Press.

Bakhtin, Mikhail 1984b: *Problems of Dostoevsky's Poetics.* Translated by Caryl Emerson. Minneapolis: University of Minnesota Press.

Bakhtin, Mikhail 1986/2004: "The *Bildungsroman* and Its Significance in the History of Realism. Towards a Historical Typology of the Novel." In Bakhtin, Mikhail: *Speech Genres & Other Late Essays.* Translated by Vern W. McGee. Austin: University of Texas Press, 10–59.

Bal, Mieke 2006: "Over-writing as Un-writing : Descriptions, World-Making, and Novelistic Time." In Moretti, Franco (ed.): *The Novel. Volume 2: Forms and Themes.* Princeton: Princeton University Press, 571–610.

Bal, Mieke 2009: *Narratology. Introduction to the Theory of Narrative.* Toronto: University of Toronto Press.

Bang, Gustav 1908: *Nykyaika. Aikamme yhteiskunta- ja sivistyselämä.* Translated by Gunnar Lindström. Porvoo: WSOY.

Barasch, Frances K. 1993: "Grotesque, theories of the." In Makaryk, Irene Rima (ed.): *Encyclopedia of Contemporary Literary Theory: Approaches, Scholars, Terms.* Toronto: University of Toronto Press, 85–90.

Barthes, Roland 1986/1997: "Semiology and the Urban." In Leach, Neil (ed.): *Rethinking Architecture. A Reader in Cultural Theory.* London: Routledge, 166–172.

Bassini, Alessandro 2012: *Notes from the Suburb: the Image of Helsinki in the Works by Kjell Westö.* Trento: University of Trento.

http://eprints-phd.biblio.unitn.it/692/1/Notes_from_the_Suburb.pdf 14.5.2013

Bataille, Georges 1929/1997: "Slaughterhouse." In Leach, Neil (ed.): *Rethinking Architecture. A Reader in Cultural Theory.* London: Routledge, 22.

Baudelaire, Charles 1863/1964: "The Painter of Modern Life." Translated by Jonathan Mayne. London: Phaidon Press.

Bell, Marjatta & Hietala, Marjatta (eds.) 2002: *Helsinki, the Innovative City. Historical Perspectives.* Helsinki: SKS.

Benjamin, Walter 2006: *The Writer of Modern Life: Essays on Charles Baudelaire.* Translated by Howard Eiland. Cambridge, MA: Harvard University Press.

Bergius, Hanne 1986: "Berlin als Hure Babylon." In Boberg, Jochen; Fichter, Tilman & Gillen, Eckhart (eds.): *Die Metropole: Industriekultur in Berlin im 20. Jahrhundert.* Munich: Beck, 102–119.

Bergson, Henri-Louis 1889/1910: *Time and Free Will. An Essay on the Immediate Data of Consciousness.* Translated by F.L. Pogson. London: George Allen & Unwin.

http://archive.org/stream/timeandfreewill00pogsgoog#page/n8/mode/2up 14.5.2013

Berman, Marshall 1982/1989: *All That is Sold Melts into Air. The Experience of Modernity.* London: Verso.

Bianchini, Franco 2006: "Introduction. European Urban Mindscapes: Concepts, Cultural Representations and Policy Applications." In Weiss-Sussex, Godela & Bianchini, Franco (eds): *Urban Mindscapes of Europe.* Amsterdam: Rodopi, 13–34.

Blom, Philipp 2008: *The Vertigo Years: Change and Culture in the West, 1900–1914.* London: Weidenfeld & Nicolson.

Borg, Alexandra 2011: *En Vildmark av Sten. Stockholm i Litteraturen 1897–1916.* Stockholm: Stockholmia Förlag.

Bradbury, Malcolm 1976/1986: "The Cities of Modernism." In Bradbury, Malcolm & McFarlane, James (eds.): *Modernism*. Harmondsworth: Penguin, 96–104.
Bridgeman, Teresa 2007: "Time and Space." In Herman, David (ed.): *The Cambridge Companion to Narrative*. Cambridge: Cambridge University Press, 52–65.
Brooks, Peter 2005: *Realist Vision*. New Haven: Yale University Press.
Brosseau, Marc 1994: "Geography's literature." In *Progress in Human Geography* 18/3, 333–353.
Buchholz, Sabine & Jahn, Manfred 2005: "Space in Narrative." In Herman, David; Jahn, Manfred & Ryan, Marie-Laure: *Routledge Encyclopedia of Narrative Theory*. London: Routledge, 551–555.
Canth, Minna 1884: "Naiskysymyksestä." In *Valvoja* 1884/4, 169–176.
Carsten, F. L. 1967/1982: *The Rise of Fascism*. Berkeley, CA: University of California Press.
Castrén, Gunnar 1947: "Helsingfors i 1800-talets skönlitteratur." In Hirn, Yrjö; Nordman, C. A.; Ekelund, Hilding & af Schultén, Marius (eds.): *Vår stad. En bok om Helsingfors*. Helsinki: Holger Schildts, 88–118.
Chanda, A. K. 1981: "The Young Man from the Provinces." In *Comparative Literature* 33/4, 321–341.
Ciaravolo, Massimo 2000: *En ungdomsvän från Sverige. Om mottagandet av Hjalmar Söderbergs verk i Finland 1895–1920*. Helsinki: Svenska litteratursällskapet i Finland.
Citron, Pierre 1961: *La Poésie de Paris dans la Littérature Française de Rousseau à Baudelaire*. Paris: Les Éditions de Minuit.
City of Helsinki Urban Facts 2012: *Helsingin väestö vuodenvaihteessa 2011/2012 ja väestönmuutokset vuonna 2011*. Helsinki: City of Helsinki Urban Facts. http://www.hel2.fi/tietokeskus/julkaisut/pdf/12_06_28_Tilastoja_23_Peuranen.pdf 14.5.2013
Daemmrich, Horst S. & Daemmrich, Ingrid 1987: *Themes & Motifs in Western Literature: A Handbook*. Tübingen: Francke Verlag.
Dannenberg, Hilary P. 2007: "Windows, Doorways and Portals in Narrative Fiction and Media." In Schenkel, Elmar & Welz, Stefan (eds.): *Magical Objects: Things and Beyond*. Berlin: Galda & Wilch, 181–198.
Dannenberg, Hilary P. 2008: *Coincidence and Counterfactuality. Plotting Time and Space in Narrative Fiction*. Lincoln: University of Nebraska Press.
Davidoff, Leonore 2003: "Gender and the 'Great Divide'. Public and Private in British Gender History." In *Journal of Women's History* 15/1, 11–27.
de Certeau, Michel 1984: *The Practice of Everyday Life*. Translated by Steven Rendall. Berkeley, CA: University of California Press.
Den Tandt, Christophe 1998: *The Urban Sublime in American Literary Naturalism*. Urbana and Chicago: University of Illinois Press.
Dennis, Richard 2008: *Cities in Modernity. Representations and Productions of Metropolitan Space, 1840–1930*. Cambridge: Cambridge University Press.
Donald, James 1999: *Imagining the Modern City*. Minneapolis: University of Minnesota Press.
D'Souza, Aruna & McDonough, Tom (eds.) 2008: *The Invisible Flâneuse? Gender, Public Space and Visual Culture in Nineteenth-Century Paris*. Manchester: Manchester University Press.
Ekelund, Erik 1937: "Joel Lehtonen. Världen och fågelnästet." In *Ord och bild* 1937/24, 369–381.
Envall, Markku 1992: "Romaani kuin kaleidoskooppi: Mika Waltarin Surun ja ilon kaupunki." In Turunen, Risto; Saariluoma, Liisa; Assmann, Dietrich (eds.): *Vaihtuva muoto. Tutkielmia suomalaisen romaanin historiasta*. Helsinki: SKS, 91–103.
Envall, Markku 1994: *Suuri illusionisti. Mika Waltarin romaanit*. Helsinki: WSOY.

Ette, Otmar 2005: *Zwischen WeltenSchreiben. Literaturen ohne festen Wohnsitz*. Berlin: Kadmos.

Finch, Jason 2011: *E. M. Forster and English Place: A Literary Topography*. Turku: Åbo Akademi University Press.

Ford, Ford Madox [Ford Madox Hueffer] 1905: *The Soul of London. A Survey of a Modern City*. London: Alston Rivers.

http://openlibrary.org/books/OL6960187M/The_soul_of_London 14.5.2013

Forsman, Jaakko; Wecksell, J. A.; Havu, I. & Salovaara, Hannes (eds.) 1925–1928: *Pieni Tietosanakirja*. Helsinki: Otava.

http://runeberg.org/pieni/ 14.5.2013

Foucault, Michel 1986: "Of Other Spaces." Translated by Jay Miskowiec. In *Diacritics* 16/1, 22–27.

Freeborn, Richard 1982: *The Russian Revolutionary Novel. Turgenev to Pasternak*. Cambridge: Cambridge University Press.

Freeman, Nicholas 2007: *Conceiving the City. London, Literature, and Art 1870–1914*. Oxford: Oxford University Press.

Freud, Sigmund 1930/2002: *Civilization and Its Discontents*. Translated by David McLintock. London: Penguin.

Friedman, Susan Stanford 2005: "Spatial Poetics and Arundhati Roy's *The God of Small Things*." In Phelan, James & Rabinowitz, Peter J. (eds.): *A Companion to Narrative Theory*. Oxford: Blackwell, 192–205.

Frisby, David 2001: *Cityscapes of Modernity*. Oxford: Blackwell.

Fussell, Paul 1980: *Abroad: British literary traveling between the wars*. New York: Oxford University Press.

Ganim, John M. 2002: "Cities of Words: Recent Studies on Urbanism and Literature." In *Modern Language Quarterly* 63/3, 365–382.

Gelfant, Blanche Housman 1954: *The American City Novel*. Norma: University of Oklahoma Press.

Gere, Cathy 2009: *Knossos & the Prophets of Modernism*. Chicago: University of Chicago Press.

Geyh, Paula E. 2006: "From Cities of Things to Cities of Signs: Urban Spaces and Urban Subjects in *Sister Carrie* and *Manhattan Transfer*." In *Twentieth-Century Literature* 52/4, 413–442.

Gillian, Rodger 1957: "Hero and Leander in Scottish Balladry." In *Comparative Literature* 9/1, 1–16.

Gleber, Anke 1999: *The Art of Taking a Walk. Flânerie, Literature and Film in Weimar Culture*. Princeton: Princeton University Press.

Goode, John 1978/1979: *George Gissing: Ideology and Fiction*. New York: Barnes & Noble.

Goodman, Nelson 1978: *Ways of Worldmaking*. Sussex: Harvester Press.

Gray, Timothy 2010: *Urban Pastoral: Natural Currents in the New York School*. Iowa City: University of Iowa Press.

Grosz, Elizabeth 1992: "Bodies-Cities." In Colomina, Beatriz & Bloomer, Jennifer (eds.) 1992: *Sexuality and Space*. Princeton: Princeton Architectural Press, 241–53.

Gumbrecht, Hans Ulrich 2006: "The Roads of the Novel." In Moretti, Franco (ed.): *The Novel. Volume 2: Forms and Themes*. Princeton: Princeton University Press, 611–646.

Gunn, Simon 2001: "The Spatial Turn: Changing Histories of Space and Place." In Gunn, Simon & Morris, Robert J. (eds.): *Identities in Space; Contested Terrains in the Western City since 1850*. Aldershot: Ashgate, 1–14.

H. S. [Herman Stenberg?] 1908: "The Tribune'n lakkaaminen." In *Päivä* 1908/7, 58.

H. S-M. 1915: "Maila Talvio, Niniven lapset." In *Valvoja* 1915/3, 257–260.

Haapala, Pertti; Löytty, Olli; Melkas, Kukku & Tikka, Marko 2008: *Kansa kaikkivaltias. Suurlakko Suomessa 1905*. Helsinki: Teos.

Hallet, Wolfgang & Neumann, Birgit 2009: "Raum und Bewegung in der Literatur: Zur Einführung." In Hallet, Wolfgang & Neumann, Birgit (eds.): *Raum und Bewegung in der Literatur*. Bielefeld: Transcript, 11–32.

Hapuli, Ritva 1995: *Nykyajan sininen kukka. Olavi Paavolainen ja nykyaika*. Helsinki: SKS.

Hapuli, Ritva; Koivunen, Anu; Lappalainen, Päivi & Rojola, Lea 1992: "Uutta naista etsimässä." In Onnela, Tapio (ed.): *Vampyyrinainen ja Kenkkuinniemen sauna. Suomalainen kaksikymmenluku ja modernin mahdollisuus*. Helsinki: SKS, 98–112.

Harvey, David 1989a: *The Condition of Postmodernity. An Enquiry into the Origins of Cultural Change*. Cambridge, MA: Blackwell.

Harvey, David 1989b: *The Urban Experience*. Baltimore: Johns Hopkins University Press.

Harvey, David 1995: "Evaluation: Geographical Knowledge in the Eye of Power: Reflections on Derek Gregory's Geographical Imaginations." In *Annals of the Association of American Geographers* 85/1, 160–164.

Harvey, David 2003: "City Future in City Past: Balzac's Cartographic Imagination." In Resina, Joan Ramon & Ingeschay, Dieter (eds): *After-Images of the City*. Ithaca: Cornell University Press, 23–48.

Hasu, Kirsi & Peltonen, Ulla-Maija (eds.) 2000: *Kirjailijoiden Helsinki*. Helsinki: Helsinki City.

Havu, I. 1965: "Helsinki kaunokirjalijoiden kuvaamana." In Rosén, Ragner et al. (eds.): *Helsingin kaupungin historia* V: 2. Helsinki: Helsinki City, 288–299.

Hawkins, Hildi & Lehtonen, Soila 2000: "Foreword." In Hawkins, Hildi & Lehtonen, Soila (eds.): *Helsinki. A Literary Companion*. Helsinki: SKS, 6–11.

Heiskanen, Outi & Santakari, Minna 2004: *Asuuko neiti Töölössä? Elämää elokuvien Helsingissä*. Helsinki: Teos.

Hellaakoski, Aaro 1922/2006: [review of Rakastunut rampa]. In Lehtonen, Joel: *Rakastunut rampa*. Helsinki: SKS, 240–241.

Hellaakoski, Aaro 1950: "Sakris Kukkelmanin asema Joel Lehtosen tuotannossa." In Hellaakoski, Aaro: *Kuuntelua: esseitä teoksista ja tekijöistä*. Porvoo: WSOY, 86–103.

Hentilä, Seppo 1995/1999: "From Independence to the End of the Continuation War, 1917–1944." In Jussila, Osmo; Hentilä, Seppo & Nevakivi, Jukka (eds.): *From Grand Duchy to Modern State. A Political History of Finland since 1809*. London: C. Hurst & Co, 101–216.

Hesse, Hermann 1920/1922: *Blick ins Chaos. Drei Aufsätze*. Bern: Seldwyla.

Hirsh, Sharon L. 2004: *Symbolism and Modern Urban Society*. Cambridge: Cambridge University Press.

Hodson, Randy 2001: *Dignity at Work*. Cambridge: Cambridge University Press.

Howlett, Jana 1985: "Petersburg – Moscow – Petropolis." In Timms, Edwards & Kelley, David (eds.): *Unreal City. Urban Experience in Modern European Literature and Art*. Manchester: Manchester University Press, 158–177.

Hubbard, Phil; Kitchin, Rob; Bartley, Brendan & Fuller, Duncan (eds.) 2002: *Thinking Geographically. Space, Theory and Contemporary Human Geography*. London: Continuum.

Huizinga, Johan 1935: *In de schaduwen van morgen. Een diagnose van het geestelijk lijden van onzen tijd*. Haarlem: H. D. Tjeenk Willink & Zoon.

Häkkinen, Antti 1995: *Rahasta – vaan ei rakkaudesta. Prostituutio Helsingissä 1867–1939*. Helsinki: Otava.

Häkkinen, Perttu & Similä, Ville 2010: "Lähteellä." In *Kuukausiliite* 2010/11, 60–69.

Häkli, Pekka 1955: *Arvid Järnefelt ja hänen lähimaailmansa*. Porvoo: WSOY.

Isomaa, Saija 2009: *Heräämisten poetiikkaa. Lajeja ja intertekstejä Arvid Järnefeltin romaaneissa* Isänmaa, Maaemon lapsia *ja* Veneh'ojalaiset. Helsinki: SKS.

J. S. 1909: "Prostitutsioni, joka 'lakkautettiin'." In *Työläisnainen* 1909/3, 17–18.

Jackson, Peter 1989: *Maps of Meaning. An Introduction to Cultural Geography.* London: Unwin Hyman.
Jacobs, Jane 1961: *The Death and Life of Great American Cities.* New York: Random House.
Janson, Ture & Kivijärvi, Erkki 1926: *Hyvä Helsinkimme.* Helsinki: Holger Schildt.
Jaye, Michael C. & Watts, Ann Chalmers (eds.): *Literature and the American Urban Experience. Essays on the City and Literature.* Manchester: Manchester University Press.
Jennings, Michael W. 2006: "Introduction." In Benjamin, Walter: *The Writer of Modern Life. Essays on Charles Baudelaire.* Translated by Howard Eiland. Cambridge, MA: Harvard University Press, 1–25.
Johnson, Jeri 2000: "Literary Geography: Joyce, Woolf and the City." In *City* 4/2, 199–214.
Josefson, Eva-Karin 2003: "Receptionen av belgiska modernister i Frankrike och Norden. Om kulturklimatet i förra sekelskiftets vänsterkretsar." In *TijdSchrift voor Skandinavistiek* 24/1, 23–46.
http://dpc.uba.uva.nl/tvs/vol24/nr01/art02 14.5.2013
Jussila, Osmo 1979: *Nationalismi ja vallankumous venäläis-suomalaisissa suhteissa 1899–1914.* Forssa: Forssan kirjapaino.
Juutila, Ulla-Maija 1984: "Matkakirja 1920- ja 1930-luvun suomalaisen kirjallisuuden kentässä." In Juutila, Ulla-Maija; Saarenheimo, Kerttu & Lappalainen, Päivi (eds.) 1984: *Hurma ja paatos: näkökulmia 1920- ja 1930-luvun kirjallisuuteen.* Turku: Turku University, 59–77.
Juutila, Ulla-Maija 1989: "Vitalismia ja naisellista luomisvoimaa – Helvi Hämäläinen." In Nevala, Maria-Liisa (ed.): *Sain roolin johon en mahdu.* Helsinki: Otava, 422–431.
Juutila-Purokoski, Ulla-Maija 2006: "Ruuan ikävä. Ruumiillisuus, ruoka ja subjektius Iris Uurron *Ruumiin ikävä* -romaanissa." In Kainulainen, Siru & Parente-Capkova, Viola (eds.): *Täysi kattaus. Ruokaa ja juomaa kirjallisuudessa.* Turku: Turku University, 101–125.
Järnström, Edw. 1908: "Eino Leinon routavuosiromaanit." In *Päivä* 1908/19, 152–155.
Järvelä, Juha 2013: *Waltari ja sukupuolten maailmat.* Helsinki: Avain.
Järvenpää, Eeva 2006: "Vasikkahaasta tuli Helsingin edustavin puisto." *Helsingin Sanomat* 10.6.2006.
http://www2.hs.fi/extrat/kaupunki/korttelisarja/43_1.html 14.5.2013
Kalajoki, Anneli 1993: "Johdannoksi." In Kalajoki, Anneli (ed.): *Helsinki rakkaani.* Porvoo: WSOY, 9–10.
Kalha, Harri 2008: *Tapaus Havis Amanda. Siveellisyys ja sukupuoli vuoden 1908 suihkulähdekiistassa.* Helsinki: SKS.
Kallinen, Ari 2011 [?]: "Kumpula kaunokirjallisuudessa."
http://kaupunginosat.net/vanha_kumpula/kol12.htm 14.5.2013
Karjalainen, Pauli Tapani 1995: "Elämä tässä talossa. Lähikartoitusta kirjallisuuden kautta." In *Alue ja Ympäristö* 24/2, 15–24.
Karjalainen, Pauli Tapani & Paasi, Anssi 1994: "Contrasting the Nature of the Written City: Helsinki in Regionalistic Thought and as a Dwelling-place." In Preston, Peter & Simpson-Housley, Paul (ed.): *Writing the City. Eden, Babylon and the New Jerusalem.* London: Routledge, 59–80.
Karkama, Pertti 1994: *Kirjallisuus ja nykyaika. Suomalaisen sanataiteen teemoja ja tendenssejä.* Helsinki: SKS.
Karkama, Pertti 1998: "Kaupunki kirjallisuudessa. Ongelmia ja näkökohtia." In Kurikka, Kaisa (ed.): *Paikkoja ja tiloja suomalaisessa kirjallisuudessa.* Turku: Turku University, 13–38.
Karkama, Pertti 2010: *Vallan orjat ja ihmisarvo. Arvid Järnefeltin ajatusmaailma.* Helsinki: SKS.

Keating, Peter 1984: "The Metropolis in Literature." In Sutcliffe, Anthony (ed.): *Metropolis 1890–1940*. London: Mansell, 129–145.

Kern, Stephen 1983: *The Culture of Time and Space 1880–1918*. Cambridge, MA: Harvard University Press.

Kervanto-Nevanlinna, Anja 2002: *Kadonneen kaupungin jäljillä. Teollisuusyhteiskunnan muutoksia Helsingin historiallisessa ytimessä*. Helsinki: SKS.

Kervanto-Nevanlinna, Anja 2003a: "Kaupungit modernisoinnin moottoreina." In Kervanto-Nevanlinna, Anja & Kolbe, Laura (eds.): *Suomen kulttuurihistoria. Oma maa ja maailma*. Helsinki: Tammi, 342–367.

Kervanto-Nevanlinna, Anja 2003b: "Esplanadi – katkelma Keski-Eurooppaa." In Kervanto-Nevanlinna, Anja & Kolbe, Laura (eds.): *Suomen kulttuurihistoria. Oma maa ja maailma*. Helsinki: Tammi, 368–369.

Keunen, Bart 1995: "The Aestheticization of the City in Modernism." In Berg, Christian; Durieux, Frank & Lernout, Geert (eds.): *The Turn of the Century: Modernism and Modernity in Literature and the Arts*. Berlin: de Gruyter, 380–391.

Keunen, Bart 1999: "The Decline of the City as Modernist Symbol: City Images in Postmodern Urban Fiction and in Collective Memory." In GUST (eds.): *The Urban Condition: Space, Community and Self in the Contemporary Metropolis*. Rotterdam: 010, 359–376.

Keunen, Bart 2000: *De verbeelding van de grootstad. Stads- en wereldbeelden in het proza van de moderniteit*. Brussels: VUB Press.

Keunen, Bart 2001: "The Plurality of Chronotopes in the Modernist City Novel: The Case of Manhattan Transfer." In *English Studies* 82/5, 420–436.

Keunen, Bart 2007: "Living with Fragments: World Making in Modernist City Literature." In Eysteinsson, Astradur & Liska, Vivian (eds.): *Modernism. Vol. 1*. Amsterdam: John Benjamins, 271–290.

Keunen, Bart 2011: "Urban Imagery between Enchantment and Disenchantment. Diagnostics of Modernity in the Urban Novel." Key note lecture, conference *Imagining Spaces / Places*, Helsinki University, 25.8.2011.

Keunen, Bart; Eeckhout, Bart & Lievens, Jeroen 2006: "De Stadsroman. Van Volvet naar Lite." In *Spiegel der Letteren* 48/2, 247–261.

Kivimaa, Arvi 1934: "Joel Lehtonen." In *Suomalainen Suomi* 1934/6, 291–292.

Klinge, Matti & Kolbe, Laura 1999: *Helsinki, Itämeren tytär: lyhyt historia*. Helsinki: Otava.

Klotz, Volker 1969: *Die Erzählte Stadt*. München: Carl Hanser.

Knuuttila, Seppo 1993: "Hiljainen kevät – miksi kansanrunouden tutkimuksessa ei oltu tietääkseenkään kansalaissodasta puoleen vuosisataan." In Ylikangas, Heikki (ed.): *Vaikea totuus: vuosi 1918 ja kansallinen tiede*. Helsinki: SKS, 46–60.

Kock, Johan 1916: *Avoin kirje herra Arvid Järnefeltille*. Helsinki: Vapaa ajatus.

Koivisto, Hanne 1999: "'Mutta nyt on kysymys maailman muuttamisesta' – Raoul Palmgrenin tulkintoja ihmisen ja yhteiskunnan suhteesta 30-luvulla." In Karkama, Pertti & Koivisto, Hanne (eds.): *Ajan paineessa*. Helsinki: SKS, 311–341.

Kopponen, Tapio 1980: "Juhani Ahon ylioppilasromaanista." In Viikari, Auli (ed.): *Kirjallisuudentutkijain seuran vuosikirja 33*. Helsinki: SKS, 71–84.

Korsberg, Hanna 2008: "Open the windows on Europe! Arvi Kivimaa's work and literary production in the 1920's and early 30's." In Jansson, Mats; Kantola, Janna; Lothe, Jakob & Riikonen, H.K. (eds.): *Comparative Approaches to Nordic and European Modernisms*. Helsinki: Palmenia, 59–78.

Kortelainen, Anna 2005: *Päivä naisten paratiisissa*. Helsinki: WSOY.

Koskela, Lasse 1999a: "Kansa taisteli – valkoiset kertoivat." In Rojola, Lea (ed.): *Suomen kirjallisuushistoria 2. Järkiuskosta vaistojen kapinaan*. Helsinki: SKS, 222–239.

Koskela, Lasse 1999b: "Täyttä nykyaikaa." In Rojola, Lea (ed.): *Suomen kirjallisuushistoria 2. Järkiuskosta vaistojen kapinaan*. Helsinki: SKS, 259–280.

Koskela, Lasse 1999c: "Nykyajan lumous särkyy." In Rojola, Lea (ed.): *Suomen kirjallisuushistoria 2. Järkiuskosta vaistojen kapinaan.* Helsinki: SKS, 310–344.
Koskenniemi, V. A. 1914: *Runon kaupunkeja.* Porvoo: Werner Söderström.
Koskenniemi, V. A. 1928: "Valtari, Mika, Suuri illusioni." In *Valvoja-Aika* 1928/4, 496–501.
Kujala, Antti 2003: "Suomen työväenliike 1899–1944." In Kervanto-Nevanlinna, Anja & Kolbe, Laura (eds.): *Suomen kulttuurihistoria. Oma maa ja maailma.* Helsinki: Tammi, 60–268.
Kunnas, Maria-Liisa 1972: *Mielikuvien taistelu. Psykologinen aatetausta Eino Leinon tuotannossa.* Helsinki: SKS.
Kunnas, Maria-Liisa 1973: "Eino Leino ja vuosi 1918." In Karonen, Vesa; Sihvo, Hannes & Tiitinen, Ilpo (eds.): *Kirjallisuudentutkijain seuran vuosikirja 27.* Helsinki: SKS, 31–47.
Kupiainen, Unto 1941: "Kaupungin kuva V. A. Koskenniemen runoudessa." In *Suomalainen Suomi* 1941/8–9, 367–376.
Kurikka, Kaisa 1998: "'Elämä on tulikuuma kultavuode...'. Irmari Rantamalan *Harhaman* dekadentti tila." In Lyytikäinen, Pirjo (ed.): *Dekadenssi vuosisadanvaihteen taiteessa ja kirjallisuudessa.* Helsinki: SKS, 127–142.
Käkelä-Puumala, Tiina 2007: "Autolla manalaan: menippolainen kuolema ja postmoderni alamaailma Thomas Pynchonin Vinelandissa." In Kivistö, Sari (ed.): *Satiiri: johdatus lajin historiaan ja teoriaan.* Helsinki: Yliopistopaino, 172–191.
Laati, Iisakki 1955: "Helsinki valtiollisten tapahtumien näyttämönä." In Rosén, Ragnar; Hornborg, Eirik; Waris, Heikki & Jutikkala, Eino (eds.): *Helsingin kaupungin historia* IV: 1. Helsinki: Helsinki City, 105–180.
Laine, Silja 2011: *"Pilvenpiirtäjäkysymys." Urbaani mielikuvitus ja 1920-luvun Helsingin ääriviivat.* Turku: Turku University.
http://www.doria.fi/bitstream/handle/10024/67365/siljalaine_doria.pdf?sequence=3 14.5.2013
Laitinen, Kai 1963: "Matti Kurjensaaren 30-lukua." In Kurjensaari, Matti: *Tie Helsinkiin. Nuoruuden toinen näytös.* Helsinki: Tammi, 5–11.
Laitinen, Kai 1965: "Tulenkantajia ja aikalaisia." In Sarajas, Annamari (ed.): *Suomen kirjallisuus V. Joel Lehtosesta Antti Hyryyn.* Helsinki: SKS, 458–470.
Laitinen, Kai 1973: "Metsästä kaupunkiin: suomalaisen proosan suuri traditio." In *Parnasso* 1973/2, 148–156.
Laitinen, Kai 1982: "Kirjallisuus." In Tommila, Päiviö; Reitala, Aimo & Kallio, Veikko (eds.): *Suomen kulttuurihistoria III.* Porvoo: WSOY, 325–361.
Laitinen, Kai 1991: *Suomen kirjallisuuden historia.* Otava, Helsinki.
Laplace, Philippe & Tabuteau, Éric (eds.) 2003: *Cities on the Margin. On the Margin of Cities. Representations of Urban Space in Contemporary Irish and British Fiction.* Besançon: Presses Universitaires Franc-Comtoises.
Lappalainen, Päivi 1984: "Kritiikki puolustusasemissa – kirjallisuustaistelu v. 1936." In Juutila, Ulla-Maija; Saarenheimo Kerttu & Lappalainen Päivi (eds.): *Hurma ja paatos: näkökulmia 1920- ja 1930-luvun kirjallisuuteen.* Turku: Turku University.
Lappalainen, Päivi 1990: "'Koko Euroopalle sa kättä annat': tulenkantajien kosmopoliittisuus ja sen yhteys modernismiin." In Takala, Tuija & Hyvärinen, Juha (eds.): *Tutkielmia suomalaisesta modernismista.* Turku: Turku University, 79–100.
Lappalainen, Päivi 1998a: "Uhattu koti." In Kurikka, Kaisa (ed.): *Paikkoja ja tiloja suomalaisessa kirjallisuudessa.* Turku: Turku University, 101–138.
Lappalainen, Päivi 1998b: "Realismi ja naisen ruumis." In Lappalainen, Päivi (ed.): *Uudessa valossa. Kirjoituksia realismin kysymyksestä.* Turku: Turku University, 77–94.
Lappalainen, Päivi 1999a: "Perhe, koti, kansa, isänmaa – kiista yhteiskunnan tukipylväistä." In Rojola, Lea (ed.): *Suomen kirjallisuushistoria 2. Järkiuskosta vaistojen kapinaan.* Helsinki: SKS, 43–73.

Lappalainen, Päivi 1999b: "Taistelu kirjallisuudesta ja moraalista." In Rojola, Lea (ed.): *Suomen kirjallisuushistoria 2.* Järkiuskosta vaistojen kapinaan. Helsinki: SKS, 324–325.

Lappalainen 2008: "Seduced Girls and Prostitutes: The Character of the Fallen Woman in Finnish Naturalist Fiction." In *Excavatio* 2008/1–2, 153–168.

Larmola, Yrjö 2000: "Helsinkiläinen Eino Leino." In *Hiidenkivi* 2000/4, 20–23.

Larmola, Yrjö 2005: "Helsinki in Literature and Illustrations." In *Virikkeitä* 2005/3, 10–15.

Lassila, Pertti 1985: "Tulenkantajan elämästä." In *Kirjallisuudentutkijain seuran vuosikirja* 38. Helsinki: SKS, 170–172.

Lassila, Pertti 1996: "'Aivan uskomaton vapautuneisuuden tunne': nuorvoimalaisuus ja ensimmäisen tasavallan nuoruus." In Hiidenheimo, Silja (ed.): *Ikaroksen perilliset*. Porvoo: WSOY, 9–16.

Laurila, Aarne 1965: "Mika Waltari." In Sarajas, Annamari (ed.): *Suomen kirjallisuus V. Joel Lehtosesta Antti Hyryyn*. Helsinki: SKS, 446–457.

Laurila, Aarne 1982a: "Elämyksiä ja historiaa: Mika Waltari Helsingin kuvaajana." In Haavikko, Ritva (ed.): *Mika Waltari: mielikuvituksen jättiläinen*. Porvoo: WSOY, 76–89.

Laurila, Aarne 1982b: "Kaupunki ja sen kirjailija." In *Eteläsuomalainen* 1982/5, 42–46.

Laurila, Aarne 2001: "450 vuotta – entä sitten? Korkea pino kirjoja Helsingistä." In *Hiidenkivi* 8/1, 36–39.

Laurila, Aili 1967: "Joel Lehtosen jäljillä Haagassa ja Lintokodossa." In *Kirjastolehti* 60, 105–107.

Lavery, Jason Edward 2006: *The History of Finland*. Westport: Greenwood Press.

Le Bon, Gustave 1896/1983: *Psychologie des foules*. Paris: Presses Universitaires de France.

Lefebvre, Henri 1974/1991: *The Production of Space*. Translated by Donald Nicholson-Smith. Oxford: Blackwell.

Lefebvre, Henri 2003: *Key Writings*. London: Continuum.

Lehan, Richard 1998: *The City in Literature. An Intellectual and Cultural History*. Berkeley, CA: University of California Press.

Leino, Eino 1910: *Suomalaisen kirjallisuuden historia*. Helsinki: Yrjö Weilin & Kumpp.

Leino, Eino 1918/1929: "Helsingin valloitus." In Leino, Eino: *Kootut teokset XV*. Helsinki: Otava, 1–90.

Leino, Eino 1960: *Kirjeet L. Onervalle*. Helsinki: Otava.

Leino, Eino 2012: *Kirjailijoiden Helsinki*. Helsinki: Gummerus.

Leino-Kaukiainen, Pirkko 1984: *Sensuuri ja sanomalehdistö Suomessa vuosina 1891–1905*. Helsinki: Suomen historiallinen seura.

Lendering, Jona & Bosman, Arjen 2010: *De Rand van het Rijk. De Romeinen en de Lage Landen*. Amsterdam: Athenaeum-Polak & Van Gennep.

Leslie, Esther 2006: "Ruin and Rubble in the Arcades." In Hanssen, Beatrice (ed.): *Walter Benjamin and the Arcades Project*. London: Continuum, 87–112.

Lilius, Henrik 1984: *Esplanadi 1800-luvulla – Esplanaden på 1800-talet – The Esplanade during the 19th century*. Nyborg: Rungsted Kyst.

Lindberg, Carolus 1931: *Helsinki, Pohjolan valkea kaupunki*. Porvoo: Werner Söderström.

Lindner, Rolf 2006: "The *Gestalt* of the Urban Imaginary." In Weiss-Sussex, Godela & Bianchini, Franco (eds): *Urban Mindscapes of Europe*. Amsterdam: Rodopi, 35–42.

Liuttu, Pentti 1963: "Helsinki suomenkielisessä taidekirjallisuudessa." In *Entisaikain Helsinki* VII. Helsinki: Helsinki-seura, 74–188.

Loivamaa, Ismo 1993: *Helsinki kaunokirjallisuudessa*. Helsinki: Kirjastopalvelu.

lrv 1908: "Eino Leino: Olli Suurpää." In *Kansankoulun lehti* 1908/11–12, 282–283.

Lynch, Kevin 1960: *The Image of the City*. Cambridge, MA: MIT Press.

Lyytikäinen, Pirjo 1997: "Ylioppilas rappion tiellä." In Aho, Juhani: *Helsinkiin*. Helsinki: SKS, vii–xvi.
Lyytikäinen, Pirjo 1998: "Dekadenssi – rappion runous." In Lyytikäinen, Pirjo (ed.): *Dekadenssi vuosisadanvaihteen taiteessa ja kirjallisuudessa*. Helsinki: SKS, 1–15.
Lyytikäinen, Pirjo 1999: "Tuhoutukoon maailma. Lopun aikojen kirjallisuutta." In Lehtonen, Tuomas (ed.): *Lopun leikit: uskon, historian ja tieteen eskatologiat*. Helsinki: Gaudeamus, 206–221.
Madsen, Peter 2001: "Imagined Urbanity. Novelistic Representations of Copenhagen." In Madsen, Peter & Plunz, Richard (eds.): *The Urban Lifeworld. Formation, Perception, Representation*. London: Routledge, 293–313.
Maironiemi, Eino 1992: "Modernismin esteet. Kirjallisuuspolitiikka suomalaisen romaanin kehityksen jarruna." In Turunen, Risto; Saariluoma, Liisa & Assmann, Dietrich (eds.): *Vaihtuva muoto. Tutkielmia suomalaisen romaanin historiasta*. Helsinki: SKS, 133–154.
Mallory, William E. & Simpson-Housley, Paul (eds.) 1987: *Geography and Literature: A Meeting of the Disciplines*. Syracuse: Syracuse University Press.
Malmio, Kristina 1999: "Älykästä sukkeluutta ja reipasta realism – 1920-luvun ajanvietekirjallisuus." In Rojola, Lea (ed.): *Suomen kirjallisuushistoria 2. Järkiuskosta vaistojen kapinaan*. Helsinki: SKS, 289–294.
Malmio, Kristina 2005: *Ett skrattretande (för)fall. Teatraliskt metaspråk, förströelselitteratur och den bildade klassen i Finland på 1910- och 1920-talen*. Helsinki: Helsinki University.
http://www.doria.fi/bitstream/handle/10024/934/ettskrat.pdf?sequence=6 15.10.2013
Marx, Karl 1867/2005: "The Fetishism of Commodities and the Secret thereof." In Marx, Karl: *Capital* vol. I.
http://www.marxists.org/archive/marx/works/1867-c1/ch01.htm#S4 14.5.2013
Massey, Doreen 1994/2008: "A Global Sense of Place." In Oakes, Timothy S. & Prise, Patricia L. (eds.): *The Cultural Geography Reader*. London: Routledge, 257–263.
Mauriala, Vesa 2005: *Uutta aikaa etsimässä. Individualismi, moderni ja kulttuurikritiikki tulenkantajien elämässä 1920- ja 1930-luvulla*. Helsinki: Gaudeamus.
Mayakovsky [Majakovski], Vladimir 1925/2010: "Minun löytämäni Amerikka." Translated by Mika Rassi. Turku: Savukeidas.
Melkas, Kukku 2009: "Palvelustyttö sivistyneistön peilinä." In Melkas, Kukku et al. (eds.) 2009: *Läpikulkuihmisiä. Muotoiluja kansallisuudesta ja sivistyksestä 1900-luvun alun Suomessa*. Helsinki: SKS, 107–134.
Melkas, Kukku et al. (eds.) 2009: *Läpikulkuihmisiä. Muotoiluja kansallisuudesta ja sivistyksestä 1900-luvun alun Suomessa*. Helsinki: SKS.
Meuwissen, Joost 2006: "De Middelpuntvliedende stad." In Dings, Mieke (eds.): *De Stad*. Rotterdam: Uitgeverij 010, 143–152.
Mikko 1893: "Kirje Helsingistä." In *Lauantai* 1893/17, 135–136.
Molarius, Päivi 1991: "Hengen maailmoista politiikan kentälle ja paitsioon. Suomalainen ylioppilaskuvaus bourdieulaisessa viitekehyksessä." In Nevala, Maria-Liisa et al. (eds.): *Avauksia: nuoret tutkijat kirjoittavat*. Helsinki: Helsingin yliopisto, 69–100.
Molarius, Päivi 1996a: "Johdanto." In Järnefelt, Arvid 1906/1996: *Veneh'ojalaiset*. Helsinki: SKS, vii–xxiii.
Molarius, Päivi 1996b: "Nuoren Apollon syöksykierre: sivistyneistö ja kansallisen ideologian murroksia." In *Kirjallisuudentutkijain seuran vuosikirja* 49/1. Helsinki: SKS, 9–29.
Molarius, Päivi 1998a: "'Veren äänen' velvoitteet: yksilö rodun, perimän ja ympäristön puristuksessa." In Härmänmaa, Marja & Mattila, Markku (eds.): *Uusi uljas ihminen: eli modernin pimeä puoli*. Jyväskylä: Atena, 94–116.
Molarius, Päivi 1998b: "Suomenruotsalaisen dagdrivare-kirjallisuuden dandy ja

modernin subjektin itsehahmotus." In Lyytikäinen, Pirjo (ed.): *Dekadenssi vuosisadanvaihteen taiteessa ja kirjallisuudessa.* Helsinki: SKS, 156-182.

Molarius, Päivi 1998c: "Minä maailmassa, maailma minussa." In Eino, Leino: *Routavuositriologia.* Helsinki: SKS, vii-xxiii.

Molarius, Päivi 2003: "'Will the Human Race Degenerate?' The Individual, the Family and the Fearsome Spectre of Degeneracy in Finnish Literature of the Late 19th and Early 20th Century." In Lyytikäinen, Pirjo (ed.): *Changing Scenes. Encounters between European and Finnish Fin de Siècle.* Helsinki: SKS, 121-142.

Moorjani, Angela B. 1980: "Madame Bovary's Eroticized Vehicle." In *Neophilologus* 64/1, 48-53.

Moretti, Franco 1983/2005: "Homo Palpitans. Balzac's Novels and Urban Personality." In Moretti, Franco: *Signs Taken for Wonders. On the Sociology of Literary Forms.* London: Verso, 109-129.

Moretti, Franco 1998: *Atlas of the European Novel 1800-1900.* London: Verso.

Moretti, Franco 2005: *Graphs, Maps, Trees: Abstract Models for a Literary History.* London: Verso.

Mulvey, Laura 1989: *Visual and Other Pleasures.* Basingstoke: MacMillan.

Mumford, Lewis 1961: *The City in History. Its Origins, Its Transformations, and Its Prospects.* New York: Harcourt, Brace & World.

Määttä, Jari 2007: "Helsingin rikollisuus kieltolain alusta sotien jälkeiseen aikaan." In Harju, Jari & Savia, Satu (eds.): *Rikospaikka: Helsinki.* Hämeenlinna: Helsingin kaupunginmuseo, 35-67.

Nead, Lynda 2000: *Victorian Babylon. People, Streets and Images in Nineteenth-Century London.* London: Yale University Press.

Niemi, Juhani 2005: *Arvid Järnefelt. Kirjailija ajassa ja ikuisuudessa.* Helsinki: SKS.

Nieminen, K. 1927: "Merenmaa, Martti, Nousuvesi." In *Valvoja-aika* 1927/3, 387-388.

Nieminen, Reetta 1974: "Kaupunkimiljöö Arvi Kivimaan varhaistuotannossa." In *Sananjalka* 16, 104-122.

Niklander, Hannu 2003: "Hajamietteitä uusmaalaisuudesta." In *Karkkilan Kotiseutuyhdistys ry:n jäsenlehti* 2003/9, 13-15.

http://www.karkkilankotiseutuyhdistys.fi/Lehdet/9-2003.pdf 14.5.2013

Nikula, Riitta 1981: *Yhtenäinen kaupunkikuva 1900-1930. Suomalaisen kaupunkirakentamisen ihanteista ja päämääristä, esimerkkeinä Helsingin Etu-Töölö ja uusi Vallila.* Helsinki: Societas scientiarum Fennica.

Nolda, Sigrid 1980: *Symbolistischer Urbanismus: zum Thema der Grosstadt im russischen Symbolismus.* Giessen: Schmitz.

Nummi, Jyrki 2002: *Aika Pariisissa. Juhani Ahon ranskalainen kausi 1889-1890.* Helsinki: SKS.

Nummi, Jyrki 2003a: "Yksin Pariisissa." In Aho, Juhani: *Yksin.* Helsinki: SKS, vii-xxii.

Nummi, Jyrki 2003b: "Between Time and Eternity. K. A. Tavaststjerna's *Barndomsvänner.*" In Lyytikäinen Pirjo (ed.): *Changing Scenes. Encounters between European and Finnish Fin de Siècle.* Helsinki: SKS, 85-120.

Nummi, Jyrki 2007: "Kaksi harakkaa: Juhani Aho ja K. A. Tavaststjerna." In Hosiaisluoma, Yrjö; Laakso, Maria; Suutela, Hanna & Tammi, Pekka (eds.): *Kirjallisia elämyksiä. Alkukivistä toiseen elämään.* Helsinki: SKS, 101-122.

Nummi, Jyrki; Rossi, Riikka & Isomaa, Saija 2011 (eds.): *Pariisista Iisalmeen. Kansainvälinen ja kansallinen Juhani Aho.* Helsinki: SKS.

Nünning, Ansgar 2009: "Formen und Funktionen literarischer Raumdarstellung: Grundlagen, Ansätze, narratologische Kategorien und neue Perspektiven." In Hallet, Wolfgang & Neumann, Birgit (eds.): *Raum und Bewegung in der Literatur. Die Literaturwissenschaften und der Spatial Turn.* Bielefeld: Transcript, 33-52.

Nünning, Vera 2010: "The Making of Fictional Worlds: Processes, Features and Functions." In Nünning, Vera; Nünning, Ansgar & Neumann, Birgit (eds.): *Cultural*

Ways of Worldmaking. Media and Narratives. Berlin: De Gruyter, 215–244.

Oates, Joyce Carol 1981: "Imaginary Cities: America." In Jaye, Michael C. & Watts, Ann Chalmers (eds.): *Literature and the American Urban Experience: Essays on the City and Literature.* Manchester: Manchester University Press, 11–34.

Oja, Outi 2007: "Hilja Kahilan *Onnelliset* ja tekijyys." In Hosiaisluoma, Yrjö; Laakso, Maria; Suutela, Hanna & Tammi, Pekka (eds.): *Kirjallisia elämyksiä. Alkukivistä toiseen elämään.* Helsinki: SKS, 123–138.

Ojajärvi, Jussi 2008: "Keväinen myrsky kirjallisuudessa." In Haapala, Pertti; Löytty, Olli; Melkas, Kukku & Tikka, Marko (eds.): *Kansa kaikkivaltias. Suurlakko Suomessa 1905.* Helsinki: Teos, 199–222.

Ojajärvi, Jussi 2009: "Eräs tulkinta sivistyneistön pettymyksestä." In Melkas, Kukku et al. (eds.) 2009: *Läpikulkuihmisiä. Muotoiluja kansallisuudesta ja sivistyksestä 1900-luvun alun Suomessa.* Helsinki: SKS, 197–235.

Olsson, Hagar 1925: *Ny generation.* Helsinki: Holger Schildts.

Onerva, L. 1909: "Arvid Järnefelt: Venehöjalaiset." In *Päivä* 1909/47, 396–398.

Osborne, Robin 2011: *The History Written on the Classical Greek Body.* Cambridge: Cambridge University Press.

Paavolainen, Olavi 1929/2002: *Nykyaikaa etsimässä. Esseitä ja pakinoita.* Helsinki: Otava.

Paavolainen, Olavi 1932: *Suursiivous eli kirjallisessa lastenkamarissa.* Jyväskylä: Gummerus.

Palmgren, Raoul 1950: "Hevosen selästä pudonnut rakuuna: Eino Leino proosakertojana." In *Ajan kirja* 1950/4, 9–23.

Palmgren, Raoul 1989: *Kaupunki ja tekniikka Suomen kirjallisuudessa. Kuvauslinjoja ennen ja jälkeen tulenkantajien.* Helsinki: SKS.

Parsons, Deborah L. 2000: *Streetwalking the Metropolis. Women, the City and Modernity.* Oxford: Oxford University Press.

Patell, Cyrus R. K. & Waterman, Bryan (eds.) 2010: *The Cambridge Companion to the Literature of New York.* Cambridge: Cambridge University Press.

Paunonen, Heikki 2000: *Tsennaaks Stadii, bonjaaks slangii. Stadin slangin suursanakirja.* Helsinki: WSOY.

Paunonen, Heikki 2010: *Stadin mestat. Ikkunoita Helsingin ja sen asukkaiden historiaan ja nykyisyyteen.* Helsinki: Edico.

Pausanias 1918: *Description of Greece.* Translated by W. H. S. Jones. Cambridge, MA: Harvard University Press.
http://www.theoi.com/Text/Pausanias10A.html#4. 14.5.2013

Peltonen, Matti 1992: "Sivistyneet, 1920-luku ja kieltolaki." In Onnela, Tapio (ed.): *Vampyyrinainen ja kenkkuinniemen sauna. Suomalainen kaksikymmenluku ja modernin mahdollisuus.* Helsinki: SKS, 61–78.

Perttula, Irma 2006: "Rakastunut rampa – illuusioiden särkymisen ja kiellon kirja." In Lehtonen, Joel: *Rakastunut rampa, eli, Sakris Kukkelman, köyhä polseviikki.* Helsinki: SKS, vii–xxi.

Perttula, Irma 2010: *Groteski suomalaisessa kirjallisuudessa. Neljä tapauskertomusta.* Helsinki: SKS.

Pesonen, Pekka 1987: *Vallankumouksen henki hengen vallankumouksessa. Tutkielma Andrei Belyin romaanista* Peterburg *ja sen aatetaustasta.* Helsinki: Helsinki University.

Pesonen, Pekka 2003: "Vajoaako ikuinen kaupunki suomalaiseen suohon? Myytti Pietarin kaupungista klassisessa venäläisessä kirjallisuudessa." In *Historiallinen aikakauskirja* 2003/3, 387–399.

Pettersson, Torsten 1986 "Det svårgripbara livet. Ett förbisett tema i dagdrivarlitteraturen." In Linnér, Sven (ed.): *Från Dagdrivare till Feminister. Studier i finlandssvensk 1900-talslitteratur.* Helsinki: Svenska litteratursällskapet i Finland, 9–40.

Phelan, James 2007: "Rhetorical Aesthetics and Other Issues in the Study of Literary Narrative." In Bamberg, Michael (ed.): *Narrative, State of the Art*. Amsterdam: John Benjamins, 103–112.
Philips, Lawrence (ed.) 2007: *A Mighty Mass of Brick and Smoke. Victorian and Edwardian Representations of London*. Amsterdam: Rodopi.
Pike, Burton 1981: *The Image of the City in Modern Literature*. Princeton: Princeton University Press.
Pleij, Herman 2009: "De Verbeelding van de Stad in de Literatuur. Van de Middeleeuwen tot Eind Negentiende Eeuw. Stadsbeeld in de Middeleeuwen." In Lucassen, Leo & Willems, Wim (eds.): *Waarom Mensen in de Stad Willen Wonen. 1200–2010*. Amsterdam: Bert Bakker, 124–133.
Pocock, Douglas C. D. 1981: *Humanistic Geography and Literature: Essays on the Experience of Place*. London: Croom Helm.
Pollock, Griselda 1988: "Modernity and the Spaces of Femininity." In Pollock, Griselda: *Vision and Difference: Femininity, Feminism and the Histories of Art*. London, Routledge, 70–127.
Porteous, J. Douglas 1990: *Landscapes of the Mind: Worlds of Sense and Metaphor*. Toronto: University of Toronto Press.
Prakash, Gyan 2010: "Introduction: Imaging the Modern City, Darkly." In Prakash, Gyan (ed.): *Noir Urbanisms. Dystopic Images of the Modern City*. Princeton: Princeton University Press, 1–16.
Prendergast, Christopher 1992: *Paris and the Nineteenth Century*. Cambridge, MA: Blackwell.
Pulkkinen, Matti P. 2004: "Oulunkylä pessimistin silmin: Joel Lehtosen Krokelby." http://kaupunginosat.net/oulunkyla/arkistot/2004/pessimisti.htm. 14.5.2013
Pääjärvi, Maaria 2006: "Flanööri Pohjolasta – V. A. Koskenniemen *Kevätilta Quartier Latinissä* ja kadun ulottuvuudet." In *Avain* 2006/3, 40–52.
Pöyhönen, Jaakko 1992: "Voimaa koneisiin, valoa kaduille ja asuntoihin." In Ahonen, Kirsi; Niemi, Marjaana & Pöyhonen, Jaakko (eds.): *Tietoa, taitoa, asiantuntemusta. Helsinki eurooppalaisessa kehityksessä 1875–1917 III. Henkistä kasvua, teknistä taitoa*. Helsinki: Suomen historiallinen seura, 183–351.
Railo, Eino [E. R.] 1907: "Kirjallisuutta [review of Jaana Rönty]." In *Nuori Suomi* 1907/21, 170–171.
Railo, Eino 1930: *Kyösti Wilkuna. Ihmisenä, kirjailijana, itsenäisyysmiehenä I*. Helsinki: Kirja.
Rajala, Panu 2008: *Unio Mystica. Mika Waltarin elämä ja teokset*. Helsinki: WSOY.
Rancken, A. W. 1932: *Helsingfors. Från småstad till storstad*. Helsinki: Söderström & C:o.
Relph, Edward 1976: *Place and placelessness*. London: Pion Limited.
Resina, Joan Ramon 2003: "From Rose of Fire to City of Ivory." In Resina, Joan Roman & Ingeschay, Dieter (eds): *After-Images of the City*. Ithaca: Cornell University Press, 75–122.
Riikonen, H. K. 1985: "Menippolainen satiiri – kirjallisuuden lajien Proteus." In *Kirjallisuudentutkijain seuran vuosikirja* 38. Helsinki: SKS, 33–51.
Riikonen, H. K. 1994: "Rikospaikkana Helsinki. Pääkaupungin kuvia suomalaisessa rikosromaanissa." In Matero, Johanna & Riikonen, H. K. (eds.): *Murhaava miljöö. Tutkielmia dekkarikirjallisuuden ympäristökuvauksista*. Turku: Turku University, 131–156.
Riikonen, H. K. 2007: "Modernism in Finnish Literature." In Eysteinsson, Astradur & Liska, Vivian (eds.): *Modernism, volume 2*. Amsterdam: John Benjamins, 847–854.
Roininen, Aimo 1999: "Työväenkirjallisuudesta vasemmistokirjallisuuteen." In Rojola, Lea (ed.): *Suomen kirjallisuushistoria 2. Järkiuskosta vaistojen kapinaan*. Helsinki: SKS, 240–242.
Rojola, Lea 1993: "Moderni elämä ja maskuliinisuuden kriisi." In Toikka, Minna (ed.):

Nykyajan kynnyksellä. Turku: Turku University, 157–181.
Rojola, Lea 1999: "Veren ääni." In Rojola, Lea (ed.): *Suomen kirjallisuushistoria 2. Järkiuskosta vaistojen kapinaan.* Helsinki: SKS, 165–183.
Rojola, Lea 2008: "Kun kansa tahtoi." In Haapala, Pertti; Löytty, Olli; Melkas, Kukku & Tikka, Marko (eds): *Kansa kaikkivaltias. Suurlakko Suomessa 1905.* Helsinki: Teos, 223–236.
Rojola, Lea 2009: "Sivistyksen ihanuus ja kurjuus – suomalaisen nousukkaan tarina." In Melkas, Kukku et al. (eds.): *Läpikulkuihmisiä.* Helsinki: SKS, 10–38.
Rossi, Riikka 2003: "Ihmisiä ja rappioita. Naturalismin henkilökuvaus." In Lyytikäinen, Pirjo & Tonteri, Päivi (eds.): *Romaanihenkilön muodonmuutoksia. Kuusi kirjoitusta henkilökuvauksesta.* Helsinki: SKS, 48–73.
Rossi, Riikka 2007: *Le naturalisme finlandais. Une conception entropique du quotidien.* Helsinki: SKS.
Rotella, Carlo 1998: *October Cities. The Redevelopment of Urban Literature.* Berkeley, CA: University of California Press.
Ruutu, Martti 1980: "Kulttuurikehityksen yleislinjat." In Tommila, Päiviö; Reitala, Aimo & Kallio, Veikko (eds.): *Suomen kulttuurihistoria. Autonomian aika.* Helsinki: WSOY, 65–134.
rv 1907: "Eino Leino: Jaana Rönty." In *Kansankoulun lehti* 1907/17–18, 464.
Räsänen, Hilma [Tuulonen, Anja] 1903: "Maalaisnaisen mietteitä pääkaupungissa." In *Pyrkijä* 1903/1, 14–16.
Rönkkö, Marja-Liisa 1992: "Töölönlahden kultalampi." In Karisto, Antti & Holstila, Eero (eds.): *Helsinki avoin kaupunki.* Helsinki: Helsingin kaupungin tietokeskus, 159–178.
Saarenheimo, Kerttu 1966: *Tulenkantajat: ryhmän vaiheita ja kirjallisia teemoja 1920-luvulla.* Porvoo: WSOY.
Saarenheimo, Kerttu 1969: "Pyramidiuni." In Saarenheimo, Kerttu (ed.): *Pyramidiuni: piirteitä tulenkantajien runoudesta.* Helsinki: SKS, 5–19.
Saarenheimo, Mikko [M.S.] 1915: "Talvio, Maila, Niniven lapset." In *Aika* 1915/5, 217–220.
Saarenheimo, Mikko 1916: "Helsinki kaunokirjallisuuden kuvastimessa." In *Aika* 1916/2, 199–208.
Saarenheimo, Mikko 1924: *1880-luvun suomalainen realismi.* Porvoo: WSOY.
Saarikangas, Kirsi 2002: *Asunnon muodonmuutoksia. Puhtauden estetiikka ja sukupuoli modernissa arkkitehtuurissa.* Helsinki: SKS.
Sadler, Simon 1998: *The Situationist City.* Cambridge, MA: MIT Pres.
Sallamaa, Kari 1995: "Naiskantaisuus ja poliittinen ruumis." In Paananen, Raija & Työlahti, Nina (eds.): *Hullu herttuatar ja muita naisia: sukupuolen konstruointia naiskirjallisuudessa.* Oulu: Oulu University, 57–68.
Salmela Markku 2012: "The Grotesque Landscape and the Naturalistic Method." In Salmela, Markku & Toikkanen Jarkko (eds.): *The Grotesque and the Unnatural.* Amherst: Cambria Press, 187–210.
Salomaa, Erkki 1965: *Viaporin kapina. 60 tuntia vallankumousta.* Helsinki: Kansankulttuuri.
Sarajas, Annamari 1962: "Routavuodet ja kansankuvan murros." In Sarajas, Annamari: *Viimeiset romantikot: kirjallisuuden aatteiden vaihtelua 1880-luvun jälkeen.* Porvoo: WSOY, 93–181.
Sarajas, Annamari 1965: "Joel Lehtonen." In Sarajas, Annamari (ed.): *Suomen kirjallisuus V. Joel Lehtosesta Antti Hyryyn.* Helsinki: SKS, 42–66.
Sarajas, Annamari 1968: *Tunnuskuvia. Suomen ja Venäjän kirjallisen realismin kosketuskohtia.* Porvoo: WSOY.
Schildt, Runar [R. Sdt.] 1912: "Helsingfors i skönlitteraturen." In *Dagens Tidning* 7.4.1912, 11–12.
Schivelbusch, Wolfgang 1979/1986: *The Railway Journey. The Industrialization of Time*

and Space in the 19th Century. Berkeley, CA: University of California Press.
Schlegel, Jean L. 1910: "Emile Verhaeren." Translated by Maija K-nniemi. In *Aika* 1910/11–12, 456–465.
Schoolfield, George C. 1998: *A History of Finland's Literature*. Lincoln: University of Nebraska Press.
Scott, Clive 1976/1986: "Symbolism, Decadence and Impressionism." In Bradbury, Malcolm & McFarlane, James (eds.): *Modernism*. Harmondsworth: Penguin, 206–227.
Searle, John R. 1969: *Speech Acts. An Essay in the Philosophy of Language*. Cambridge: Cambridge University Press.
Selén, Kari 2010: *Madame. Minna Craucherin levoton elämä*. Helsinki: Helsinki kirjat.
Sennett, Richard 1994: *Flesh and Stone. The Body and the City in Western Civilization*. New York: W.W. Norton & Company.
Sharpe, William Chapman 1990: *Unreal Cities. Urban Figuration in Wordsworth, Baudelaire, Whitman, Eliot and Williams*. Baltimore: Johns Hopkins University Press.
Sielaff, Steffen 2004: *Die postmoderne Odyssee. Raum und Subjekt in den Romanen von Paul Auster*. Berlin: Freie Universität Berlin.
http://www.diss.fu-berlin.de/diss/receive/FUDISS_thesis_000000001413 14.5.2013
Siipi, Jouko 1962: "Pääkaupunkiyhteiskunta ja sen sosiaalipolitiikka." In Rosén, Ragner et al. (eds.): *Helsingin kaupungin historia V*: 1. Helsinki: Helsinki City, 137–380.
Simmel, Georg 1903/1969: "The Metropolis and Mental Life." In Sennett, Richard (ed.): *Classic Essays on the Culture of Cities*. Englewood Cliffs: Prentice Hall, 47–60.
Simpson, Tyrone 2011: "The City in Fiction." In O'Donnell, Patrick; Madden, David W. & Nieland, Justus (eds.): *The Encyclopedia of Twentieth-Century Fiction Vol. II*. Oxford: Wiley-Blackwell, 500–505.
Sintobin, Tom & Rymenants, Koen 2007: *Aan dezelfde zee. Oostende in de Nederlandse literatuur*. Leuven: Davidsfonds.
Smeds, Kerstin 1996: *Helsingfors-Paris. Finland på världsutställningarna 1851–1900*. Helsinki: Svenska litteratursällskapet i Finland.
Soja, Edward W. 1989: *Postmodern Geographies. The Reassertion of Space in Critical Social Theory*. London: Verso.
Spengler, Oswald 1918/1926: *The Decline of the West. Form and Actuality*. Translated by Charles Francis Atkinson. London: George Allen & Unwin Ltd.
http://www.archive.org/stream/declineofwest01spenuoft#page/n5/mode/2up 14.5.2013
Stead, W. T. 1885: "The Maiden Tribute of Modern Babylon I: the Report of our Secret Commission." In *The Pall Mall Gazette* 6.6.1885.
http://www.attackingthedevil.co.uk/pmg/tribute/#sthash.iWqXn4Sb.dpbs 14.5.2013
Steele, Jeffrey 2012: "Invisible City: Antebellum Writers and Urban Space." In Castronovo, Russ 2012 (ed.): *The Oxford Handbook of Nineteenth-Century American Literature*. Oxford: Oxford University Press, 179–197.
Steiner, Rodney 1981: *Los Angeles, the Centrifugal City*. Dubuque, IA: Kendall/Hunt.
Steinman, Lisa M. 2012: "Flexible Genealogies and Romantic Poetics." In Sandy, Mark (ed.): *Romantic Presences in the Twentieth Century*. Farnham: Ashgate, 43–56.
Stierle, Karlheinz 1993/2001: *La capitale des signes. Paris et son discours*. Translated by Marianne Rocher-Jacquin. Paris: Éditions de la Maison des sciences de l'homme.
Suolahti, Eino E. 1948/1981: "Historiallinen romaanimme." In Suolahti, Eino E.: *Esseitä*. Porvoo: WSOY, 125–144.
Suolahti, Eino E. 1949: *Helsingin neljä vuosisataa*. Helsinki: Otava.
Suolahti, Eino E. 1960/1981: "Maila Talvion helsinkiläisromaanien todellisuustausta." In Suolahti, Eino E.: *Esseitä*. Porvoo: WSOY, 245–157.
Swain, Virginia E. 2004: *Grotesque Figures: Baudelaire, Rousseau, and the Aesthetics of Modernity*. Baltimore: Johns Hopkins University Press.

Söderhjelm, Werner 1916/1920: *Kotimaisia kulttuurikuvia*. Translated by Helle Cannelin. Helsinki: Otava.
Talvio, Maila 1936: "Onko Helsingillä historiaa?" In *Entisaikain Helsinki* I. Helsinki: Helsingin historiayhdistys, 5–14.
Talvio, Maila 1936/1951: "Pieni puhe meidän Helsingille." In Talvio, Maila: *Kootut teokset* XII. Porvoo: WSOY, 479–487.
Tani, Sirpa 1995: *Kaupunki Taikapeilissä. Helsinki-elokuvien mielenmaisemat – maantieteellisiä tulkintoja*. Helsinki: Helsingin kaupungin tietokeskuksen tutkimuksia.
Tapioharju, Taru 2010: *Tyttö kaupungissa. Uuden naisen diskurssi Mika Waltarin 1920- ja 1930-luvun Helsinki-romaaneissa*. Tampere: Tampere University. http://tampub.uta.fi/handle/10024/66599 14.5.2013
Tarkiainen, Viljo [V. T.] 1907: "Eino Leino, *Jaana Rönty*." In *Valvoja* 1907/7–8, 493–496.
Tarkka, Pekka 1965: "'Henkien taistelun' ihmisiä ja eläimiä." In *Kirjallisuudentutkijain seuran vuosikirja* 21. Helsinki: SKS, 88–97.
Tarkka, Pekka 2012: *Joel Lehtonen II. Vuodet 1918–1934*. Helsinki: Otava.
Thacker, Andrew 2003/2009: *Moving through Modernity. Space and Geography in Modernism*. Manchester: Manchester University Press.
Thum, Reinhard H. 1994: *The City. Baudelaire, Rimbaud, Verhaeren*. New York: Peter Lang.
Tilastollinen päätoimisto 1909: *Pääpiirteet Suomen väestötilastosta vuosina 1750–1890*. Helsinki: Tilastollinen päätoimisto.
Toftegaard Pedersen, Arne 2007: *Urbana odysseer. Helsingfors, staden och 1910-talets finlandssvenska prosa*. Helsinki: Svenska litteratursällskapet i Finland.
Tommila, Päiviö & Hirn, Sven 1980: "Kaupunkikulttuuri." In Tommila, Päiviö; Reitala, Aimo & Kallio, Veikko (eds.): *Suomen kulttuurihistoria. Autonomian aika*. Helsinki: WSOY, 475–502.
Tonsor, Stephen J. 1988: "City." In Seigneuret, Jean-Charles (ed.): *Dictionary of Literary Themes and Motifs Vol. 1*. Westport: Greenwood Press, 257–264.
Trilling, Lionel 1948: "Introduction." In James, Henry: *The Princess Casamassima*. New York: Macmillan, v–xlviii.
Tuan, Yi-Fu 1974: *Topophilia. A Study of Environmental Perception, Attitudes, and Values*. Englewood Cliffs: Prentice Hall.
Tuan, Yi-Fu 1977: *Space and Place. The Perspective of Experience*. Minneapolis: University of Minnesota Press.
Tuan, Yi-Fu 1978: "Literature and Geography: Implications for Geographical Research." In Ley, David & Samuels, Marwyn (eds.): *Humanistic Geography: Prospects and Problems*. Chicago: Maaroufa Press, 194–206.
Tunturi, Janne 1996: "'Fazer? Sanoi Eeva': Mary Marckin nuortenkirjojen Helsinki." In *Narinkka*. Helsinki: Helsingin kaupunginmuseo, 160–172.
Turunen, Markku 2006: "Ontuva paholainen: kirjallisuuden rujo sankari kiehtoo ja kammottaa." In *Parnasso* 56/7, 26–31.
Vaaskivi, Tatu 1938: *Huomispäivän varjo. Länsimaiden tragedia*. Jyväskylä: Gummerus.
Vaaskivi, Tatu 1941: "Helvi Hämäläisen taiteilijavoitto." In *Suomalainen Suomi* 1941/6–7, 318–327.
Vaittinen, Pirjo 1995: "Erään kirjailijan jälkikesä. Helvi Hämäläisen *Säädyllinen murhenäytelmä* ja suomalainen julkisuus." In Ahokas, Pirjo; Lappalainen, Otto & Saariluoma, Liisa (eds.): *Proosan taiteesta. Leevi Valkaman juhlakirja*. Turku: Turku University, 97–123.
Valkama, Leevi 1960/1983: *Proosan taide. Viisi tutkielmaa*. Helsinki: WSOY.
Vattulainen, Saara 1998: "Eino Leino politiikan puolustajana vuosina 1905–1908." In *Tiedepolitiikka* 1998/4, 41–44.
Veivo, Harri 1997: "Visioista sirpaleisiin – kaupunki kirjallisuudessa." In *Hiidenkivi* 1997/4, 28–30.

Viinikka-Kallinen, Anitta 1997: "Itsensä hukannut nousukas. Keskusarvojen menettäminen vuosisadanvaihteen proosassa." In *Virke* 97/5, 22–26.
Viljanen, Lauri 1959: *Lyyrillinen minä ja muita kirjallisuuskatkelmia.* Helsinki: WSOY.
Viljanen, T. V. 1955: "Helsinki sotien jaloissa." In Rosén, Ragnar; Hornborg, Eirik; Waris, Heikki & Jutikkala, Eino (eds.): *Helsingin kaupungin historia* IV: 1. Helsinki: Helsinki City, 181–210.
Väre, Vappu 1946: "Iris Uurto: nerokas syrjästäkatsoja." In Aaltonen, Toini; Aarnio, Paavo; Suolahti, Aili & Vuorela, Erkki (eds.): *Kerho 33.* Helsinki: Otava, 24–39.
Walkowitz, Judith R. 1992: *City of Dreadful Delight. Narratives of Sexual Danger in Late-Victorian London.* London: Virago.
Wall, Cynthia 2011: "London and Narration in the Long Eighteenth Century." In Manley, Lawrence (ed.): *The Cambridge Companion to the Literature of London.* Cambridge: Cambridge University Press, 102–118.
Waltari, Mika 1937: *Helsinki kautta vuosisatojen. Historiallisia lukukappaleita.* Helsinki: Otava.
Waltari, Mika 1980: *Kirjailijan muistelmia.* Porvoo: WSOY.
Waltari, Mika & Blomberg, A. 1941: *Kotikaupunkimme Helsinki.* Helsinki: Otava.
Warf, Barney 2008: *Time-Space Compression: Historical Geographies.* New York: Routledge.
Warhol, Robin 2005: "Gaze." In Herman, David; Jahn, Manfred & Ryan, Marie-Laure (eds): *Routledge Encyclopedia of Narrative Theory.* London: Routledge, 194.
Waris, Heikki 1932/1973: *Työläisyhteiskunnan syntyminen Helsingin Pitkänsillan pohjoispuolelle.* Helsinki: Weilin+Göös.
Whitman, Cedric 1958: *Homer and the Heroic Tradition.* Cambridge, MA: Harvard University Press.
Williams, Raymond 1973: *The Country and the City.* London: Chatto & Windus.
Williams, Raymond 1985: "The Metropolis and the Emergence of Modernism." In Timms, Edwards & Kelley, David (eds.): *Unreal City. Urban Experience in Modern European Literature and Art.* Manchester: Manchester University Press, 13–24.
Willman, Elvira 1906: "Prostitutsiooni sosiaalisena luokka-ilmiönä ja sen poistaminen sosiaalis-valtiollisilla keinoilla." In *Työmiehen illanvietto* 1906/27–28, 211–214.
Wilson, Elizabeth 1991: *The Sphinx in the City. Urban Life, the Control of Disorder, and Women.* London: Virago Press.
Wilson, Elizabeth 1992: "The Invisible Flâneur." In *New Left Review* I/191, 90–110.
Wilson, Elizabeth 1995: "The Rhetoric of Urban Space." In *New Left Review* I/209, 146–160.
Wirth-Nesher, Hana 1996: *City Codes. Reading the Modern Urban Novel.* Cambridge: Cambridge University Press.
Wohl, Richard R. & Strauss, Anselm L. 1958: "Symbolic Representation and the Urban Milieu." In *American Journal of Sociology* 63/5, 523–532.
Wolff, Janet 1985: "The Invisible *Flâneuse*. Women and the Literature of Modernity." In *Theory, Culture & Society* 1985/2(3), 37–46.
Woolf, Virginia 1905/1986: "Literary Geography." In McNeillie, Andrew (ed.): *The Essays of Virginia Woolf Volume I 1904–1912.* London: The Hogarth Press, 32–35.
Wuolle, Aino 1979/1981: *Finnish-English Dictionary.* Porvoo: WSOY.
Zoran, Gabriel 1984: "Towards a Theory of Space in Narrative." In *Poetics Today* 5/2, 309–335.
Zukin, Sharon 1991: *Landscapes of Power. From Detroit to Disney World.* Berkeley, CA: University of California Press.

Unpublished sources

Ameel, Lieven 2006: *Koettu ja kuviteltu Helsinki Eino Leinon romaaneissa* Olli Suurpää ja Jaana Rönty. Master's thesis. Helsinki University.

Hannula, Petri 1998: *Joel Lehtosen* Rakastunut rampa *ja ruumiillisuus eurooppalaisessa kirjallisuudessa*. Master's thesis. Jyväskylä University.
https://jyx.jyu.fi/dspace/handle/123456789/9038 14.5.2013

Liuttu, Pentti 1950: *Helsinki suomalaisessa kirjallisuudessa*. Laudatur thesis. Helsinki University.

Molarius, Päivi 1993: *Opin sauna autuas aina? Vallan ja vieraantumisen teemat autonomian ajan suomalaisessa ylioppilaskuvauksessa.* Licenciate thesis. Helsinki University.

Timonen, Ville 2011: *Irmari Rantamalan* Harhaman *dekadentti tematiikka, Tolstoi ja Nietzsche*. Master's thesis. Tampere University.
http://tutkielmat.uta.fi/pdf/gradu05424.pdf 14.5.2013

Lieven Ameel

Helsinki in Early Twentieth-Century Literature
Urban Experiences in Finnish Prose Fiction 1890–1940

Helsinki in Early Twentieth-Century Literature analyses experiences of the Finnish capital in prose fiction published in Finnish in the period 1890–1940. It examines the relationships that are formed between Helsinki and fictional characters, focusing, especially, on the way in which urban public space is experienced. Particular attention is given to the description of movement through urban space. The primary material consists of a selection of more than sixty novels, collections of short stories and individual short stories. This study draws on two sets of theoretical frameworks: on the one hand, the expanding field of literary studies of the city, and on the other hand, concepts provided by humanistic and critical geography, as well as by urban studies.

This study is the first monograph to examine Helsinki in literature written in Finnish. It shows that rich descriptions of urban life have formed an integral part of Finnish literature from the late nineteenth century onward. Around the turn of the twentieth century, literary Helsinki was approached from a variety of generic and thematic perspectives which were in close dialogue with international contemporary traditions and age-old images of the city, and defined by events typical of Helsinki's own history. Helsinki literature of the 1920s and 1930s further developed the defining traits that took form around the turn of the century, adding a number of new thematic and stylistic nuances. The city experience was increasingly aestheticized and internalized. As the centre of the city became less prominent in literature, the margins of the city and specific socially defined neighbourhoods gained in importance.

Many of the central characteristics of how Helsinki is experienced in the literature published during this period remain part of the ongoing discourse on literary Helsinki: Helsinki as a city of leisure and light, inviting dreamy wanderings; the experience of a city divided along the fault lines of gender, class and language; the city as a disorientating and paralyzing cesspit of vice; the city as an *imago mundi*, symbolic of the body politic; the city of everyday and often very mundane experiences, and the city that invites a profound sense of attachment – an environment onto which characters project their innermost sentiments.

Index

Ackroyd, Peter 185
af Ursin, Nils Robert 112
Ahlund, Claes 187
Aho, Juhani 5, 12, 16, 26, 31–42, 46–47, 49–50, 58, 60–61, 63, 76–77, 80, 89, 98, 102, 122, 124, 161, 164, 179, 186–194, 205, 207
Ahokas, Jaakko 178, 198, 211
Alkio, Santeri 52
Alter, Robert 20, 50, 88, 105–106, 126, 142, 207, 213
Anttila, Aarne 13, 86, 187, 200
Augé, Marc 214
Augustine, Saint 19, 22
Bakhtin, Mikhail 39, 83, 87, 151–153, 156, 186, 210, 212
Bal, Mieke 25, 135, 186
Balzac, Honoré de 14, 83, 88, 108, 200
Bang, Gustav 159
Bassini, Alessandro 13
Bataille, Georges 159
Baudelaire, Charles 15, 26–27, 33, 61, 65, 74–77, 79–80, 100, 105, 120–121, 128
Bely, Andrei 106
Benjamin, Walter 15, 27, 50, 65, 75, 80, 105–106, 186, 196
Bergbom, Kaarlo 113
Bergroth, Kersti 183, 206
Bergson, H. L. 130, 207
Berman, Marshall 37, 75, 94
Borg, Alexandra 26–27, 50, 64, 70, 77, 113, 156, 184, 185
Bridgeman, Teresa 25
Brooks, Peter 31, 65, 184
Calvino, Italo 14
Canth, Minna 194, 207
Cassirer, Ernst 186
Chanda, A. K. 25, 38–40, 42, 180, 189
Chesterton, G. K. 128

Conrad, Joseph 126
D'Annunzio, Gabriele 88
Dannenberg, Hilary P. 25, 41
Davidoff, Leonore 26
de Certeau, Michel 27–28, 57, 61, 63, 69, 82–83, 85–86, 161, 186, 197
de Goncourt, Edmond & Jules 156
Dickens, Charles 14, 20, 22, 31, 88, 99, 102, 126
Donald, James 20
Dostoevsky, Fyodor 10, 14, 20, 197
Dreiser, Theodore 167, 185, 212
Eliot, T. S. 126
Engels, Friedrich 88
Ette, Otmar 25
Flaubert, Gustave 106, 135, 187, 213
Flecker, James Elroy 127
Foucault, Michel 88–89, 186, 199
Freeman, Nicholas 84, 128, 184, 199, 207
Freud, Sigmund 158
Garborg, Arne 32
Gelfant, Blanche H. 112, 177
Goethe, Johann Wolfgang von 94, 161
Gogol, Nikolai 88, 197
Goodman, Nelson 15, 161
Gumbrecht, Hans Ulrich 25, 47, 73
Harvey, David 12, 20, 64, 92, 167, 171, 186, 190, 198
Hauptmann, Gerhart 88
Haussmann, Georges-Eugènes 64
Hesse, Hermann 158
Huizinga, Johan 158
Häkkinen, Antti 68, 188, 195
Hämäläinen, Helvi 6, 16, 111, 118, 129, 136–146, 148, 163–165, 167, 169, 171–172, 176–177, 181, 204, 209–210
Ibsen, Henrik 88
Isomaa, Saija 89, 97, 108, 111, 196–199, 201–202

Ivalo, Santeri 39–42, 45, 56, 64, 67, 76, 78–79, 89, 93, 161, 164, 188–190, 194, 205
Jackson, Peter 186
Jacobs, Jane 185
James, Henry 38, 199
Jooss, Kurt 212
Joyce, James 17, 20, 51, 54, 88, 126, 211
Järnefelt, Arvid 6, 16, 31, 39–40, 44–45, 47–49, 52, 57–58, 62, 68, 75–77, 79, 81–94, 97–99, 101–102, 104, 106–113, 120, 129, 162–163, 165, 175, 179–180, 187–191, 193, 195–199, 201, 212
Järvelä, Juha 215
Kafka, Franz 14
Karjalainen, Pauli Tapani 14, 51
Karkama, Pertti 14, 37, 52, 111, 126, 191, 195, 197, 201
Karri, Unto 74, 95–96, 117, 123–124, 132, 135, 145, 158, 179, 189, 206
Keating, Peter 184
Kern, Stephen 188
Kervanto-Nevanlinna, Anja 43, 53, 115, 192
Keunen, Bart 31, 83, 102, 118, 121, 142, 184–186, 189, 205, 207
Kivijärvi, Erkki 189, 206
Kivimaa, Arvi 50, 95–96, 117, 122, 124, 131–132, 134–137, 145, 154, 164, 170, 175, 179–180, 185, 189, 192–193, 205–208, 214
Kivimies, Yrjö 183
Kock, Johan 88, 198
Koskenniemi, V. A. 9–11, 13, 21, 77, 86, 96, 111, 122, 162, 183, 204–205
Kurjensaari, Matti 124, 172, 187, 189
Laine, Silja 13–14, 109, 134, 200, 204–205
Laitinen, Kai 10, 18, 77, 122, 169, 172, 203–204, 207
Lang, Fritz 212
Lappalainen, Päivi 34, 69, 72, 124, 131, 164, 187, 195, 204
Laurila, Aarne 13–14, 122, 204, 208
Le Bon, Gustave 107
Lefebvre, Henri 22–25, 35, 63–64, 66, 69, 90, 119, 143, 150, 153, 169, 176, 186, 211, 213–214
Lehan, Richard 17, 19, 22, 88, 92, 118, 120–121, 126, 143, 169, 184–186, 190–191, 207
Lehtonen, Joel 6, 16, 21, 77, 79, 95, 124, 147–161, 165, 168–171, 176–179, 181, 205–206, 210–211
Leino, Eino 5, 16, 21, 31, 45, 48, 52, 54–57, 59–62, 65–67, 69–73, 80, 82, 89–90, 93, 96–97, 101–104, 106–107, 111, 133, 145, 164–165, 179–180, 184, 189, 192–195, 198
Leino, Kasimir 58–60, 73, 195
Levertin, Oscar 156
Liuttu, Pentti 13, 30, 145, 200, 214
Loivamaa, Ismo 184
Lomas, Herbert 188
Lotman, Yuri 186
Lynch, Kevin 22, 27
Lyytikäinen, Pirjo 32, 70, 97, 100, 107, 191, 194
Mannerheim, C. G. E. 55
Marx, Karl 23–24, 88, 103, 198
Mayakovsky, Vladimir 159
Merenmaa, Martti 146
Molarius, Päivi 33, 45–46, 77, 80, 87, 187, 191–192
Moll, Albert 52
Moorjani, Angela B. 135
Moretti, Franco 25, 49–50
Mumford, Lewis 20, 22, 185–186
Nash, John 64
Niemi, Juhani 85, 197–198
Nieminen, Reetta 14, 122
Noponen, Alpo 193
Nummi, Jyrki 14, 26, 124, 187, 189, 205
Olsson, Hagar 127, 160
Onerva, L. 35, 56, 92, 96, 108, 152, 163, 191–193, 205
Paavolainen, Olavi 117, 137–138, 158, 178, 205–206, 208–209
Palmgren, Raoul 13, 53–54, 165, 171, 178, 192, 200, 209, 214
Perttula, Irma 147, 149, 153–154, 169, 206, 210–211
Pessoa, Fernando 14
Pike, Burton 14, 17–20, 81, 94, 184, 186
Poe, Edgar Allan 26, 74, 120
Pollock, Griselda 26, 194
Prendergast, Christopher 22, 27, 61, 83, 99, 104, 184, 186, 197
Procopé, Hjalmar 113
Proust, Marcel 14, 120
Pushkin, A. S. 101, 197
Rantamala, Irmari 185
Relph, Edward 176–177, 186, 214
Rimminen, Mikko 51
Rodenbach, Georges 101
Rojola, Lea 33, 72, 187, 194, 200
Runeberg, Johan Ludvig 57, 76, 104, 191
Saarenheimo, Mikko 13, 32, 52, 162, 189

Schildt, Runar 13, 21, 66, 70, 144, 162
Schivelbusch, Wolfgang 188
Schlegel, Jean 112
Shakespeare, William 90
Sharpe, William 14–15, 18
Sibelius, Jean 113, 197
Simmel, Georg 50, 213
Sinervo, Elvi 144, 148, 163, 165, 167, 171–172, 176–177
Soini, Elsa 124, 136, 214
Soja, Edward 186
Spengler, Oswald 96, 124, 157–159
Strauss, Anselm 20, 57, 180
Strindberg, August 10, 31, 183
Söderberg, Hjalmar 77, 156
Talvio, Maila 9, 13, 21, 31, 39–42, 44–46, 48, 51–52, 68–69, 76–77, 79, 82, 84, 92–94, 96–97, 100, 111, 136, 146, 179, 183, 186, 188–189, 191, 193, 195–196, 200, 205, 207
Tarkiainen, Viljo 67
Tarvas, Toivo 52, 74, 78–79, 82, 93–95, 97, 106, 109–112, 128, 131–132, 134–135, 144–145, 162, 172, 179–180, 188–189, 191, 199–200, 204–205, 210
Tavaststjerna, K. A. 32, 36, 187, 205
Tihlä, Hilda 13, 40, 42, 48, 56, 64, 186, 196
Toftegaard Pedersen, Arne 13, 36, 77, 184, 193, 206
Topelius, Zacharias 21, 30, 113, 183, 192

Trilling, Lionel 38
Tuan, Yi-Fu 24, 91, 186
Uurto, Iris 79–80, 122–125, 128–129, 144, 148, 163, 166–169, 172–173, 176–177, 179–181, 189, 195–196, 204, 206
Vaaskivi, Tatu 158, 209, 212
Vala, Katri 213
Vandervelde, Émile 112
Verhaeren, Émile 112
Viljanen, Lauri 140, 211
Waltari, Mika 6, 10, 13, 16, 50–51, 94, 96, 106, 110–112, 117–131, 133–134, 136–137, 142, 145–146, 158, 162, 164–166, 170–175, 179–180, 189, 191, 201, 204–208, 210, 212–215
Waris, Heikki 162
Westö, Kjell 13, 54, 185
Whitman, Cedric 18
Wilkuna, Kyösti 31, 39, 42–43, 45, 49, 56, 67–68, 71, 76, 79, 101, 104–106, 165, 175, 187–190, 196
Williams, Raymond 18, 153, 184–185, 213
Wilson, Elizabeth 22, 65, 83, 89, 103, 134, 184, 186, 196
Wirth-Nesher, Hana 36, 184–185
Wohl, Richard 20, 57, 180
Wolff, Janet 26, 65, 78, 145
Woolf, Virginia 14, 17, 142
Zola, Émile 14, 22, 31, 47, 83, 156, 213
Zukin, Sharon 154

Studia Fennica Ethnologica

Memories of My Town
The Identities of Town Dwellers and Their Places in Three Finnish Towns
Edited by Anna-Maria Åström, Pirjo Korkiakangas & Pia Olsson
Studia Fennica Ethnologica 8
2004

Passages Westward
Edited by Maria Lähteenmäki & Hanna Snellman
Studia Fennica Ethnologica 9
2006

Defining Self
Essays on emergent identities in Russia Seventeenth to Nineteenth Centuries
Edited by Michael Branch
Studia Fennica Ethnologica 10
2009

Touching Things
Ethnological Aspects of Modern Material Culture
Edited by Pirjo Korkiakangas, Tiina-Riitta Lappi & Heli Niskanen
Studia Fennica Ethnologica 11
2009

Gendered Rural Spaces
Edited by Pia Olsson & Helena Ruotsala
Studia Fennica Ethnologica 12
2009

Laura Stark
The Limits of Patriarchy
How Female Networks of Pilfering and Gossip Sparked the First Debates on Rural Gender Rights in the 19th-century Finnish-Language Press
Studia Fennica Ethnologica 13
2011

Where is the Field?
The Experience of Migration Viewed through the Prism of Ethnographic Fieldwork
Edited by Laura Hirvi & Hanna Snellman
Studia Fennica Ethnologica 14
2012

LauraHirvi
Identities in Practice
A Trans-Atlantic Ethnography of Sikh Immigrants in Finland and in California
Studia Fennica Ethnologica 15
2013

Studia Fennica Folkloristica

Pertti J. Anttonen
Tradition through Modernity
Postmodernism and the Nation-State in Folklore Scholarship
Studia Fennica Folkloristica 15
2005

Narrating, Doing, Experiencing
Nordic Folkloristic Perspectives
Edited by
Annikki Kaivola-Bregenhøj, Barbro Klein & Ulf Palmenfelt
Studia Fennica Folkloristica 16
2006

Mícheál Briody
The Irish Folklore Commission 1935–1970
History, ideology, methodology
Studia Fennica Folkloristica 17
2008

Venla Sykäri
Words as Events
Cretan Mantinádes in Performance and Composition
Studia Fennica Folkloristica 18
2011

Hidden Rituals and Public Performances
Traditions and Belonging among the Post-Soviet Khanty, Komi and Udmurts
Edited by Anna-Leena Siikala & Oleg Ulyashev
Studia Fennica Folkloristica 19
2011

Mythic Discourses
Studies in Uralic Traditions
Edited by Frog, Anna-Leena Siikala & Eila Stepanova
Studia Fennica Folkloristica 20
2012

Studia Fennica Historica

Medieval History Writing and Crusading Ideology
Edited by
Tuomas M. S. Lehtonen &
Kurt Villads Jensen with
Janne Malkki and Katja Ritari
Studia Fennica Historica 9
2005

Moving in the USSR
*Western anomalies
and Northern wilderness*
Edited by Pekka Hakamies
Studia Fennica Historica 10
2005

DEREK FEWSTER
Visions of Past Glory
*Nationalism
and the Construction
of Early Finnish History*
Studia Fennica Historica 11
2006

Modernisation in Russia since 1900
Edited by Markku Kangaspuro
& Jeremy Smith
Studia Fennica Historica 12
2006

SEIJA-RIITTA LAAKSO
Across the Oceans
*Development of Overseas
Business Information
Transmission 1815–1875*
Studia Gennica Historica 13
2007

Industry and Modernism
*Companies, Architecture
and Identity in the Nordic
and Baltic Countries during the
High-Industrial Period*
Edited by Anja Kervanto
Nevanlinna
Studia Fennica Historica 14
2007

CHARLOTTA WOLFF
Noble conceptions of politics in eighteenth-century Sweden (ca 1740–1790)
Studia Fennica Historica 15
2008

Sport, Recreation and Green Space in the European City
Edited by Peter Clark,
Marjaana Niemi & Jari Niemelä
Studia Fennica Historica 16
2009

Rhetorics of Nordic Democracy
Edited by Jussi Kurunmäki &
Johan Strang
Studia Fennica Historica 17
2010

Studia Fennica Anthropologica

On Foreign Ground
*Moving between Countries
and Categories*
Edited by Minna Ruckenstein &
Marie-Louise Karttunen
Studia Fennica Anthropologica 1
2007

Beyond the Horizon
*Essays on Myth, History,
Travel and Society*
Edited by Clifford Sather &
Timo Kaartinen
Studia Fennica Anthropologica 2
2008

Studia Fennica Linguistica

Minimal reference
The use of pronouns in Finnish and Estonian discourse
Edited by Ritva Laury
Studia Fennica Linguistica 12
2005

ANTTI LEINO
On Toponymic Constructions as an Alternative to Naming Patterns in Describing Finnish Lake Names
Studia Fennica Linguistica 13
2007

Talk in interaction
Comparative dimensions
Edited by Markku Haakana, Minna Laakso & Jan Lindström
Studia Fennica Linguistica 14
2009

Planning a new standard language
Finnic minority languages meet the new millennium
Edited by Helena Sulkala & Harri Mantila
Studia Fennica Linguistica 15
2010

LOTTA WECKSTRÖM
Representations of Finnishness in Sweden
Studia Fennica Linguistica 16
2011

TERHI AINIALA, MINNA SAARELMA & PAULA SJÖBLOM
Names in Focus
An Introduction to Finnish Onomastics
Studia Fennica Linguistica 17
2012

Studia Fennica Litteraria

Changing Scenes
Encounters between European and Finnish Fin de Siècle
Edited by Pirjo Lyytikäinen
Studia Fennica Litteraria 1
2003

Women's Voices
Female Authors and Feminist Criticism in the Finnish Literary Tradition
Edited by Lea Rojola & Päivi Lappalainen
Studia Fennica Litteraria 2
2007

Metaliterary Layers in Finnish Literature
Edited by Samuli Hägg, Erkki Sevänen & Risto Turunen
Studia Fennica Litteraria 3
2008

Aino Kallas
Negotiations with Modernity
Edited by Leena Kurvet-Käosaar & Lea Rojola
Studia Fennica Litteraria 4
2011

The Emergence of Finnish Book and Reading Culture in the 1700s
Edited by Cecilia af Forselles & Tuija Laine
Studia Fennica Litteraria 5
2011

Nodes of Contemporary Finnish Literature
Edited by Leena Kirstinä
Studia Fennica Litteraria 6
2012

White Field, Black Seeds
Nordic Literacy Practices in the Long Nineteenth Century
Edited by Anna Kuismin & M. J. Driscoll
Studia Fennica Litteraria 7
2013

LIEVEN AMEEL
Helsinki in Early Twentieth-Century Literature
Urban Experiences in Finnish Prose Fiction 1890–1940
Studia Fennica Litteraria 8
2014

www.ingramcontent.com/pod-product-compliance
Lightning Source LLC
Chambersburg PA
CBHW080803300426
44114CB00020B/2812